£48

The Law of Partnership

The Law of Partnership

Terence Prime BA, PhD

Solicitor, Lecturer in Law,
University of Liverpool

Gary Scanlan LLB

Solicitor, Lecturer in Law,
University of Liverpool

Butterworths
London, Dublin, Edinburgh
1995

United Kingdom	Butterworths, a Division of Reed Elsevier (UK) Ltd, Halsbury House, 35 Chancery Lane, LONDON WC2A 1EL and 4 Hill Street, EDINBURGH EH2 3JZ
Australia	Butterworths, SYDNEY, MELBOURNE, BRISBANE, ADELAIDE, PERTH, CANBERRA and HOBART
Canada	Butterworths Canada Ltd, TORONTO and VANCOUVER
Ireland	Butterworth (Ireland) Ltd, DUBLIN
Malaysia	Malayan Law Journal Sdn Bhd, KUALA LUMPUR
New Zealand	Butterworths of New Zealand Ltd, WELLINGTON and AUCKLAND
Puerto Rico	Butterworth of Puerto Rico, Inc, SAN JUAN
Singapore	Butterworths Asia, SINGAPORE
South Africa	Butterworths Publishers (Pty) Ltd, DURBAN
USA	Butterworth Legal Publishers, CARLSBAD, California and SALEM, New Hampshire

A CIP Catalogue record for this book is available from the British Library.

ISBN 0 406 02512 6

Typeset by M Rules, London
Printed by Clays Ltd, Bungay, Suffolk

PREFACE

Despite the preference for the limited liability company which characterises the modern world, there remains a significant amount of business transacted through the partnership medium, and, in practice, most lawyers and most accountants have everyday experience of the form (not to mention the participants in the relationship for whom the form is as real as their marriages, and occupies perhaps more of their conscious working hours). In the view of the authors, however, the available literature is not that which is appropriate to a major subject.

In short we felt that there was a major gap in the literature, and we have endeavoured to fill it. We have sought to provide a readable text, which rests partnership law on its main principles, but which at the same time provides sufficient details in the text and footnotes for it to be a work to which reference can usefully be made in resolving detailed issues. We hope that it is sufficiently clearly expressed to be of use not merely to the practising legal profession, but also postgraduate students, accountants, and those intelligent laymen who have also chosen to be partners and feel the need for a work which explains the legal consequences of the relationship to which they have committed themselves. We hope that our endeavour will be of benefit to them all.

The endeavour has not been ours alone. We must mention in particular the hard work of Mrs Amanda Clare and Miss Marian Hoffmann who took our jumbled efforts and reduced them to a typescript on the word processor. At the very end of the production of the book we also received help from Miss Lisa Smith. The patient support of our publishers continues to be a model of the relationship which should exist between publishers and authors, but is in fact only achieved in the best run publishing houses. Finally, we note the uncomplaining patience of our families and our wives Mary Prime and Kim Scanlan in the loss of our society while we were in our respective studies. Whether the lack of complaint arose from patient forbearance or sheer relief at our withdrawal we have found it politic not to enquire! We simply remain grateful to them all.

We have endeavoured to state the law accurately at the end of February 1995. We have deliberately incorporated full accounts of the most recent developments in partnership law, namely, the Partnerships and Unlimited Companies (Accounts) Regulations 1993, the important tax changes introduced by the Finance Act 1994, and the very recent insolvency changes brought about by the Insolvent Partnerships Order 1994. We believe that this will increase the usefulness of the work.

Any author is aware that there may be limitations in his work which only the disinterested eye of third parties will detect and reveal to him. We are no exceptions to this principle and, so far from being shy of suggestions, we welcome them. We are therefore always interested in hearing from anyone whose views or insights differ from our own.

Terence Prime   31 March 1995
Gary Scanlan

CONTENTS

TABLE OF STATUTES

References in this Table to *Statutes* are to Halsbury's Statutes of England (Fourth Edition) showing the volume and page at which the annotated text of the Act may be found.

TABLE OF STATUTORY INSTRUMENTS

TABLE OF CASES

A

C

xl *Table of cases*

L

1 Table of cases

CHAPTER 1

DEFINITION AND BACKGROUND

BACKGROUND

The law of partnership is a creation of the common law and equity,[1] but the basis on which we now have it is statutory, for in 1890 Parliament enacted the Partnership Act of that year[2] which remains the foundation of the modern law.[3] Nevertheless the origins of the law dictate that the law of partnership is an area rich in illustrative case law which illuminates the application of its principles in practical situations, and which remains worthy of consideration and attention. Further, although the Act codified much of the existing law, the codification was substantial rather than complete. It is not possible to find the answer to *all* problems arising in respect of a partnership in its provisions, although most solutions to issues of partnership law will be found there.

Indeed the intervention of the legislature was nevertheless carried out in a way which recognised that the origins of partnership law were judge-created. It made very little amendment to the body of judge-made rules already in place, and included specific provision within the legislation for the preservation of the rules of common law and equity, except in so far as such rules conflicted with the express provisions of the legislation.[4] A recent example of the consequences of the preservation of the rules of law and equity can be found in the Canadian case of *Geisel v Geisel*.[5] There a farm was

---

[1] See generally Formoy *The Historical Foundations of Modern Company Law* (1923); CA Cooke *Corporation, Trust and Company* (1950); Holdsworth *History of English Law*, vol 8.

[2] Partnership Act 1890 (53 & 54 Vict c 39).

[3] Unless the liability of one or more of the partners is limited, in which case the Limited Partnerships Act 1907 will also apply. Limited partnerships are discussed below, Chapter 14.

[4] 1890 Act, s 46.

[5] (1990) 72 DLR 245.

operated by two brothers in partnership, one of whom was killed in a farm accident. The deceased partner's widow and children sought to bring an action under the Fatal Accidents Act against the surviving brother. The claim was met with an argument based on the Canadian equivalent of s 10 of the Partnership Act 1890. This provides that where any wrongful act or omission of any partner acting in the ordinary course of the business of the firm causes loss or injury to any person *not being a partner in the firm* the firm is liable to the same extent. Thus, the partner is jointly and severally liable with his co-partners for everything for which the firm becomes liable under s 10 while he is a partner. It was contended that, taken together, the effect of these provisions is that all partners are jointly and severally liable for all torts committed by any of the partners in the ordinary course of business, but only 'to any person not being a partner in the firm'. Therefore, it was argued, there is no provision within the legislation for a partner to sue his partners in tort. The court concluded that the purpose of the provision was merely to make it clear that in the circumstances covered by it the firm would be liable as well as an individual partner. It was not therefore a provision inconsistent with the applicability of the general rules of law and equity (including tort) required by s 46. Consequently, the action could be maintained.

The Act itself is structured into five parts under the following heads:

(1)   nature of partnership (ss 1–4);
(2)   relations of partners to persons dealing with them (ss 5–18);
(3)   relations of partners to one another (ss 19–31);
(4)   dissolution of partnership, and its consequences (ss 32–44);
(5)   supplemental (ss 45–50).

The presentation undertaken in this book will broadly follow the sequence established in the Act, since it is as logical as any other, and, given that the subject now has a legislative base, the balance of convenience must lie in favour of following the order of the primary source material.

DEFINITION AND NATURE OF PARTNERSHIP

Identifying the partnership relationship

Before moving to the definitions and identifying characteristics of a partnership, it is valuable to stand back and briefly consider the situations in which the characterisation of a commercial relationship as a partnership is likely to be decisive in the resolution of a legal problem. There appear to be three such situations:

(1) a non-participant in the alleged partnership may be anxious to establish that a partnership in fact exists and includes as many potential defendants as possible because, if a partnership does exist, each partner carries unlimited legal liability for the responsibilities of the firm;[6]

(2) a participant in the alleged partnership may wish to establish its existence because the responsibilities owed by partners to each other are not merely contractual and tortious, but also fiduciary, with the result that they are more extensive than those generally owed outside the relationship;[7]

(3) partnerships have their own taxation regime and it may well be an issue between the taxpayer and the Revenue as to whether he is or is not a partner with regard to particular activities.[8]

In considering the application of the rules and principles discussed hereafter to any particular situation it should always be remembered that the burden of proof in these situations lies on the one who alleges that a partnership exists.[9] The bearing of the burden of proof can inevitably be decisive, and its incidence is therefore important, both in understanding the existing case law and in considering the application of the rules to new situations.

The implications of this can be enormous. A cautionary example is the case of *Saywell v Pope*.[10] The case concerned a well-established partnership between Mr Saywell and Mr Pope, which had for a number of years carried on the business of selling and repairing tractors and other agricultural machinery. In January 1973 the firm obtained a marketing franchise from the international company, Fiat. Up to this date the firm had employed the partners' wives in the firm to do a small amount of work. The accounts for the years 1972 and 1973 both showed small salaries being paid to the wives in respect of this work. By April 1974 the franchise was causing more work to be created, and the wives became more active in the business.

The partnership had never had a formal partnership agreement. At the suggestion of the firm's accountant an agreement was eventually entered into between Mr Saywell, Mrs Saywell, Mr Pope and

---

6 See Chapter 6.
7 See Chapter 8.
8 See Chapter 15.
9 *Saywell v Pope* [1979] STC 824; *IRC v Williamson* (1928) 14 TC 335.
10 [1979] STC 824.

Mrs Pope, which was not, however, done until June 1975. This declared, inter alia, that the partnership commenced in April 1973, and set out the division of profits between the partners. However, the bank mandate in force prior to April 1973 under which Mr Saywell and Mr Pope had authority to sign cheques was left unchanged, and no notice of any change in the membership of the partnership was given to either the bank or the various creditors of the business. Neither of the wives introduced any capital to the business, nor did they have any facilities to draw from the partnership bank account. On the other hand, the accounts for the period April to December 1973 and the 1974 year were prepared on the basis that the wives were partners, although there was no evidence as to when the accounts were drawn up, or on whose instructions they were prepared. The shares of profits shown as attributable to the wives were not drawn out by them. The two families claimed that a partnership existed prior to the signing of the partnership agreement by them in 1975, as the family tax positions would be more beneficial on that basis. The Revenue denied the existence of a partnership. Given the equivocal nature of the evidence in support of the contention that a partnership had been created, and, in particular, the fact that the profits shown in the accounts as attributable to the wives were never in fact drawn by them, the court held that the General Commissioners were entitled to conclude that the tax payers had failed to discharge the burden on them to show that a partnership existed, and that the two families should be taxed on the basis that no partnership had existed prior to the agreement being signed. The moral is obvious. Businesses should be genuinely operated as partnerships from the moment they are intended to assume that form, and the partnership agreement entered into not later than that moment.

Definition

The 1890 Act begins with a definition of partnership. The definition has two aspects. First, a general definition is provided, and this is followed by specific provision that certain relationships do not constitute a partnership. In general terms, partnership is the relation which subsists between persons carrying on a business in common with a view to profit.[11] Specifically, the relation between members of any company or association is not a partnership in three specific

---

[11]   Section 1(1).

circumstances. These arise where the company or association is:

(1) registered as a company under any Act of Parliament for the time being in force relating to the registration of joint stock companies;

(2) formed or incorporated by, or in pursuance of, any other Act of Parliament or letters patent or royal charter; or

(3) a company engaged in working mines within and subject to the jurisdiction of the Stannaries.[12]

Clearly, whilst the exceptions must be borne in mind, it is the general definition which is fundamental. So important is it that it merits detailed consideration. Indeed, every part of that definition of partnership as 'the relation which subsists between persons carrying on a business in common with a view to profit' inevitably contributes to the meaning which the definition carries. Each part will be considered separately.

1. THE RELATION WHICH SUBSISTS

Partnership depends on an existing subsisting relationship. That relationship is consensual, and therefore under English law must depend on a contract for its creation. In the words of Jessel MR:[13]

'. . . it is a *contract* of some kind undoubtedly – a contract, like all contracts, involving the mutual consent of the parties; a contract for the purpose of carrying on a commercial business – that is a business bringing profit in some shape or another between the partners.'

However, while partnership requires a contract between parties relating to the carrying on of a business, not every such agreement will create a partnership. In particular, partnership is about the present conduct of business together. An agreement to carry on business in the future does not create the parties to the agreement partners, at least until the business begins to be actively undertaken.[14] On the other hand, if an agreement exists satisfying all the requirements of the statutory definition of partnership a partnership is created, and this is not prevented by the inclusion in the agreement of a term that the parties had no intention of creating such a relationship.[15] While the intention of the parties will no doubt be

---

[12] Section 1(2).
[13] *Pooley v Driver* (1876) 5 Ch D 458 at 471.
[14] Per Parke J in *Dickinson v Valpy* (1829) 10 B & C 128 at 141, 142.
[15] Per Cozens-Hardy MR in *Weiner v Harris* [1910] 1 KB 285 at 290.

taken in account by the courts, it is not what they intended by their agreement, but what they achieved, which is decisive.

2. BETWEEN PERSONS

Partnership is a relationship between *persons* for the purpose of operating a business. It follows that for a partnership to exist its business must be carried on by two or more persons. It is not possible to create a partnership around a business which has a 'sole partner', for such a business is not a partnership, and the sole partner will, in fact, be sole proprietor of the business. On the other hand an arrangement whereby one person carried on business on behalf of himself and others is a perfectly effective partnership,[16] the one being the active partner, the others 'sleeping' or 'dormant' partners, who take no part in the day-to-day running of the business, but who are entitled to a share of the profits, are bound by the actions of the active partners in the ordinary course of business and, usually, have a say in how in general the business is conducted. Commonly a sleeping or dormant partner will have contributed substantially to the capital which underpins the business.

While it is necessary that two or more persons carry on business for a partnership to be constituted, there is no requirement that the participants should be natural persons. It is perfectly possible for a partnership to be constituted between companies, or between companies and natural persons.[17]

Thus, in *Hugh Stevenson & Sons Ltd v Aktiengesellschaft für Cartonnagen-Industrie*[18] a partnership was entered into between an English company and a German company, in 1907, to carry on in England the business of the manufacture and sale of metal edges for cardboard boxes. The partnership was for a period of five years, and thereafter until the expiration of six months' notice given by either party. In fact, the partnership continued until the beginning of the 1914–18 war, the outbreak of which operated to dissolve the partnership. After the outbreak of war the English company continued to operated the business and use the partnership plant for that purpose. The House of Lords held that since it was partnership property which was used to generate the profits after the dissolution of the partnership, the German company was entitled to a share of them.

---

[16] *Wallace v Wallace's Trustees* (1906) 8 F 558.
[17] See the judgment of Blackburn J in *Cox v Hickman* (1860) 8 HL Cas 268.
[18] [1918] AC 239; see also *Newstead v Frost* [1979] 2 All ER 129, CA; affd [1980] 1 All ER 363, HL.

3. CARRYING ON A BUSINESS

The concept of partnership is of a business medium, and the statutory definition requires that a business be 'carried on'. Unfortunately, the Act does not attempt to define 'business', although it does expressly include 'every trade, occupation or profession'.[19] As has been pointed out judicially, 'the word "business" is an etymological chameleon; it suits its meaning to the context in which it is found'.[20] The basis of a business association is that it operates on commercial lines and requires skill and/or effort to bring its commercial operations to a successful conclusion. This seems to be the underlying assumption of the courts as they strive to draw the distinction between business and non-business activities on an almost case-by-case basis. Provided that these commercial requirements are satisfied, a partnership will exist even though no repeated trading is envisaged, and the business consists of a single venture.[1] Thus, in *Winsor v Schroeder*[2] a house purchaser – who had the misfortune to find herself committed to the purchase of two houses when she could only afford one – joined with a local property developer and purchased the houses jointly under an agreement whereby the profits intended to be generated on resale would be divided equally. Whilst recognising that one-off transactions would be less likely to be viewed as partnership ventures by the courts, Woolf J concluded that the particular venture had all the qualities of joint profit-making endeavour to constitute a partnership, and categorised it as such.

On the other hand, where the necessary commercial input cannot be found the judges will conclude that no business exists. An illustrative case is *Customs and Excise Comrs v Lord Fisher*[3] which concerned the chargeability of pheasant shoots to VAT. A gentleman had arranged shoots, to which he invited friends and relatives on a paying basis. Without the contributions it was unlikely that the shooting could be maintained. The court concluded that no business was being carried on, despite the fact that the financial contributions were considerable, and the gentleman put a very considerable amount of planning and organisation into the shoots. The facts that financial contributions were involved, and that the

---

[19] Section 45.
[20] Per Lord Diplock in *Town Investments Ltd v Department of the Environment* [1977] 1 All ER 813 at 819.
[1] *Re Abenheim, ex p Abenheim* (1913) 109 LT 219.
[2] (1979) 129 NLJ 1266.
[3] [1981] 2 All ER 147.

shooting activities generated money for the organiser, were not in themselves conclusive. On the other hand the facts that the shoot was restricted to friends and relatives, and that the shooting was not undertaken with the intensity usually associated with a 'commercial' shoot, was probably decisive. If the shoot had been operated more intensively, and advertised to the general public, the result might well have been otherwise.

Equally, the absence of profit does not in itself mean that there is no business. If the particular activity is carried out in a commercial manner and with essentially commercial operations, there may still be a *business*, as where accommodation is provided on a non-profit-making basis for students or some other group of the population.[4] However, such a business could not be carried on *in partnership*, because of the separate requirement of partnership law that the business be carried on with a view to profit. Of course, if a commercial operation is carried on with a view to making profits, but has, as yet, produced only losses, there *is* a business, and one of a type which can be carried on in partnership. A business is no less a business because it is, as yet, unsuccessful. Nevertheless, for a business to exist it must have been formed. Thus, the promoters of a company working together to get the company formed and running are not partners in their activities, since the company is intended to be the business, and no trading is envisaged until it has been formed.[5]

In the categorisation of activities as business or non-business it is important to bear in mind that the categorisation is carried on by judges, who do not leave behind them their legal training and ways of thought. Thus, in *Smith v Anderson*[6] the Court of Appeal held that the trustees of the nineteenth-century forerunner of a unit

---

4   *Customs and Excise Comrs v Morrison's Academy Boarding Houses Association* [1978] STC 1.

5   *Keith Spicer Ltd v Mansell* [1970] 1 WLR 333; *Wood v Argyll (Duke of)* (1844) 6 Man & G 928; *Reynell v Lewis* (1846) 15 M & W 517; *Capper's Case* (1850) 1 Sim (NS) 178; *Hutton v Thompson* (1851) 3 HL Cas 161; *Norris v Cottle* (1850) 2 HL Cas 647; *Bright v Hutton* (1852) 3 HL Cas 341, 28 LJ Ch 404; *Hamilton v Smith* (1859) 5 Jur NS 32. The cases of *Holmes v Higgins* (1822) 1 B & C 74; *Lucas v Beach* (1840) 1 Man & G 417 and *Barnett v Lambert* (1846) 15 M & W 489 are anomalous and clearly wrongly decided, since they are in accordance with neither authority nor principle. They were criticised subsequently in *Norris v Cottle*. Of course, if the promoters were in the business of forming companies together and making profit from their *formation* and the provision of property to them, the position would be otherwise: *Royal Victoria Palace Syndicate* (1873) 29 LT 668; affd (1874) 30 LT 3; *Wood v Argyll (Duke of)* (1844) 6 Man & G 928; *London Financial Association v Kelk* (1884) 26 Ch D 107.

6   (1880) 15 Ch D 247.

trust were not partners, since they were not carrying on a business, although they were paid on a proper commercial basis for the activities which they undertook. James LJ took the view[7] that:

'nothing that is done under this deed by the trustees comes within the ordinary meaning of "business", any more than what is done by the trustees of a marriage settlement who have large properties vested in them, and who have very extensive powers of disposing of the investments, charging the investments, and selling them and re-investing in other investments according to their discretion and judgement, with or without the consent of their cestuis que trust. That is not a business.'

As Cotton LJ pointed out:[8]

'The trustees . . . are the only persons who are dealing with the investments, and they are dealing, not as agents for some principal, but as trustees in whom the property and management of it are vested, and who have the power of changing the investments and securities.'

4. IN COMMON

For a partnership to be created not only must two persons be co-operating commercially, they must also be acting in common in relation to a single business, so that the business is jointly constituted. In deciding whether a single business is being carried on by two persons so that a partnership is created, regard must be had to all the circumstances. While co-operation in a single venture may constitute two or more participants partners, it more frequently does not. Such collaboration may not amount to collaboration in a business, because all they might be achieving by their collaboration is the proper administration or exploitation of assets vested in them jointly. It is only if the collaboration is of a type which is so structured as to be commercial that a partnership will result. Consequently, if the owner of a business dies and his personal representatives operate his business in accordance with the terms of the will as part of the administration of the estate, they do not become partners by their actions. Thus, in *Re Fisher and Sons*[9] a man carried on business as sole proprietor, under the firm name of EW Fisher and Sons. By his will he appointed executors and gave them power to carry on the trading of the business for the benefit of his wife for

---

[7] At 276.
[8] At 284.
[9] [1912] 2 KB 491.

her life. After his death the executors carried on the business in the firm's name, pursuant to the power given to them. Some time later a creditor sued the firm for goods supplied. He sought to make the executors liable as partners in the firm. Phillimore J held that they were not partners, since they had exercised their powers as executors, not as partners in the firm.[10] If, however, the executors are also the beneficiaries of the estate and continue to operate the business after the estate has been administered, they will then constitute themselves partners. Their activities have then stretched beyond the administration of an asset vested in them, and have become a commercial operation from which they each intend to reap profit.

Further, several businesses may co-operate in a single project, such as the building of a large bridge, without creating a partnership, because no common business is created. While each business intends to obtain a profit by their participation in the building of the bridge there is no attempt to create and carry on a single common business. Each business is, and remains, separate.[11] Contractual provisions determine which business is responsible for which operations, and what each will receive for those operations. The profits achieved by any particular participant will be represented by its individual receipts less its individual overheads. If, however, the businesses were to undertake the activity on the basis that all receipts would be pooled and all overheads deducted to create a common profit which would then be divided between the businesses in agreed proportions, then they would probably have constituted themselves partners in the venture.

It follows from this that where commercial co-operation can be shown between businesses the important considerations in determining whether or not a partnership is created are (1) whether capital is held in common, and (2) whether profits are achieved in common prior to division. As has been noted, if the other requirements are met for a partnership to be created, it is not essential that all participants be active in the day-to-day running of the business. The position of a 'dormant' or 'sleeping' partner is acknowledged in partnership law, such a partner usually being admitted to the partnership because of his contribution to capital. However, in legal theory it does appear that a participant can be such a partner even if he contributes no capital. Here the important considerations

---

[10] See also *Holme v Hammond* (1872) LR 7 Ex Ch 218. Had the executors been sued as *executors* rather than as *partners*, they would have been liable since they had entered into the contracts.

[11] Eg *Coope v Eyre* (1788) 1 Hy Bl 37; *Tyser v Shipowners Syndicate (Reassured)* [1896] 1 QB 135.

are whether, despite his lack of provision of capital or everyday participation, he has the rights of a partner, in particular the right to participate in the profits the business is expected to generate. However, it must not be thought that participation in profit alone will constitute the participator a partner in the business if the sharing of profits was intended merely to measure his remuneration in respect of services provided to the business, and not to be his return on partnership participation. Thus, in *Strathearn Gordon Associates Ltd v Comrs of Customs and Excise*[12] a company acted as management consultant for other businesses. It also entered into seven property developments with various other businesses, under which it either acted as consultant or agreed to manage or supervise the development. In return, each property development agreement provided that the company should receive substantial fees, usually calculated as a percentage of the profits generated. The various agreements were found not to create partnerships. Since the other parties and the projects were different in each case, and no continuing relationship was created, they were more of the nature of single acts of supervision in individual developments. Therefore, the essence of each agreement was the provision of services by the company for a consideration, and the fact that such consideration was measured by reference to a share of the net profits did not convert the arrangement into a partnership. Nor will participation in profits constitute a wife a partner in her husband's business if she does not really participate in it, and the agreement is only a domestic arrangement and not intended to create a legally binding partnership between them.[13]

Commencement of business

There are implications in this for the commencement of business. If it is intended that a formal partnership agreement be drawn up, it appears that no partnership will usually be taken to have commenced between the parties until the agreement is signed, unless all the prospective partners actively participate in the management and operations of the business.[14] Again, it is possible that a business may be commenced, or a continuing business undertaken, on the basis that one individual receives as a reward not a partnership but an option to become a partner at some future date. In such a

---

[12] [1985] VATTR 79.
[13] *Britton v Comrs of Customs and Excise* [1986] VATTR 209; see also *Saywell v Pope* p 3, above.
[14] *Saywell v Pope* [1979] STC 824.

situation, provided that the option represents the true position, and is not a cover for a partnership which in fact already exists,[15] the option holder is not a partner, and only becomes one in exercising the option in accordance with its terms.[16]

Of course, even where the agreement between the parties is bona fide and intended to create only an option to become part of the business, the option holder may constitute himself a partner by holding out. Thus, in *Courtenay v Wagstaff*[17] the plaintiff had been employed as parliamentary reporter for a newspaper and claimed to have been wrongfully dismissed. He sought to make the defendant liable for the wrongful dismissal on the basis that the defendant was a partner in it. The defendant's connection with the newspaper was based on an agreement with a Mr Holt, who ran it. Pursuant to this agreement, the defendant advanced money to fund the venture on stringent terms, under which the defendant was given unlimited control over the publication and the option of declaring himself a partner at any time within 12 months, and was to trust solely to the profits of the venture for the repayment of the loan and its interest. As the activities of the newspaper proceeded the defendant involved himself increasingly in its management, and allowed Holt to hold him out as a partner in the venture. While the court concluded (somewhat surprisingly) that the defendant had not been a partner in the venture at its commencement, it also concluded that subsequently he had assumed that responsibility by holding out.

5. WITH A VIEW TO PROFIT

Profit is at the heart of partnership. The essential concept of partnership, so far as the law is concerned, is that of a joint enterprise carried on for the sake of gain. This has the support of both judicial pronouncement and scholarly writing:

> 'I cannot find any authority throwing any doubt on the accuracy of the passage in Lindley on Partnership, which makes the participation in profits essential to the English idea of partnership, and states that, although in former times the word "copartnership" was used in the sense of "co-ownership," the modern usage has been to confine the meaning of the term to societies formed

---

[15] *Courtenay v Wagstaff* (1864) 16 CBNS 110.
[16] *Ex p Turquand* (1841) 2 Mont D & De G 339; *Gabriel v Evill* (1842) 9 M & W 297; *Price v Groom* (1848) 2 Ex Ch 542; *Ex p Davis* (1863) 4 De GJ & SM 523; *Re Young, ex p Jones* [1896] 2 QB 484. See also by analogy *Howell v Brodie* (1839) 6 Bing NC 44; *Burnell v Hunt* (1841) 5 Jur 650.
[17] (1864) 16 CBNS 110.

for gain. A number of definitions given by writers from all parts
of the world are appended to the passage, and in all of them the
idea involved appears to be that of joint operation for the sake of
gain.'[18]

The basic concept of profit is that of net profit, ie gross income less
overheads incurred to generate them reflected in the increasing
assets of the business between the two account dates.[19] As a consequence, where an agreement provides for the division of gross
receipts, such as publishing agreements between publisher and
author and some performance agreements between film actor and
film company, there is no creation of a partnership.

It follows, of course, that the undertaking of a joint enterprise
without any view to the generation of a commercial profit will not
create a partnership.[20] Thus, societies or associations formed for
charitable or social purposes will not create a partnership,[1] so that
a non-profit-making railway preservation society[2] will not constitute
a partnership.

An important issue which arises here is whether a group of people
operating some form of club thereby constitute themselves a partnership. This issue arose in the case of *Pitreavie Golf Club v
Penman*.[3] The Pitreavie Golf Club was constituted in Scotland as an
unincorporated association for the purpose of playing golf. Under
its rules its affairs were managed by a council consisting of the cap-
tain, vice-captain, secretary, and treasurer, and not more than nine
other members. As such it was constituted as a normal members'
club. In common with such clubs it was never intended that the
club should generate a profit, although it was contemplated that it
would generate an income sufficient to cover its expenses.
Unfortunately, this did not prove to be the case, and some considerable debts were created. One of the creditors sought to put the
club into insolvency. This was only possible under Scots law if the
club was either a company or a partnership. Since it was not a
company, and the intention that profits should not be generated
meant that it was not a partnership, the creditor was unsuccessful in
his attempt.

Unincorporated associations, including members' clubs, are

[18] Per Lord Coleridge in *R v Robson* (1885) 16 QBD 137 at 140.
[19] For a discussion of the meaning of profit see Chapter 11, p 253, below.
[20] *Lyon v Knowles* (1863) 3 B & S 556, 7 LT 670; affd (1864) 10 LT 876.
[1] Per Lord Lindley in *Wise v Perpetual Trustee Co* [1903] AC 139 at 149.
[2] *Goddard v Mills* (1929) Times, 16 February.
[3] 1934 SLT 247.

therefore not partnerships.[4] However, not all clubs are members' clubs. Some clubs are proprietory clubs where the proprietors operates the club to generate profit for themselves. This, of course, is a very different form of operation to a members' club, and the result is a business, operated by profit, which will give rise to a partnership where several proprietors are acting in common to operate the club. If such a club has but one proprietor he will be a sole trader.

However, it should be noted that a partnership entered into to make a profit does not cease to be a partnership merely because it fails to generate a profit. This has considerable implications for the use of partnership as a mechanism of tax avoidance where the partnership is given some overseas connection to avoid the payment of UK taxes. The issue arose in *Newstead (Inspector of Taxes) v Frost*.[5] The litigation concerned a partnership agreement entered into between David Frost, the television personality, and a Bahamian resident company. The central point of the scheme was that, if a partnership was created, UK tax would only be imposed on such part of his income as was remitted to the UK. If no partnership was in reality created, tax would be imposed on all income generated whether remitted to the UK or not. Inevitably the Inland Revenue argued that no partnership resulted from the arrangement. The basis of their argument was that the relationship established between Frost and the company was not one which had at its heart the generation of profits, but rather the avoidance of tax. David Frost would have derived income overseas from the exploitation of his talents whether he entered into the partnership arrangement or not.

The Court of Appeal drew a distinction between, on the one hand, transactions entered into wholly to avoid tax and, on the other, those entered into partly for the purposes of commercial operations and partly to avoid tax. The former did not create a partnership, but since the creation of profit was part of the function of the latter it did.[6] Roskill LJ[7] quoted the judgment of Megarry J in *FA and AB Ltd v Lupton* at first instance:[8]

---

[4] See also *Blackpool Marton Rotary Club v Martin (Inspector of Taxes)* [1988] STC 823.

[5] [1979] 2 All ER 129, CA; affd [1980] 1 All ER 363, HL.

[6] This allowed the court to distinguish previous decisions of its own and of the House of Lords that arrangements entered into to avoid tax did not create a partnership in *Bishop v Finsbury Securities Ltd* [1966] 1 WLR 1402, HL and *FA and AB Ltd v Lupton* [1972] AC 634, HL.

[7] [1979] 2 All ER 129 at 138–139.

[8] [1968] 2 All ER 1042 at 1051.

'If on analysis it is found that the greater part of the transaction consists of elements for which there is some trading purpose or explanation (whether ordinary or extraordinary), then the presence of what I may call "fiscal elements", inserted solely or mainly for the purpose of producing a fiscal benefit, may not suffice to deprive the transaction of its trading status. The question is whether, viewed as a whole, the transaction is one which can fairly be regarded as a trading transaction. If it is, then it will not be denatured merely because it was entered into with motives of reaping a fiscal advantage. Neither fiscal elements nor fiscal motives will prevent what in substance is a trading transaction from ranking as such. On the other hand, if the greater part of the transaction is explicable only on fiscal grounds, the mere presence of elements of trading will not suffice to translate the transaction into the realms of trading. In particular, if what is effected is predominantly an artificial structure, remote from trading and fashioned so as to secure a tax advantage, the mere presence in that structure of certain elements which by themselves could fairly be described as trading will not cast the cloak of trade over the whole structure.'[9]

If partnership depends on the generation of profit is it also a requirement that the profit should be divisible amongst the participants? Lord Lindley, in his authoritative work on partnership law, came to the tentative view that it did not despite considerable judicial dicta to the contrary dating from before the 1890 Act.[10] The question is perhaps almost truly academic, because, in practice, men and women enter into partnership arrangements with the view of conducting a business to generate profit for individual gain. However, it is submitted that Lord Lindley's views are wrong for five basic reasons:[11]

(1) at the conceptual level, co-operation in business for mutual advantage seems to be the central concept of partnership, both in ordinary language and within the Act;

(2) the idea of mutual participation in profit and loss as the central plank of partnership law was articulated clearly by the judges prior to the enactment of the 1890 legislation;

[9] An example of a case where an apparent 'partnership' was merely a tax-saving measure constructed around a partnership, with no true purpose of profit creation, can be found in *E Rennison & Son v Minister of Social Security* (1970) 114 Sol Jo 952.

[10] *Lindley and Banks on Partnership* (16th edn, 1990) p 11.

[11] Sir Frederick Pollock, who drafted the Act, certainly did not share Lord Lindley's view.

(3)   section 46 of the Act preserves the principles of common law and equity except so far as they are inconsistent with the express terms of the Act. The Act has no express terms inconsistent with the principle outlined;

(4)   in fact, the Act contains two words which support the principle, namely 'in common'. The logical deduction of a requirement that a business be carried on in common by its participants is that its profits should be divisible between them;

(5)   the concept set out in (1) seems implicit in the provision of s 24(1) that, prima facie, all partners are entitled to share equally in the capital and profits of the business.

Of course, the mere fact that no partnership subsists between the partners does not prevent a person from becoming liable to third parties on the basis that he has allowed himself to be held out as a partner.

SPECIFIC RULES FOR DETERMINING THE EXISTENCE OF A PARTNERSHIP

Over and above the definition of partnership with its specific exceptions the 1890 Act also sets out specific rules to apply in determining the existence of a partnership in doubtful circumstances. It must, however, be always remembered that the provisions of s 2 are merely aimed at helping the courts assess the true intentions of the parties and the legal effect of the arrangements which they have made. The actual intentions and purposes of the parties are more important than the provisions. More important than either the expressed intentions and purposes of the parties and the statutory provisions is the actual effect of the arrangements made and intended. If the arrangements made have the actual characteristics of a partnership the courts will hold that a partnership exists even though the express terms of the agreement deny that one is to be created.[12]

However, the existence or non-existence of a partnership must be deduced from the whole circumstances of the relations between

---

[12]   Per Lord Halsbury in *Adam v Newbigging* (1888) 13 App Cas 308 at 315; per Cozens-Hardy MR in *Weiner v Harris* [1910] 1 KB 285 at 290; *Ex p Delhasse* (1878) 7 Ch D 511; *Moore v Davis* (1879) 11 Ch D 261; *Pooley v Driver* (1876) 5 Ch D 458; *Fenston v Johnstone (Inspector of Taxes)* (1940) 23 TC 29; *Stekel v Ellice* [1973] 1 WLR 191.

the parties and the terms of their arrangement.[13] This does not necessarily meant that, if a partnership is found not to exist, liability is avoided. Thus, in *Swiss Air Transport Co Ltd v Palmer*[14] the defendant operated a business in which he imported wigs from Malta, which he then sold world-wide. He had a business relationship with a Mr Paris, whom he authorised to act on his behalf on three previous occasions in arranging the freight of goods by air. While the defendant was in southern Africa, Paris made arrangements with the plaintiff for the carriage by air of two cargoes, one of wigs and the other of clothes. In both cases the defendant was named as the shipper. Subsequently, Paris also obtained an air ticket from the plaintiff, whom he instructed to invoice the defendant in London. The defendant refused to pay, and the plaintiff brought an action against him, Paris having by this time died. The evidence established that, in the previous dealings involving the plaintiff, the defendant and Paris, the defendant had behaved as though he and Paris were operating together to achieve a common purpose. Swanwick J concluded that there was a business relationship between Paris and the defendant, but the evidence was not sufficiently conclusive to show that that relationship was one of partnership, and that he could not conclude that a partnership existed. However, by the previous course of dealing in which the defendant had acquiesced by permitting Paris to pledge his credit on the three previous occasions, the defendant had held out Paris as his *agent* with general authority to pledge his credit for the cost of the freight of goods. The defendant was therefore liable as principal for the freight in respect of the two consignments of goods, but not for the price of the air ticket.

The specific rules for ascertainment of a partnership are contained in s 2 and concern:

(1)   joint tenancy and tenancy in common;
(2)   the sharing of gross returns; and
(3)   the receipt by a person of a share of profits.

---

[13]   *Tyser v Shipowners Syndicate (Reassured)* [1896] 1 QB 135; and by analogy *Eames v Stepnell Properties Ltd* [1967] 1 WLR 593; *Scott v Ricketts* [1967] 1 WLR 828; *Johnston v Heath* [1970] 1 WLR 1567; *Vater v Tarbuck* (1970) 214 EG 267. The use of the words 'partner' or 'partnership' are not conclusive: *Goddard v Mills* (1929) Times, 16 February; *Newstead v Frost* [1980] 1 WLR 135; *Minister of Public Works of the Government of Kuwait v Sir Frederick Snow & Partners* [1981] Com LR 103; *Norton Warburg Holdings Ltd v Perera* (1982) 132 NLJ 296.

[14]   [1976] 2 Lloyd's Rep 604.

Joint tenancy and tenancy in common

Joint tenancy, tenancy in common, joint property, common property or part ownership does not itself create a partnership as to anything so held or owned, whether the tenants or owners do or do not share any profits made by the use thereof.[15] Whilst a partnership does not, therefore, arise simply because of co-ownership of property, its exploitation, if trading occurs, with a view to profit may give rise to partnership. The dividing line seems to be whether the co-owners merely divide the profits which naturally follow from the ownership of the property,[16] or *actively* pursue a genuine *business* exploitation of the property.[17] The distinction is not easy to draw and apply to concrete situations. If a partnership occurs, the jointly owned property may or may not be part of the partnership property depending on terms of the agreement between the participants. Thus, in *Davis v Davis*[18] two sons inherited equally as tenants in common a business and three freehold houses from their father on his death. They let one of them and used the rent which they received to enlarge workshops attached to the two other houses. They continued to carry on the business, taking a weekly sum each as drawings and also dividing any rent not used for the building operations. The court concluded that there was a partnership in the business, but not in the houses.

The sharing of gross returns

The sharing of gross returns does not itself create a partnership, whether the persons sharing such returns have or have not a joint or common right or interest in any property from which, or from the use of which, the returns are derived.[19] This makes perfectly clear the point made above, that partnerships involve the carrying on of a business in common and the division of the net returns. Hence it is, as noted above, that the usual agreements between authors and publishers do not create a partnership.

---

[15] Section 2(1).
[16] *Helme v Smith* (1831) 7 Bing 709; *French v Styring* (1857) 2 CBNS 357; *Ex p Harrison* (1814) 2 Rose 76; *Green v Briggs* (1848) 6 Hare 395; *Lyon v Knowles* (1863) 3 B & S 556.
[17] *Ex p Young* (1813) 2 Ves & B 242; *A-G v Borrodaile* (1814) 1 Price 148; *Campbell v Mullett* (1819) 2 Swan 551.
[18] [1894] 1 Ch 393.
[19] Section 2(2).

This distinction between the sharing of gross returns and the division of net profits was the basis of the decision of the Court of Appeal in *Sutton and Co v Grey*.[20] In this case the court decided that an agreement between a firm of stockbrokers and a Mr Grey – under which Grey was to receive half commission on business introduced by him and bear half of any losses sustained on such business – did not go to create a partnership, because the commission received by Grey in respect of any transaction might not be clear profit since he might have expenses and overheads to bear from his share.

As the mere sharing of gross returns does not create a partnership, such an agreement does not carry the corollary that any losses sustained must also be shared as is the case in partnership. For general losses also to fall on all of the participants express agreement to that effect is necessary in the agreement, as was the position in *Sutton*. If a partnership is created, the sharing of losses follows automatically.

The rule concerning the sharing of gross returns antedated the 1890 Act. Thus, prior to the introduction of the Act it was decided that the letting of a theatre to the producer of a play, on the terms that the theatre owner is paid by reference to the number of seats sold, does not create a partnership between producer and theatre owner.[1] In *Cox v Coulson*,[2] decided after the introduction of the Act, the defendant was the manager of a theatre and had agreed with the producer of a play to provide the theatre, and to pay for the lighting and the play bills. The producer of the play was to provide the company of performers, the support staff and the scenery. The defendant was to receive 60% of the gross takings, and the producer of the play 40%. The plaintiff was injured by a shot fired by an actor in a performance of the play at the theatre. She sued the defendant, basing her argument that he was liable, inter alia, on the basis that he was the partner of the producer of the play. Her argument was rejected on the basis that what had been agreed between the defendant and the producer of the play amounted only to an agreement to share gross returns, and did not of itself create a partnership.

---

[20] [1894] 1 QB 285.
[1] *Lyon v Knowles* (1863) 3 B & S 556.
[2] [1916] 2 KB 177.

Sharing of profits

A question which had arisen prior to the 1890 Act was whether the mere sharing of profits alone could create a partnership.[3] If partnership necessarily followed from the sharing of profits, someone who lent money to a business on the basis that he was paid in relation to the profits of the business, or someone who was an employee on similar terms, would find themselves categorised by the courts as a partners and fixed with unlimited liability for the obligations of the business.

It cannot be said that early case law articulated a clear answer to the central question of whether partnership automatically arose in such a situation despite the real intentions of the parties. However, it was felt that the very confusion was an obstacle to commercial development and, indeed, in 1854 the Mercantile Law Commission drew specific attention to the problem, expressly referring to the desirability –

'of enabling capitalists to lend money to traders at a rate of interest, and agents and servants to receive remuneration for their services by money payments, varying with the profits of the business, without being exposed to the hazard of being rendered liable as partners to the creditors of the concern.'[4]

It took a decision of the House of Lords to impose some clarity and order upon a confused scene. In *Cox v Hickman*[5] the House expressly repudiated the notion that participation in profits necessarily created a partnership relation. The House had before it for consideration an arrangement whereby a trader assigned his property to trustees representing creditors of his business, so that the trustees might control the running of the business to allow the creditors to be paid off out of profits. It concluded that such an arrangement did not lead to the creation of a partnership between the debtor and his creditors. The central plank of the House of Lords decision that partnership is not the inevitable consequence of a receipt of net profits was followed thereafter.[6]

---

[3] As in *Waugh v Carver* (1793) 2 Hy Bl 235.
[4] First Report of Mercantile Law Commission (1854).
[5] (1860) 8 HL Cas 268.
[6] While the House did not expressly overrule earlier authorities to the contrary such as *Bloxham v Pell* (1775) cited at 2 Wm Bl 999; *Grace v Smith* (1775) 2 Wm Bl 998; *Waugh v Carver* (1793) 2 Hy Bl 235 a new principle was established, and there has been no reversion to the old. This is probably due to the alacrity and consistency with which *Cox v Hickman* was followed. See *Kilshaw v Jukes* (1863) 3 B & S 847; *Re English and Irish Church and University Assurance Society (No 2)* (1863) 1 Hem & M 85; *Bullen v Sharpe* (1865) LR 1 CP 86; *Holme v Hammond* (1872) LR 7 Ex Ch 218; *Mullwo, March & Co v Court of Wards* (1872) LR 4 PC 419.

The 1890 Act would seem to embody the result of the decision in *Cox v Hickman* as transmuted by Bovill's Act and interpreted by subsequent case law.[7] Section 2(3) provides generally that –

'the receipt by a person of a share of the profits of a business is prima facie evidence that he is a partner in the business, but the receipt of such a share or of a payment contingent on or varying with the profits of a business, does not of itself make him a partner in the business.'

After these general words (which are the most significant part of the provision) the subsection goes on to provide that certain specific situations, in which a receipt of a share of the profits of a business occurs, do not create a partnership. These are:

(1) a payment of a debt by instalments;
(2) a contract for the remuneration of a servant or agent;
(3) payment of annuities to a widow or child of a deceased partner;
(4) a loan to a partnership;
(5) the sale of the goodwill of a business.

These specific situations will be discussed later.[8] Here, it is the general words which merit attention. At first sight, the subsection appear to create a clear presumption that, where profits are shared, a partnership arises unless there is sufficient rebutting evidence to the contrary. However, the words have been given a more subtle interpretation than this. The technical effect of s 2(3) appears to have been accurately explained by North J in the following words:[9]

'Adopting then the rule which was laid down before the Act, and which seems . . . to be precisely what is intended by s 2(3) of the Act, the receipt by a person of a share of the profits of a business is *prima facie* evidence that he is a partner in it, and, if the matter stops there, it is evidence upon which the court must act. But, if there are other circumstances to be considered, they ought to be considered fairly together; not holding that a partnership is proved by a receipt of a share of the profits, unless it is rebutted by something else; but taking all the circumstances together, not

---

[7] See *Syers v Syers* (1876) 1 App Cas 174; *Pooley v Driver* (1876) 5 Ch D 458; *Re Howard, ex p Tennant* (1877) 6 Ch D 303; *Re Megevand, ex p Delhasse* (1878) 7 Ch D 511; *Badeley v Consolidated Bank* (1888) 38 Ch D 238.
[8] See p 25, below.
[9] *Davis v Davis* [1894] 1 Ch 393 at 399. See also *Re Young, ex p Jones* [1896] 2 QB 484; *Walker West Developments Ltd v FJ Emmett Ltd* (1979) 252 Estates Gazette 1171; *Saywell v Pope* [1979] STC 824.

attaching undue weight to any of them, but drawing the inference from the whole.'

It follows from this that if there is *no* other evidence beyond the sharing of profits, the court *must* rule that a partnership was created, but if there is any evidence beyond the sharing of profits, no presumption in reality arises, and the matter must be determined from all the relevant facts. In practice there are always other factors to be looked at in the circumstances which led to the profits being shared, and consequently the presumption never falls to be applied. Thus, North J was also able to adopt the succinct test of Lindley LJ that 'ever since *Cox v Hickman* what we have to get at is the real agreement between the parties'.[10]

The reason why the sharing of profits is not conclusive evidence of partnership is that the conceptual fundamentals of partnership lie elsewhere. The law of partnership is, in fact, a branch of the law of agency; the branch which governs the activities of persons working together to generate profits for a business organisation of which they are all part. Consequently, the test of partnership is not simply whether an alleged partner is to receive a share of profits, but whether he constituted his alleged co-partners his agents for the carrying on of the business. The receipt of profits is only important as a consequence of the activities of the agency, and is therefore only a significant indicator of the existence of a partnership, but not in itself conclusive.

It follows that each particular set of circumstances will be considered on its own merits to determine whether or not a partnership has been achieved. Thus, if money is advanced as a loan to finance a venture and secured on assets of the business the result will not cease to be a genuine loan merely because the lender is entitled both to interest on the advance and to a share of the net profits of the venture.[11] If, however, an agreement which is ostensibly a loan has provisions in it giving unusual rights to the 'lenders', and makes provision in the event of the lender's insolvency which are more consistent with partnership than lender status, the court may well decide that the arrangement is in fact a partnership.[12] In the latter case the arrangement was characterised by Jessel MR[13] as 'an

---

[10]   *Badeley v Consolidated Bank* (1888) 38 Ch D 238 at 258.
[11]   *Re English & Irish Church and University Assurance Society (No 2)* (1863) 1 Hem & M 85; *Kilshaw v Jukes* (1863) 3 B & S 847; *Bullen v Sharp* (1865) LR 1 CP 86; *Holme v Hammond* (1872) LR 7 Ex Ch 218.
[12]   *Badeley v Consolidated Bank* (1888) 38 Ch D 238.
[13]   *Pooley v Driver* (1876) 5 Ch D 458. See also *Ex p Delhasse* (1877–78) 7 Ch D 511.

ingenious contrivance, for giving these contributors the whole of the advantages of partnership, without subjecting them . . . to any of the liabilities'.[14] The ingenious contrivance failed.

A modern example of profit sharing not resulting in the creation of partnership is that of the taxi trade. Certainly it is possible for taxi owners to carry on business together with a view to profit, thereby creating a partnership, but the more general result is to create an employer/employee relationship. This is illustrated by the Canadian case of *Seamone v Boehner*.[15] The plaintiff was licensed to carry on a taxi business. He hired the defendant as a taxi driver using his own vehicle. Under the arrangement the defendant was to pay to the plaintiff 25% of his takings, the defendant retaining the balance. The plaintiff supplied all the capital and assets of the business, and the whole of the management of the business was in his hands. Subsequently, the plaintiff's business licence expired, and the defendant discovered that the plaintiff's lease of the premises from which the business was carried on was invalid. The plaintiff refused or neglected to obtain a new licence, which prompted the defendant to obtain a valid lease of the business premises and eject the plaintiff from it, carrying on the business from the premises himself under the firm name. The plaintiff claimed, inter alia, a share of the profits on the basis that he and the defendant had been partners, and the profits were generated from partnership property. The court rejected the contention. No partnership had been created, and the relationship between the parties prior to the plaintiff's ejection had been that of employer/employee.

Nevertheless, it should be emphasised that the decision in the end is very factual and all the circumstances of the particular arrangement fall to be considered. If the truth of the arrangement is that a partnership is created, and was in reality intended, the courts will categorise it as such, and it matters not that it is dressed up and referred to as something different. An example is *Walker West Developments Ltd v FJ Emmett*,[16] where property developers and builders had entered into an agreement relating to a development project to be undertaken jointly in which profits were to be shared. The terminology of the agreement was not such as one would usually find in a partnership agreement, and one of the participants was designated to handle the receipts of the project and from them reimburse expenses incurred by the other. Nevertheless, the Court of Appeal took the view that the venture was essentially a trading

---

[14] (1876) 5 Ch D 458 at 493.
[15] [1951] 1 DLR 777.
[16] (1979) 252 Estates Gazette 1171. See also the facts of *Davis v Davis* [1894] 1 Ch 393.

venture, the net profits of which were to be divided, and categorised
it as a partnership. Indeed, it is certainly true that there is, in general, a greater willingness for the courts today to conclude that an
arrangement under which several people are to participate in profits in some way is a partnership than was the case 150 years ago,
and some of the old cases would now be decided differently on
their facts, even though the principles remain unchanged.

If the division of profits is now a somewhat ambiguous indicator
of the existence of a partnership, an agreement to share losses as
well as profits is a much stronger pointer, for, in commercial reality,
perhaps the real consequence of partnership to businessmen is the
assumption of the commercial risks which it entails. Consequently,
any agreement under which net profits *and losses* are to be shared
will be a strong indicator of the existence of partnership.[17] Although
it is a strong indicator, however, it is not necessarily decisive if there
are counter-indications arising from the arrangement between the
parties such as an absence of any right for one of the parties to participate in the management of the firm, or, perhaps, seek its
dissolution, because these are powers customarily bestowed on partners.[18] However, an agreement under which net profits are stated to
be shared, but not losses, will not necessarily lead to the conclusion
that partnership is absent.[19]

Even where a partnership exists there may be exceptional circumstances in which the activities of members may be individual
and not partnership activities, even if undertaken in association
with the use of the firm name. Thus, in *Alberni String Quartet v
Comrs of Customs and Excise*[20] the members of the famous string
quartet gave masterclasses for a week at a university, concluding
with a concert on the last day, which was an integral part of the
instruction. The quartet was registered as a partnership. One issue
was whether the masterclasses were part of the partnership activities. It was held that they were, since they had been undertaken

---

17   *Green v Beesley* (1835) 2 Bing NC 108; *Greenham v Grey* (1855) 41 CLR 501;
      Brett v Beckwith (1856) 3 Jur NS 31, 26 LJ Ch 130; *Moore v Davis* (1879) 11 Ch
      D 261; *Pawsey v Armstrong* (1881) 18 Ch D 698; *Fenston v Johnstone* (1940) 23
      TC 29; *Northern Sales (1963) Ltd v Ministry of National Revenue* (1973) 37 DLR
      (3d) 612.
18   *Walker v Hirsch* (1884) 27 Ch D 460; *Hawksley v Outram* [1892] 3 Ch 359;
      Sutton & Co v Grey [1894] 1 QB 285; *English Insurance Co v National Benefit
      Assurance Co (Official Receiver)* [1929] AC 114; *Pratt v Strick* (1932) 17 TC 459.
19   *Kilshaw v Jukes* (1863) 3 B & S 847.
20   [1990] VATTR 166. Similar issues may arise in the case of a pop group in rela-
      tion to their separate performance and song-writing activities: see, eg *Stuart v
      Barrett* (1992) 8 EIPRD 162.

Definition and background 25

collectively and concluded with the concert. If, however, they had been undertaken individually then they would not have been part of the partnership activities even though the quartet's name (the firm name) would have been referred to, unless the partners were agreed that such activities were partnership and not individual activities.

The specific provisions

The five specific provisions in the 1890 Act, previously noted, must now be considered. In each case the particular arrangements referred to do not *of themselves* create a partnership, although the court may conclude from the particular facts that in fact a partnership does exist.

1. PAYMENT OF A DEBT BY INSTALMENTS

The receipt by a person of a debt or other liquidated amount by instalments or otherwise out of the accruing profits of a business does not itself make him a partner in the business or liable as such.[1]

Thus, if L lends to B £20,000 to establish a business on terms that it is repaid from profits by instalments of £4,000 per annum, the arrangement does not, in itself, make L the partner of B. An example can be found in *Kilshaw v Jukes*.[2] Here, one A advanced money and supplied goods to B and C to finance a building development. It was agreed that he would be repaid out of profits, the remainder of which would be divided between B and C. The court concluded that A did not become a partner with B and C by virtue of the arrangement.

2. REMUNERATION OF A SERVANT OR AGENT

A contract for the remuneration of a servant or agent of a person engaged in a business by a share of the profits of the business does not of itself make the servant or agent a partner in the business or liable as such.[3] This prevents an employee whose pay is directly related to the profits generated by the partnership, or who is paid a

---

[1] Section 2(3)(a). *Cox and Wheatcroft v Hickman* (1860) 8 HL Cas 268 was an example of this situation. See also *Ex p Jones* [1896] 2 QB 484.
[2] (1863) 3 B & S 847.
[3] Section 2(3)(b). This encapsulates the pre-existent case law: see *Ross v Parkyns* (1875) LR 20 Eq 331; *Rawlinson v Clarke* (1846) 15 M & W 292; *Stocker v Brockelbank* (1851) 3 Mac & G 250; *Shaw v Galt* (1864) 16 ICLR 357; *Radcliffe v Rushworth* (1864) 33 Beav 484; *Ex p Tennant* (1877) 6 Ch D 303.

salary plus a bonus which is related to the profits of the business, being classed as a partner.[4] The reason why an employee should not be a partner merely by reason of receiving a share of the profits is that he does not in reality enjoy the status of a partner, since he has no say in the way in which the business is operated. The question of whether, on the one hand, a partnership has arisen or whether, on the other, the relationship which subsists is an employment contract is often raised before an industrial tribunal in relation to the rights conferred on employees in the modern world,[5] but may arise through much more roundabout means.[6]

Of course, it should always be remembered that, even though an employee is not a partner,[7] he may be treated as a partner in dealings with third parties if he allows himself to be held out as a partner by the firm.[8]

The salaried partner

A feature of the growth of the modern professional partnership – with its very considerable number of partners operating within a large scale business run on very hierarchical lines – has been the creation of an intermediate rank of professional. Designated as salaried partners, these operate in a middle rank between the true partners and the purely salaried employees. From the point of view of the economic analysis of the business organisation a salaried partner has his foot on the rung of the promotion ladder, which leads from employment to full partnership on his way up the hierarchy of the firm.[9] The basic characteristics of his position are that he is held out to the world as being a partner, but in fact he receives a salary – plus, perhaps, a bonus – by way of remuneration, rather than a share of the profits.[10] The basic legal issue which arises is whether or not he is a partner, and, if he is a partner, what his rights are.

.[4] Several examples have been met in the case law already discussed where the issue of whether a partnership or employment had been created: see, eg *Saywell v Pope* [1979] STC 824.
[5] *Palumbo v Stylianou* [1966] 1 ITR 407; *E Rennison & Son v Ministry of Social Security* (1970) 114 Sol Jo 952.
[6] Similar issues may arise in the case of a pop group in relation to their separate performance and song-writing activities: see, eg *Stuart v Barrett* (1992) 8 EIPRD162.
[7] *Briggs v Oates* [1990] ICR 473.
[8] As may a retired partner, see p 153, below.
[9] He may, however, be on the way down the hierarchy and be occupying a consultancy status prior to retirement: see *Re Hill* [1934] Ch 623; *Marsh v Stacey* (1963) 107 Sol Jo 512.
[10] Per Megarry J in *Stekel v Ellice* [1973] 1 All ER 465 at 472.

On analysis, there can be little doubt that the basic issue in fact encompasses separate issues:

(1) is the salaried partner a partner for the purposes of outsiders dealing with the firm? The answer to this question is that almost certainly he will be, since by his inclusion in the letter heading of the firm's correspondence and elsewhere he will have allowed himself to be held out as such. From this he will have ostensible authority to bind the firm, and the usual liability of a partner in respect of the obligations of the firm;[11]

(2) is the salaried partner a partner for the purposes of dealing with his fellow partners? Does he have the status of a partner to be able to apply for the firm to be wound up? It appears that a salaried partner may either be a true partner or an employee depending on the rights conferred on him by the partnership agreement, and whether these point to a contract of partnership or one of employment.[12] If he is a true partner it is likely that he will have both actual and ostensible authority to bind the firm;

(3) even if a salaried partner is a true partner it may be that the terms of the partnership agreement will severely limit the rights of salaried partners within the partnership as compared with the full partners. Where this is so then the terms of the partnership agreement will operate to restrict the salaried partner accordingly.[13]

3. PAYMENT OF AN ANNUITY TO A WIDOW OR CHILD OF A DECEASED PARTNER

A person being the widow or child of a deceased partner and receiving by way of annuity a portion of the profits made in the business in which the deceased person was a partner is not by reason only of such receipt a partner in the business or liable as such.[14] In understanding this provision it must be appreciated that a common way in which in the past provision might be made for the widow or children of a partner in the event of his death was a clause in the partnership agreement requiring an annuity to be paid to them thereafter from the profits of the business. Today, it is much more usual to deal with the problem by other means, such as personal insurance, but such

---

[11] Per Megarry J in *Stekel v Ellice* (above) at 472; *Re Hill* (above).
[12] Compare *Stekel v Ellice* with *Briggs v Oates* [1990] ICR 473.
[13] As in *Stekel v Ellice*.
[14] Section 2(3)(c).

clauses are still found.[15] Of itself, such an agreement does not make the widow or children partners in the business.

4. LOAN THE INTEREST OF WHICH VARIES WITH PROFITS

The advance by way of a loan to a person engaged or about to engage in any business on a contract with that person that the lender shall receive a rate of interest varying with the profits, or shall receive a share of profits arising from the carrying on of the business, does not of itself make the lender a partner with the person or persons carrying on the business or liable as such, provided that the contract is in writing and signed by, or on behalf of, all the parties thereto.[16]

This provision is complex, and gives rise to a real difficulty. It will be remembered that category (1) also dealt with situations which could include loans. The difference between them is that in category (1) the debt payable out of profits may well not be a loan at all or, if a loan, the amount ultimately payable is not related to the profitability of the business, whereas in category (4) the money payable is in relation to a loan to the business and either the interest or the amount payable is related to the profitability of the business. This further connection with the business would make it perhaps inherently more likely that the lender might be a partner.

The difficulty which arises from the provision derives from the proviso. If the situation covered by the fourth category is inherently nearer to partnership than the first the effect of the words 'provided that the contract is in writing and signed by or on behalf of all parties thereto' is that an *informal* arrangement of the type mentioned in category (4) is automatically a partnership. Smith LJ in an obiter dictum in the Court of Appeal certainly took this view,[17] but it is submitted that this is wrong. An informal arrangement of this type does not fall within category (4) but may still escape classification as a partnership by virtue of the general part of s 2(3).[18] However, it may well be that the lender will have a lot of explaining to do, including the absence of a formal agreement, and the court may well be much less easily persuaded than where category (4) can be relied on.

In any event, even where a formal agreement falling within category (4) is prepared, care should be taken over its drafting. It goes

---

[15] A comparable clause for the payment of a fixed sum rather than a proportion of profits of a business was at the heart of the litigation in the well-known case of *Beswick v Beswick* [1968] AC 58.

[16] Section 2(3)(d).

[17] *Re Fort, ex p Schofield* [1897] 2 QB 495 at 501.

[18] Discussed at p 21, above.

without saying that the advance must genuinely be a loan. It should be remembered that an essential characteristic of a loan is a personal responsibility on the borrower to repay it. An arrangement under which repayment is *only* to be made from partnership profits is therefore not a loan.[19] The agreement should avoid all provisions and expressions peculiar to partnership agreements,[20] on no account should the lender take a share of capital, and there should be no provision that the loan should not be employed as part of the capital of the partnership.[1]

5. SALE OF GOODWILL

A person receiving by way of annuity or otherwise a portion of the profits of a business in consideration of the sale by him of the goodwill of the business is not, by reason only of such receipt, a partner in the business or liable as such.[2] An example of this is afforded by the facts of *Pratt v Strick*,[3] which concerned the sale of a doctor's practice. Under the terms of the assignment of the business it was agreed that the seller would continue to reside in the house from which the practice was run for three months and introduce the patients of the practice to the purchaser. During the three months the earnings and expenses of the practice were to be shared equally. On these facts the court decided that the practice became the purchaser's at the date of the assignment, and seller and purchaser were not partners in the practice as it continued for the three months.

It is important that a business transaction should be closely scrutinised before concluding that it falls within the provision. Thus, in *Re Gieve, ex p Shaw*[4] the widow of a businessman sold the business to Gieve and Wills, who carried on the business. Under the terms of the arrangement she was to be paid a substantial annuity. Subsequently Gieve died and Wills became insolvent. The issue arose as to whether her claim was postponed or could be pursued.[5] The Court of Appeal concluded that the transaction was not a sale of goodwill in return for a share of profits, but a sale of goodwill for

---

[19] *Re Megavand, ex p Delhasse* (1878) 7 Ch D 511.
[20] However, mere terminology cannot, in itself, prevent a partnership from arising when that is the substance of the arrangement. See *Kilshaw v Jukes* (1863) 3 B & S 847; *Bullen v Sharp* (1865) LR 1 CP 86; *Ross v Parkyns* (1875) LR 20 Eq 331.
[1] *Holme v Hammond* (1872) LR 7 Ex Ch 218.
[2] Section 2(3)(e). For a discussion of goodwill see Chapter 9, p 201, below.
[3] (1932) 17 TC 459.
[4] [1899] WN 41, per Wright J; [1899] WN 72, CA.
[5] Pursuant to s 3 of the 1890 Act, discussed at p 31, below.

the provision of an annuity. The mere fact that the annuity could only be paid from the profits of the business did not affect the reality of what had been effected.

Categorisation not exclusive

It should not be thought that the categorisation attempted by the 1890 Act is productive of mutually exclusive situations. A particular arrangement may fall into more than one of the categories. An example is afforded by the case of *Re Young, ex p Jones*.[6] Jones and Young entered into an agreement under which Jones agreed to lend Young £500 in consideration of the payment to Jones of £3 per week from profits. So far the agreement would have fallen within category (1). However, the agreement went on to provide that Jones was to assist in the office, to have control over the money advanced and also to be able to draw bills of exchange. Further, if he wished to do so, he had the right to enter into a partnership agreement within seven months. These further provisions made the situation one for which the appropriate provisions would appear to be category (2). In any event the court concluded that such an arrangement did not in itself create a partnership, and as there was nothing further to indicate the existence of a partnership, Jones had not become a partner in the venture. On the other hand, as one might expect, an arrangement under which a creditor agrees not to call in a debt in consideration of the payment of a share of the profits to a third person does not fall within the fourth category.[7]

A further illustration is the case of *Walker v Hirsch*.[8] The plaintiff was a clerical employee of the firm. He then entered into an arrangement whereby he agreed to advance £1,500 to the firm. In return he was to be paid a salary of £180 pa and one-eighth of the net profits. If losses were generated by the business he was to bear one-eighth of these. What was the nature of the arrangement? Was it a partnership? Was it a contract of employment? Was it a contract of loan? In reality it had features of all of these forms of agreement. It falls to the courts to decide on the particular circumstances of each case whether such an arrangement is, or is not, a partnership.[9]

---

[6] [1896] 2 QB 494.
[7] *Re Pinto Leite and Nephews* [1929] 1 Ch 221.
[8] (1884) 27 Ch D 460.
[9] The Court of Appeal concluded that the particular arrangement litigated before them was a contract of employment.

Postponement in insolvency

The advantage of praying in aid s 2(3) to avoid classification as a partnership is that the successful person is not liable for the losses and liabilities of the business if it proves to be unsuccessful. However, the success is modified by s 3 of the 1890 Act, which postpones the position of the non-partner in certain circumstances on the insolvency of the business.[10] Section 3 operates where the non-partner has made finance available to the partnership. Whilst he is not directly responsible for the losses of the business, his right to recover in respect of the finance is postponed until the claims of other creditors for money's worth have been satisfied. He is thus put at risk, but not a risk of unlimited liability.

More precisely, s 3 provides:

'In the event of any person to whom money has been advanced by way of loan upon such a contract as is mentioned in the last foregoing section, or of any buyer of a goodwill in consideration of a share of the profits of the business, being adjudged a bankrupt, entering into an agreement to pay his creditors less than one hundred pence in the pound, or dying in insolvent circumstances, the lender of the loan shall not be entitled to recover anything in respect of his loan, and the seller of the goodwill shall not be entitled to recover anything in respect of the share of profits contracted for, until the claims of the creditors or buyer for valuable consideration in money or money's worth have been satisfied.'

The effect of this is that a creditor who has advanced money by way of a loan, or who has transferred goodwill within the terms of s 2(3), cannot claim with the other creditors. For this purpose, it is irrelevant that the creditors were not creditors at the time the loan was made or the goodwill transferred, or that the other creditors gave credit to the partners individually rather than to the business. If the circumstances set out in the section are met, the particular creditor's claim is postponed, and cannot recover anything on the insolvency of the debtor until all of the other creditors have been satisfied.[11]

It is important, therefore, to determine precisely what the circumstances are in which the section will be brought into operation. If the creditor has advanced separate sums, some on circumstances falling within s 3 and some at fixed rates of interest, he will be

---

[10] This will be referred to again in Chapter 13 which deals with insolvency.
[11] *Re Grason, ex p Taylor* (1879) 12 Ch D 366; *Re Mason* [1899] 1 QB 810.

postponed with regard to the former but not the latter.[12] However, if further sums *relating to that loan* are advanced on a loan falling within the section, all sums are postponed. Likewise, where a loan falling with the section was made to a partnership in circumstances falling within s 3, and continued to one of the partners who subsequently took over the business on the dissolution of the partnership, the creditor remained postponed on the insolvency of the continuing partner.[13] The principle is that, once caught by the provision, a loan remains within its ambit. Only a new loan will escape. Thus, a lender with a loan which entitles him to a share of the profits does not remove the loan from the ambit of the section by agreeing to accept a fixed rate of interest. Only the repayment of the old loan and the making of a new loan will have this effect.[14]

On the other hand, if that part of the agreement which provided for sharing in profits is so vague as to be void and can be severed from the rest of the agreement, the agreement will be enforceable as a simple loan agreement and the lender will not be postponed.[15]

It has been argued that an informal loan or advance made within the circumstances set out in s 2(3)(d) is not postponed in the case of insolvency since it does not meet the formal requirements of the proviso.[16] The position with regard to such informal loans was considered by the Court of Appeal in *Re Fort*.[17] One S had advanced £3,000 to Fort under an agreement which had not been put into writing so that Fort could set up business as a jeweller. Under the agreement Fort was to receive interest at 5%, plus a half of the profits of the business. Fort became insolvent, and S sought to recover his debt. He argued that since his loan agreement was not in writing it fell within the proviso to s 2(3)(d), and so outside the terms of the subsection, so that s 3 did not apply and the agreement was not postponed to the claims of the creditors. The court disagreed. Section 3 refers to such a contract as is mentioned in s 2(3)(d) and the type of contract mentioned is a contract of loan giving a return by way of a share of the profits, which precisely covered the agreement before it. The proviso relates only to those seeking to rely on the subsection to avoid becoming partners and who therefore have a contract of the particular type. In the words of Lord Esher:[18]

12 *Re Tew, ex p Mills* (1873) 8 Ch App 569; *Re Mason* [1899] 1 QB 810.
13 *Re Mason* [1899] 1 QB 810.
14 *Re Grason, ex p Taylor* (1879) 12 Ch D 366; *Re Stone* (1886) 33 Ch D 541; *Re Hildesheim* [1893] 2 QB 357; *Re Mason* (above).
15 *Re Vince* [1892] 2 QB 478.
16 Discussed at p 28, above.
17 [1897] 2 QB 495.
18 At 500.

'Such a contrast [an informal loan] comes within the words of s 2 of the Act, describing the contract dealt with in the section. The proviso is no part of such description.'

The postponement achieved by s 3 is postponement of priority amongst unsecured creditors. The section does not operate to remove any priority achieved by the creditor in taking security for the loan. In the words used in *Re Vince*[19] it does not 'deprive the lender of his right to retain any security he may take for his money; nor of his right to foreclose such security'.[20]

---

[19] [1892] 2 QB 478.
[20] The legislation carries on the changes introduced by the Partnership Act 1865, s 5 and cases decided under that legislation are to similar effect: see, eg *Ex p Corbridge* (1876) 4 Ch D 246; *Ex p Sheil* (1877) 4 Ch D 789; *Badeley v Consolidated Bank* (1888) 38 Ch D 238.

CHAPTER 2

FORMATION OF PARTNERSHIP

The foundation stone of the vast majority of partnerships is the voluntary agreement of the partners to enter into such a relationship.[1] In general, the law recognises that the capacity of an individual to enter into a partnership agreement is the same as the capacity of a party to enter into any contractual relationship with another.[2] Accordingly, as a matter of principle, anyone of full age and mental capacity is capable of becoming a party to a partnership agreement. Certain factors may, however, affect a party's ability to enter into partnership, or the conditions upon which he may enter into, or remain within, a partnership. These are discussed below.

Minors

The capacity of a minor to become a partner in an enterprise is subject to special rules and restrictions.[3] A minor may enter into a partnership with others but, in doing so, he will in general incur no liability either to his partners, or to third parties, during his

---

[1] The above statement is subject to the comparatively rare cases where the law implies a partnership between parties in the absence of an express agreement. See p 55, below.

[2] Statute and public policy may restrict the capacity of certain parties to enter into a partnership. For these special cases see pp 36–38, below. For ease of exposition, reference in the text to an individual includes all legal persons including corporations unless the context excludes this.

[3] A minor is a party below the age of majority. Since the Family Law Reform Act 1969 and the Age of Majority (Scotland) Act 1969 the age of majority in the UK has been 18. On attaining that age a party attains full legal capacity. The practical importance of this aspect of the law has accordingly been much reduced.

minority.[4] In the case of *Lovell and Christmas v Beauchamp*[5] the House of Lords determined that a minor is, on becoming a partner, entitled to a share of the profits of the enterprise. However, during his minority he cannot be sued for the partnership debts in his personal capacity.[6] The adult partners are nevertheless fully liable for debts incurred by the minor on behalf of the partnership.[7]

A minor may repudiate a partnership agreement to which he is a party at *any* time prior to his attaining his majority. Once he attains his majority he can repudiate the partnership agreement, but only within a *reasonable time after* he has attained his majority.[8] He must then repudiate the partnership agreement in its entirety, and not seek to claim *any* share of the profits of the partnership.[9] If the minor, on attaining his majority, fails within a reasonable time to repudiate the partnership agreement[10] he will risk incurring liability as a partner for any debts sustained by the partnership *after* the lapse of this reasonable period, by virtue of the doctrine of holding out.[11]

Where a minor repudiates a partnership agreement, and there has been a total failure of consideration[12] for any premiums paid by him, he is entitled to recover any such sums.[13] The adult partners

---

4 See *Re A and M* [1926] Ch 274, where both partners were minors.

5 [1894] AC 607.

6 A party commencing an action for debt against a partnership where one of the partners is a minor should generally do so in the partnership's trading or business name. Any judgment subsequently obtained should be 'against the defendant firm other than A a minor'. If the action for debt is brought against the partners individually, ie not in the partnership's business or trading name, the minor should not be joined as a defendant: see *Chandler v Parkes* (1800) 3 Esp 79; *Harris v Beauchamp* [1893] 2 QB 534.

7 In such cases, the adult partners may utilise any capital contributed by the minor to the partnership in the satisfaction of the partnership debts. They may also deduct any losses incurred by the partnership from the minor's undrawn or future share of profits: see *Lovell v Beauchamp* (fn 5, above). As an *alternative*, the adult partners may seek a restitution order under s 3 of the Minors' Contracts Act 1987.

8 Co Litt 380b, *Newry and Enniskillen Railway v Coombe* (1849) 3 Ex Ch 565.

9 *Lovell v Beauchamp* (fn 5, above); *North Western Rly Co v McMichael* (1850) 5 Ex Ch 114.

10 Eg by retaining a share in the partnership, or by failure either to affirm or disaffirm the partnership agreement. What is a reasonable time is, of course, a question of fact.

11 See Partnership Act 1890, s 14; *Goode v Harrison* (fn 8, above). For the doctrine of holding out see p 55, below.

12 See p 43, below for a discussion of the consideration which may support a partnership agreement.

13 *Corpe v Overton* (1833) 10 Bing 252; *Steinberg v Scala (Leeds) Ltd* [1923] 2 Ch 452.

can in the circumstances noted above seek a restitution order against the minor in respect of any property which the latter has acquired by virtue of the partnership agreement.[14]

Minors and third parties

Although not strictly an issue of capacity, it may be convenient at this stage to consider a minor's liability for the debts of the partnership, where the minor is held out as a partner.[15] It would appear that the minor would, in such a case, still be free from liability for the partnership debts so incurred.[16]

A minor who is a partner will not be held responsible for the tortious acts of his adult partners. However, in accordance with general principles of tort, an action may lie against a partnership for the acts of a minor partner, where such acts are fraudulent or negligent and are carried out by him on behalf of and for the benefit of the partnership.[17] However, where a party seeks to enforce against a minor partner what is essentially a contractual claim by an action in tort, the courts will not permit such an action to lie.[18] Where a minor partner in the course of partnership business perpetrates an act which is fraudulent he will, however, remain liable to a third party affected by such an act, and may be the subject of a consequential action for restitution.[19] In such cases the relevant party will also be able to seek appropriate equitable relief.[20]

Persons suffering from mental disorder

In accordance with the general principles of contract, a person entering into a partnership agreement, who is suffering from a mental disorder, will be bound by such an agreement, but only in so far as the following conditions are satisfied:

---

[14] See Minors' Contracts Act 1987, s 3.
[15] See p 55, below for a consideration of the doctrine of holding out.
[16] *Price v Hewitt* (1853) 8 Ex Ch 146; *Johnson v Pye* (1665) 1 Sid 258; *Vin Ab Enfant* H2 pl 16; *Glossop v Colman* (1815) 1 Stark 25; *Green v Greenbank* (1816) 2 Marsh 485.
[17] Including negligent or fraudulent misstatements or misrepresentations. An action may lie between an adult partner and a minor partner for any tortious act committed by the latter.
[18] *R Leslie Ltd v Sheill* [1914] 3 KB 607 at 620, per Kennedy LJ.
[19] Minors' Contracts Act 1987, s 3; *Wright v Snowe* (1848) 2 De G & Sm 321.
[20] *Lempriere v Lange* (1879) 12 Ch D 675; *Woolf v Woolf* [1899] 1 Ch 343.

(1) that the other partner(s) were unaware of the mental incapacity of their fellow partner at the time the partnership was formed;[1]
(2) that the other partner(s) entered into the partnership agreement in good faith;
(3) that at the time of the making of the partnership agreement no receiver had been appointed under the Mental Health Act 1983 to administer the mentally incapacitated partner's affairs and property.[2]

In such cases the incapacitated partner, though suffering from a mental disorder, will accordingly have the benefit of, and be subject to, any rights or liabilities arising from the partnership.

A judge of the Court of Protection in administering the property and affairs of a patient[3] may direct that any partnership of which the patient is a member be dissolved.

Supervening mental illness

A partner who has entered into a partnership with an unimpaired mental capacity may subsequently suffer a supervening mental incapacity. In such cases the mentally incapacitated partner will still be entitled to his share of the profits of the enterprise.[4] It inevitably follows from the above that such a person will also remain liable as a partner for the acts of his co-partners.[5] However, the position of such a partner may be effected as has been noted above by any action undertaken on his behalf by the Court of Protection under the Mental Health Act 1983.

Aliens

A person who is not a citizen of the United Kingdom, a Commonwealth citizen, British protected person, or a citizen of the Irish Republic as classified by the British Nationality Act 1981[6] is an alien. Such individuals are, however, capable of becoming

---

[1] See *Hart v O'Connor* [1985] AC 1000 and the authorities cited therein.
[2] Mental Health Act 1983, s 99; *Re Marshall* [1920] 1 Ch 284.
[3] See Mental Health Act 1983, s 94(1), as amended by Public Trustee and Administration of Funds Act 1986, s 2(2). See also Mental Health Act 1983, s 96.
[4] *Jones v Noy* (1833) 2 My & K 125.
[5] *Sadler v Lee* (1843) 6 Beav 324.
[6] Section 50(1).

partners in an enterprise with British citizens.[7] Nevertheless, there is a qualification to the above. In cases where an alien is either (a) resident or (b) carrying on business in a country which is at war with the UK, then in accordance with general principles of contract and public policy, in the absence of a Crown licence, any partnership between such an enemy alien and a British citizen in existence at the time of the outbreak of war will automatically be dissolved.[8] Furthermore, in the circumstances noted above, the formation of such a partnership during hostilities is illegal and, consequently, such a partnership is incapable of creation. A British citizen who is resident, or carrying on a business, in a country which is at war with the UK will be in the same position as an enemy alien, at least for the purposes of his involvement in the continuation or creation of a partnership with any person (including a British citizen) who is resident or carrying on business in the UK during those hostilities.

Although an enemy alien cannot[9] maintain an action against a party in the UK, he may without restriction be a defendant to an action. In such a case, his position is no different from that of any other defendant in an equivalent action.

Spouses

Despite the removal of the disabilities to which a wife was formerly subject, a wife and husband who are in partnership may find that their partnership is subject to special consideration because of the ties of marriage.[10] If the marriage and the partnership enterprise are inexorably linked, conduct which may lead to the breakdown of the marriage relationship may well also affect the partnership relationship.[11] Special provision is made where a person lends money to a partnership (for the purposes of the partnership business) and their

---

[7] Even aliens otherwise protected by diplomatic immunity under the Diplomatic Privileges Act 1964 may be subject to actions in the United Kingdom in respect of liabilities incurred as partners of firms which carry on business in the UK. See Diplomatic Privilege Act 1964, Sch 1, art 31.

[8] Partnership Act 1890, s 34; *R v Kupfer* [1915] 2 KB 321; *Hugh Stevenson and Sons v Aktiengesellschaft* [1918] AC 239; *Rodriguez v Speyer Bros* [1919] AC 59.

[9] In the absence of a licence granted by the Crown: see *Porter v Freudenberg* [1915] 1 KB 857; see also *The Mowe* [1915] P1.

[10] Such a relationship may be less readily inferred by the law where the parties are married, *Nixon v Nixon* [1969] 1 WLR 1676.

[11] Furthermore, on the breakdown of the marriage, the partnership assets may be subject to the jurisdiction of the Family Division.

spouse is a member of that partnership. In such cases, if an insolvency order is made against the partnership, the lender spouse's rights to recover the sum lent will be postponed, both to the creditors of the partnership and to the insolvent spouse's separate creditors.[12]

Companies

A company, being a legal person, may enter into partnership with any other legal person, including another company.[13] However, the company's ability to enter into a partnership will depend principally on the terms of its memorandum and articles of association, which must expressly or impliedly permit such an action.[14] Even where, because of limitations within its memorandum and articles of association, a company could not lawfully enter into a partnership, but it has nevertheless done so, the position of third parties who may have dealt with such a company on the basis that it is a partner in the relevant enterprise is not affected.[15]

The restrictions upon a UK citizen trading with an enemy alien, or entering into, or remaining in, partnership with such a person, also remain valid for, and applicable to, enemy alien companies. In such cases the determination of a company's status as an enemy alien is ultimately a matter of applying the test of control, and not merely determining the company's country of incorporation.[16]

Bankrupts

A person who is bankrupt and who obtains credit[17] for a partnership of which he is a member, without disclosing to the person

---

[12] Cf the situation where such a loan is made to a partnership of which the bankrupt spouse *was* a partner; though in such cases the bankrupt spouse's separate creditors may still be preferred creditors as against the lender spouse: see Insolvency Act 1986, s 329.

[13] See Partnership Act 1890, s 1(1) and Interpretation Act 1978, s 5, Sch 1.

[14] But see *Newstead v Frost* [1980] 1 WLR 135 at 141; *Hugh Stevenson & Son v Aktiengesellschaft etc Industrie* [1918] AC 239. It is unlikely that a company which has a modern memorandum and articles of association would be prohibited from entering into a partnership.

[15] Companies Act 1985, s 35, as amended.

[16] In identifying the seat of control of a company the courts will lift the 'corporate veil', to determine whether the controlling agents of the company are resident in an enemy country, or are controlled by the enemy: see *Daimler Co Ltd v Continental Tyre Co* [1916] 2 AC 307 at 345 and 346; *Kuenigl v Donnersmarck* [1955] 1 QB 515.

[17] Above a prescribed amount: see the Insolvency Proceedings (Monetary Limits) Order 1986, SI 1986/1996.

from whom the credit is obtained his insolvent status, commits an offence.[18] Furthermore, a bankrupt cannot lawfully engage in a partnership which carries on its business under a name, other than that in which the bankrupt was adjudged bankrupt, unless he discloses the fact of his bankruptcy to persons dealing with that partnership.[19]

Trustees and personal representatives

Trustees and personal representatives may, in their respective capacities, enter into a partnership.[20] However, in doing so they incur all the liabilities of a partner.[1] Nevertheless, if in becoming members of a partnership such individuals are acting within the scope of their powers and duties as trustees and/or personal representatives, they will be entitled to an indemnity out of any trust fund or estate respectively. It would seem that in the circumstances noted above, a trustee by entering into a partnership would not constitute any cestui que trust a partner in such an enterprise.[2]

THE SIZE OF A PARTNERSHIP

Although the position at common law remained unclear, it does not appear that the common law ever unambiguously recognised any restriction on the number of persons who could be members of a partnership.

Statute has, however, imposed restrictions on the size of partnerships. The relevant current legislation is s 716(1) of the Companies Act 1985. This provision restricts a company, association or partnership to no more than 20 persons, if such an organisation has for its object the acquisition of gain, either for that enterprise or for its individual members. Any organisation with more than 20 members engaged in such an object must, in principle, be a registered company, ie registered under the Companies Acts or by letters patent.[3]

---

[18] Insolvency Act 1986, s 360(1).
[19] Ibid.
[20] See Chapter 12 for a consideration of this issue.
[1] *Muir v City of Glasgow Bank* (1879) 4 App Cas 337.
[2] Where a bare nominee enters into a partnership on behalf of his principal, he will constitute his principal the actual partner in the enterprise.
[3] There are special rules relating to limited partnerships, see Chapter 14, the Limited Partnerships Act 1907, s 4(2) and the Companies Act 1985, s 717.

Section 716(2), however, provides exceptions to the above restriction upon partnership size, and permits the formation of partnerships of more than 20 members in cases where the partnership is formed to carry on a professional practice within a firm of solicitors or accountants. In such cases each partner must be a member of the relevant profession.[4] Similar exemption from s 716(1) exists under s 716(2) for persons who carry on the profession of stockbroker within a partnership, but only where the parties are members of a recognised stock exchange. Such a partnership must consist entirely of persons who are members of such a stock exchange.[5]

Further, by virtue of regulations made under s 716(2)(d)[6] certain professional firms may be excepted from the operation of s 716(1) and may therefore operate in partnerships of more than 20 members.[7] These professional firms include:

(1) partnerships of patent and registered trade mark agents, where each partner is a registered trade mark or patent agent;[8]

(2) partnerships of surveyors, auctioneers, valuers, estate agents, and estate managers, where not less than three-quarters of the total number of partners are members of one or more of the relevant professional bodies;[9]

(3) partnerships of actuaries, where all the partners are either Fellows of the Institute of Actuaries or Fellows of the Faculty of Actuaries;[10]

---

4 For the definition of 'solicitor' for the purposes of s 716 see Companies Act 1985, s 716(3) as amended by the Companies Act 1989, Sch 19, para 15(3); see also SI 1991/2729 which permits partnerships formed for the purpose of carrying on the profession of practising lawyers, which are multinational partnerships, to exceed 20 persons. For the definition of 'accountants' for the same purposes see Companies Act 1985, s 716; Companies Act 1948, s 161(11)(b) and Companies Act 1989, s 50(1). See also Companies Act 1989 (Eligibility for Appointment as Company Auditor) (Consequential Amendments) Regulations 1991, SI 1991/1997, reg 2, Sch, para 53(1), (3).

5 For the definition of recognised stock exchange for the purposes of s 716(2) see Companies Act 1985, s 716(4) as substituted by the Companies Act 1989, Sch 19, para 15(3). See also SI 1992/1028 which exempts from s 716(1) partnerships which are members of the International Stock Exchange; see also SI 1992/1027 which provides the same exemption for limited partnerships.

6 Inserted by the Companies Act 1989, Sch 19, para 15.

7 Depending on a prescribed number of partners being professionally qualified.

8 SI 1992/644. See also the Patent Agents and Registered Trade Mark Agents (Mixed Partnerships and Bodies Corporate) Rules 1994, SI 1994/362 and 363.

9 See the Partnerships (Unrestricted Size) No 1 Regulations 1968, SI 1968/1222. The specified bodies are the Royal Institution of Chartered Surveyors, the Chartered Lands Agents' Society, the Chartered Auctioneers' and Estates Agents' Institute and the Incorporated Society of Valuers and Auctioneers.

10 See SI 1992/1439.

(4)   partnerships of consulting engineers, where the majority of partners are recognised by the Council of Engineering Institutions as chartered engineers;[11]

(5)   partnerships of what may be described as building designers, ie persons who are involved in the professions involved in building design, where not less than three-quarters of the partners are either registered under the Architects (Registration) Act 1931 or are recognised by the Council of Engineering Institutions as a chartered engineer or by the Royal Institution of Chartered Surveyors as a chartered surveyor;[12]

(6)   partnerships of loss adjusters where not less than three-quarters of the total number of partners are members of the Chartered Institution of Loss Adjusters.[13]

Consequences of contravening section 716

A partnership may contravene s 716 of the Companies Act 1985, or any regulations made under that section, with the consequence that it is an illegal partnership. This may be because it simply exceeds the number of permitted partners, ie 20 under s 716(1). Furthermore, a partnership which has been formed to practice a profession may be illegal because it includes within its members one or more partners who may not be professionally qualified. Such a partnership may, however, carry on its profession or business, and though it exceeds 20 members, it may nevertheless, if there are a minimum or prescribed number of partners professionally qualified, be legal by virtue of regulations made under s 716(2)(d) (see above). In cases where partnerships are illegal, they cannot be lawfully created or, if they are in existence at the time of contravention, continue to exist.[14]

---

[11] See the Partnerships (Unrestricted Size) No 10 Regulations 1992, SI 1992/1439.

[12] See the Partnerships (Unrestricted Size) No 4 Regulations 1970, SI 1970/1319. See also SI 1992/1438 which amends SI 1970/1319 and which replaces a reference to a designated body by a reference to a successor body in any of the regulations.

[13] See the Partnerships (Unrestricted Size) No 5 Regulations 1982, SI 1982/530.

[14] A number of individuals may operate a business enterprise through a single trustee or nominee, and thus circumvent s 716(1). For a consideration of the general consequences that flow from the illegality of a partnership see p 45, below.

CONSIDERATION FOR A CONTRACT
OF PARTNERSHIP

A partnership agreement is only a species of contract. As a general principle of English contract law, such an agreement must therefore be supported by consideration if it is to be enforceable by a party. Consideration may be furnished by a party to the partnership agreement by his agreeing to or actually providing capital and/or his skills to the partnership enterprise. Furthermore, in accordance with the concept of consideration, any act or omission which is a detriment to a party (eg it involves him incurring a liability to a third party) will constitute consideration so as to support a partnership agreement.[15] Agreeing to be bound by the terms of a partnership agreement will also clearly constitute such consideration.

The courts (again in accordance with general principles of contract) will not examine the adequacy of such consideration vis-à-vis the partners.[16] Accordingly, a partnership in which one or more of the partners agree to indemnify other partners against losses (though all agree to share any profits) is a valid partnership agreement.[17]

Where a party agrees to the payment of a premium as part of a condition to his entry to a partnership, and for his membership of that partnership for a specified time, his failure to make such a payment will render him liable to an action for recovery of such a premium by his potential partners. However, the recovery of the premium is conditional upon the plaintiff(s) being ready and willing to take the defendant into the relevant partnership in accordance with the agreement.[18]

Since all successful businesses generate goodwill, a party wishing to enter into partnership with a person or persons who are already carrying on a successful business may have to provide consideration to purchase a share of the goodwill of the enterprise. The value of such consideration may be governed by the terms of the partnership agreement, either by placing an exact value on the goodwill (or the share of the goodwill) or by providing a means of valuation of the

[15] *The Herkimer* (1840) Stuart Adm 17 at 23; *Anderson's Case* (1877) Ch D 75.
[16] *Dale v Hamilton* (1846) 5 Hare 369 at 393, per Wigram VC.
[17] *Geddes v Wallace* (1820) 2 Bligh 270; *Walker West Developments Ltd v FJ Emmett Ltd* (1979) 252 Estates Gazette 1171. Cf *Brophy v Holmes* (1828) 2 Mol 5.
[18] Recovery of premiums where there is a premature termination of such a partnership is governed by the Partnership Act 1890, s 40. There can be no recovery of a premium or any part of a premium where a partnership at will is ended. For partnerships at will see p 45, below.

goodwill. Although professional partnerships, including medical practices, will have goodwill, it is an offence under s 54 of the National Health Service Act 1977 to require an incoming partner to a medical practice carried on under the auspices of the National Health Service to provide any consideration in respect of goodwill, or for such a partnership to sell goodwill[19] to a purchaser of such a practice.

Although (as has been noted above) the adequacy of the consideration supplied by a party for entry into a partnership will not be examined by the courts, the value of such consideration may be pertinent to the question of taxation. In particular, the adequacy of such consideration supplied by an incoming partner may be material in determining whether partnership assets to which that party subsequently become entitled on the death, retirement or expulsion of another partner is to be regarded as a chargeable transfer to him (whether exempt or not) for the purposes of inheritance tax.[20]

FIXED TERM PARTNERSHIP

A partnership agreement may provide that the partnership is to endure for a set length of time. Provision may also be made in the agreement for a partnership to terminate on the occurrence of a prescribed event, which is more or less certain to occur.

Any partnership which may be terminated in either of the above circumstances can be regarded as a fixed term partnership.[1] Such a partnership can only be terminated, apart from the expiration of time or the occurrence of a prescribed event on which its continuation is conditional (or in accordance with any provision in the partnership agreement) by the unanimous agreement of the partners, by the terms of the Partnership Act, or by order of the court.

Thus s 32(a) of the Partnership Act 1890 provides that, subject to any agreement between the partners, a fixed term partnership is automatically dissolved on the expiration of that term.

---

[19] See *Lindley and Banks on Partnership* (16th edn, 1991) p 94 for a full discussion of this provision for definitions of goodwill, See also *Cruttwell v Lye* (1810) 17 Ves 335 and *Trego v Hunt* [1896] AC 7.

[20] For a consideration of tax issues and partnerships see Chapter 16.

[1] A fixed term partnership can also be created where there is a reference within the partnership agreement to terms which may bring about the dissolution of the partnership and which are based on any criterion of a most variable kind or even a condition or event which may be certain or uncertain to occur. Thus any term, no matter how vague or tenuous, which sets limits to the duration of the partnership will constitute such a partnership a fixed term partnership. This view it is submitted is supported by *Moss v Elphick* [1910] 1 KB 846.

By s 32(b) of the 1890 Act a partnership which is entered into for a single venture or undertaking is dissolved by the termination or completion of that undertaking or venture. This provision is subject to any contrary agreement between the parties. This provision may overlap with s 32(a), noted above.

PARTNERSHIPS AT WILL

No fixed term or undefined time partnerships

A partnership agreement may make no provision as to the duration of the partnership. Such a partnership may be regarded as a partnership at will. A partnership at will may be terminated by one partner giving notice to this effect to the other partners.

Two statutory provisions are relevant to such partnerships. Section 26(1) of the Partnership Act provides that:

(1) where no fixed term has been agreed upon for the duration of the partnership, any partner may determine the partnership at any time on giving notice of his intention so to do to all the other partners;
(2) where the partnership has originally been constituted by deed, a notice in writing, signed by the partner giving it, shall be sufficient for this purpose.

Section 32(c) of the Partnership Act is similar in scope and effect to s 26(1) and provides that, subject to any contrary agreement between the partners, where a partnership has been entered into for an undefined time it may be terminated by a partner giving notice to the other or others of his intention to dissolve the partnership.

In the last-mentioned situation the partnership is dissolved as from the date mentioned in the notice as the date of dissolution, or, if no date is so mentioned, as from the date of the communication of the notice.

Both of the above provisions thus appear to legislate for a partnership at will, ie a partnership which makes no provision for setting limits to its duration. Both legislative provisions provide that partnerships at will can be terminated by the giving of notice of termination by one partner to the other partner(s).

Nevertheless, there are differences between the two legislative provisions. Section 26(1) seems to give a mandatory right to a partner to terminate a partnership at will[2] but in s 32(c) the right of a partner to terminate a partnership at will is manifestly subject to any contrary agreement between the parties. Furthermore, neither provision refers to partnerships at will, but only to a partnership where *no fixed term* has been agreed in s 26(1) or in s 32(c) to a partnership for an '*undefined time*'. However, it may be cogently argued that since s 32(a) of the Partnership Act does refer to a fixed term partnership then the reference to a partnership for an *undefined time* in s 32(c) is to be construed as the exact opposite, ie a partnership for *no fixed time*. To sum up, it is submitted that both terms in ss 26(1) and 32(c) are no more than synonyms and both sub-sections apply to partnerships at will.[3]

In *Moss v Elphick*[4] the Court of Appeal determined that s 26(1) could only apply to partnerships where the partnership deed was silent with regard to terms which sets limits to the duration of a partnership. Thus, any provision in the partnership deed, no matter how tenuous or vague, which sets such limits to the duration of a partnership, must constitute a partnership a fixed term partnership, and therefore an enterprise which is outside the ambit of s 26(1).[5] Furthermore, it is suggested that any such provision in a partnership agreement would also amount to a contrary agreement between the partners for the purposes of s 32(c)[6] also taking such a partnership outside the terms of this sub-section.

The practical effect of such arguments is that any provision in a partnership agreement which sets limits to the duration of the partnership will prevent the partnership from being one at will. Accordingly, such partnerships cannot be terminated by notice either under s 26(1) or s 32(c). Only where the partnership agreement is entirely silent on such a point will the partnership be constituted a partnership at will. It may then be terminated by one of the partners giving notice to the other(s) under either of the above statutory provisions. Thus, the effect of the reasoning of the

---

[2] However, the editor of *Lindley and Banks on Partnership* (16th edn, 1991) at p 134 argues that s 26(1) must take effect subject to the contrary agreement of the partners by virtue of s 19 of the Partnership Act.

[3] See Morse *Partnership Law* (2nd edn, 1986) p 32.

[4] [1910] 1 KB 846.

[5] Since the partnership would not be one where there was no fixed term, as required by s 26(1).

[6] And thus exclude such partnerships from the ambit of s 32(c), which can only operate where there is no contrary agreement between the partners. It may also be argued that any such provision in a partnership agreement prevents the partnership from being for an undefined term as required by s 32(c). What effect such an argument has on the operation of s 32(b), noted above, remains unclear and is perhaps of little practical importance.

Court of Appeal in *Moss v Elphick*, noted above, is that the seemingly mandatory s 26(1) is not in conflict with the clearly permissive s 32(c), and that the apparent mandatory effect of the former provision is practically negated. Thus the philosophy behind the Partnership Act 1890, that the agreement of the partners is generally paramount in a partnership relationship, is maintained.

An example of the practical application of the above principles would be where, under the express provision of a partnership deed, one partner alone had the right to terminate the partnership. The effect of such a provision would be to exclude the operation of both s 26 and s 32. The partnership could then only be dissolved by reference to the relevant provisions of the partnership deed, by operation of law, or by order of the court.

A partnership at will will be presumed unless some agreement to the contrary can be proved.[7] Such agreement may be express, as noted above, or even implied by or from the conduct of the partners. Therefore, the terms of the partnership agreement, or the conduct of the partners, must be inconsistent with the right which a partner would otherwise expect of being able to determine the partnership by notice.

Circumstances which the courts have regarded as relevant to determining whether a partnership is a fixed term partnership or one at will are as follows:

(1) the continuation of a fixed term partnership beyond the expiration date will result in the creation of a new partnership which, in the *absence* of evidence as to the intended duration of such a new partnership, will be deemed to be a partnership at will;[8]
(2) the admission of a new partner to a fixed term partnership will terminate the earlier partnership and create a new one. If the earlier partnership agreement does not envisage the admission of new partners, the new partnership will be one at will. However, if the old agreement does provide for new partners, and the new partner agrees expressly or by implication to be bound by that agreement, the new partnership will be a fixed

---

[7] See *Moss v Elphick* [1910] 1 KB 846 at 849, per Farwell LJ; *Abbott v Abbott* [1936] 3 All ER 823 at 826, per Clauson J, approving a statement of principle first formulated by Lord Lindley. The burden of proof lies on the party alleging the agreement: see *Burdon v Barkus* (1862) 4 De GF & J 42.
[8] *Walters v Bingham* [1988] 1 FTLR 260; *Neilson v Mossend Iron Co* (1886) 11 App Cas 298; *Featherstonhaugh v Fenwick* (1810) 17 Ves 298; Partnership Act 1890, s 27.

term one.[9] It is in such cases in part a question of construction of the original partnership deed or agreement;

(3)   a partnership entered into for the sole purpose of completing a single undertaking or venture will, in general, be inferred as a fixed term partnership, terminating when that undertaking or venture is completed.[10]

Certain circumstances are neutral, or even militate against construing a partnership as being a fixed term business relationship. Thus, the fact that debts, even of a long term nature, have been incurred, or that property such as a lease of premises has been obtained by a partnership, are not sufficient in themselves to negative the presumption that a partnership is one at will.[11]

Termination by notice

Section 32 of the Partnership Act 1890 provides that a partnership entered into for an undefined time may be dissolved by a partner giving notice to the other partner(s) of his intent to dissolve the partnership. In such a case the partnership is dissolved as from the date mentioned in the notice. Where no date is mentioned in the notice, the date of dissolution is from the date of the communication of the notice.

Under s 26 of the Partnership Act 1890 the termination of a partnership at will merely requires a partner to give notice of termination to all the other partners. Where the partnership has been constituted by a formal deed of partnership, a notice in writing need only be signed by the partner giving notice.

---

[9]   The same position may arise in cases where the parties agree to be bound by a provisional partnership agreement pending the execution of a new formal partnership deed. Though a matter of construction of such an agreement, in general such a provisional agreements will create fixed term partnerships. See *Walters v Bingham* [1988] 1 FTLR 260; *Zamikoff v Lundy* (1970) 9 DLR (3d) 637.

[10]   See *Reade v Bentley* (1858) 4 K & J 656. Of course, certain such limited enterprises may not be construed by the courts as constituting a partnership between the parties. For the dissolution of partnerships entered into for a single venture or undertaking, see p 45, above and the Partnership Act 1890, s 32(b).

[11]   See *King v Accumulative Assurance Co* (1857) 3 CBNS 151; *Featherstonhaugh v Fenwick* (1810) 17 Ves 298; *Jeffreys v Smith* (1820) 1 Jac & W 298; *Alcock v Taylor* (1830) Taml 506; *Burdon v Barkus* (1862) 4 De GF & J 42; *Crawshay v Maule* (1818) 1 Swan 495; *Syers v Syers* (1876) 1 App Cas 174.

ILLEGAL PARTNERSHIPS

Consideration has already been given[12] to partnerships which are illegal. Thus, partnerships between British citizens and an enemy alien, or partnerships which (in certain circumstances) consist of more than a prescribed number of partners, are illegal. The law recognises further grounds which will render a partnership illegal. These will now be considered in turn, and the consequences that flow from a partnership being illegal will then be discussed.

Criminal activity

A partnership formed for the purpose of deriving profit from criminal activity will be illegal.[13]

Public policy

It has long been held that a partnership will be illegal if it is formed for a purpose which is contrary to present notions of morality, religion or public policy.[14] Since concepts of morality are constantly changing this ground of illegality is clearly an amorphous and uncertain one, and little guidance on its application can be gleaned from past authority. The present status of this ground therefore remains unclear.

Partnerships with enemy aliens

See the discussion above for a consideration of this ground for declaring a partnership illegal.

European aspects

It has been suggested that parties may in some situations, in entering into a partnership, breach art 85 of the EC Treaty by that simple

---

[12] See pp 37 and 40, above.
[13] See the celebrated 'Highwayman' case of *Everet v Williams* (1725); *Pothier on Obligations* and 9 LQR 197. See also *Ashhurst v Mason* (1875) LR 20 Eq 225 at 230; *Sykes v Beadon* (1879) 11 Ch D 170 at 195; *Biggs v Lawrence* (1789) 3 Term Rep 454 and *Stewart v Gibson* (1838) 7 Cl & F 707. It is, however, generally irrelevant that the activity of a partnership is illegal by reference to the laws of a friendly state. The courts *may* in such cases still be prepared to strike down such a partnership: see *Foster v Driscoll* [1929] 1 KB 470.
[14] See *Herring v Walround* (1682) 2 Cas in Ch 110: an enterprise to exhibit a human freak for profit was declared illegal.

act.[15] This prospect would seem most unlikely, however, in view of the comparative smallness of the vast majority of the business enterprises which constitute partnerships in the UK.

It would also seem unlikely that a UK partnership could, by its mere existence, breach the provisions of the Competition Act 1980. Nevertheless, such possibilities must be considered in respect of partnerships between large corporations. Such corporate partnerships may constitute business enterprises, which may have a significant impact upon the operation of particular business activities or markets.[16]

Illegality and statute

A statute may provide that a partnership which infringes any of its provisions is an illegal enterprise.[17] By way of contrast, a statute may merely impose a sanction or penalty upon the partnership and/or its members for breach of any of its provisions, but not otherwise constitute the partnership illegal. Each case is a question of statutory interpretation.[18] The above may be illustrated by the following examples.

Professions and illegal partnerships

It is an offence for a person to act as or pretend to be a solicitor.[19] It has been determined, therefore, that a partnership which seeks to practice as a firm of solicitors and is a partnership which is

[15] See *Lindley* (16th edn, 1991) p 109. Article 85 renders null and void agreements between parties which may affect trade between the member states of the EC in so far as the agreements may prevent, restrict, or distort competition within the EC.

[16] Frequently, agreements between significant business enterprises concerning their joint co-operation in a business activity take the form of a joint venture, and not a partnership.

[17] This may arise because the statute by its provisions forbids the very purpose(s) for which the partnership was formed. See p 51, below and in particular fns 2 and 4, p 51, below. For other cases of statutory illegality of partnerships see also the Companies Act 1985, s 716 discussed at p 40, above.

[18] *SCF Finance Co Ltd v Masri (No 2)* [1987] QB 1002; *Hudgell Yeates & Co v Watson* [1978] QB 451; *Phoenix General Insurance Co of Greece SA v Halvanon Insurance Co Ltd* [1988] QB 216; *Re Cavalier Insurance Co Ltd* [1989] 2 Lloyd's Rep 430; *R v Hall* [1891] 1 QB 747; *R v Kakelo* [1923] WN 220.

[19] For a person to act as a solicitor he must be admitted to the roll of solicitors. He must also hold a current practising certificate, see the Solicitors Act 1974, ss 1, 20, 21.

comprised of a solicitor or solicitors together with an unqualified partner is illegal.[20] A similar situation has been arrived at where the members of a partnership are carrying on the practice of dentistry and one or more of the partners is unqualified.[1]

Purpose forbidden by statute

A statute may prohibit any person from undertaking a prescribed activity under pain of criminal sanction. A partnership formed to carry out such a prohibited activity may under those circumstances be illegal.[2] The rationale behind this principle is that in such cases the partnership is illegal because it has been formed with the intention of committing or deriving profit from a criminal or illegal act. However, a statute may by its provisions preclude such a drastic consequence, and merely impose a sanction upon each of the members of the partnership for breach of its provisions.[3]

Whether a breach of a statutory provision by a partnership renders the members of that partnership subject to a penalty, or whether the partnership is rendered illegal, must remain a question of interpretation of the individual statute. As a general rule, however, it may be said that a partnership formed with the unambiguous intent to contravene, circumvent or thwart the provisions of a statute which regulates a profession or business enterprise or activity will in general be an illegal enterprise.[4]

---

[20] *Williams v Jones* (1826) 5 B & C 108; *Scott v Miller* (1859) John 220. Where a qualified partner becomes unqualified, eg by omitting to renew his practising certificate, he becomes an unqualified person and the partnership of which he is a member becomes illegal; *Hudgell Yeates & Co v Watson* [1978] QB 451; *Edmonson v Davis* (1801) 4 Esp 14. In *Hudgell Yeates & Co v Watson* [1978] QB 451 at 462, per Bridge LJ it was suggested that where a qualified partner in a firm of solicitors ceases by accident to be qualified, the partnership, though illegal and automatically dissolved (see Partnership Act 1890, s 34) will be reconstituted when the unqualified partner becomes qualified again.

[1] See the Dentists Act 1984.

[2] Eg a partnership which is formed with the intent of carrying on an unlicensed credit business contrary to the Consumer Credit Act 1974: *SCF Finance Co Ltd v Masri (No 2)* [1987] QB 1002.

[3] Under the Consumer Credit Act 1974 a firm carrying on a consumer credit hire or an ancillary credit business must possess a standard licence issued by the Director General of Fair Trading. Each partner will commit an offence under the Act if the partnership carries out an activity not authorised by its own licence: see ss 39(1), 167 and Sch 1 to the Act. However, such a breach of the Act would not render the partnership illegal, see s 170(1) of the 1974 Act, fn 2 above.

[4] Cf the case where the illegality occurs without such intent and appears to be incidental. See *Dungate v Lee* [1969] 1 Ch 545.

Consequences of illegality

A partnership which is illegal ab initio or which subsequently becomes illegal is subject to immediate automatic dissolution by operation of law.[5]

It follows from the above that partners in an illegal partnership may not maintain actions as between themselves so as to enforce any rights under their partnership agreement which are tainted by any such illegality.[6] The inability of partners to enforce such rights under the partnership agreement is only a particular illustration of the general principle that a partner of an illegal partnership may not maintain an action, or enforce rights against his co-partners, in respect of any matters which affect or are related to that partnership, or his interest in that enterprise.[7] Although the illegality of a partnership may be raised as a defence by a partner in respect of any action brought against him by a co-partner, the defence in general must be specifically pleaded.[8] However, the court is not precluded on its own motion from raising the issue of illegality, and

---

[5] See Partnership Act 1890, s 34. In the case of a partnership which is illegal ab initio the dissolution occurs at the moment of creation.

[6] This principle also applies to prospective partners in an illegal partnership. Thus a premium paid over to an illegal partnership by a party as a condition to that party becoming a member of that partnership is irrecoverable by the prospective partner: *Williams v Jones* (1826) 5 B & C 108; *Harse v Pearl Life Assurance Co* [1904] 1 KB 558; *Duvergier v Fellows* (1832) 1 Cl & Fin 39. Any agreement between partners to an illegal partnership if tainted by the illegality is also unenforceable through court action: see *Ewing v Osbaldiston* (1837) 2 My & Cr 53. In the recent case of *Tinsley v Milligan* [1993] 3 All ER 65 the House of Lords recognised that where property interests are acquired as a consequence of an illegal transaction, a party (notwithstanding their participation in the illegal transaction) may recover a share, or all, of such property from one holding that property by virtue of the former's enjoyment of a legal or equitable proprietary interest. Such recovery is, however, dependent on the establishment of title to the property independently of and without reliance on any illegality to which the person seeking recovery is a party. In such cases it would be irrelevant that the title to the property on which the person seeking recovery relies was acquired in the course of carrying through an illegal transaction. This decision would appear to be limited to recovery of property through title, eg by virtue of a constructive or resulting trust of which the person seeking to recover is a beneficiary. The case would not seem to affect the text above. See also *Bowmakers Ltd v Barnet Instruments Ltd* [1944] 2 All ER 579; *Saunders v Edwards* [1987] 2 All ER 651; *Euro-Diam Ltd v Bathurst* [1988] 2 All ER 23; *Howard v Shirlstar Container Transport Ltd* [1990] 3 All ER 366, the latter authority was doubted in *Tinsley*, see also the cases cited in *Tinsley v Milligan*.

[7] *Foster v Driscoll* [1929] 1 KB 470; *Sykes v Beadon* (1879) 11 Ch D 170. The illegality must, however, relate to the partnership and the agreement which sustains it, see below.

[8] See RSC Ord 18, r 8(1).

in appropriate cases may therefore refuse the parties to an action the remedies they seek.[9]

The principal actions which are denied to a partner of an illegal partnership against his co-partners are actions for account,[10] or on an account stated, and an action for a contribution where one partner has met the liabilities of the partnership at the express request of his co-partner(s).[11] Despite the above, a partner who is a member of an illegal partnership may in certain circumstances maintain an action against his co-partners to enforce his rights under the partnership agreement. Thus, if he has been induced to enter into the partnership as a result of his co-partners' fraudulent misrepresentations as to the legality of the partnership, he may by action enforce any rights which accrue to him by virtue of the partnership agreement. In such cases the partner maintaining such an action must be unaware at the time he enters into the partnership that the partnership is illegal.[12]

An illegal act within a legal partnership

An illegal partnership taints all activities carried out by the partners in the furtherance of the purposes of the partnership, and yet it does not follow that the converse is true. Thus, an illegal act of a partner or partners on behalf of a lawful partnership does not per se taint that partnership. Accordingly, where a partner is engaged in an illegal act, which is in furtherance of the purposes of the partnership, a fellow member of that partnership (whether or not he is a party to any such illegal act) may enforce his rights under the partnership agreement, and recover a share of any profits produced by that illegal act. This remains the case even though the consequence is that he has obtained a benefit from an illegal act. A partner who receives money as a consequence of an illegal act carried out by him in the

---

[9] See Partnership Act 1890, s 34. See also *Lipton v Powell* [1921] 2 KB 51; *Rawlings v General Trading Co* [1921] 1 KB 635.

[10] On an action for account see Chapter 10 and *Knowles v Haughton* (1805) 11 Ves 168; *Armstrong v Armstrong* (1834) 3 My & K 45; *Harvey v Collett* (1846) 15 Sim 332; *Farmers' Mart Ltd v Milne* [1915] AC 106; cf *Greenberg v Cooperstein* [1926] Ch 657.

[11] For an action for a contribution see Chapter 10 and *De Begnis v Armistead* (1833) 10 Bing 107; *Fisher v Bridges* (1854) 3 E & B 642.

[12] Misrepresentations of any kind which do not relate to the supposed legality of an illegal partnership or its purposes will not permit a partner to enforce his rights under the partnership agreement although he claims he was induced to enter the partnership on the basis of the representations: see *Shelley v Paddock* [1980] QB 348; *Saunders v Edwards* [1987] 2 All ER 651.

course of the partnership business can only retain (as against his co-partners) such sums of that money as he would be entitled to as his share under the terms of the partnership agreement. In such a case any other partner(s) can maintain actions against him to recover their share of such moneys.[13]

Where a member or members of a partnership are engaged in an illegal enterprise, which remains partially or entirely inchoate, and which will involve the transfer of partnership assets, an action by any partner to recover such property, whether those assets are in the hands of third parties or in the hands of other partners, may be maintained. However, the money or property must not have been actually applied in furtherance of the illegal enterprise.[14]

It seems that the fruits or profits of any illegal enterprise accruing to a partnership, which is not itself illegal, cannot be solely or wholly retained by a partner as against his co-partner(s), if the latter can claim under the terms of the partnership agreement that he or they are entitled to a share of any such fruits or profits. A share of the profits of an illegal enterprise accruing to a partnership can be recovered by the creditors or beneficiaries of a deceased partner's estate, where the deceased partner's estate (including the right to a share of the profits of the illegal transaction) is vested in his personal representative(s).[15] Lindley suggests, however, that where no account has been settled between partners in respect of the profits of an illegal transaction, a personal representative of a deceased partner who holds any such profits as part of the deceased partner's estate can rely on the illegality of the transaction as if he were a partner of the business, so as to resist a claim for an account in respect of those profits by the estate's creditors and beneficiaries.[16]

Illegal partnerships and third parties

It only remains to consider the question of illegal partnerships, and the relationship between such enterprises and third parties. An

---

[13] As an adjunct to an action to recover any moneys a partner is entitled to an account. A fortiori a partner may recover such moneys which are in the hands of a third party: see *Farmers Mart Ltd v Milne* [1915] AC 106 at 113; *Euro-Diam Ltd v Bathurst* [1990] 1 QB 1; *Re Cavalier Insurance Co Ltd* [1989] 2 Lloyd's Rep 430. Cf *Gordon v Comr of Police* [1910] 2 KB 1080 and *Whiteman v Sadler* [1910] AC 514.

[14] *Taylor v Lendey* (1807) 9 East 49; *Barclay v Pearson* [1893] 2 Ch 154; *Herman v Jeuchner* (1884) 15 QBD 561; *Strachan v Universal Stock Exchange (No 2)* [1895] 2 QB 697.

[15] *Joy v Campbell* (1804) 1 Sch & Lef 328; *Hale v Hale* (1841) 4 Beav 369.

[16] The editor cites the cases of *Ottley v Browne* (1810) 1 Ball & B 360 and contrasts this case with *Sharp v Taylor* (1849) 2 Ph 801.

illegal partnership, eg one formed for an illegal purpose which supplies goods or services to a third party in pursuance of that purpose, cannot subsequently maintain an action to recover either the price of such goods or any fee for any services supplied.[17] Conversely, where a third party supplies goods or services to an illegal partnership, in circumstances where the relevant transaction is tainted by that illegality, such a party can nevertheless enforce his or its rights to be paid for such goods and services against the partnership. This right to payment is restricted, however, to situations where the third party is unaware of the illegality of the transaction and of the partnership at the time the third party performs his or its part of the transaction.[18]

INFORMAL PARTNERSHIPS

A partnership must not be confused with the creditor/business relationship. Conversely a relationship defined by an agreement in such terms may in reality constitute in law a partnership. These issues are considered in Chapter 1.

PARTNERSHIP BY ESTOPPEL

In certain instances an individual who has left a partnership is nevertheless represented or allows himself to be represented to third parties as if he were still a partner within that enterprise. Furthermore a party associated with a partnership may make or permit representations to be made as to his status within the partnership. The above cases may give rise to a partnership by estoppel, which is considered in Chapter 6.

---

[17] *Biggs v Lawrence* (1789) 3 Term Rep 454; *Shaw v Benson* (1883) 11 QBD 563; *Jennings v Hammond* (1882) 9 QB 225.
[18] *Re South Wales Atlantic SS Co* (1876) 2 Ch D 763; *Newland v Simons & Willer (Hairdressers) Ltd* [1981] ICR 521; *Phoenix General Insurance Co of Greece SA v Halvanan Insurance Co Ltd* [1988] QB 216; *Re Cavalier Insurance Co Ltd* [1989] 2 Lloyd's Rep 430.

CHAPTER 3

THE PARTNERSHIP AGREEMENT

INTRODUCTION

The agreement which underpins the consensual arrangement essential to partnership can be made entirely informally,[1] but it does not follow that partnership should be based on an informal arrangement, nor usually is it. Contract is the usual form for the regulation of arrangements in business. This is as true of the arrangements that are made with regard to business organisations as it is in relation to the arrangements which those businesses in turn make with other businesses by way of trade. However, in partnership law it is usual for the partnership contract to be covered by a formal and fairly comprehensive written agreement, entered into by the partners after each has obtained legal advice.

The purposes of such a partnership agreement, or 'articles of partnership' as it is often known, are various. First, although the Partnership Act 1890 does set out a list of rules governing the relations between partners, the statutory rules are not, and were not intended to be, comprehensive. A formal agreement can, therefore, make provision for matters not dealt with by the Act itself. Further, the rules contained in the Act are often not suitable for the particular partnership arrangement. Since the rules in the Act are not mandatory, partners can make other arrangements, and thus produce a partnership agreement which is in line with their real needs and aspirations. Finally, the partnership agreement will seek to deal with as many potential issues as possible so that, if disputes arise, there is a common point of reference by which the

---

[1] Thus, it can arise from a course of dealings between the participants, provided they are genuinely in agreement that a partnership is created by their activities: contrast *Jackson v White* [1967] 2 Lloyd's Rep 68 with *Dungate v Lee* [1967] 1 All ER 241.

matter can be clearly and decisively resolved. Indeed, in this last respect it is quite usual for express provision to be included in the formal agreement even in respect of matters to be dealt with on terms identical to the provisions of the Partnership Act, so as to draw all agreed terms into one single document bearing the signature of all partners.

It follows that today it is exceptional for partnership to be consciously undertaken without a formal partnership agreement being prepared. It also follows that the terms contained in the agreement will be entirely related to the needs of the individual partnership, and that the terms of partnership agreements vary widely, partly in accordance with the type of profession or trade to be carried on by the partnership, and partly in relation to their individual needs. However, while the document is drawn to meet the anticipated needs of the particular partnership, and is created to be as comprehensive as possible, it will neither be, nor be intended to be, completely comprehensive. It is impossible to anticipate and cover every eventuality and, however careful the partners and their lawyers may be, circumstances may always arise which can be resolved only by reference to general principles of partnership law.

It is therefore impossible to produce an account of all the terms which may be found in partnership agreements. Instead this chapter will give an account of partnership clauses in two sections. The first section will deal with those terms commonly included in partnership agreements; the second with the provisions of the Partnership Act regulating matters often covered with by agreements. However, attention must first be given to two preliminary issues, namely (1) the construction of a partnership agreement and (2) the continuation of a partnership governed by a formal agreement after the period fixed for its termination.

CONSTRUCTION OF AGREEMENTS

A written partnership agreement is a document and falls to be construed in the same manner as any other document with the application of the normal principles of construction.[2] It is, perhaps, worth noting that the approach of the courts to the construction of documents has become progressively less technical in recent years, and the courts are now much more willing to adopt constructions which will give effect to the intention of the parties as

[2] As to which see Odgers *Construction of Deeds and Statutes* (5th edn, 1967) (ed G Dworkin).

discovered from the document taken as a whole. In fact, the achievement of the purposes of the partners may well always have been a primary purpose of construction of partnership agreements. In the view of Lord Lindley, '[t]he attainment of the objects which the partners have declared they have in view is always regarded as the first importance'.[3] The literal meaning of a provision must be made to bow to the manifest objectives of the partners where these can be ascertained. Thus, in one case a court confronted with a provision in a partnership agreement which required the signature of the senior partner to all expulsion notices declined to hold that the provision applied to an expulsion noticed served on him by his fellow partners.[4]

Over and above this there are perhaps two principles to be borne in mind, namely (1) that the agreement is not comprehensive and (2) that the partners owe duties of good faith to each other.

The agreement is not comprehensive

The principle that the written partnership agreement does not represent a comprehensive expression of the obligations of the partners both to each other and to outsiders is deep-seated in partnership law and predates the Partnership Act 1890. Thus, in *Smith v Jeyes*[5] Lord Langdale summed up the position as follows:

'The transactions of partners with each other cannot be considered merely with reference to the express contract between them. The duties and obligations arising from the relation between the parties are regulated by the express contract between them, so far as the contract extends and continues in force; but if the express contract, or so much of it as continues in force, does not reach to all those duties and obligations, they are implied and enforced by the law . . .'[6]

It follows, therefore, that the mere fact that express provision is made by the agreement with regard to one matter does not mean that another related matter is excluded from the partnership relationship and, consequently, neither the maxims *expressum facit cessare*

---

[3] *Lindley and Banks on Partnership* (16th edn, 1990) p 140 citing *Chapple v Cadell* (1822) Jac 537.
[4] *Hitchman v Crouch Butler Savage Associates Services Ltd* (1983) 127 Sol Jo 441. See also *Sykes v Land* (1984) 271 Estates Gazette 1264.
[5] (1841) 4 Beav 503.
[6] At 505.

tacitum[7] nor *expressio unius est exclusio alterius*[8] can be readily applicable to the construction of an express partnership agreement.[9] The principle that the agreement is not comprehensive is of significance in any situation to the solution of which the construction of the partnership agreement and the applicability of general principles of law is relevant. Not least it may be of great importance in deciding whether or not one partner is entitled to dissolve the partnership because of the activities of another. As Lord Langdale went on to point out in *Smith v Jeyes*:[10]

'When it is insisted that the conduct of one partner entitles the other to a dissolution, we must consider not merely the specifications of the express terms, but also the duties and obligations which are implied in every partnership contract.'[11]

Not least among those duties and obligations owed by one partner to another is that of good faith.[12]

The duty of good faith

The powers conferred on the partners as individuals by the partnership agreement are presumed to have been conferred by the agreement with a view to the benefit of the firm as a unit, and not for the individual benefit of the partner concerned. As such, powers must be exercised in good faith and for the benefit of the firm as a whole. There are two consequences of this. First, provisions within the agreement will, where possible, be construed in such a way as to prevent one partner being able to rely on it to defraud another. Thus, the exercise by a partner of a power conferred on him by the partnership articles will be treated by the courts as ineffective if it is used by him to conceal or hide that partner's fraud.[13] In one case the courts refused to give effect to a provision in a partnership agreement to the effect that the accounts of the firm became final and binding once signed by all partners when it was

---

7   Co Litt 210a, 183b: 'When there is express mention of certain things, then anything not mentioned is excluded.'
8   Co Litt 210a: 'The express mention of one thing implies the exclusion of the other.' The two maxims are thus interchangeable and enunciate one of the first principles applicable to the construction of written documents, per Lord Denman in *Line v Stephenson* (1838) 5 Bing NC 183. Partnership documents are therefore exceptional in this respect.
9   *Nelson v Bealby* (1862) 4 De GF & J 321; *Browning v Browning* (1862) 31 Beav 316.
10 (1841) 4 Beav 503.
11 At 505.
12 This was precisely the issue in *Smith v Jeyes*.
13 Per Brown Wilkinson VC in *Walters v Bingham* [1988] 1 FTLR 260 at 267–268.

shown that the set of accounts which had been signed were false and had been fraudulently prepared by one of the partners.[14]

The second consequence of the principle is that the partnership agreement will be construed, where possible, by the courts in such a way as to prevent one partner using it as a means of exploiting his power and obtaining an unfair advantage. Such actions are inconsistent with the close working relations and mutual trust at the heart of the partnership relation, which depends on the good faith exercised by the partners in their dealings with each other. Thus, a power of expulsion or compulsory retirement will not be allowed to be exercised if its implementation would secure a financial or other benefit at the cost of the outgoing partner.[15]

CONTINUATION AFTER EXPIRY OF FIXED TERM

If the partners in a firm continue its operations after the expiration of the term fixed for its duration it is presumed that they continue on the terms of their original agreement. The law is contained in s 27 of the Partnership Act 1890, which provides, first, that where a partnership entered into for a fixed term is continued after the term has expired, and without any express new agreement, the rights and duties of the partners remain the same as they were at the expiration of the term, *so far as is consistent with the incidence of a partnership at will.*[16] A continuance of the business by the partners or such of them as habitually acted therein during the term, without any settlement or liquidation of the partnership affairs, is presumed to be a continuance of the partnership.[17]

For the provision to be displaced it is necessary that a new agreement should have been entered into. Whether or not this has occurred is essentially a question of fact.[18]

---

[14] *Oldaker v Lavender* (1833) 6 Sim 239.
[15] *Blisset v Daniel* (1853) 10 Hare 493, where the exercise of the power was intended to lead to the appropriation of the share of the expelled partner at less than its true value.
[16] Section 27(1) (emphasis added).
[17] Section 27(2). Section 27 gives effect to the law established by the cases: see *Crawshay v Collins* (1808) 15 Ves 218; *Featherstonhaugh v Fenwick* (1810) 17 Ves 298; *Booth v Parks* (1828) 1 Mol 465, Beatty 444; *Neilson v Mossend Iron Co* (1886) 11 App Cas 298.
[18] The mere fact that a new draft partnership deed has been prepared does not constitute a new agreement: *King v Chuck* (1853) 17 Beav 325; *Neilson v Mossend Iron Co* (above); *Stekel v Ellice* [1973] 1 WLR 191), unless, of course, the partners have agreed to continue on the basis that the new draft applies: *Walters v Bingham* [1988] 1 FTLR 260.

Continuation under the old agreement has a bearing upon the interpretation of the partnership agreement for references to the partnership term will be construed as references to the partnership term as continued.[19] However, an issue arises as to which clauses of the original agreement do continue because, while the original terms apply, they do so only so far as is consistent with a partnership at will.[20] The courts have drawn a broad distinction between provisions relating to the manner in which a partnership may be terminated and other provisions, holding that the former are inconsistent with a partnership at will and therefore not part of the agreement by which the partnership continues.[1] A power to expel a partner is plainly inconsistent with a partnership at will, at least where there are only two partners, and therefore is not part of the continuing partnership arrangements.[2] For as Lord Westbury LC pointed out:

'. . . there is good . . . reason for holding that this particular stipulation in the written agreement is gone after the expiration of the term, from the fact that the new contract being for no specified time, but determinable at the will of either party, the power to determine the partnership is not wanted.'[3]

On the other hand, provisions which will continue into the ongoing arrangement include a right to acquire a partner's share,[4] an arbitration clause,[5] and a clause restricting competition. It is, however, necessary to consider the precise terms of the particular clause in every case.

---

[19] *Essex v Essex* (1855) 20 Beav 442; *Cox v Willoughby* (1880) 13 Ch D 863; *McLeod v Dowling* (1927) 43 TLR 655.

[20] *Cox v Willoughby* (above); *McLeod v Dowling* (above).

[1] *Campbell v Campbell* (1893) 6 R 137; *Neilson v Mossend Iron Co* (1886) 11 App Cas 298.

[2] *Clark v Leach* (1863) 1 De GJ & SM 409. See also the comments of Stirling J in *Daw v Herring* [1892] 1 Ch 284 at 290. Whilst the comments of Stirling J were obiter, so are comments to the contrary by Browne-Wilkinson V-C in *Walters v Bingham* [1988] 1 FTLR 260 at 268, which seem based on no clear legal principle.

[3] (1863) 1 De GJ & S 409 at 415.

[4] *Essex v Essex* (1855) 20 Beav 442; *King v Chuck* (1853) 17 Beav 325; *Cox v Willoughby* (1990) 13 Ch D 863; *McLeod v Dowling* (1927) 43 TLR 655; *Daw v Herring* [1892] 1 Ch 284; *Brooks v Brooks* (1901) 85 LT 453; *M'Gown v Henderson* 1914 SC 839.

[5] *Gillett v Thornton* (1875) LR 19 Eq 599: see also by analogy *Morgan v William Harrison Ltd* [1907] 2 Ch 137.

CLAUSES COMMONLY INCLUDED IN PARTNERSHIP AGREEMENTS

There is no such thing as a standard partnership agreement. Indeed, one of the great strengths of the legal framework of partnership is its adaptability to the particular needs of each particular business and the parties undertaking it. However, while partnership agreements vary widely, there are 13 clauses which will be found almost universally in partnership agreements. These are:

(1)   the parties;
(2)   the nature and place of business;
(3)   the name of the firm;
(4)   the commencement and duration of the partnership;
(5)   the provision of the capital;
(6)   the calculation and division of profits;
(7)   the management of the business;
(8)   the firm's bank account and the drawing of cheques;
(9)   the accounts of the partnership;
(10)   the death or retirement of a partner;
(11)   expulsion of a partner;
(12)   changes in the members of the firm;
(13)   the protection of the goodwill of the practice;
(14)   arbitration.

It is true that the majority of the provisions of the Partnership Act 1890 apply unless the particular agreement contains an express or implied provision inconsistent with its particular counterpart within the Act. It might be thought, therefore, that, if the partners are satisfied with the arrangements of the 1890 Act on a particular point, no express provision need be included in the agreement, reliance instead being placed on the relevant statutory regime. However, it should be always remembered that partners are businesspeople and not lawyers and will not necessarily be conversant with the provisions of the 1890 Act. It is, therefore, better and more usual practice to include express provision in the partnership agreement even though this is merely a reproduction of the position which would arise in any event under the Partnership Act 1890. Indeed, even in the case of a partnership among lawyers this has much to recommend it, as it is possible even for a lawyer to overlook a provision of the legislation given that, as with many professional people, priority is often given to the needs of clients rather than to the professional's own affairs.[6]

---

[6] Further, some of the partners may well have little experience in the field of partnership law in this time of great specialisation.

The usual clauses in a partnership agreement will now be considered in sequence.

Parties

The parties to the agreement should all be clearly identified together with their precise partnership standing. Thus, full partners should be distinguished from dormant partners, and, in the case of a limited partnership, the limited partners should be distinguished from the full partners. In the case of a complex, large, modern partnership (with a mixture of 'equity partners' entitled to participate in the management of the firm, 'non-equity partners' not entitled to take a part in management but entitled to a share of profits, and 'salaried partners' entitled to share neither in management nor profits) the various groups and their respective rights should be distinguished from each other.[7]

Nature and place of business

The nature of the business should be clearly stated. This is important for a number of reasons. First, it is that business, and that business alone, which the partners have agreed to carry on, and with regard to which each partner is the agent of the firm, and can therefore bind his partners.[8] Secondly, the partnership business on which the partners have agreed can only be changed by unanimous decision.[9] The business to be carried on by the partnership is thus fundamental to its operation.

The place of business is also likely to be of importance both to the partners and, possibly, to the ultimate success of the business. Further, it is at the place of business that the partnership books are to be kept.[10] Where the premises are owned by one or more of the partners, care should be exercised to ensure that the partnership has adequate rights of occupation to protect the firm's commercial needs in relation to its place of business. In the case of many businesses a proportion of their goodwill may well attach to the premises with which they are associated and, if they are forced to sever their

---

[7] In the case of the large modern practice with its multitude of partners it is perhaps best to schedule the names and addresses of each category of partners so that additions and subtractions can be easily implemented.

[8] Partnership Act 1890, s 5.

[9] Section 24(8).

[10] Section 24(9).

connection with the premises, the growth of the business may be checked, at least in the short to medium term. The mere fact that premises are indispensable to the operations of the partnership will not give rise to a presumption that the partnership has rights of occupation when none have been expressly granted.[11] Sloppy, undefined arrangements under which the firm merely relies on the goodwill and generosity of the partners who own the premises from which the business is carried on are dangerous, and can be injurious to the business and even fatal to relations between the partners.

Firm name

The firm name is clearly of importance since it is the means by which the business can be identified and, therefore, the identity around which the goodwill of the business will collect. Often, in the case of a small business, the partners will choose to use their own names. However, in the case of a large partnership this is impracticable, and even in the case of small businesses a firm name may be chosen which is not related in any way to the names of the partners.

In general, the partners are free to choose any name that they wish. To this general rule there are two restrictions. First, the choice must comply with the rules on names set out in the Business Names Act 1985.[12] Second, the name chosen must not cause confusion in the minds of the public with some other established business, or that business may successfully maintain an action for passing off.[13] Indeed, where such confusion amongst the public would arise, an action may be maintained for passing off even though its effect is to prevent persons from trading under their own names. In *Croft v Day*[14] the plaintiffs were the makers of blacking in Holborn, London under the well-known name of Day & Martin, with a long- and well-established goodwill. The original founders of the firm, Mr Day and Mr Martin, were long since dead, and the firm contained no partner of either name. A real Mr Day and a real Mr Martin, with no connection with the established firm, formed a partnership and started trading as makers of blacking under the partnership of Day & Martin. The plaintiffs successfully applied for an injunction

---

[11]   See the discussion on partnership property in Chapter 9, p 187, below.
[12]   Discussed in Chapter 5, p 91, below.
[13]   The requirements for a successful passing off action have been authoritatively stated in recent years in *Erven Warnink v Townend* [1980] RPC 31. See also C Wadlow *The Law of Passing Off* (1990); J Dryesdale and M Silverleaf *Passing Off, Law and Practice* (1986).
[14]   (1843) 7 Beav 84.

to prevent the operations of the interlopers. Their goodwill was affected, their trade would be prejudiced and confusion was being created in the mind of the purchasing public.[15] It is not true, however, that a person will invariably be prevented from using his own name by the use of the passing off action. In *Croft v Day* the use of their name by the defendants was clearly fraudulent, and done in the hope that it would result in the public becoming confused. In general, in the early cases, the courts were prepared to prevent a defendant from using his own name only if it was satisfied that his use of his own name was not bona fide, and was done with an ulterior motive.[16] If the defendant was acting bona fide the courts would not intervene.[17] However, by the end of the century the courts had adopted an approach which allowed them to find a lack of bona fides in any case because, they reasoned, even if the defendant started his activities innocently, it was considered fraudulent for him to continue once he was put on notice of confusion with the plaintiff.[18]

The modern law derives from *Parker Knoll Ltd v Knoll International Ltd*,[19] a decision of the House of Lords. Unfortunately, the reasoning of their Lordships was such that not all the issues were clearly settled. The action was one brought by the English furniture manufacturers against a subsidiary of a US company, and concerned whether or not the defendants could use the mark 'Knoll International' as a trade mark on their furniture. It was not disputed that the defendants had acted in good faith. It should be noted that the use of the mark in question was on goods, not as a firm name. It is a more injurious thing to prevent the use of one's own name as a firm name than it is to prevent its use as a mark on goods. The following propositions seem to flow from the decision of the House of Lords:

(1) the courts will not allow the use of one's own name when the use is *not* bona fide, and is motivated by the hope that confusion will result;

(2) the courts will not allow the *bona fide* use of one's own name when the use is in relation to goods;

---

[15] This, of course, is an aspect of goodwill which is more fully discussed in Chapter 9, p 201, below.

[16] Apart from *Croft v Day* see also the earliest case of passing off at common law of *Sykes v Sykes* (1824) 3 B & C 541.

[17] See, eg *Burgess v Burgess* (1853) 3 De G Mac G 896; *Turton v Turton* (1889) 42 Ch D 128.

[18] *Reddaway (Frank) & Co Ltd v George Banham & Co Ltd* [1896] AC 199; *Spalding v Gamage* (1915) 32 RPC 273.

[19] [1962] RPC 265.

(3)   *possibly* the courts will allow the *bona fide* use of one's own name when the use is as a firm name.

If this is what the House of Lords meant, then the rules in relation to passing off are not entirely in accord with the situation which obtains when the original mark is protected by registration under the Trade Marks Act 1994[20] and an action is brought for infringement instead of a passing off action. Here the legislation is quite clear in providing that a registered trade mark is not infringed by the use by a person of his own name and address, provided that the use is in accordance with honest practices in industrial or commercial matters.[1] Under the legislation, therefore, the issue depends not on any distinction based upon whether the mark is used in relation to goods or as the firm name, but on whether the use is or is not bona fide, that is in accordance with honest practices in industrial or commercial matters.

It may well be that the provisions of the new legislation will cause the courts quickly to evolve the principles of passing off so as to achieve a similar result, a desirable clarification and simplification of the law. In *Erven Warnink v Townend*[2] Lord Diplock said:

> 'Where, over a period of years, there can be discerned a steady trend in legislation which reflects the view of successive Parliaments as to what the public interest demands in a particular field of law, development of the common law in that part of the same field which has been left to it ought to proceed upon a parallel rather than a diverging course.'[3]

The reform of trade mark law occurs too infrequently for any steady trend in legislation to be discernable, but when the reforms are undertaken with the amount of deliberation and consideration shown in the most recent reforms, and when the purpose of the reform is to achieve a degree of harmonisation of the various national systems of trade mark law across Europe, Lord Diplock's conclusion is no less wise than it is in relation to the differing circumstances in an adjacent legal area which led him to articulate it. The mere fact that English judges so rarely articulate the policy considerations which underpin their judgments does not mean that their decisions are not, in fact, often prompted by them.

Once chosen the name is the identity of the partnership and

---

[20]   This possibility is discussed in Chapter 9, p 205, below.
[1]   Section 11(2)(a).
[2]   [1980] RPC 31.
[3]   At 94.

should be used on all documents and name plates and in connection with all operations of the business.

Commencement and duration of partnership

Normally, the partnership agreement will contain provision for the date on which it is to commence, and for its duration. It is indeed essential that its terms should establish expressly and precisely the commencement date of the partnership, since that is the date from which each partner has the usual authority to bind his co-partner and from which, therefore, each may find himself bound by the others with unlimited liability for the debts and obligations of the firm. The agreement may be backdated to the date of actual commencement if the business has, in fact, been carried on in partnership for some time. Alternatively, if the business has yet to be commenced, a date for the commencement of the partnership in the future can be specified. To avoid argument, misunderstandings and confusion, the date of actual commencement should always be shown.

If no commencement date is shown in the deed the partnership is *presumed* to have commenced from the execution of the deed. In this connection it should be borne in mind that a deed takes effect from the time of its execution, and not from the date shown on its face.[4] It follows that if it is established that the deed was executed on some date other than that shown on its face the partnership will be taken as having commenced from that date,[5] unless it is proved that in fact the partnership commenced on some other date.[6]

Whilst it is possible to provide that the partnership shall continue for the duration of the joint lives of the partners, or for a fixed term of years, it is more normal for provision to be made that the partnership shall continue until determined by one or other of the partners giving a specified period of notice. Such a provision would be of general application, and enables the partnership to be determined merely because it has become inconvenient to one or other of the partners. In addition, there is always the possibility that dissolution may become desirable because of one of the parties' misconduct, insolvency, or neglect or refusal to perform his duties. Separate provision is usually made for these circumstances by

---

[4] *Goddard's Case* (1584) 2 Co Rep 4b; *Clayton's Case* (1585) 5 Co Rep 1a, Shep Touch 72; *Hall v Cazenove* (1804) 4 East 477; *Steele v Mart* (1825) 4 B & C 272.
[5] Per Patterson J in *Browne v Burton* (1847) 5 Dow & L 289 at 292.
[6] The presumption that the partnership commences from the execution of the deed is precisely that, merely a presumption: see *Malpas v Clements* (1850) 19 LJQB 435; *Morgan v Whitmore* (1851) 6 Ex Ch 716.

including a power for the other partners to expel the guilty one. No general power of expulsion is implied in partnership law.

Further, in all cases the articles should provide for what is to happen on the death of one of the partners, or the retirement of the partners, and for protracted illness preventing a partner from undertaking the partnership business for a substantial period of time.

Provision for partnership capital and property

No business can operate without capital and the capital of a partnership business must inevitably be contributed by the partners. Clear provision should be made in the partnership agreement to cover this. The proportions in which the capital is to be subscribed by the partners should be stated in terms of sums of money, even if the actual contribution of one or more partners is to be in specie. It may well be that the partnership capital will be contributed unequally. In any event, the agreement should set out clearly what capital each partner is entitled to have returned to him on the dissolution of the partnership. In the case of an unequal contribution of capital it is sensible that there be a provision that interest be paid on capital out of the profits of the business prior to calculation of net profits for division. In the absence of a specific provision with regard to payment of interest on capital, there is no such entitlement under English partnership law.

An important matter for the partnership agreement to address is the entitlement to the increasing capital of the business. Let us suppose that the initial capital is £200,000, which is used to acquire assets including land and buildings. After ten years' trading the assets of the business stand at £2,000,000, partly because of increased value of the land and buildings, and partly because of the production of a substantial goodwill for the business arising from its successful trading. The partners contributed the capital unequally, but under the terms of the partnership agreement they are entitled to a division of profits on the basis of equality. Is the accretion to the capital of the business to be divided amongst the partners in proportion to their original contribution of capital or to the proportions in which they divide profits? The matter should be clearly dealt with in the partnership agreement. If there is no clear provision the accretion of capital will be divisible equally.[7] Even if this is the result which is desired, inclusion of a specific provision in the partnership agreement enables the matter to be dealt with by the

---

[7] Section 24(1).

partners reminding each other of what was expressly agreed should misunderstandings and potential disputes arise.

It may be that a partner's right to participate in the profits and management of the business is conditional on the introduction of his capital contribution. If this is the intention of the parties it should be clearly set out in the partnership agreement, since the courts will not easily make such an inference. Thus, in one case the parties agreed that one would bring in £2,000 and perform certain actions and the other would bring in £5,000. When the second party did not bring in the £5,000 it was held that the other could maintain an action against him in respect of this sum, even though he had not brought in his own £2,000 or performed the promised actions.[8]

Another area which has proved fertile ground for misunderstandings and disputes between partners is the identification of partnership property forming the capital of the partnership itself. If a partner allows the use of some asset owned by him (eg a set of offices), his partners may assume that it is intended that the premises should be part of the partnership capital and assets, whilst he may equally understand that the premises are to remain his with the partnership use being a matter of mere grace and favour. The partnership agreement should be quite specific on such matters.[9] All items which are intended to be part of the capital of the business, and therefore partnership property, should be clearly stated to be so. Any items of property used by the partnership which are not intended to be partnership property should also be clearly and specifically so labelled. Where assets are to be retained in the individual ownership of one or more of the partners but used by the partnership for its purposes, the basis of the firm's use should be set out. Care should be taken to ensure that the firm's needs to use the property in the future are fully protected by the acquisition of the necessary legal rights to ensure continued access and use. This applies to all forms of property including land and buildings and intellectual property.

Calculation and division of profits

Profits are important to any business, since it is only from the profits that the expenses of the administration of the business can be met. Further, in the case of partnership it is from the profits that the

---

[8] *Kemble v Mills* (1840) 1 Man & G 757 (whether covenants are independent or conditional is a matter of construction). By contrast see *Stavers v Curling* (1836) 3 Bing NC 355.

[9] Partnership property is discussed below, Chapter 9.

partners receive their rewards and living. The partnership agreement will provide that the net profits are divisible amongst the partners in specified proportions. The net profits are the gross profits less the business expenses and outgoings incurred in securing it.[10] If the partnership agreement makes no provision, either express or implied, as to the proportions in which profits are divisible, the profits will be divided equally.[11]

The basic principle of law is that, in the absence of agreement to the contrary, the net profits of any year are calculated on the basis of money actually received during the year less those moneys which are actually paid out in the year, regardless of when the work was done which led to the particular income or outgoings.[12] It may well be that, in the case of a particular business, this is not the position which the partners would choose to see obtain. If so, specific provision can be included in the partnership agreement allowing for the value of the work in hand to be included in the calculation of profit each year.[13]

In the calculation of profits, any increase in the value of goodwill, or of the other capital assets of the business, is taken as an accretion to capital and not a contribution to profits. Profits which are generated in any year and left in the business remain as undrawn profits, and may be withdrawn by the partner entitled to them at any time. If they are to become part of capital it is necessary that the partners should formally so resolve.

It is usual for the partnership accounts to be drawn up on a yearly basis and the profits then divided. The partners necessarily have to live in the meantime, and it is usual for a provision to be included permitting the partners each month to draw a specified figure on account of the profits anticipated at the end of the year.

Partnerships are made under which only some of the partners are obliged to give their full time efforts to the partnership with other partners being dormant or sleeping partners. The other partners are included within the business because their capital is needed or, alternatively, they have expertise on which it is useful to draw on an

---

[10]   Per Fletcher Moulton LJ in *Re Spanish Prospecting Co Ltd* [1911] 1 Ch 92 at 99; *Vulcan Motor and Engineering Co v Hampson* [1921] 3 KB 597; *Naval Colliery Co (1897) Ltd v IRC* (1928) 138 LT 593.

[11]   Partnership Act 1890, s 24(1).

[12]   Per Turner LJ in *Maclaren v Stainton* (1861) 3 De GF & J 202 at 214; *Badham v Williams* (1902) 86 LT 191; *JP Hall & Co Ltd v IRC* [1921] 3 KB 152.

[13]   It does not follow, of course, that where a *new* partnership is formed to carry on an *old* business the new partners share in the existing unpaid accounts. In the absence of agreement to the contrary they do not, per Kekewich J in *Badham v Williams* (above) at 192. They will, however, take over the uncompleted work in hand at an appropriate valuation.

occasional basis. In such circumstances, consideration should be given to a provision for a salary for those members of the partnership who give their full time efforts to it, to be paid prior to the calculation of divisible profits.

Bank accounts and the drawing of cheques

Money is the oxygen of business activity, and within any business the control of the money confers power on the controller. Money is also the most easily disposable of all business assets and, therefore, the partnership asset most likely to be targeted by a dishonest or unscrupulous partner.

The partnership agreement usually specifies the bank, and also provides that all cheques and money received by the firm should be paid into the bank account without delay. Provision is also made as to who may sign cheques. In the absence of agreement to the contrary each partner can sign cheques on the partnership account. This may not accord well with the particular circumstances of a business. Thus, if a business has been well established by the senior partner, who is in effect the provider of the capital of the business, it may well be that, if he chooses to take a young partner, it is appropriate that provision should be made that his signature be necessary on any cheques. Further, in a partnership of several partners it may be a useful check on potential dishonesty or carelessness to provide that the signatures of two partners are necessary for a cheque. If any such provision is made in a partnership agreement, it should be precisely duplicated in the mandate to the partnership bankers when the partnership bank account is opened.

Management of the partnership business

In the absence of a stipulation to the contrary, each partner is entitled to participate in the management of the partnership business.[14] This may or may not accord with the needs of the particular business. It is usual, therefore, to specify whether all or some only of the partners are to participate in the management of the business, and also to specify that the partner or partners who do so are to give their full time to the business over which they have management rights. Dormant or 'sleeping' partners are not usually given management rights in the day-to-day running of the business.

14 Partnership Act 1890, s 24(5).

It is usual to provide that management decisions will be taken by majority vote amongst the partners entitled to participate in the management of the business. However, the majority is not usually the majority in relation to the number of partners, but is ascertained in accordance with the respective partnership shares of the net profits. The partnership agreement may exclude some of the partners from some of the activities of management, eg hiring and firing of staff. In any event it is important that, whatever the detail, there should be specific provision within the agreement whereby the firm can achieve clear and effective decisions in the operation of its affairs.

Further, the day-to-day job of management may be delegated (by the partners entitled to participate) to an office manager who undertakes the work in accordance with policy guidelines laid down by them. This is a very common arrangement between the largest partnerships which now occur in the professions such as solicitors or accountants.

The provision that a partner should devote his whole time to the partnership business may well be buttressed by further provisions specifying the amount of holidays to which he is entitled, and further providing that he cannot hold any outside office or business appointment without the consent of his co-partners. If, subsequently, such a partner were to obtain an outside office or appointment which his partners were disposed to allow him to take up, it is important that a clear agreement be reached as to whether the income generated should be part of the partnership income, or should be left as the income of the particular partner alone.

Accounts

Since partnership is the relationship formed by the carrying on of a business with a view of profit, with the profits being divided amongst the partners, it may seem obvious that proper partnership accounts should be kept. Nevertheless, the partnership agreement should make specific provision for the keeping of accounts, including the keeping of a balance sheet. Nor indeed is the usefulness of this confined to the relationship between the partners themselves. As Lord Lindley points out:

> 'The object of taking partnership accounts is two fold, viz. (1) to show how the firm stands as regards strangers, and (2) to show how each partner stands towards the firm.'[15]

---

[15] *Lindley and Banks on Partnership* (16th edn, 1990) p 161.

It is necessary, therefore, that the accounts required to be kept should be such as will accomplish both objects. The accounts required include both the day-to-day books in which all receipts and payments are entered as and when they are received or made, and the full final yearly accounts, showing the assets and liabilities of the firm and what is due to each creditor, and also what is due to each partner in respect of both his capital and portion of profits including any undrawn profits. Seen against this background, therefore, proper partnership accounts are essential to the practical working out of the implications of partnership law.

In addition to provisions requiring the accounts to be maintained, the partnership agreement should also provide that the books should be kept at a particular place and also specify which of the partners shall have access to them. This is a useful provision because any unauthorised attempt by one partner to remove the books of account from their designated place will be restrained by the court on the application of another.[16]

The partnership accounts will be prepared from the partnership books at periodical (probably annual) intervals. The agreement should specify (1) the dates on which accounts are to be prepared, (2) the person or persons who are to prepare them and (3) the accounting basis on which they are to be prepared (eg as to whether work in hand and goodwill are to be included). It should also require the partners to sign the accounts once they have been approved.

Death or retirement of a partner

The desirability of express provision dealing with the dissolution of partnership has already been noted. It is underpinned by s 33(1) of the 1890 Act, which provides that, subject to any agreement between the partners, every partnership is dissolved as regards all the partners by the death of any partner.

In fact, this is clearly not the solution which most partners would wish to result, since a well-established business with extensive goodwill is quite capable of being carried on by the surviving partners continuing it, either alone, or with a new replacement partner. Any disruption to the continuation of the business can only be detrimental to it, and affect the value of the goodwill. However, s 33(1) does allow for the partners to incorporate an alternative provision in their agreement, and it is usual for provision to be

---

[16] *Taylor v Davis* (1842) 3 Beav 388n; *Greatrex v Greatrex* (1847) 1 De G & Sm 692.

made for the continuation of the firm by the surviving partner or partners, notwithstanding the death of one or more partners. Supporting this are provisions setting out how the value of the deceased partner's share of the assets is to be ascertained, which sum will be paid to his personal representatives. Thus, the business continues undisturbed while, at the same time, the estate of the deceased partner is properly protected. Usually, the clause will provide for the ascertainment of the sum due by reference to the last full year's balance sheet and accounts, in respect of a financial year, completed within the preceding 12 months.

Many variations with regard to these provisions are possible. Provision can be made for a calculation of the profits to be distributed from the date of the last complete accounting year to the date of death to cover any period of trading in between. Alternatively, the provision might give rise to a fixed allowance or rate of interest in respect of this period. Sometimes provision may be made that the personal representatives take over the deceased partner's share as sleeping partners until such time as the sum due to the estate is paid. Provision may also be made for the payment of an annuity to the deceased partner's surviving spouse from the future profits of the business.[17]

Expulsion of a partner

Retirement is a voluntary withdrawal from a partnership. In the absence of an express power within the partnership agreement, no partner can be forced out of the partnership against his will. Given that the consequence of this is that, if one partner so conducts himself that his fellow partners feel unable to continue with him, their only remedy is to seek dissolution of the partnership, the desirability of including an express power of dissolution becomes clear. In practice, most well-drawn agreements contain a power for a partner to be expelled in certain circumstances. The grounds for expulsion need to be clearly expressed and, in both drawing and operating the provision, it must be remembered that the clause will be strictly construed, both with regard to the circumstances covered and with regard to the precise observance of any procedural steps which it requires to be taken with regard to its manner of exercise.[18]

---

[17] This type of provision is less common than it once was, because of the tax advantages given to the establishment of personal pension plans. The spouse does not become a partner by accepting the annuity (1890 Act, s 2(3): see Chapter 1).

[18] Expulsion is discussed in Chapter 12, p 277, below.

Changes in the members of the firm

Partnership is a personal relationship between business people who, by entering into the arrangement, commit themselves to work very hard and closely together in pursuit of a common vision. It has, with some justification, been compared to marriage. The underlying nature of partnership is recognised by s 24(7) of the 1890 Act, which requires the consent of all the existing partners to the introduction of a new partner, so that the personnel cannot be changed unless everyone agrees. It is, of course, open to the partners to agree something different within their particular agreement. One possibility is to allow a new partner to be introduced if the majority of the partners are in agreement on the introduction of the individual concerned. Often, however, the underlying principle of the Partnership Act on this matter is not modified. Where it is modified, a more modern adaptation is to allow one partner or his personal representatives to nominate his successor, subject to the successor being a fit, qualified and proper person to participate in the partnership arrangement.

Goodwill[19]

Partners do, of course, disappear from a partnership for reasons other than death. Fortunately, most partners do manage retirement! However, by the time they have reached retirement, they will have occupied a prominent position within the firm for many years, and a great deal of their customers' goodwill might be to them personally and, therefore, only indirectly that of the firm. Accordingly, when they retire from the firm it would be very damaging if they were allowed to compete by setting up a business in competition with the firm and, indeed, if they have received payment in respect of the goodwill of the business, it would be unfair to the remaining partners. Accordingly, it is normal to include a restrictive covenant within the partnership agreement prohibiting former partners from competing with the partnership business. In principle, such provisions are perfectly acceptable. However, it should be remembered that, if such a provision is drawn wider, either in geographical extent or duration of protection, than is necessary for the protection of the goodwill of the business, it will be unreasonable and struck down as being in restraint of trade.[20] Such clauses are usually strictly

---

[19] Goodwill is discussed further in Chapter 9, p 201, below.
[20] *Whitehill v Bradford* [1952] 1 All ER 115; *Macfarlane v Kent* [1965] 2 All ER 376; *Lyne-Pirkis v Jones* [1969] 3 All ER 738.

construed, and if too wide will confer no protection at all. An example is *Peyton v Mindham*,[1] which concerned a clause within the partnership agreement of two medical practitioners which provided that if the partnership came to an end in certain circumstances, the partner who did not continue the practice was prohibited from professionally advising, attending, prescribing or treating any person, who was, or had at any time been, a patient of the partnership, or any member of the household of such a patient. The clause also provided that the erstwhile partner should not endeavour directly or indirectly to prevent any such person from employing the continuing partner in the way of profession or practice. The erstwhile partner was, however, allowed to act as locum under the terms of the clause.

Sadly, one of the partners became incapacitated so that he could not perform his fair share of the work, and this led to the termination of the partnership, and his fellow partner continuing the practice alone. The continuing doctor sought to enforce the covenant against his incapacitated partner. The clause was struck down as being unreasonable, since on its wording it would prevent the incapacitated partner, who had largely recovered, from acting as a consultant to patients of the practice, and not merely as general practitioner. Since the wording of the covenant was too wide, the covenant was totally unenforceable.

Arbitration

Partnership is a relationship which is both personal and commercial, and it is not surprising to find that in general partnership agreements provide that disputes should be resolved by arbitration rather than by legal proceedings in the courts. To cover this, an arbitration clause needs to be placed in the terms of the agreement. The clause should be clear as to whether it is to apply only while the partnership is a going concern, or whether disputes arising or continuing after dissolution are also to be resolved by arbitration.[2]

VARIATION OF PARTNERSHIP AGREEMENT

As the partners can reach agreement that their relations should be governed by terms other than those set out in the Partnership

---

[1] [1971] 3 All ER 1215.
[2] In general, in the absence of clear indication to the contrary, an arbitration agreement will be taken to continue where a partnership is continued beyond a fixed initial period: *Gillett v Thornton* (1875) LR 19 Eq 599.

Act, so they may also subsequently vary, by mutual consent, the terms set out in the partnership agreement. This right is expressly recognised by s 19 of the Partnership Act 1890 which provides that –

> 'the mutual rights and duties of partners whether ascertained by agreement or defined by the Act may be varied by the consent of all the partners, and such consent may be either expressed or inferred from a course of dealing.'

Thus, variation can arise quite informally, and this in itself is something of a potential trap for partners, who may not see the possible long term implications of their actions and arrangements.

RELATIONS BETWEEN THE PARTNERS UNDER THE PARTNERSHIP ACT 1890 ALONE

Where the terms of the partnership deed make no express provision governing relations between the partners the 1890 Act is left to operate alone. It is worthwhile setting out the rules found there at this point.

Capital and profits

All the partners are entitled to share equally in the capital and profits of the business, and must contribute equally towards the losses, whether of capital or otherwise sustained by the firm.[3]

A partner making, for the purpose of the partnership, any actual payment or advance beyond the amount of capital which he has agreed to subscribe is entitled to interest at the rate of 5% per annum from the date of payment or advance.[4]

A partner is not entitled, before the ascertainment of profits, to interest on the capital subscribed by him.[5]

Management of the business

Every partner may take part in the management of the partnership business.[6]

---

[3] Section 24(1).
[4] Section 24(3).
[5] Section 24(4).
[6] Section 24(5).

No partner shall be entitled to remuneration for acting in the partnership business.[7]

The introduction of new partners

No person may be introduced as a partner without the consent of all existing partners.[8]

Partnership decisions

Any difference arising as to ordinary matters connected with the partnership business may be decided by a majority of the partners, but no change may be made in the partnership business without the consent of all existing partners.[9]

Partnership books and accounts

The partnership books are to be kept at the place of business of the partnership (or the principal place, if there is more than one), and every partner may, when he thinks fit, have access to and inspect and copy any of them.[10]

Expulsion of a partner

No majority of the partners can expel any partner unless a power to do so has been conferred by express agreement between the partners.[11]

Duty of partner not to compete with firm

If a partner, without the consent of the other partners, carries on any business of the same nature as and competing with that of the firm, he must account for and pay over to the firm all profits made by him in that business.[12]

---

[7] Section 24(6).
[8] Section 24(7).
[9] Section 24(8).
[10] Section 24(9).
[11] Section 25.
[12] Section 30.

Dissolution of a partnership

Subject to any agreement between the partners, a partnership is dissolved if:

(1)   entered into for a fixed term, by the expiration of that term; or
(2)   entered into for a single venture or undertaking, by the termination of that venture or undertaking; or
(3)   entered into for an undefined time, by the partner giving notice to the other or others of his intention to dissolve the partnership.

In the last-mentioned case, the partnership is dissolved as from the date mentioned in the notice as the date of dissolution or, if no date is so mentioned, as from the date of the communication of the notice.[13]

Subject to any agreement between the partners, every partnership is dissolved as regards all the partners by the death or bankruptcy of any partner. A partnership may, at the option of the other partners, be dissolved if any partner suffers his share of the partnership property to be charged for his separate debt.[14]

A partnership is in every case dissolved by the happening of any event which makes it unlawful for the business of the firm to be carried on, or for the members of the firm to carry on in partnership.[15]

On the application by a partner the court may decree a dissolution of the partnership in five cases:

(1)   when a partner, other than the partner suing, becomes in any way permanently incapable of performing his part of a partnership contract;
(2)   when a partner, other than the partner suing, has been guilty of such conduct as, in the opinion of the court, regard being had to the nature of the business, is calculated to affect prejudicially the carrying on of the business;
(3)   when a partner, other than the partner suing, wilfully or persistently commits a breach of the partnership agreement, or otherwise so conducts himself in matters relating to the partnership business that it is not reasonably practicable for the other partner or partners to carry on the business in partnership with him;
(4)   when the business of the partnership can only be carried on at a loss;

---

[13]   Section 32.
[14]   Section 33.
[15]   Section 34.

(5)   whenever in any case circumstances have arisen which, in the opinion of the court, renders it just and equitable that the partnership be dissolved.[16]

Right of outgoing partner to share in profits after dissolution

Where any member of a firm has died, or otherwise ceased to be a partner, and the surviving or continuing partners carry on the business of the firm with its capital or assets, without any final settlement of accounts as between the firm and the outgoing partner or his estate, then in the absence of any agreement to the contrary the outgoing partner or his estate is entitled at the option of himself or his representatives to such share of the profits made since the dissolution as the court may find to be attributable to the use of his share of the partnership assets, or to interest at the rate of 5% per annum on the amount of his share of the partnership assets. This provision is, however, modified where, by the partnership agreement, an option is given to surviving or continuing partners to purchase the interest of a deceased or outgoing partner, and they exercise the option. Here, the estate of the deceased partner, or the outgoing partner or his estate, is not entitled to any further or other share of the profits. However, to escape the payment of profits the surviving or continuing partner must comply in all material respects with the terms of the option so as to observe fully all its requirements.[17]

---

[16] Section 35.
[17] Section 42.

CHAPTER 4

CORPORATE, SUB- AND GROUP PARTNERSHIPS

INTRODUCTION

Partnerships are a flexible form of business enterprise. The membership of a partnership may consist of any form or combination of forms of legal person, including corporations. Partnerships which consist solely of corporations are usually known as corporate partnerships. Conversely, partnerships may enter into partnership with other partnerships and such business associations are commonly known as group partnerships. The nature of these forms of partnership, together with the sub-partnership, and the advantages of and reasons for their creation are the subject of this chapter.

CORPORATE PARTNERSHIPS

In strict terms, a corporate partnership (or 'consortium', as it is sometimes called) is a business organisation where all the members of the partnership are corporations.[1] Nevertheless, the expression 'corporate partnership' has been applied to partnerships which include at least one corporate member, but whose membership is not solely restricted to such legal persons.[2]

---

[1] Such corporations are usually those registered under the Companies Act 1985, as amended. However, there would in general be no legal bar on corporations other than those registered under the Companies Act from entering into partnerships. In this part of the chapter references to companies will, unless stated to the contrary, be assumed to be limited liability companies registered under the Companies Act 1985.

[2] The existence of corporate partnerships has been given statutory recognition. See, eg Income and Corporation Taxes Act 1988, ss 114–116, as amended. Case law has given consideration to corporate partnerships: see *Re Rudd and Son Ltd* [1984] Ch 237; *Pinkney v Sandpiper Drilling Ltd* [1989] ICR 389. These cases involved partnerships whose members were all companies: see also *Newstead v Frost* [1980] 1 WLR 135, where the partnership was between a company and an individual.

A corporate partnership is essentially the same as any other form of partnership, but the special nature of the corporation as a legal person determines that a corporate partnership may, on occasion, exhibit certain characteristics and limitations which are not shared by other partnerships. To begin with, each corporate member of a partnership must be empowered by its memorandum and articles of association to enter into a partnership.[3]

A partnership, by its very nature, must have more than one member. Corporate partnerships must also share this requirement. However, there would seem to be no objection to a corporate partnership between two companies, both of which are 'single member companies' and which are effectively owned and controlled by a single individual.[4] Partnerships can also be formed between companies within a corporate grouping. Lindley suggests there is a possibility of securing a certain advantage when forming a corporate partnership the membership of which consists exclusively of group companies.[5] Such a partnership can be so constructed that the partnership agreement or deed provides that, on the presentation of a winding up petition, or the making of such an order against one of the members of the corporate partnership, the partnership can be terminated. In such cases, the partnership deed or agreement can provide that the insolvent corporate partner's share of the partnership assets will accrue *automatically* to the continuing partner or partners.[6] Lindley[7] also suggests that such an accrual of the partnership assets to the continuing partner(s) cannot be set aside under s 127 of the Insolvency Act 1986.[8] Nevertheless, such

---

[3]   The strictness of the ultra vires rule which restricted the activities of a company to those permitted by its memorandum and articles of association is now considerably reduced. In any event, a company may alter its memorandum and articles of association so as to empower it to enter into a partnership where it previously had no such power. See Companies Act 1985, ss 4–6 and 9. See also *Newstead v Frost*, fn 2 above.

[4]   The single member company was created by Council Directive 12/93 and SI 1992/1699. See also *Lee v Lee's Air Farming* [1961] AC 12 for a consideration of the 'one man' company.

[5]   *Lindley and Banks on Partnership* (16th edn, 1971) pp 241–242.

[6]   See Chapter 12 on dissolution and winding up of a partnership and Chapter 13 on insolvency. It is thus advisable for the partnership agreement or deed to provide for the expulsion of the company from the partnership *before* the making of a winding up order in addition to providing for the automatic accrual of the insolvent corporate partner's share to the continuing partners in the circumstances prescribed in the text. It can be argued that such provisions constitute a limitation inherent in any corporate partner's share of the partnership assets.

[7]   Ibid.

[8]   Section 127 of the Insolvency Act 1986 provides that any disposition of a corporate partner's property *after* the presentation of a winding up petition is avoided, *unless* the court orders otherwise: see also s 129(2).

an arrangement could only be upheld if it was justifiable on purely commercial grounds. Furthermore, there must be no suspicion that the insolvent corporate partner was insolvent at the formation of the corporate partnership.[9]

Advantages of corporate partnerships

The advantages for companies in entering into corporate partnerships is that they may engage in particular business ventures which require joint expertise, or the aggregation of resources, with the minimum of formality. The partnership can be automatically terminated by the partnership agreement or deed on the completion of the venture or project.[10] One potential advantage for the shareholders of the companies involved in a corporate partnership is that they may effectively participate in a venture, and yet remain protected by limited liability. Furthermore, the insolvency of a corporate partner(s), although it may result in the winding up of the corporate partnership, will still not deprive the respective shareholders of the corporate partner(s) of their protection of limited liability.[11] A corporation must, as in the case of real persons, ensure that it does not enter into a partnership unintentionally. If a company supplies capital to another party, in order that the latter may engage in an enterprise, the company should ensure that such a financial association is not construed or inferred as creating a partnership between the company and the recipient of the capital.[12] In conclusion it must be noted that private individuals may enter into a limited partnership[13] with a corporate partner, with the

---

[9] See the Insolvency Act 1986, s 423, which empowers a court to set aside transactions (which would include transfers of assets under the automatic accrual provisions noted above) if such transactions are intended to defraud a company's creditors. See also s 238, which permits any transactions made by a company within two years of the company becoming insolvent to be set aside where the transaction provided for the company to receive no consideration. Such transactions may not be set aside, notwithstanding the above, if the transaction was entered into in good faith and for the purposes of carrying on the company's business, and at the time of the transaction there were reasonable grounds for believing the transaction would benefit the company.

[10] See Chapter 2 for a consideration of the duration of partnerships.

[11] Note, however, that the courts may always be prepared to pierce the corporate veil where they regard the corporate partner(s) as being no more than a facade and therefore treat the proprietor(s) of a company and the company as a single entity.

[12] See Chapter 1, where the creation of a partnership by financial association is considered.

[13] For a consideration of the nature of limited partnerships see Chapter 14.

latter being the general partner. Such an association will create a partnership with limited liability. It is, however, difficult to envisage circumstances where such an association would have any advantages over a limited liability company in which all interested parties were shareholders.[14]

One of the possible uses of the corporate partnership is to circumvent the general restriction on the maximum size of partnerships.[15]

Despite what has been said above, corporate partnerships share the principal characteristics of a partnership between non-corporate individuals. Thus, a corporate partnership is governed by the Partnership Act 1890 and by the express or implied agreement of the parties.[16] However, consideration must be given to the fact that a partnership agreement governing a corporate partnership must recognise that a corporate partner has no physical existence.[17] Such an agreement must, therefore, deal with the important matters of the expulsion of a corporate partner and the rights of the other corporate partners in the event of the dissolution of a corporate partner. The most important grounds justifying the expulsion of a corporate partner should be its actual or possible insolvency.

The events which can therefore be regarded as justifying the expulsion of a corporate partner from a corporate partnership and which should be referred to in the partnership deed will include:

(1)   the appointment of an administrative or other receiver in respect of all or part of a corporate partner's assets under the Insolvency Act 1986: see ss 8, 13, 33 and 29;

(2)   the directors of a corporate partner proposing a voluntary arrangement in respect of the company under the Insolvency Act 1986, s 1;

(3)   the making of an administration order against a corporate partner under the Insolvency Act 1986, s 8;

---

14   It must be emphasised that the limited partners who become members of the corporate partnership and who endeavour to control its affairs may lose their limited partnership status. In such cases the courts may be willing to pierce the corporate veil and determine that the proprietors of the company and the limited partners are one and the same.

15   See Chapter 2 for a consideration of the restriction of the maximum size of certain partnerships.

16   See Partnership Act 1890, s 19.

17   Accordingly, clauses in a partnership agreement which deal with the death or physical or mental incapacity of a partner are clearly inappropriate to a corporate partner.

(4) the passing of a resolution for the voluntary winding up of an
insolvent corporate partner under the Insolvency Act 1986,
s 84;[18]
(5) a winding up order being made against a corporate partner
under the Insolvency Act 1986, s 125;
(6) the presentation of a winding up petition against a corporate
partner but where there is no concurrent petition presented
against the partnership.[19]

A corporate partner who is subjected to any of the above situations
may impose upon the corporate partnership a considerable
restraint in the carrying out of its business affairs. Where a petition
for winding up has been presented, the status of the corporate
partner remains uncertain. If, on the subsequent hearing of the
petition, it follows that an order is made, the winding up of the
corporate partner is deemed to have commenced on the date when
the petition was presented.[20] In such cases, as has been noted
above, any dispositions of a corporate partner will be void unless
the court orders otherwise. If a corporate partner is subjected to
any of the legal processes considered above the practical consequences will be that the affected corporate partner will not be
able to function unhindered as a partner, nor will the corporate
partner be an effective member of the corporate partnership.
Accordingly, the power to expel a corporate partner in such circumstances must be an option that is available to the remaining
partners in the enterprise.[1]

This power of expulsion is all the more important in view of the
trenchant observation of the learned editor of *Lindley*[2] who has
noted that a winding up order per se will not dissolve the corporate
partnership.

The power to expel a *solvent* corporate partner which enters into
a voluntary winding up should also be inserted into the partnership
agreement. Despite the solvency of such a corporate partner, the
same problems as noted above may arise for a partnership which

---

[18] For the position where such a resolution is passed in respect of a solvent corporate partner see Chapter 12.
[19] For a consideration of the presentation of concurrent petitions against a partnership and individual partners see Chapter 13.
[20] See the Insolvency Act 1986, s 129(2).
[1] Even the appointment of an interim liquidator under the Insolvency Act 1986,
s 135(1) may considerably worsen the working relationship between the partners
of the business enterprise. The power to expel in such circumstances should
remain an option.
[2] See *Lindley* (16th edn, 1971) p 244 and Partnership Act 1890, s 33.

continues to carry on its business affairs with a corporate partner which is nevertheless in the process of winding up its own affairs.[3]

Expulsion of a corporate partner is clearly a drastic remedy.[4] Furthermore, the power of expulsion need not be exercised by the remaining partners. An alternative power should therefore be inserted in the partnership agreement to dissolve the partnership in any of the circumstances noted above.

Although the expulsion of a corporate partner from a partnership, or the dissolution of the same, has been considered generally in the context of the financial health of the relevant corporate partner(s), such powers may be exercised in other circumstances.

A partnership is, in general, a personal business relationship between private individuals. In such cases, the peculiar abilities, characters or skills of the members of the enterprise take on a particular importance. Superficially, such matters may not be considered as of any great importance where corporations constitute, in whole or in part, the members of a partnership. Such a view, however, ignores the fact that a company may be little more than an 'incorporated' 'one-man' business enterprise, ie a single member company[5] or an 'incorporated' partnership. Where such companies are constituted members of a corporate partnership, their director(s) (who are generally also the principal shareholders) are the directing minds and persona[6] of the relevant enterprise. Accordingly, the active and beneficial membership of such companies within a corporate partnership may be dependent on the continued personal involvement of such directors or persons in the partnership.[7] Furthermore, the skills or abilities of such persons may be of prime importance to the continued viability of the partnership. It would in such cases be prudent for the partnership

---

[3] It should be noted that the Insolvency Act 1986, s 87(1) provides that a company from the commencement of the winding up must cease to carry on its business (including its involvement in any partnership), except in so far as is required for its beneficial winding up.

[4] Particularly if the expulsion of the corporate partner results in the automatic accrual of the corporate partner's share of the partnership assets to the remaining partners. See p 82, above.

[5] See fn 4, p 82, above.

[6] On the concept of the directing mind of a company see Lord Denning in *Tesco Supermarkets v Nattrass* [1972] AC 153.

[7] There is no legal reason why the personal involvement of a director(s) of any company within a partnership, irrespective of the size of the company, should not be of prime importance to the partnership, even where the corporate partner is a large and complex business enterprise. The corporate partnership may depend on the personal involvement of the board of directors or a management team of a corporate partner.

agreement to empower the partnership to expel a corporate partner, or to dissolve the partnership, if the services of such person(s) are for any reason discontinued or lost.[8]

Although there are special rules applicable to both the insolvency and the taxation of corporate partners and corporate partnerships these matters are discussed in Chapters 12 and 13.

SUB-PARTNERSHIPS

A sub-partnership is, in essence, a partnership within a partnership. Such an enterprise, although it constitutes a share in another partnership, and is derived from the latter, nevertheless operates outside the confines of that principal partnership. Such a sub-partnership was first recognised by Lord Eldon in *Ex p Barrow*.[9] Any agreement to share the profits of the sub-partnership will constitute or bring about a partnership only between those who are a party to the agreement.

Bray v Fromant[10] emphasised the principle that the partners who are solely partners in the respective sub- and main partnership are not thereby constituted partners inter se.[11] Accordingly, in the Australian case of *New Zealand Banking Group v Richardson*,[12] it was held that such a sub-partner could not be fully responsible for the losses of the main partnership. Nevertheless, such a sub-partner had to bear a *proportion* of any such losses which had to be borne by the sub-partners, who were also partners in the main partnership.

On the creation of a sub-partnership, it does not follow that any of the terms of the main partnership agreement will by implication be incorporated into the sub-partnership agreement, or be regarded as governing that enterprise. The duration of the sub-partnership will not therefore necessarily endure for the same term as the main partnership.[13]

---

8 Thus the death or disability of such persons would be pertinent to the exercise of the power of expulsion of a corporate partner or the dissolution of the corporate partnership. Changes in the voting control of a corporate partner may also constitute grounds for the exercise of the powers of expulsion or dissolution noted above. The exercise of such powers in the above cases may be regarded as analogous to the situation whereby no person may be introduced as a partner without the consent of all existing partners, see the Partnership Act 1890, s 24(7).

9 (1815) 2 Rose 255.

10 (1821) 6 Madd 5: see also *Ex p Dodgson* (1830) Mont & M 445.

11 On the basis of the maxim *socius mei socii socius meus non est*, ie 'my partner's partner is not necessarily my partner'.

12 [1980] Qd R 321. See also *Fletcher* (1981) 55 ALJ 687.

13 See *Frost v Moulton* (1856) 21 Beav 596. For the duration of partnerships see Chapter 2.

GROUP PARTNERSHIPS

The group partnership is an entity which consists of a partnership between two or more partnerships. Although such an enterprise may bear a superficial resemblance to a sub-partnership, *each* member of *each* individual partnership is a constituent member of the group partnership, which is not the case in sub-partnerships.

The advantage of the group partnership is that partnerships may share facilities, resources and/or expertise without total loss of autonomy (although such autonomy and financial independence may in practical terms be lost). However, it must be borne in mind that none of the respective partnerships enjoys a separate personality, independent of its constituent members, and the group partnership consists of the collective membership of all the partners of the respective constituent partnerships. Accordingly the general statutory restrictions on the formation of partnerships of more than 20 members is of considerable consequence to group partnerships.[14] Apart from this restriction, a group partnership differs in no way from any other form of partnership. Such a partnership is therefore governed by the Partnership Act 1890 and by the agreement express or implied of its members.

Each constituent partnership may continue to carry out its duties and responsibilities within the group partnership under its own name, but the group partnership may, as an alternative, operate under a common group name. The prior approval of the Secretary of State is required in either case under the Business Names Act 1985.[15]

The group partnership may pose difficult managerial problems for its members.[16] A group partnership may become an unwieldy business organisation. The group partnership agreement should therefore allocate responsibility and decision-making powers between the group partnership and the various constituent partnership members. Such allocation should reflect the perceived role of the group partnership, and the required independence or autonomy of each of the constituent partnership members.[17]

---

[14] See Chapter 2 for a consideration of the restriction on the maximum size of partnerships and the exceptions to this provision. There is, of course, no prohibition per se on companies becoming members of a group partnership.

[15] See ss 2 and 3 of the Business Names Act 1985.

[16] Eg in the allocation of goodwill between the group partnership and the constituent partnerships.

[17] Although the allocation of responsibility and decision-making powers should be specified in the group partnership agreement, such allocation should principally be determined by the nature and purpose of the business which it is intended the group partnership is to undertake.

The group partnership agreement may thus provide that decisions which fall to be decided by the group partnership shall be determined by a simple or qualified majority of *all* the partners. Such a mechanism will also require a prescribed quorum at partners' meetings where such decisions are to be made. Where the group partnership consists of partnerships which are not subject to the general statutory restriction on membership numbers, such a decision-making process may prove cumbersome.

An alternative procedure for determining group partnership matters is what may be regarded as a form of bloc vote system. In such cases each constituent partnership is treated as a single entity for the purposes of voting on group partnership matters. Each constituent partnership's vote may be weighted so as to reflect the number of partners in each constituent partnership. Such a system can be incorporated into a formal group partnership management committee.

The group partnership agreement

The group partnership agreement may provide for a number of mechanisms for determining group partnership matters, dependent on the nature of the matter to be determined. The mechanisms may be a combination of the procedures noted above.[18]

The group partnership agreement should specify the division between the assets of the constituent partnerships and the group partnership assets. The ownership of the goodwill of the group partnership should always be a matter for express determination in the group partnership agreement. Furthermore, the terms and conditions upon which the assets of constituent partnerships or individual partners may be used by the group partnership should also be clearly specified.

As in all well-drafted partnership agreements, express provision should be made in the group partnership agreement for the expulsion of a partner, and for the dissolution of the partnership.[19] The special characteristic of the group partnership requires that provision is made for the automatic expulsion or retirement of a group partner who has ceased, for whatever cause, to be a member of a constituent partnership.

---

[18] Thus, matters may be determined by a majority vote of all partners, although such voting may need to take place within a formal management committee system.

[19] For a consideration of the possible grounds justifying the expulsion of a partner or for the dissolution of a partnership see Chapter 12.

Provision should also be made in the group partnership agreement for a constituent partnership to retire voluntarily from the group partnership. Such a constituent partnership should also be subject to automatic expulsion from the group partnership if it becomes insolvent,[20] or if any of the individual or corporate members of such a partnership become insolvent. Finally the group partnership agreement should provide for the dissolution of the group partnership and the distribution of the group partnership assets to the members of the constituent partnerships.

As in the case of a corporate partnership, concurrent petitions for winding up an insolvent group partnership may be presented against the group partnership and two or more of the constituent partnerships. The procedures governing and the effects of such petitions on partnerships in general will be considered in Chapter 13.

---

[20] Other grounds for expulsion of an individual or corporate partner or constituent partnership should include the conduct or reputation of individual partners and/or constituent partnerships, or criteria which have been agreed between individual members of the group partnership, such as the professional qualification of individual members.

CHAPTER 5

PUBLIC AND PRIVATE CONTROLS ON PARTNERSHIP AND PARTNERS

This chapter will consider certain statutory and common law restrictions imposed upon both the partnership as a business organisation and the members of a partnership. The first such restriction to consider is that imposed upon a partnership which seeks to conduct its business under a business name which does not consist of the surnames or corporate names of all the members of the partnership. Such a partnership may be subject to the provisions of the Business Names Act 1985.[1]

Section 1 of the Business Names Act 1985 identifies the partnerships which will be subject to the provisions of the Act. Thus, a partnership which has its place of business and which carries on business in Great Britain under a business name which does not consist solely and exclusively[2] of the names of the partners must comply with the terms of the 1985 Act.

BUSINESS NAMES ACT 1985, SECTION 4

Disclosure required of persons using business name

A partnership which is subject to the 1985 Act must state in legible characters on all business correspondence[3] the name of each

---

[1] This Act is based on ss 28-32 of the Companies Act 1981. These provisions replaced the registration system for business names contained in the Registration of Business Names Act 1916.

[2] With permitted additions which consist only of the forename(s) of individual partners or the initials of these forenames, or where two or more individual partners have the same surname, the addition of 's' at the end of the surname. Furthermore, any addition to the business name of the partnership which merely indicates that the business is carried on in succession to a former owner of the business is also permitted without reference to or regulation under the 1985 Act.

[3] Such correspondence includes: (i) business letters; (ii) written orders for goods

---

91

partner. Furthermore, such correspondence should state, in relation to each member of the partnership, an address in Great Britain at which service of any document, relating in any way to the business, will be effective.[4] Furthermore, a partnership subject to the provisions of the 1985 Act must, on any premises on which the business of the partnership is carried on, and to which the customers of the business or the suppliers of any goods or services to the business have access, display in a prominent position a notice containing the names and addresses of the partners.[5] Any customer of or supplier of goods and services to the partnership is entitled to ask for a written list of the information so displayed, which must be supplied by the partnership immediately.[6]

Clearly, partnerships with a large number of partners would find compliance with the above rules, particularly the provisions regarding the partnership correspondence, difficult and certainly impractical. Accordingly, s 4(3) of the 1985 Act provides that a partnership comprising *more* than 20 partners need not list the names and relevant addresses[7] on all business correspondence, if two conditions are satisfied. The first condition is that all business correspondence[8] of such a partnership must[9] state in legible characters the address of the partnership's principal place of business at which a list of all of the partners' names is open to inspection.[10] The second condition is that such a partnership's business correspondence must not contain the names of any partners except as signatories.

All partnerships which are subject to the provisions of the 1985 Act must make the prescribed list of the partner's names available for inspection during office hours.[11] Any such list should comply with any regulations made under s 4(5) of the 1985 Act, which

---

or services to be supplied to the business; (iii) invoices and receipts issued in the course of the business; (iv) written demands for payment of debts arising in the course of the business.
4   See s 4(1)(a).
5   See s 4(1)(b).
6   Section 4(2).
7   Ie the addresses of each of the partners at which service of any document relating in any way to the business will be effective, see p 91 above.
8   The relevant provision of the Act, ie s 4(3) refers to business documents. This term, however, is clearly a synonym for the business correspondence listed in s 4(1)(a) and which is listed in fn 3, above.
9   As an alternative to compliance with s 4(1)(a) of the Act.
10 Such a partnership must therefore still maintain such a list at its principal place of business as in the case of partnerships of less than 20 members.
11 Section 4(4): such a list is defined as a notice within the Act.

determine the form of such lists, or how they are to be displayed.[12] It is an offence for any partner(s) to fail without reasonable excuse to comply with any of the provisions of s 4 of the 1985 Act relating to the disclosure of information on business correspondence. It is also an offence under s 4 of the Act to refuse anyone the right of inspection of the list of partners when requested.[13]

Civil remedies for breach of section 4

In addition to criminal sanctions for failure to comply with the provisions of s 4, s 5 of the 1985 Act also imposes upon a recalcitrant partnership certain disabilities in connection with any civil proceedings which arise out of any contract entered into by the partnership in the course of business. Section 5 imposes, in essence, a statutory estoppel in respect of any such litigation undertaken by the partnership to enforce contractual rights where the 'disclosure' requirements of s 4 have not been satisfied. In such cases, an action in contract instigated by the partnership arising out of any business undertaken by the partnership may be dismissed if the defendant can establish either:

(1)   that he has a claim against the partnership arising out of the contract which he has been unable to pursue by reason of the partnership's breach of s 4; or

(2)   that he has suffered some financial loss in connection with the contract by reason of the partnership's failure to comply with the provisions of s 4.

However, the court has a discretion to allow any such action to proceed if it considers it just and equitable,[14] but this provision is without prejudice to the right of the partnership to enforce the rights under such a contract as the partnership may have against another in any proceedings brought by the latter.[15]

---

[12]   See s 6 of the Act for the procedural matters that may arise out of any regulations which relate to business names made by the Secretary of State.
[13]   For the penalties relating to, and procedures for prosecution of, the offences under the Act see s 7. Note that, under s 7(3) of the Act, repeated transgressions can lead to a cumulative default fine.
[14]   Section 5(1).
[15]   Section 5(2).

BUSINESS NAMES ACT 1985, SECTION 2

Prohibition of use of certain business names

Section 2(1) of the 1985 Act prohibits a partnership carrying on its business under certain business names, unless the prior written approval of the Secretary of State has been secured.

The prohibition relates to any business name which:

(1)   would be likely to give the impression that the business is connected with government departments or local authorities; or

(2)   which includes any word or expression for the time being specified by regulations made under s 3 of the Act.[16]

Section 2 is not retrospective, and does not apply to the business names of partnerships which were in existence and use prior to 26 February 1982,[17] and which continue to operate under that business name. Furthermore, s 2(2) granted a 12-month period of grace where a business had been transferred after 26 February 1982 and the new owner continued to use that business name.

It is an offence to contravene the provisions of s 3 of the Act, which provides that the use of certain words and expressions within or as a business name may by virtue of regulations made by the Secretary of State require the latter's consent.[18] Such regulations may specify a government department or other body as a body which may object to the use of such word(s) or expressions.

Where a partnership proposes to carry on a business under a business name which is, or which includes, a word or expression to which a specified body may object, the partnership should contact that body in writing to see if it has any objection to the proposed use of such words or expressions by the partnership. The partnership should also notify the Secretary of State of any such approach, and of any response made by the relevant body.

Sexual/racial discrimination

The admission of a new partner to a partnership is governed principally by the Partnership Act.[19] Nevertheless, where a partnership

---

[16]   See below.
[17]   The section is based on the Companies Act 1981, s 28(2).
[18]   See above.
[19]   See the Partnership Act 1890, s 24(7).

is considering the admission of a new partner the present members must also consider the question whether their criteria for admission breach the statutory provisions which prohibit discrimination on the grounds of sex and race. Consideration will first be given to the statutory provisions which prohibit discrimination on the grounds of sex.

1. THE SEX DISCRIMINATION ACT 1975

This Act makes unlawful, inter alia, discrimination on the grounds of sex, or marital status, or by way of victimisation in a wide range of activities including employment.

Discrimination takes place against a woman[20] for the purposes of the 1975 Act if, on the ground of her sex:

(1)   she is treated less favourably than a man in the same circumstances;[1] or

(2)   a condition or requirement is applied to a woman which is also applied to a man; but

    (a)   the proportion of women who can comply with such requirements or conditions is considerably smaller than the proportion of men who can comply with it; and

    (b)   such a condition or requirement cannot be justified irrespective of the sex of the person to whom it is applied; and

    (c)   which is detrimental to the woman because she cannot comply with it.[2]

Section 1(2) of the 1975 Act provides that for the purposes of comparison in the case of direct discrimination[3] where a man is treated differently because of his married or unmarried status, then the treatment accorded to a woman *must* be compared to that which is given to a man with the same marital status.

Discrimination of either the direct or indirect form is made relevant to partnerships by virtue of s 11(1) of the Sex Discrimination Act 1975. This subsection[4] provides that:

---

[20]   See s 1 of the 1975 Act. Although discrimination may take place against a man the text has considered discrimination against a women for ease of exposition.

[1]   This form of discrimination may be called direct discrimination.

[2]   This form of discrimination may be called indirect discrimination. Under s 2 of the 1975 Act a man under the same circumstances may be subject to direct and indirect discrimination. The text will, for the purposes of ease of exposition, refer to sex discrimination against women.

[3]   See above.

[4]   As amended by the Sex Discrimination Act 1986, s 1(3).

'It is unlawful for a firm in relation to a position as partner in the firm, to discriminate against a women –

(a)   in the arrangements they make for the purpose of determining who should be offered that position, or

(b)   in the terms on which they offer her that position, or

(c)   by refusing or deliberately omitting to offer her that position, or

(d)   in a case where the woman already holds that position –

(i)   in the way they afford her access to any benefits, facilities or services, or by refusing or deliberately omitting to afford her access to them, or

(ii)   by expelling her from that position, or subjecting her to any other detriment.'

It should be noted that all partnerships are subject to the provisions of s 11(1) of the 1975 Act. Section 11(1) applies, however, to potential partnerships as well as existing partnerships.[5] There are, nevertheless, qualifications to the application of s 11(1) to partnerships. It is not unlawful for a partnership to discriminate against a woman either:

(1)   in the arrangements it makes for the purposes of determining who should be offered the position of partner; or

(2)   in refusing or deliberately omitting to offer her such a position,

but, in either of the above cases, only where the position as partner is a case where being a man would be a genuine occupational qualification for that position.[6]

It is also lawful to discriminate on the grounds of sex with regard to the terms on which:

(1)   a position as partner is offered; or

(2)   where a woman already holds such a position –

(a)   in the way the partnership affords her access to benefits, facilities, or services, or refuses or deliberately omits to afford her such access; or

(b)   by expelling her from her position as partner, or subjecting her to any other detriment. If such can be regarded as provision made in relation to death.

In general such actions, carried out by a partnership against a woman partner, would, although discriminatory, also be lawful if

[5] Section 11(2).
[6] Section 11(3).

they were made as provision in relation to retirement. But the grounds upon which any such provision relating to retirement would be lawful are more restricted than in the case of provision made by a partnership in relation to death.

Where a partnership makes provision in relation to *retirement* it is unlawful for the partnership to discriminate[7] against a woman, in such of the terms on which they offer her a position as partner, in so far as they provide for her expulsion, or by expelling her from that position, or by subjecting her to any detriment which results in her expulsion.[8] It thus remains lawful to discriminate against a woman in respect of provision in relation to retirement which may concern access to benefits, facilities, or services, or which subject her to detriment not leading to expulsion.

Section 11(1) applies in full to limited partnerships, as it applies to partnerships governed by the Partnership Act 1890.

2. RACIAL DISCRIMINATION

By s 1 of the Race Relations Act 1976 a person discriminates against another if:

(1) he treats a person less favourably on racial grounds;[9] or

(2) he applies a requirement or condition to a person of a racial group which he applies or would apply equally to other parties not of the same racial group[10] as that person; but

(3) the proportion of individuals of that person's racial group who can comply with the conditions or requirements applied to parties of other racial groups is considerably smaller than the proportion of individuals not of that person's racial group who can so comply *and* it cannot be shown such an action is justifiable irrespective of racial grounds, and where such actions cause detriment to the member of that racial group because that person cannot so comply.

Unlike the case of sexual discrimination, it is only unlawful for a

---

[7] For a definition of discrimination see p 95, above.

[8] Section 11(4) as amended by the Sex Discrimination Act 1986, s 2(2).

[9] Such discrimination may be defined as direct discrimination. 'Racial grounds' is defined by s 3(1) of the 1976 Act as grounds based on colour, race, nationality, or ethnic or national origins.

[10] Such discrimination may be defined as indirect discrimination. 'Racial group' means a group of persons defined by reference to colour, race, nationality or ethnic or national origins, and references to a person's racial group refer to any racial group into which he falls. See the Race Relations Act 1976, s 3(1). A racial group may for the purposes of the 1976 Act comprise two or more distinct racial groups: see s 3(2).

firm of six or more partners to discriminate on racial grounds against a person in relation to a position as partner in the firm either:[11]

(1)   in the arrangements they make for the purpose of determining who should be offered that position; or
(2)   in the terms on which they offer him that position; or
(3)   by refusing or deliberately omitting to offer him that position; or
(4)   in a case where the person already holds that position –
      (a)   in the way they afford him access to any benefits, facilities or services, or by refusing or deliberately omitting to afford him access to such benefits, facilities, or services; or
      (b)   by expelling him from that position, or subjecting him to any other detriment.

Such discriminatory actions are unlawful if carried out by nascent as well as existing partnerships. The above provisions also apply to limited partnerships as well as to partnerships governed by the Partnership Act 1890.[12]

The 1976 Act renders certain discriminatory action lawful in relation to a partnership although such exceptions are more restricted than in the case of sexual discrimination. Thus discrimination is permitted either:

(1)   in the arrangements made for the purpose of determining who should be offered a partnership; or
(2)   in the refusal or deliberate omission to offer such a position,

but in each case only where being a member of a particular racial group would be a genuine qualification for the position.[13]

3. CONSEQUENCES OF DISCRIMINATION

Where a woman is a party to an act of sexual discrimination, eg by virtue of the operation of a discriminatory provision in a partnership agreement, the term will nevertheless be unenforceable against her notwithstanding that she is a partner. If she was not a party to the

---

[11]   Section 10(1), Race Relations Act 1976. See also ibid s 73 whereby the number of partners specified for the purposes of s 1 may be altered by an order made by the Secretary of State.
[12]   Section 10(2) and (4).
[13]   Section 10(3).

discriminatory act any relevant term in the partnership agreement will be void.[14]

COMPETITION LEGISLATION

Partnerships, like all business enterprises, may engage in anti-competitive practices. In such cases the provisions of the Competition Act 1980 may apply to them. A partnership, therefore, either by its mere creation or in the conducting of its business, may be the subject of a reference to the Monopolies and Mergers Commission. The ultimate sanction in such a case is an order being made against the partnership under s 10 of the 1980 Act prohibiting the members of the partnership from engaging in the anti-competitive practices.[15] The application of the 1980 Act to partnerships may be more theoretical than actual. Even less likely to affect a partnership is art 85 of the EC Treaty.[16] This provision renders null and void any agreement between undertakings[17] which may affect trade between member states of the European Union where such agreements have as their object or effect the prevention, restriction or distortion of competition within the European Union. It may be argued that virtually all partnerships involve the members agreeing not to compete with the business of the partnership and such an agreement may be regarded as an agreement which is contrary to art 85. It is unlikely, however, that a partnership could ever command or control a given business activity or area of enterprise within a market so as to attract the attention of the Commission of the European Communities.[18]

---

[14] See the Sex Discrimination Act 1975, s 77(1) and (2). For the consequences of racial discrimination in respect of partnerships see Race Relations Act 1976, s 72. Both sections have been amended by the Trade Union Reform and Employment Rights Act 1993, Sch 6.

[15] For a definition of anti-competitive practices see s 2(1) of the 1980 Act. For the procedures to be followed before the making of an order under s 10 see ss 3–9.

[16] Article 85 renders null and void agreements between parties which may affect trade between the member states of the EC in so far as the agreements may prevent, restrict, or distort competition within the EC.

[17] Undertakings would, for the above purposes, include partnerships as well as the individual members of a partnership, whether private individuals or corporations. See, however, *Gottfried v BASF AG* [1976] 2 CMLR D44 (76/743/EEC).

[18] Since art 85 would require the relevant undertakings to enjoy a significant share of the relevant market or enterprise it is unlikely that partnerships, even corporate partnerships, would be subject to the article.

The controls or restrictions upon partnerships which are imposed by statutes regulating, inter alia, insolvency proceedings against individual partners or partnerships, or the payment of taxes are considered in Chapters 13 and 15.[19]

NON-STATUTORY RESTRICTION ON PARTNERSHIPS

The contractual basis of a partnership is emphasised, inter alia, by the necessity for persons intending to be partners to be of sound mind and full capacity when they enter into a partnership agreement. Partners as well as potential partners also stand in a fiduciary relationship with one another.[20] Such principles are most clearly illustrated when a partnership is created or a new partner is admitted to a partnership. Partners or intending partners must ensure, on the creation of a partnership or on the admission of a new partner, that no individual has, in becoming a partner, been subjected to undue influence. Thus, where a person can be shown to have entered or been admitted into a partnership on terms which are clearly unfavourable to him, and such terms have been negotiated in circumstances which amount to that person having been the subject of undue influence, the partnership agreement to which he is a party may be declared void as against him.[1]

In *O'Sullivan v Management Agency and Music Ltd*,[2] the Court of Appeal held that a party upon whom undue influence has been exerted while entering into an unfavourable agreement[3] could pursue against the other party or parties to the agreement either contractual remedies or equitable remedies. Such a party is not barred under the principles of equity from having such an agreement set aside, merely because *restitutio in integrum* is no longer possible because the agreement has been fully executed.[4] Thus, a

---

[19]   See also RSC Ord 81, which governs the procedures for a partnership to undertake proceedings and to be sued in the firm name.

[20]   See Chapter 8 for a consideration of this duty.

[1]   And not merely voidable through mistake or fraudulent misrepresentation: see per Lord Denning MR in *Lloyds Bank Ltd v Bundy* [1974] 3 All ER 757 at 763, [1975] QB 326 at 337.

[2]   [1985] 3 All ER 351: and see the cases cited therein.

[3]   The case involved agreements relating to the management of a performing artiste and composer. Nevertheless, the principles set out in the case are, it is suggested, applicable to partnership agreements.

[4]   A fortiori when the partnership is still in an inchoate or subsisting state.

partnership agreement entered into by a party in circumstances where there has been a breach by the other partner(s) of the fiduciary duty owed to him can be set aside in equity, notwithstanding that it is not possible to place any of the parties to the agreement in the precise position they had been in before they entered into the partnership agreement. However, in order that a partnership agreement can be set aside in such circumstances, the court must be satisfied that it can achieve practical justice between the parties. To this end the court must first do justice to the party seeking to have the agreement set aside by obliging the partners who are in breach of their fiduciary duties to give up any profits or advantages they gained under the agreement. Nevertheless, the court should in such cases also consider whether it would be appropriate to compensate the partners who are in breach of their fiduciary duties for their contribution to the partnership enterprise during the subsistence of the partnership. In considering the question of compensation for such partners, the court should have regard to what amounts to reasonable remuneration, which may include a profit element for the work done by the relevant partner or partners where the partnership has been successful through their efforts. It may well be that compensation will only be considered by the courts in such cases where the contribution of the relevant partner(s) to the success of the partnership has been significant.[5]

Where a partnership agreement is set aside, any sums recovered by the party seeking such an order may be subject at the order of the court to the payment of interest.[6]

RESTRAINT OF TRADE

A partnership agreement may provide that a partner must attend full time to partnership affairs[7] and not engage in activities outside the partnership which are inimical to the interests of the business. In addition, a partnership agreement usually provides that a partner who leaves the business is prohibited from competing with the

[5] See *O'Sullivan v Management Agency* [1985] 3 All ER 351 at 365; *Erlanger v New Sombrero Phosphate Co* (1878) 3 App Cas 1218, [1874–80] All ER 271.

[6] See *Regal (Hastings) Ltd v Gulliver* [1942] 1 All ER 378, [1967] 2 AC 134. See also *Adam v Newbigging* (1888) 13 App Cas 308, [1886–90] All ER Rep 975.

[7] Such a duty or responsibility is also considered in Chapter 8.

partnership. Such a provision within a partnership agreement will restrict the activity of a former partner in the manner noted above for a specified time, and/or within a stated geographical area.[8] Although such a provision should on the face of it be regarded as entirely a matter of agreement between the partners[9] such a provision may by struck down on the ground that it is unreasonable and in restraint of trade. As a general principle, such clauses are regarded as being against the public interest[10] and therefore prima facie unreasonable.

In *Deacons v Bridge*[11] Lord Fraser of Tullybelton determined that, in construing the reasonableness of a 'restraint of trade' clause within a partnership agreement, regard must first be had to what legitimate interests of the remaining partners ought to be protected by the enforcing of such a clause on behalf of a partnership. What constitutes such legitimate interests depends on the facts of the particular case, though the nature of the firm, its size, and the position the former partner held in the partnership business are clearly pertinent factors in determining such an interest. Though his Lordship did not directly address the issue of the size and influence of the partnership within a particular sphere of business activity, such a matter must also be relevant in determining the legitimate interest of a partnership in enforcing a restraint of trade clause against a former partner. The courts, it is suggested, must always have regard to the prospect of a partnership utilising a restraint of trade clause so as to obtain a practical or virtual monopoly within a given locality or within a sphere or area of business.

Lord Fraser considered that, once the legitimate interest of a partnership in enforcing a restraint of trade clause contained in a partnership agreement had been established, the particular clause should then be examined. If the clause provides adequately for the protection of the legitimate interests of the partnership, then it is a reasonable clause and enforceable against former partners. Conversely, if the clause is wider than necessary for the protection

---

[8] Such clauses, ie restraint of trade clauses within partnership agreements, are considered in Chapter 3.

[9] See the Partnership Act 1890, s 19, but note the possibility of the agreement being declared void if it has been imposed upon a party by means of undue influence.

[10] Since they prevent or restrict an individual from engaging in a profession or business activity.

[11] [1984] 2 All ER 19.

of the legitimate interests of the business, it will be struck down in its entirety and rendered totally unenforceable.[12] Particular case law examples of the forms of restraint of trade clauses which have been held to be enforceable show little consistency in approach. Many of the cases predate *Deacons v Bridge*. Nevertheless, it appears that a medical partnership which encompasses both a private and National Health practice may protect the goodwill which attaches to the NHS part of its practice through a restraint of trade clause.[13] Such a clause may therefore prevent an ex-partner from becoming the medical practitioner to the NHS patients of his former partnership, although only within the constraints imposed by the relevant clause.

It has been held that an attempt by a partnership to impose a blanket restriction upon a former medical practitioner partner by a restraint of trade clause from engaging in medical practice in the practice area of the partnership must render such a clause unenforceable.[14] However, in *Clarke v Newland*[15] a clause in a medical partnership agreement not to practise in the practice area within three years of the termination of the partnership was held by the Court of Appeal to be enforceable. The court was of the opinion that the clause had to be construed in the light of 'the factual matrix' at the time the agreement was made and the object which the clause sought to obtain for the partnership (or in the actual case the plaintiff, who was after the termination of the partnership a sole practitioner). The object of the clause was the protection of the plaintiff's medical practice and it was therefore enforceable. It should be noted that the defendant was a salaried partner. It follows that if the clause is wider than is necessary to protect the legitimate

---

[12] His Lordship in *Deacons v Bridge* rejected the use by analogy of the principles utilised by the courts in the consideration of the enforceability of restraint of trade clauses used in employer/employee agreements or in vendor/purchaser sale of a business and goodwill agreements. Semble the position of a salaried partner? It would appear that the above principles noted in the main body of the text would not apply to a restraint of trade clause which a partnership seeks to enforce against a salaried partner who leaves the partnership if he is subsequently determined as being an employee: see *Briggs v Oates* [1990] ICR 473. It would appear in such cases that a restraint of trade clause would be construed strictly against the partnership.

[13] See *Kerr v Morris* [1987] Ch 90, overruling *Hensman v Traill* (1980) Times, 22 October.

[14] *Lyne-Pirkis v Jones* [1969] 1 WLR 1293: but see *Clarke v Newland* [1991] 1 All ER 397 (considered in the text below) where *Lyne-Pirkis v Jones* was distinguished on contextual grounds.

[15] [1991] 1 All ER 397.

interests of the partnership it will be unenforceable.[16] By way of contrast a restraint of trade clause that provided that the former partner was not to 'carry on or be interested or concerned in carrying on the business or profession of medicine, surgery, midwifery or pharmacy or any branch thereof within 10 miles and for a period of 21 years' was held reasonable[17] and enforceable against the former partner.

Thus any prohibition imposed upon a former partner by a partnership from competing with the latter, or from attempting to gain the latter's goodwill and clients or customers, which is limited in time and/or geographical area is prima facie reasonable. However, in considering the question of geographical restriction which may be imposed by a restraint of trade clause in a partnership agreement, the courts must have regard to the number of competing businesses within such an area, or the number of actual or potential customers or clients who may be available to, or who may wish to, use the services supplied by the partnership. If a restraint of trade clause, although restricted by geographical area, in fact covers such a large number of competing business that an ex-partner is effectively prevented from carrying on his livelihood or profession, then it would seem such a clause will be held to be unreasonable and unenforceable.[18]

It has been held in the recent past by the Court of Appeal that a restraint of trade clause in a legal practice partnership agreement was contrary to public policy when it sought to prevent a solicitor from acting for a client of the partnership of which he was formerly a member.[19] Such an opinion was based, it seems, on the special

---

[16] Eg by preventing the former partner from engaging in consultancy work, where he has never engaged in such an activity while a partner: see *Peyton v Mindham* [1972] 1 WLR 8.

[17] *Whitehill v Bradford* [1952] 1 All ER 115.

[18] See *Dallas McMillan & Sinclair v Simpson* 1989 SLT 454. In the case of *Deacons v Bridge* the restriction as to geographical area though covering the whole of Hong Kong was held to be reasonable, since it only prevented the ex-partner from practising as a solicitor for any *client* of the partnership or any *person who had been a client of the partnership in the three years before the ex-partner left the partnership*. The restraint of trade clause did not therefore prevent him from engaging in the practice of a solicitor in Hong Kong. Such a provision would it is suggested have been held to be unreasonable. The actual provision in *Deacons v Bridge* was regarded by the court as being in the public interest, since it encouraged professional partnerships to take on new partners, while it still permitted such a partnership to protect its goodwill and clientele. This was beneficial to the clients of the partnership since they were able to rely on the continuity of the firm as a successful enterprise.

[19] See *Oswald Hickson Collier & Co v Carter-Ruck* [1984] 2 All ER 15.

and fiduciary relationship that exists between a solicitor and his client, which transcends the relationship the solicitor may enjoy with any professional colleague. A further rationale behind this opinion was that the public interest required that a person should be able to seek the advice and services of the solicitor he wishes to act for him. However, this view has been doubted.[20] It is suggested, therefore, that the practice of the profession of a solicitor cannot in this respect be distinguished from that of the practice of any other profession. Accordingly, the reasonableness of a restraint of trade clause in a legal practice partnership agreement, which prevents an ex-partner from acting for the present or former clients of the partnership in limited and prescribed circumstances, must be judged solely on the principles of the legitimate interest of the partnership as enunciated in *Deacons v Bridge*. It is the application of such a principle, together with the court's examination of the scope of the particular restraint of trade clause, which should determine whether such a clause is enforceable against an ex-partner of a legal practice partnership.

---

[20] See the Court of Appeal decision in *Edwards v Worboys* [1984] AC 724n. Furthermore, in the Privy Council decision of *Deacons v Bridge* the court was of the opinion that it must respectfully and emphatically decline to agree with *Oswald's* case. The Privy Council felt that case could not be justified either on the authorities or on principle.

CHAPTER 6

RELATIONS OF PARTNERS TO OUTSIDERS

THE AGENCY BASIS TO LIABILITY

It is plainly impractical for the activities of the partnership to require that they all be carried out by the partners acting together. A partnership, like a limited company, is a trading entity,[1] which can only carry out its activities through individuals. In the case of companies, the principle major activities of the company are carried out by directors; in the case of partnerships, the same activities are carried out by the partners. The basis by which individual directors bind a company, and individual partners bind a partnership, is the law of agency. The applicable principles were drawn by the courts from the law of agency and applied to partnership prior to the passing of the Partnership Act 1890. As Lord Cranworth said in *Cox v Hickman*,[2] 'The liability of one partner for the acts of his co-partners is in truth the liability of a principal for the acts of his agent'.[3] Where two or more persons are engaged as partners in ordinary trade, each has an implied authority from the others to bind them all by contracts entered into in the usual course of business in that trade. Every partner in trade is, for the ordinary purposes of trade, the agent of his co-partner, and all are liable for the ordinary trade contracts of the others. Partners may stipulate among themselves that one of them only shall enter into particular contracts, or into any contracts, or that as to certain of their contracts none shall be liable except those by whom they are actually made; but with such private arrangements, third persons dealing with the firm without

---

[1] A limited company does, of course, have a distinct legal personality.
[2] (1860) 8 HL Cas 268 at 234.
[3] For leading modern cases on the law of agency dealing with the authority of company directors see *Freeman & Lockyer (a firm) v Buckhurst Park Properties (Mangal) Ltd* [1964] 2 QB 480 and *Hely-Hutchinson v Brayhead Ltd* [1968] 1 QB 549.

notice have no concern. The public has a right to assume that every partner has authority from his co-partner to bind the whole firm in contracts made according to the ordinary usages of trade. As Lord Cranworth makes clear, there are two great strands to agency law. On the one hand there is the actual authority of the agent to bind the principal, which is based upon the agreement between principal and agent.[4] This regulates the relations of principal and agent inter se. Beyond this there is the apparent authority of the agent, ie the authority which the agent will apparently have in the eyes of third parties with whom he deals. This is the principle which controls the extent to which the agent may bind the principal with the third party. It is, of course, primarily the principles developed within the latter strand which control the relations of the partners with third parties. Again, the applicable principles were developed by the courts prior to the enactment of the 1890 Act. At common law, whatever limitation might exist on the authority of the agent arising from the terms of the agreement between principal and agent, every third person who does not know the limitations on the agent's actual authority is allowed to assume that each partner has authority to do for the firm whatever is necessary for the transaction of its business as demonstrated by the manner in which that type of business is usually carried on by others.[5]

In fact, the actual and apparent authority of a partner will often be equally extensive. As the stranger is entitled to assume that a partner has authority to undertake transactions in the ordinary course of the partnership business, so it is also implied that his partners have agreed that he has such authority, and therefore his actual authority would, without more, be this extensive. Whilst actual authority is defined by the agreement between the partners, it must be remembered that the full terms of an agreement arise both from what is expressly agreed by the parties *and* from the terms to which they, as reasonable people, must be taken to assent impliedly.

However, it may be that in a particular partnership the partners do not wish such wide actual authority to arise. This may be because they do not want any partner to be able to carry out all the activities which would normally be within the normal course of business without the sanction of the others. Alternatively, it may be

---

[4] Except, of course, in cases of agency of necessity. However, situations of agency of necessity arise very rarely in the modern world.

[5] See the remarks of James LJ in *Re Agriculturist Cattle Insurance Co, Baird's Case* (1870) 5 Ch App 725 at 733; see also *Hawken v Bourne* (1841) 8 M & W 703.

that there is a young, junior, and inexperienced partner whose authority, and whose authority alone, the partners wish to circumscribe. In either situation the appropriate limitation can be introduced by express provision within the partnership agreement. Thus, for instance, it is possible to include a provision under which no partner might accept a bill of exchange on his own initiative, even though such an activity would be normal in the course of a business of that type.[6] In such a situation the actual authority is now restricted, while the apparent authority necessarily continues to its full extent. Consequently, if a bill of exchange is accepted, the partnership will be bound, even though the individual partner will have acted outside his actual authority, and thereby breached his agreement with his partners and made himself potentially liable to an action by them.

RESTRICTIONS ON A PARTNER'S AUTHORITY

There is only one situation in which the restriction on a partner's apparent authority will operate to prevent the partnership being bound to a third party who has dealt with an individual partner as partner. This arises where the third party is aware of the restriction or prohibition in the partnership agreement. In such a situation the third party is well aware that the partner has no authority to act in the way in which he has. Indeed, the Partnership Act 1890 makes express provision for this in s 8, which provides that if it has been agreed between the partners that any restriction should be placed on the power of any one or more of them to bind the firm, no act done in contravention of the restriction is binding on the firm with respect to persons having notice of the agreement.[7]

A person may have notice of a restriction on the power of an individual partner either by being given express notice[8] or by implication from the circumstances of the particular transaction.[9] In particular, if the transaction appears to be undertaken for the private purposes of the partner as, by *either* accepting a bill of exchange

---

[6] *Gallway v Mathew and Smithson* (1808) 10 East 264.

[7] Giving effect to dicta of Lord Ellenborough in *Gallway v Mathew and Smithson* (1808) 10 East 264 at 266, and *Alderson v Pope* (1808) 1 Camp 404n.

[8] *Minnit v Whinery* (1721) 5 Bro Parl Cas 489; *Gallway v Mathew and Smithson* (above); *Willis v Dyson* (1816) 1 Stark 164; *Rooth v Quin and Janney* (1819) 7 Price 193; *Vice v Fleming* (1827) 1 Y & J 227; *Ex p Holdsworth* (1841) 1 Mont D & De G 475.

[9] *Bignold v Waterhouse* (1813) 1 M & S 255; *Kendal v Wood* (1870) LR 6 Ex Ch 243; *Heilbut and Rocca and Briggs v Nevill* (1870) LR 5 CP 478.

in the firm name,[10] *or* pledging or charging partnership property for payment for his own debts,[11] notice will be implied from the circumstances of the transaction.

COMMENCEMENT AND DURATION OF AUTHORITY

Commencement of agency

Since the authority of a partner is, under general agency principles, derived from the existence of the partnership it follows inevitably that in general the authority commences with the commencement of the partnership itself.[12] Prior to the commencement of the partnership one intended participant may confer on another their authority to do an act or acts, and thereby constitute him his agent for a particular transaction or transactions. But the existence of the agency and, therefore, of the agent's authority, depends on actual authority specifically conferred, whether arising expressly or by implication.

It follows that if transactions are entered into by A in the early stages of the formation of a partnership involving A, B, and C, B and C will only be bound if *either* the court infers that the partnership had commenced when the transactions were undertaken,[13] *or* the court infers that B and C actually authorised A to enter into the transactions on behalf of all three.[14] The principles are clear, although the actual application of them in particular circumstances often seems somewhat arbitrary and inconsistent.

Further, where in the initial formation of a partnership individual partners undertake liabilities to raise capital for the use of the partnership it is important to determine on whose behalf they are

---

[10] *Green v Deakin* (1818) 2 Stark 347; *Frankland v M'Gusty* (1830) 1 Knapp 274; *Ex p Thorpe* (1836) 3 Mont & A 716; *Ex p Austen* (1840) 1 Mont D & De G 47; *Miller v Douglas* (1840) 3 Ross LC 500; *Leverson v Lane* (1862) 13 CBNS 278; *Re Riches* (1865) 4 De GJ & SM 581.

[11] *Snaith v Burridge* (1812) 4 Taunt 684; *Re Riches* (above).

[12] *Lindley and Banks on Partnership* (16th edn, 1990) p 329, citing *Ex p Jackson* (1790) 1 Ves 131; *Young v Hunter* (1812) 4 Taunt 582; also by analogy citing cases affecting promoters of a company, *Beale v Mouls* (1847) 10 QB 976; *Kerridge v Hesse* (1839) 9 C & P 200; *Whitehead v Barron* (1839) 2 Mood & Rob 248; *Beech v Eyre* (1843) 5 Man & G 415; *Bremner v Chamberlayne* (1848) 2 Car & Kir 560; *Newton and Watkins v Belcher* (1848) 12 QB 921.

[13] *Saville v Robertson and Hutchinson* (1792) 4 Term Rep 720; *Gouthwaite v Duckworth* (1810) 12 East 421; *Kilshaw v Jukes* (1863) 3 B & S 847.

[14] *Hutton v Bullock* (1874) LR 9 QB 572.

incurred. If incurred on behalf of the partnership when in existence, the partners will be bound. If, however, they are entered into by the partner personally to raise his own contribution to the partnership property, they are his individual transactions and only he will be liable.[15]

Termination of agency

A partner's *actual* authority stems from the partnership agreement. Accordingly, it continues until the partnership is dissolved pursuant to the terms of the agreement or the partner agrees to give it up.[16] The only possible exception to this would arise if the partnership agreement both conferred authority and also expressly gave the other partners authority to terminate or limit it by notice in particular circumstances, eg a term which allows the other partners to require by notice that all cheques drawn thereafter should require the signature of two or more partners where each partner hitherto had authority to sign.

By contrast, a partner's ostensible authority to bind the firm is based on the perceptions of third parties dealing with the firm. As such it may continue after the termination of the partnership, and will be brought to an end only by notice pursuant to provisions discussed below.[17]

PARTNERSHIP ACT 1890, SECTION 5

The common law principles of agency were incorporated into the Partnership Act 1890. The Act provides in s 5 that:

'Every partner is an agent of the firm and his other partners, for the purpose of the business of the partnership; and the acts of every partner who does any act of carrying on in the usual way business of the kind carried on by the firm of which he is a member by the firm bind the firm and his partners, *unless* the partner so acting in fact has no authority to act for the firm in a particular matter, and the person with whom he is dealing either knows

---

[15] *Greenslade v Dower and Colman* (1828) 7 B & C 635; *Dickinson v Valpy* (1829) 10 B & C 128; *Smith v Craven and Thompson* (1831) 1 Cr & J 500; *Fisher v Tayler* (1843) 2 Hare 218; *Heap v Dobson* (1863) 15 CBNS 460.

[16] Discussed in Chapter 12, p 261, below.

[17] See 'Future dealings after dissolution', p 151, below.

that he has no authority, or does not know or believe him to be a partner.'[18]

It follows from this provision that for a third person to be able to hold the partnership liable for the activities of an individual partner, it is necessary that the following be satisfied:

(1) the activities must be done in relation to the business of the partnership;
(2) the activities must be such as would be usual for carrying on that business in the usual way;
(3) the act must be done by the individual as partner, and not as an individual in his own right, and so understood by the third party. It follows that if a partner undertakes an activity as an individual, and the third party is aware of this, the firm will not be bound by the transaction.[19]

If these requirements are not met in one or other particular, the act is not done by a partner on behalf of the firm in the course of carrying on the partnership business in the usual way and, therefore, in the absence of express authority or the subsequent ratification of the partners, will not bind the firm.[20] On the other hand, if the requirements are satisfied, the firm will be bound even though the activities of the individual partner constitute a fraud on his co-partners, unless the third party is privy to the fraud.[1]

It should be noted that, while an individual partner is the agent of the partnership, there are no converse rules that the firm is an agent of the individual partners. Therefore, whilst payment to an individual partner of a debt due to the partnership will usually discharge the debt, the payment of a sum to the partnership to discharge a debt due to an individual partner will, in general, have no similar effect.[2]

---

[18] Emphasis added. It follows that the third party does not rely on the partnership when he does not know that the person with whom he deals is a partner, just as he does not if he does not believe him to have authority: per Cockburn CJ in *Nicholson v Ricketts* (1860) 2 E & E 497 at 524; per Cleasby B in *Holme v Hammond* (1872) LR 7 Ex Ch 218 at 233.

[19] *British Homes Assurance Corpn Ltd v Paterson* [1902] 2 Ch 404.

[20] *Dickinson v Valpy* (1829) 10 B & C 128; *Crellin v Brook* (1845) 14 M & W 11.

[1] *Bond v Gibson and Jephson* (1808) 1 Camp 185; *Wintle v Crowther and Combes* (1831) 1 Cr & J 316; *Thicknesse v Bromilow* (1832) 2 Cr & J 425; *Lewis v Reilly and Watson* (1841) 1 QB 349; *Ex p Bushell* (1844) 3 Mont D & De G 615; *Bank of Bengal v Macleod* (1849) 7 Moo PCC 35; *Bank of Bengal v Fagan* (1849) 7 Moo PCC 61; *Bryant, Powis and Bryant Ltd v Quebec Bank* [1893] AC 170; *Hambro v Burnand* [1904] 2 KB 10.

[2] *Powell v Brodhurst* [1901] 2 Ch 160.

Before considering these principles in detail, two separate issues should be noted.

Normal agency principles continue to apply

The actual authority of partners to bind the firm when acting in the ordinary course of its business is, in fact, an application of ordinary principles of agency. It should be remembered that the ordinary principles of agency continue to apply in respect of all activities of the partners. If, therefore, the partners confer on an individual partner the power to undertake a transaction beyond the ordinary course of the partnership business (eg to constitute his partners into partners with other persons in a separate business), the individual partner is thereafter fully empowered to do this, and if he proceeds his partners will be fully bound, even though this is not an activity within the normal course of the partnership business. They are bound because of the application of normal agency principles, which will bind them to what they have expressly authorised.

Similarly, if an agent undertakes an activity which is unauthorised the principal may step in and ratify the transaction which his agent has undertaken on his behalf. The application of this principle means that a partnership confronted with a partner who has acted beyond the scope of his authority may ratify the partner's transaction, and thereafter they will be bound under normal agency principles.

The sleeping or dormant partner

It will be remembered that a sleeping or dormant partner is one who takes no part in the business of the partnership but who is nevertheless a partner, usually having provided business capital. Playing no active role in the business, the sleeping or dormant partner is not, apparently, a partner. If an active partner does something within the actual agreed authority, the sleeping or dormant partner is bound under normal agency principles. However, since the dormant partner is not apparently a partner, is he bound by an act done by an active partner within the scope of the apparent authority of that partner, but beyond the scope of the actual authority? There are two views as to the answer to this question. In *Watteau v Fenwick*[3] Wills J expressed the view that, in the case of a dormant partner, any limitation of authority between the dormant and the

---

[3]   [1893] 1 QB 346 at 349.

active partner would be ineffective to protect the sleeping partner from being bound by actions within the ordinary authority of the active partner. The Partnership Act 1890, s 5 makes clear provision that an act is binding on the other partners unless the person with whom the active partner was dealing 'does not know or believe him to be a partner'. Applying this literally, it could be said that the activities of the active partner in the ordinary course of business bind the dormant partner, unless the third party did not know or believe the active individual to be a partner.

On the other hand, it can be argued that s 5 is merely a specific expression of a deeper principle. Apparent authority turns upon the reasonable assumptions and knowledge of the third party. In general, one active partner acting in the course of business will bind the other active partners because the third party will believe himself to be dealing with the partnership and the active partners, of whom he might well be aware, behind it. However, dormant partners being dormant, he will not probably know of them and have similar expectations in respect of them. Why, then, should they be bound? The principle which informs s 5 would suggest that the dormant partner should not be bound, even though s 5 itself makes no provision for this particular situation.[4]

ACT IN RELATION TO THE BUSINESS OF THE PARTNERSHIP

The act or activity which is undertaken must be one which is done in relation to the partnership business for the partnership to be bound. If partners carry on business as greengrocers, and one of the partners enters into a contract for a large supply of bathroom fittings, the partnership will not be bound since the transaction would not be one which is in the ordinary course of the business of a greengrocer, although it would be one in the ordinary course of business of a hardware store. What is within the ordinary course of a business depends on the type of business involved. How then is the classification of the type of business derived? To an extent the classification is achieved by the partners within the partnership agreement itself. In the example given, the partners characterised their business as a greengrocers. However, the courts will only allow the partners to classify in broad terms. A greengrocers' shop is not a hardware store. If, however, the partners were to attempt to restrict the partnership business to only certain aspects of the

[4] *Lindley* (16th edn, 1990) p 250.

normal greengrocery business, or agree that it was to be a green-grocers' business which was only to be carried out in a certain way, the courts will still simply classify the business as a greengrocers' business and infer that the partners are to have all the powers usually associated with such a business. The reason is not hard to see. Third parties, with whom the business will deal, will themselves classify in this general manner, and draw the normal deductions that follow. Such is the way of the world. It is from the position of third parties that apparent authority is judged.

This is neatly illustrated by *Mercantile Credit Co Ltd v Garrod*,[5] which involved an active partner, A, and a dormant partner, D. A and D had entered into an agreement for the letting of garages and the carrying on of a motor repair business. The agreement expressly excluded the buying and selling of motor cars. Without D's knowledge and approval, A purported to sell a car, to which he had no title, to a hire purchase company for the sum of £700. The hire purchase company understood that it was dealing with the partnership. The credit company brought an action seeking to make D liable. D argued that the transaction was not binding because there was no authority to buy or sell motor cars in the partnership deed. Mocatta J preferred to paint with a broader brush, looking at the matter from the point of view of the outside world. From that point of view the business which was being undertaken was that of a garage business, and in selling a motor car A was doing an act within the usual course of such a business. Consequently, D was held liable.

What constitutes the usual course of a business clearly depends on the nature of the particular business. There are, for instance, numerous decisions on the usual activities of the practice of a solicitor, many of them very elderly,[6] but it should be borne in mind that what is usual in the carrying on of a particular business or profession changes with the passing years, and therefore old case law is an untrustworthy guide in this area.[7] What is usual can be shown by evidence called to the hearing, and expert evidence may well prove to be decisive in resolving particular cases.[8]

An area of particular significance to solicitors is that of solicitors' undertakings on behalf of the firm. These are given by solicitors to

---

[5] [1962] 3 All ER 1103.
[6] The two most modern cases are *Re Bell's Indenture* [1980] 1 WLR 1217 (solicitor has implied authority to receive trust funds as agent of trustees, but not to accept office as trustee) and *United Bank of Kuwait Ltd v Hammoud* [1988] 1 WLR 1051.
[7] Per Staughton LJ in *United Bank of Kuwait Ltd v Hammoud* [1988] 1 WLR 1051 at 1063.
[8] Ibid.

facilitate their clients' affairs but, if given unwisely, have the potential to leave the firm with very considerable liabilities. Of course, whether given by an employee or partner, the firm is likely to raise the issue of whether their undertaking was given in the ordinary course of business in answer to any attempt to enforce an undertaking against it, when it has been unwise enough to give the undertaking without ensuring that it will be put in funds by its client to discharge the partnership responsibility which it creates by giving the undertaking. An example arises from the recent case of *United Bank of Kuwait v Hammoud*.[9] Here a solicitor had given two very unwise undertakings on behalf of his firm while representing a dishonest client. He undertook in each case to pay to a bank a very large sum of money, which in fact he could not be sure of receiving. At the time of giving one undertaking he was an employee, and at the time of giving the other a salaried partner. Since in either event he was the agent of the firm the question in each case was whether he was acting in the ordinary course of business of the firm in giving the undertakings. The court concluded that an undertaking given as security for a loan was within the ordinary business of a solicitor where it was given in the context of an underlying transaction of the type which solicitors usually undertake, and where the funds which the solicitor undertook to pay to the third party might reasonably be expected to come under the control of the firm on whose behalf the undertaking was given. The fact that the solicitor giving the undertaking might know of circumstances making the transaction unusual is irrelevant. The issue is to be considered on the basis of the transaction as it appeared to an outsider. Since the evidence showed that, viewed from an outsider's perspective, the transaction was one falling within the usual course of business of a firm of solicitors, the firm would be made liable on the undertakings.

Pledging of credit

These principles lie behind the Partnership Act 1890, s 7 which provides that –

'. . . where one partner pledges the credit of the firm for a purpose apparently not connected with the firm's ordinary course of business, the firm is not bound, unless he is in fact especially authorised by the other partners; but this section does not affect any personal liability by an individual partner.'

---

[9] [1988] 1 WLR 1051.

The last two lines of this provision retain usual agency law. While the firm and the other partners are not bound where a partner acts outside the firm's ordinary course of business, the individual partner may nevertheless be liable under ordinary principles of agency law, either by making himself personally liable in respect of the transaction with the third party or, alternatively, to an action by the third party for breach of warranty of authority. Indeed, the proviso can be seen as superfluous because, since this area of partnership law rests upon agency principles, all those principles will be applicable unless the Partnership Act provided to the contrary.

ACT OF CARRYING ON BUSINESS IN USUAL WAY

Not only must the activity be one for the carrying on of the particular business, it must be activity for carrying on the business in the usual way. The activity in issue must be both within the ordinary business of the partnership and undertaken in the ordinary course of such business. Thus, in one case a partnership was formed for the purpose of promoting a trawler company. One of the partners was held to have ostensible authority to employ agents to manage one of the vessels.[10]

This general proposition brings us to a much more difficult question to resolve in most concrete situations. It is usually a fairly simple matter to decide whether or not the activity in question was one foreign to the usual business of a firm of that particular type. The second issue, however, is more complicated, because the activity is one which is certainly part of the usual activity of the business of the particular type (otherwise the liability of the partnership is settled by the answer to the first issue), but what is being alleged is that it is not an activity which is undertaken *by a single partner* in businesses of the relevant type. Unfortunately, the 1890 Act itself is not of the greatest assistance in resolving the second issue since, beyond merely providing that the acts for which a partner has usual authority are acts 'for carrying on *in the usual way* business of the kind carried on by the firm', it is sadly silent on this important issue. However, considerable case law has evolved (some of it dating from before the 1890 Act) to which reference may usefully be made, provided that it is remembered that the way in

---

[10] *Lindern Trawler Managers v WHJ Trawlers (a firm)* (1949) 83 Ll L Rep 131. Another example is *Mercantile Credit Co v Garrod* (above).

which businesses are carried on evolves with the passing years as does their nature.[11]

The case law seems to produce three categories:

(1) powers normally held by all partners in any form of partnership;
(2) powers normally held by partners in a trading partnership; and
(3) powers not normally held by partners in any form of partnership.

This analysis produces a distinction between trading and non-trading partnerships. A trading partnership is one whose business is based upon the buying and selling of goods belonging to the firm.[12] Non-trading partners are, therefore, those who provide services of one kind or another such as professional services, painters and decorators, or hirers of plant and equipment.[13]

Powers normally held by all partners in any form of partnership

Every partner in any form of partnership is presumed to have authority to bind the firm in the following ways:

(1) he may sell goods or chattels belonging to the firm. This extends beyond the firm's stock in trade, and includes all goods belonging to the partnership;[14]
(2) he may receive payment made to the firm in respect of debts due to it, and the receipts or releases which he gives in respect of payment will release the payer from further liability in respect thereof.[15] The principle continues in respect of partnership debts even after dissolution of the firm so far as necessary to wind up the affairs of the firm.[16] However, if the partner giving the receipt acts in fraud of his fellow partners in

---

[11] See p 134.
[12] *Wheatley v Smithers* [1906] 2 KB 321; *Higgins v Beauchamp* [1914] 3 KB 1192.
[13] It would also include lessors of property if carried on as a partnership business.
[14] *Lambert's Case* (1614) Godb 244.
[15] See the remarks of Best CJ in *Stead v Salt* (1825) 3 Bing 101 at 103; see also *Anon* (1701) 12 Mod Rep 447 (Case 777); *Jacaud v French* (1810) 12 East 317; *Henderson and Smith v Wild* (1811) 2 Camp 561; *Hawkshaw v Parkins* (1819) 2 Swan 539; *Powell v Brodhurst* [1901] 2 Ch 160.
[16] Partnership Act 1890, s 38; *Duff v East India Co* (1808) 15 Ves 198; *Bristow and Porter v Taylor* (1817), 2 Stark 50; *Porter and Bristow v Taylor* (1817) 6 M & S 156; *King v Smith* (1829) 4 C & P 108; by analogy *Brasier v Hudson* (1837) 9 Sim 1; *Powell v Brodhurst* [1901] 2 Ch 160.

118   *Chapter 6*

giving the receipt[17] or in collusion with the debtor,[18] his fellow partners will not be bound;

(3) he may purchase goods for the firm of a kind usually employed in its business. If he does so, *and the supplier of the goods understands that they are being supplied to the partnership*, the partnership is bound,[19] even though the individual partner who purchases the goods on behalf of the firm proceeds to misapply them and absconds with the proceeds.[20] Further, it follows that while in a non-trading firm a partner has no general authority to borrow money on behalf of the firm, he may nevertheless bind his firm by the purchase of goods on credit on its behalf;

(4) an individual partner may take on employees for the purpose of the partnership business.[1] It would follow that an individual partner has power also to dismiss an employee;

(5) if an individual partner has power to take on and discharge employees, he also has implied authority to employ an agent or terminate the agent's contract.[2] Certainly an individual partner may employ a solicitor to defend an action brought against the firm. If he does so, the solicitor has authority to take all steps necessary to defend the matter, including acknowledging service in the names of each of the partners, and he is not obliged to inform each partner individually as to the progress of the action.[3] It follows logically that a single partner could employ a solicitor to bring an action on behalf of the firm.[4]

Powers normally held by partners in a trading partnership

Partners in trading firms have been held to have wider powers than those in non-trading firms. It is not immediately obvious why this

17 *Henderson v Wild* (1811) 2 Camp 561; *Farrar v Hutchinson* (1839) 9 Ad & El 641.
18 *Henderson v Wild* (above); *Aspinall v London and North Western Rly* (1853) 11 Hare 325.
19 *Hyat v Hare* (1696) Comb 383; *Gardiner v Childs* (1837) 8 C & P 345.
20 *Bond v Gibson and Jephson* (1808) 1 Camp 185.
1 *Beckham v Drake* (1841) 9 M & W 79, affd on this point (1843) 11 M & W 315.
2 *Ex p Mitchell* (1808) 14 Ves 597; *Ex p Hodgkinson* (1815) 19 Ves 291.
3 *Tomlinson v Broadsmith* [1896] 1 QB 386. This may include undertaking appeals in tax matters, *Customs and Excise Comrs v Evans* [1982] STC 342 at 349.
4 The capacity to bring or defend proceedings thus rests on the extent of the partner's authority under partnership law. By contrast a partner has a right *as an individual* to appeal against a partnership tax assessment to the General or Special Commissioners, or from them to the High Court. He may therefore exercise his right to appeal in such circumstances notwithstanding that the wishes of his partners are to the contrary, *Sutherland v Gustar (Inspector of Taxes)* [1994] 4 All ER 1.

should be so, but nevertheless the distinction between trading and non-trading partnerships is consecrated by the case law, and the extra powers inherent in the trading partnership have received judicial acknowledgment. In *Higgins v Beauchamp*[5] a partner in a cinema was held to have no general power to borrow on the credit of the firm. The partnership deed contained a clear prohibition on such borrowing by an individual partner. It was alleged that an implied power to borrow existed, but this was rejected by the court on the basis that a cinema is not a trading business, and consequently the particular partner concerned lacked the implied authority usual in the case of a trading business.

Perhaps the classic exposition of the powers of an individual partner is to be found in the words of the celebrated US academic and Justice of the Supreme Court Joseph Story in his *Treatise on Agency*[6] where the position is summarised as follows:

'each partner is propositus negotiis societatis; and may consequently bind all the other partners by his acts, in all matters which are within the scope and objects of a partnership. Hence, if the partnership be of a general commercial nature, he may pledge or sell the partnership property; he may buy goods on account of the partnership; he may borrow money, contract debts and pay debts on account of the partnership; he may draw, make, sign, endorse, accept, transfer, negotiate and procure to be discounted, promissory notes, bills of exchange, cheques and other negotiable paper in the name and of account of the partnership . . . The restrictions of this implied authority to bind the partnership are apparent from what has already been stated. Each partner is an agent only in and for the business of the firm; and, therefore, his acts beyond that business will not bind the firm. Neither will his acts done in violation of his duty to the firm bind it, when the other party to the transaction is cognizant of, or co-operates in, such breach of duty.'[7]

It will be noted that the expression used here is 'partnership of a general commercial nature', but in subsequent case law this has been equated with the concept of 'trading partnership'.

The powers thus traditionally held by individual partners within

[5] [1914] 3 KB 1192.
[6] 1839, Chapter 6, ss 124 and 125.
[7] Quoted with approval by the Privy Council in *Bank of Australasia v Breillat* (1847) 6 Moo PCC 152 at 193.

a trading partnership, extending beyond those normally held within any partnership, therefore, include the following:

(1) power to borrow money on account of the firm,[8] provided, of course, that the borrowing is for the purposes of the firm's business;[9]

(2) power to pledge the partnership goods.[10] This follows from the power of the partner to borrow. This is so even though the individual partner concerned in the transaction subsequently misapplies the money to his own purposes,[11] provided, of course, that the third party was not aware of the partner's intention.[12] It makes no difference that the pledge is given for antecedent debts.[13] Traditionally, there is no such power for a partner in a non-trading partnership.[14]

It will be observed that these powers arise naturally and by implication in the case of trading partnerships. In the case of non-trading partnerships this is not so and here it is necessary to show that such powers are within the normal course of dealing usual to the particular type of business.[15]

This is potentially inconvenient. Accordingly, s 23(2) of the Bills of Exchange Act 1882 makes specific provision with regard to the drawing and endorsement of cheques by providing that 'the signature of the name of a firm is equivalent to the signature by the person so signing of the names of all persons liable as partners in that firm'. If the name of the firm is also the name of an individual partner in the firm (which is often the case) the signature of the individual partner prima facie binds the firm unless his co-partners can show that the signature was given by the partner in his personal capacity, and not on behalf of the firm.[16]

---

[8] *Lane v Williams* (1692) 2 Vern 277; *Ex p Bonbonus* (1803) 8 Ves 540.
[9] Partnership Act 1890, s 7.
[10] *Ex p Howden* (1842) 2 Mont D & De G 574; *Gordon v Ellis* (1844) 7 Man & G 607; *Brownrigg v Roe* (1850) 5 Ex Ch 489; *Butchart v Dresser* (1853) 4 De GM & G 542; *Langmead's Trust* (1855) 20 Beav 20; affd (1855) 7 De GM & G 353; *Brown v Kidger* (1858) 3 H & N 853.
[11] *Longmead's Trust* (above).
[12] *Ex p Bonbonus* (above).
[13] *Re Patent File Co* (1870) 6 Ch App 83; *Re Clough* (1885) 31 Ch D 324.
[14] *Higgins v Beauchamp* [1914] 3 KB 1192.
[15] *Greenslade v Dower and Colman* (1828) 7 B & C 635 (farmers); *Hedley v Bainbridge* (1842) 3 QB 316 (solicitors); *Wheatley v Smithers* [1906] 2 KB 321 (auctioneer).
[16] *Yorkshire Banking v Beatson* (1880) 5 CPD 109.

An individual partner may make an equitable mortgage for partnership purposes of land or chattels belonging to the firm by deposit of title deeds or otherwise.[17] However, a single partner does not have power to execute a deed so as to bind the firm by way of legal mortgage.[18]

Powers not usually held by individual partners

A partner, whether in a trading firm or not, does not have apparent authority in a number of matters:

(1) an individual partner cannot bind his firm by executing a deed unless authority is expressly confered on him by power of attorney.[19] However, if a deed is executed by one partner in the presence of his co-partners using the firm name, it is implied that he has their express authority, and the document is deemed to have been executed by all.[20] Nevertheless, in other cases, whilst the signature of the deed will be ineffective as an execution of the deed by all the partners, it may operate to bind the partners to the underlying transaction, provided that it was one for which the partner had authority to undertake.[1] An illustration of the principle that a deed executed by a partner within the scope of his ostensible authority in pursuance of a transaction is not necessarily totally devoid of legal effect is the case of *Re Briggs & Co*.[2] In that case the partner had executed a deed which was to effect a legal assignment of book debts belonging to his firm. As has been noted, the individual partner's authority does not extend to executing deeds on behalf of the firm. The deed was therefore ineffective as a deed completing the legal assignment, which was the result intended. However, an equitable assignment does not require a properly executed deed to be effective, and the signed document was therefore effective to create an equitable assignment of the book debts;

---

[17] *Re Clough* (1885) 31 Ch D 324; *Re Bourne* [1906] 2 Ch 427.
[18] See below.
[19] *Steiglitz v Eggington* (1815) Holt NP 141; *Harrison v Jackson* (1797) 7 Term Rep 207; *Merchant v Morton, Down & Co* [1901] 2 KB 829.
[20] *Ball v Dunsterville* (1791) 4 Term Rep 313; *Burn v Burn* (1798) 3 Ves 573; *Orr v Chase* (1812) 1 Mer 729; *Brutton v Burton* (1819) 1 Chit 707.
[1] *Davis v Martin* [1894] 3 Ch 181; *Marchant v Morton, Down & Co* [1901] 2 KB 829. It may operate to confer an equitable interest on a third party: *Re Briggs & Co, ex p Wright* [1906] 2 KB 209.
[2] [1906] 2 KB 209.

(2)   individual partners cannot bind the firm by giving a guarantee in the firm's name in the absence of a trade custom to that effect.[3] In the absence of authority of the partner the firm will only be bound if they ratify,[4] or if they so conduct themselves as to give rise to an estoppel.[5] If the other partners knew of the guarantee and allowed the firm to act as though the firm was bound, ratification will be inferred or an estoppel will arise;[6]

(3)   an individual partner has no power to bind the company by accepting property (eg fully paid up shares in a company) in lieu of money in satisfaction of a debt due to a firm;[7]

(4)   an individual partner has no power to make his partners into partners with other persons in another business.[8] However, he may have power to enter into a partnership for a single venture on behalf of the firm;[9]

(5)   an individual partner has no authority to authorise a third person to make use of the firm's name in legal or other proceedings;[10]

(6)   An individual partner has no authority to bind the firm by a submission to arbitration.[11] However, this restriction relates to ad hoc submissions, and should not restrict a partner's authority to enter into a normal trading contract which happens to contain an arbitration clause.

THE IMPORTANCE OF CATEGORISATION

It will be immediately clear from this analysis that the categorisation of a particular transaction as to type may well be fundamental to the

---

[3] *Crawford v Stirling* (1802) 4 Esp 207; *Duncan v Lowndes and Bateman* (1813) 3 Camp 478; *Hasleham v Young* (1844) 5 QB 833; *Brettel v Williams* (1849) 4 Exch 623; *Simpson's Claim* (1887) 36 Ch D 532. See also the Partnership Act 1890, ss 5 and 18.

[4] *Sandilands v Marsh* (1819) 2 B & Ald 673.

[5] *Amalgamated Investment & Property Co Ltd (In Liquidation) v Texas Commerce International Bank Ltd* [1982] QB 84.

[6] Ibid; *Sandilands v Marsh* (above).

[7] *Niemann v Niemann* (1889) 43 Ch D 198.

[8] Per James LJ in *Re European Society Arbitration Acts, ex p British Nation Life Assurance Association* (1878) 8 Ch D 679 at 704; *Singleton v Knight* (1888) 13 App Cas 788.

[9] *Mann v D'Arcy* [1968] 1 WLR 893.

[10] *Marsh v Joseph* [1897] 1 Ch 213.

[11] *Antram v Chace* (1812) 15 East 209; *Stead v Salt* (1825) 3 Bing 101; *Adams v Bankart* (1835) 1 Cr M & R 681; *Hatton v Royle* (1858) 3 H & N 500.

resolution of the issue of whether or not the individual partner has bound his firm. Modern judges may well categorise more from the overall effect of the transaction than from a straightforward approach applying entirely traditional legal analysis. The point is well illustrated by *Mann v D'Arcy*.[12] The defendant, D'Arcy, was a partner in a firm of produce merchants, D'Arcy and Co. He purported to commit his firm to a joint venture with the plaintiff in respect of a portion of a cargo of potatoes. His firm argued that they were not bound, since no partner possesses authority to make his partners co-partners in a different business. Megarry J agreed that the joint venture did create a partnership. However, he did not rank it as another business. In his view the arrangement was merely one way of buying and selling goods within the firm business, which the partner had authority to do. He was only mitigating the expense inherent in the particular transaction, and sharing the profit from the particular transaction.

CHANGING BUSINESS PRACTICE

It cannot be over-emphasised that business practice evolves and changes. As commercial practice evolves, so the decisions of the court will evolve to meet it. The customary principles set out in case law can do no more than offer guidance to the modern courts in the absence of specific evidence as to practice today. Where evidence of modern practice is adduced it is probable that individual cases will be decided on the basis of that evidence, and not on the basis of precedent established in the last century, or in the early part of this.[13]

ACT MUST BE DONE AS A PARTNER

It is also important to bear in mind that the principles which have been considered apply where an individual partner has acted in the transaction as partner of the firm. If he enters into the transaction in his own right and without reference to the firm, he does not bind the firm, even though the transaction relates to a matter which is within the scope of the partnership business and, indeed, is within his actual and apparent authority. The principle is, in fact, now

12 [1968] 1 WLR 893.
13 See p 134, below.

expressed in the Partnership Act 1890, s 6,[14] and runs through the workings of the whole statute.

As Gurney B recognised 150 years ago in *Beckham v Drake*,[15] the issue in each case is whether the individual partner is acting for himself alone or on behalf of the firm. If he was acting for himself, and was understood to be so acting, his partners will not be bound.

The fact that the firm benefited from the arrangement does not alter the position. The firm is only bound if it was understood that the transaction was entered into on the part of the firm.[16] The benefit to the firm is only some evidence that this was the nature of the arrangement.[17]

MONEY LENT TO A PARTNER

If a partner borrows money in his own right and uses this for the purposes of the firm, the loan is owed by the partner and not the firm.[18] However, while the creditor has no right against the firm directly from the loan agreement itself, an equivalent right arises by way of equitable subrogation.[19] Under the principles of subrogation, if the loan is made available for the partnership's business in such a way as to relieve the partnership from legitimate obligations which it owes or in such a way as to increase its assets, the creditor will be able to claim from the firm the amount of the loan which is used to these ends.[20]

---

[14] Discussed below.

[15] (1841) 9 M & W 79 at 99; see also *Wilson v Whitehead* (1842) 10 M & W 503.

[16] *Gallway v Mathew* (1808) 10 East 264; *Loyd v Freshfield* (1826) 2 C & P 325; *Beckham v Drake* (1841) 9 M & W 79; *Kingsbridge Flour Mill Co v The Plymouth Grinding Co* (1848) 2 Ex Ch 711.

[17] Per Rolfe B in *Beckham v Drake* (1841) 9 M & W 79 at 100.

[18] *Smith v Craven and Thomson* (1831) 1 Cr & J 500; *Hawtayne v Bourne* (1841) 7 M & W 595; *Fisher v Tayler* (1843) 2 Hare 218; *Ricketts v Bennett and Field* (1847) 4 CB 686; *Re Worcester Corn Exchange Co* (1853) 3 De GM & G 180.

[19] *Ex p Chippendale (The German Mining Co's Case)* (1854) 4 De GM & G 19; *Blackburn Building Society v Cunliffe Brooks & Co* (1884) 9 App Cas 857, (1885) 29 Ch D 902; *Bannatyne v D & C McIver* [1906] 1 KB 103.

[20] *Athanaeum Life Assurance Society v Pooley* (1858) 3 De G & J 294; *Re Cork and Youghal Rly Co* (1866) 4 Ch App 748; *Baroness Wenlock v River Dee Co* (1883) 36 Ch D 675n, (1887) 19 QBD 155; *Reid v Rigby & Co* [1894] 2 QB 40; *Orakpo v Manson Investments Ltd* [1978] AC 95.

FORMAL CONTRACTS

The principle that to bind the firm a contract must be entered into by a partner with that intention, and not with the intention of binding himself, is clearly set out in s 6 of the Partnership Act 1890. This provides that an act or instrument relating to the business of the firm done or executed in the firm name, or in any other manner showing an intention to bind the firm, by any person thereto authorised, whether a partner or not, is binding on the firm and all the partners. However, the provision is not to affect any general rule of law relating to the execution of deeds or negotiable instruments.

The statutory provision applies to all contractual responsibilities, whether contained in a document or purely oral. It also sets out the position with regard to contracts negotiated by anyone having authority from the firm, whether as partner, employee, or simple agent. Nevertheless, it is perhaps in cases of formal contracts that discussion is most required, since the provision seems to assume that the document itself will show clearly whether or not it is entered into on behalf of the firm, and this is often not the case. There are three types of obligations commonly entered into by partnerships, namely written contracts, bills of exchange and deeds.

1. WRITTEN CONTRACTS

The written form of the contract will often be some indication of whether or not the contract is entered into on behalf of the firm. Indeed, it may contain provisions which clearly negative the conclusion that it is entered into to make the firm a contracting party. However, the mere fact that it appears to be a contract between the third party and some only of the partners is not necessarily decisive and, if the intention of the parties was that in fact the firm itself was becoming a party to the contract, it is the firm which will be bound.[1]

Some forms of contract are required to be in writing and signed by the party who is sought to be made liable, especially contracts for

---

[1] *Drake v Beckham* (1843) 11 M & W 315. However, if a person is described as the owner of certain property, and it is a term of the contract that he should contract as owner of that property, extrinsic evidence is not available to show that he is a partner with, or agent on behalf of, others who are the principals of the contract: *Humble v Hunter* (1848) 12 QB 310; *Formby Bros v Formby* (1910) 102 LT 116; *Fred Drughorn Ltd v Raderiaktiebolaget Trans-Atlantic* [1919] AC 203; *O/Y Wasa SS Co v Newspaper Pulp and Wood Exports Ltd* (1949) 82 Ll L Rep 936.

the sale of land and contracts of guarantee. In such cases a careful construction of the statute is necessary to determine whether signature by an agent is permissible. If it is not permissible, only those partners who sign will be bound.[2]

2. BILLS OF EXCHANGE

In principle, a bill of exchange must be drawn, indorsed, or accepted in the firm name by someone with authority to bind the firm for the firm to be liable for it.[3] It follows that if the business is carried on in the name of one partner only, and he draws a bill in his name for his own purposes so that the bill is his own personal bill, the firm will not be bound.[4]

It also follows that if there are two firms of the same name with a common partner, the potential responsibilities of the partners of the two concerns have to be resolved by asking in respect of each firm whether the signatory had authority to use the name of that particular firm and whether it had been used. If both questions can be answered in the affirmative in respect of either concern, the partners of that firm will be liable; if in respect of both, the partners of both firms will be liable.[5]

If a bill is not drawn in the name of the firm the partners will not be liable.[6] The issue remains as to whether or not the firm name has been used in any particular set of circumstances. While the court's approach is strict, it allows some deviation. If the name used differs from that of the firm, the issue is whether the name used, although inaccurate, substantially describes the firm, or whether it so far differs that the indorser must be taken to have issued the note on his own account,[7] or that of some other firm. Thus, whilst a firm carried on in the name of Brown and Smith will be bound by the signature of one partner using both their full names (eg Ben Brown and Sally Smith),[8] a firm carried on the name of Ben Brown will not be liable on a bill drawn in the name of Brown and Co.[9]

---

[2] *Swift v Jewsbury* (1874) LR 9 QB 301.
[3] *Usher v Dawncey* (1814) 4 Camp 97; *South Carolina Bank v Case* (1828) 8 B & C 427; *Stephens v Reynolds* (1860) 5 H & N 513; *Ringham v Hackett* (1980) Times, 9 February, (1980) 124 Sol Jo 201; *Central Motors (Birmingham) v PA & SNP Wadsworth (Trading as Pensagain)* (1982) 133 NLJ 555, [1983] CLY 80.
[4] *Ex p Law* (1839) 3 Deac 541; *Re Adansonia Fibre Co, Miles' Claim* (1874) 9 Ch App 635; *Yorkshire Banking Co v Beatson* (1880) 5 CPD 109.
[5] *Swan v Steele* (1806) 7 East 210.
[6] *Williams v Thomas* (1806) 6 Esp 18; *Lloyd v Ashby* (1831) 2 B & Ad 23.
[7] *Faith v Richmond* (1840) 11 Ad & El 339.
[8] *Norton v Seymour* (1847) 3 CB 792.
[9] *Kirk v Blurton and Habershon* (1841) 9 M & W 284.

If, however, a firm *habitually* carries on business in a name other than its firm name, and the name used in the bill is that which is habitually used, the firm will be estopped from denying the name habitually used as its own, and will be bound.[10] Of course, where a wrong name is used so that the firm itself escapes liability, the partners who sign the instrument will still be liable.[11] Similar principles apply in the case of promissory notes.[12]

3. DEEDS

A partner has no implied authority to bind the firm by deed.[13] Accordingly, for the firm to be bound it is necessary that a partner should have express authority to execute the deed on behalf of the firm. Even though a partner does have express authority, however, the firm will *only* be bound if he signs in the firm name, despite the fact that the deed discloses that he is acting for the firm.[14] The partner or partners who have signed will, of course, themselves be bound.[15] Any covenants in a deed intended to be made by the firm should be expressed in those terms, and not in terms that they are made by a partner in the name of the firm. Only in the former case will the firm be bound.[16]

LIABILITY OF THE FIRM FOR WRONGS OTHER THAN THE MISAPPLICATION OF OTHER PEOPLE'S PROPERTY

Civil liability under English law can arise either in contract or in tort. If we turn now from consideration of the firm's liability in contract to consider the firm's liability in tort, we find that the firm, and therefore the partners within it, will be liable for a tort committed by one of the partners on a third party in two situations.

---

[10] *Williamson v Johnson* (1823) 1 B & C 146.
[11] *Wilde v Keep* (1833) 6 C & P 235; *Owen v Van Uster* (1850) 10 CB 318; *Odell v Cormack* (1887) 19 QBD 223 at 226.
[12] *Clerk v Blackstock* (1816) Holt NP 474; *Shipton v Thornton* (1838) 9 Ad & El 314; *Ex p Buckley* (1845) 14 M & W 469; *Maclae v Sutherland* (1854) 3 E & B 1; *Bottomley v Fisher* (1862) 1 H & C 211; *Murray v Somerville* (1809) 2 Camp 98n.
[13] See above.
[14] *Hall v Bainbridge* (1840) 1 Man & G 42; *Pickering's Claim* (1871) 6 Ch App 525.
[15] *Appleton v Binks* (1804) 5 East 148.
[16] *Combe's Case* (1613) 9 Co Rep 75a; *Wilks v Back* (1802) 2 East 142; *John Bros Abergarw Brewing Co v Holmes* [1900] 1 Ch 188.

First, liability can arise where the tortious activities of the individual have been authorised by his fellow partners. Secondly, liability can arise because the tortious activity has been committed in the course of the partnership business. Therefore, under the second potential prong of partnership tort liability, liability can arise where one of the partners negligently injures a third person whilst going about the partnership business such as by driving his motor car. The basic rules governing liability in these situations are contained in the Partnership Act 1890, s 10 which provides:

> 'Where, by any wrongful act or omission of any partner acting in the ordinary course of the business of the firm, or with the authority of his co-partners, loss or injury is caused to any person not being a partner in the firm, or any penalty is incurred, the firm is liable therefore to the same extent as the partner so acting, or omitting to act.'

The first potential prong of liability, that the tortious act was authorised by the actor's fellow partners, can be briefly disposed of, since whether or not authorisation was given in any particular set of circumstances is inevitably a question of fact.

Similarly, whether or not a tort has been carried out in the ordinary course of business is also essentially factual, but a few illustrations may be helpful here. Thus, a professional firm will be liable for the negligent advice of one of the partners.[17] A partnership running a garage business would be liable for injury arising from the negligence of one of the partners in repairing or servicing a customer's car. Similarly, liability has also been imposed on the firm for the negligent driving of a coach,[18] and for the negligent handling of a client's affairs by a professional man.[19]

The range of conduct is thus as large as the range of the law of tort and duties imposed by statute.[20] Perhaps a little less obviously, in one case a partner in a firm of grain merchants, who bribed a clerk in a rival firm to give him confidential information relating to the rival, was held to be acting in the course of the partnership business on the basis that it is in the ordinary course of business to

---

[17] *Blyth v Fladgate* [1891] 1 Ch 337; *Midland Bank Trust Co Ltd v Hett Stubbs and Kempe* [1979] Ch 384.

[18] *Moreton v Hardern* (1825) 4 B & C 223.

[19] *Blyth v Fladgate* (above); *Welsh v Knarston* 1972 SLT 96.

[20] *A-G v Stranyforth* (1721) Bunb 97; *A-G v Burges* (1726) Bunb 223; *A-G v Weeks* (1726) Bunb 223; *R v Manning* (1739) 2 Com 616; *Duke of Brunswick v Slowman* (1849) 8 CB 317; *Mellors v Shaw and Unwin* (1861) 1 B & S 437; *Ashworth v Stanwix and Walker* (1861) 3 E & E 701; *Steel v Lester and Lilee* (1877) 3 CPD 121.

obtain information about a competitor. As a consequence, the partnership firm was held liable for the losses suffered by the competitor.[1] In establishing the liability of the firm it matters not that the tort of the partner was intentional,[2] nor that the firm itself could not have committed the tort.[3] On the other hand, where the individual partner is acting in an unusual manner or for his own purposes, he will not be acting in the course of the partnership business. If, therefore, without the knowledge and authority of his co-partners the individual seeks to collect a partnership debt by use of violence or the threat of violence, he will not be acting in the ordinary course of the firm's business, because businesses are not customarily run in this manner. Similarly, where an individual wrongfully brought a malicious prosecution for an alleged theft of partnership property it was held that his action was not in the ordinary course of the partnership business, and no liability attached to his partners.[4] The fact that the act was committed for the benefit of the individual rather than the partnership as a whole is not decisive in showing that the partner was acting outside the ordinary course of the firm's business, but it is a factor to be taken into account in considering the issue.[5]

Particular issues arise with regard to liability of the firm for fraud and fraudulent misrepresentation perpetrated by a partner. Provided that the fraud is undertaken in the ordinary course of the partnership business the firm is liable under the general principles discussed.[6] However, it must be remembered that common law fraud is not constructive fraud, but depends on a truly deceitful act. Therefore, if one partner innocently makes a false statement or innocently undertakes an action but another partner knows the true facts there is no fraud because there is no true deceit.[7] If, however, the partner with the knowledge expressly[8] or by implication[9] authorises his co-partner to make the representation or undertake

---

[1] *Hamlyn v Houston & Co* [1903] 1 KB 81; *Janvier v Sweeney* [1919] 2 KB 316.
[2] *Limpus v London General Omnibus Co* (1862) 1 H & C 526; *Citizens Life Assurance Co v Brown* [1904] AC 423.
[3] *Kirkintilloch Equitable Co-operative Society Ltd v Livingstone* 1972 SLT 154.
[4] *Arbuckle v Taylor* (1815) 3 Dow 160.
[5] *Lloyd v Grace Smith & Co* [1912] AC 716.
[6] Ibid.
[7] *Armstrong v Strain* [1952] 1 KB 232.
[8] *London County Freehold Properties Ltd v Berkeley Property Investment Co Ltd* [1936] 2 All ER 1039.
[9] *Ludgate v Love* (1881) 44 LT 694.

the activity his action is deceitful, and fraud is made out, for which the firm will be liable, if it is undertaken in the ordinary course of the partnership business.[10]

The availability of the action for fraud of course determines whether or not damages can be recovered for losses sustained. Where the firm has obtained property or money due to the misrepresentation of one of the partners, it can be compelled to return it, even though the misrepresentation was innocent under the usual principles of misrepresentation.[11]

Fraudulent representations relating to the character or credit of a third party

There is a statutory provision restricting the circumstances in which proceedings can be brought against a partnership on the basis of fraudulent representations relating to the character or credit of a third party which should be noted at this point. The Statute of Frauds (Amendment) Act 1828, s 6 expressly prohibits the bringing of any action –

'whereby to charge any person upon or by reason of any representation or assurance made or given concerning or relating to the character, conduct, credit, ability, trade, or dealing of any other person, to the intent or purpose that such other person may obtain credit, money, or goods upon, unless such representation or assurance be made in writing, signed by the party to be charged therewith.'

It would appear that the provision applies to misrepresentations as to the character or credit of the third party, which are fraudulent,[12] but not those which were made negligently[13] and in respect of which liability might potentially attach either at common law[14] or by statute.[15] The provision is therefore very limited in scope. Where it does apply the section requires that the representation should be in writing, and signed by each person against whom proceedings are to be brought. To meet the requirement, therefore, the partners

---

[10] *Lovell v Hicks* (1837) 2 Y & C Ex 472; *Rapp v Latham and Parry* (1819) 2 B & Ald 795.
[11] *Blair v Bromley* (1847) 2 Ph 354; *Moore v Knight* [1891] 1 Ch 547.
[12] *Banbury v Bank of Montreal* [1918] AC 626.
[13] *WB Anderson & Sons Ltd v Rhodes (Liverpool) Ltd* [1967] 2 All ER 850.
[14] Under the principle arising from *Hedley Byrne & Co Ltd v Heller & Partners Ltd* [1964] AC 465.
[15] Under the Misrepresentation Act 1967, s 2.

against whom the proceedings are brought must have signed the written representation individually; signature of one only using the firm name will not bind his co-partners.[16]

MISAPPLICATION OF MONEY OR PROPERTY OF A THIRD PERSON

While s 10 of the 1890 Act sets out the general principles of partnership liability in tort, s 11 deals with two specific situations involving the receipt of money or property from a third party and its misapplication. The situations are (1) where money or property is received by a partner, and (2) where money or property is received by the firm.

Receipt by partner

Where one partner, acting within the scope of his apparent authority, receives the money or property of a third person and misapplies it, the firm is liable to make good the loss.[17]

It should be noted that this provision deals with only one situation where firm liability can arise through the default of the partner – that of the receipt by a partner of the money or property whilst acting within the scope of his apparent authority.[18] There is another principle which can give rise to liability which the Act treats as being so fundamental and obvious that it does not state it at all, namely the receipt of the money or property by the partner whilst acting within his actual authority. If, therefore, property is received by a partner in circumstances in which it is *within the custom of the particular partnership* that partners shall receive money or property,

---

[16] *Williams v Mason* (1873) 28 LT 232; *Swift v Jewsbury* (1874) LR 9 QB 301; *Hirst v West Riding Union Banking Co* [1901] 2 KB 560; *Keene v Mear* [1920] 2 Ch 574. However, an agent acting within the scope of his authority may sign so as to bind a corporation since a corporation can only act through an agent: see *UBAF Ltd v European American Banking Corpn, The Pacific Colcotronis* [1984] QB 713.

[17] Section 11(a).

[18] Cases in which the firm has been held liable in such circumstance include *Willet v Chambers* (1778) 2 Cowp 814; *Brydges v Branfil* (1842) 12 Sim 369; *Harman v Johnson* (1853) 2 E & B 61; *Todd v Studholme* (1857) 3 K & J 324; *Atkinson v Mackreth* (1866) LR 2 Eq 570; *Dundonald v Masterman* (1869) LR 7 Eq 504; *Rhodes v Moules* [1895] 1 Ch 236. If the property is received by the individual partner as partner the firm is liable even though his co-partners know nothing of the transaction: *St Aubyn v Smart* [1868] 3 Ch App 646 and the cases cited above.

the firm will be liable if the money or property is subsequently mis-applied by the partner, even though it is not customary in businesses of the particular type for partners to receive money or property from third parties in those circumstances. This liability arises from the actual authority of the partner arising by implication, not his apparent authority. Thus, in one case, it was held that the receipt of a sum of money by one partner in a firm of solicitors for the purpose of investing it as soon as he found a good investment in which to place it was not within the scope of his apparent authority so as to render the firm liable for its misapplication, for such a transaction was not part of the business of a solicitor.[19] If, however, it had been shown that it was customary in the particular firm for partners to receive money from clients and deal with it in this way, the receipt would have been within his actual authority, and the firm would become liable for the misapplication of the money.

It must be borne in mind that, for the firm to be liable, the third party must deal with the individual partner as a partner in the firm, and not as an individual in his own right. Thus, in one case a company whose activities were centred on the provision of finance for mortgages appointed one Atkinson, a solicitor in a firm called Atkinson & Atkinson, to act for it in mortgage transactions. Two years later Atkinson took Paterson into partnership, and gave notice of this to the company. On Paterson being taken into partnership the name of the firm was changed to Atkinson & Paterson. Some three weeks later the company sent Atkinson a cheque payable to Atkinson & Atkinson to allow a mortgage to be completed. Atkinson misappropriated this cheque, and the company sought to make Paterson liable in respect of its loss. The court concluded that the company had intended to deal with Atkinson personally on the basis that the cheque was not made out in favour of the new firm, and that consequently Paterson was not liable.[20]

Receipt by firm

Where a firm in the course of its business receives money or prop-erty of a third person, and the money or property so received is

---

[19] *Harman v Johnson* (1853) 2 E & B 61. See also *Plumer v Gregory* (1874) LR 18 Eq 621; *Cleather v Twisden* (1884) 28 Ch D 340; *Re Bell's Indenture* [1980] 1 WLR 1217. The receipt by solicitors of money from clients for the purpose of conducting the clients' *legal* affairs is received in the course of the solicitors' pro-fessional business; and the firm will be bound: *Earl of Dundonald v Masterman* (1869) LR 7 Eq 504.

[20] *British Home Assurance Corpn Ltd v Paterson* [1902] 2 Ch 404.

misapplied by one or more of the partners while it is in the custody of the firm, the firm is liable to make good the loss.[1] Here the issue between the stranger and the firm which he wishes to make liable for the partner's activities is whether or not the money or property at the heart of the dispute was received in the ordinary course of the firm's business. Thus in another case concerning solicitors, *Rhodes v Moules*,[2] Rhodes was in need of money and obtained a loan on the security of a mortgage on his property. He was told by one Rew, a partner in a firm of solicitors, that the mortgagees wanted additional security. To satisfy this demand he handed to Rew share warrants payable to bearer. Rew misappropriated them, and Rhodes brought an action against the firm and succeeded, for Rew had received the warrants in the ordinary course of the firm's business.[3]

The underlying concept behind the statutory provision would seem to be the receipt by the partner of the money or property in the ordinary course of the firm's business, and the use of the custody so obtained to misapply that which should be held for the client. The courts have indeed interpreted the provision in this way and, consequently, for the firm to be liable the initial receipt must be in the course of the firm's business *and* the misapplication of the property must occur whilst it is in the custody of the firm as a result of the initial receipt. The point is well illustrated by *Sims v Brutton and Clipperton*.[4] In that case a firm of solicitors accepted money from a client to invest it in a particular mortgage. The investment was duly made and, inevitably, at that point the money passed out of the custody of the solicitor. Subsequently, one of the partners acted fraudulently to induce the mortgagor to repay the money to him, and not to the client. His receipt of the repayment was outside the ordinary business of the partnership. The court held that the firm was not liable since the misapplication of the money was not made whilst it was in the custody of the firm. It should, however, be noted that once the firm has accepted custody of the money or property, liability will still attach even if the partner

---

[1] PA 1890, s 11(b).

[2] [1895] 1 Ch 236.

[3] Other examples are *Devaynes v Noble, Clayton's Case* (1816) 1 Mer 572; *Devaynes v Noble, Baring's Case* (1816) 1 Mer 611; *Devaynes v Noble, Warde's Case* (1816) 1 Mer 624; *Vulliamy v Noble* (1817) 3 Mer 593; *Stone v Marsh* (1827) 6 B & C 551; *Ex p Bolland* (1828) 1 Mont & A 570; *Hume v Bolland* (1832) 1 Cr & M 130; *Keating v Marsh* (1834) 1 Mont & A 592; *Sadler v Lee* (1843) 6 Beav 324; *Blair v Bromley* (1847) 2 Ph 354; *Re Biddulph, ex p Barnewall* (1849) 3 De G & Sm 587; *Eager v Barnes* (1862) 31 Beav 579; *Moore v Knight* [1891] 1 Ch 547.

[4] (1850) 5 Ex Ch 802. See also *Bishop v The Countess of Jersey* (1854) 2 Drew 143; *Coomer v Bromley* (1852) 5 De G & Sm 532.

who subsequently misapplies it has been appointed trustee of it, provided that he continues as a partner in the firm and the money or property remained in its custody.[5]

A more difficult case is *Tendring Hundred Waterworks Co v Jones*,[6] where a solicitor, Garrard, was a partner in a firm of solicitors and as part of the business of the partnership was also secretary to the waterworks company. The company wished to purchase a large estate and employed the solicitors to undertake the purchase for them. For their own convenience, the company arranged for the property to be conveyed into the name of their secretary, and not their own. The vendors handed the title deeds to Garrard, who proceeded to raise money by mortgaging them to a third party. The company, when matters came to light, brought action against Garrard's partner, Jones. The court held that the title deeds had never been received by the firm as such, since Garrard's activities in receiving the title deeds were connected with his being trustee of the property for the company and not with his activities in the business of the partnership. This decision seems extremely weakly founded, since the trusteeship was undertaken in connection with his activities as secretary of the company, which in turn was part of the partnership business. It is thought that a modern judge would be likely to take a more robust view. Nevertheless, while the applicable principles may have been misapplied in this case, their existence cannot be doubted.

IMPROPER EMPLOYMENT OF TRUST PROPERTY FOR PARTNERSHIP PURPOSES

Since trust property is not partnership property, the responsibility of the partners in respect of it might have been left to general trust law. However, the Partnership Act 1890 makes specific provision for the liability of partners for trust property. It recognises that it is not uncommon for a partner, particularly partners in professional firms such as accountants and solicitors, to be appointed trustees, thus giving rise to issues of liability should he then employ trust property within the partnership business. Section 13 provides that if a partner,

---

[5] *La Marquise De Ribeyre v Barclay* (1857) 23 Beav 107. The particular decision can, however, be criticised on the basis that the bonds were no longer held by the firm but the individual partner as trustee, and were, therefore, no longer in the custody of the firm.

[6] [1903] 2 Ch 615. See the more robust view taken in *Re Bell's Indenture* [1980] 1 WLR 1217.

being a trustee, improperly employs trust property in the business or on the account of the partnership, no other person is liable for the trust property to the persons beneficially interested therein. To this general proposition there are two provisos. First, the provision does not affect any liability incurred by reason of any other partner having notice of a breach of trust.[7] Secondly, the provision does not prevent trust money from being followed and recovered from the firm, if it is still in its possession or under its control. The effect of the provision is therefore to allow general trust principles to continue to apply. The use, by an individual partner/trustee, of trust property within the business can hardly be viewed as part of the normal business activities of the partnership, and no liability attaches to any of his other partners as a consequence.[8] For liability to attach to individual partners, the individual partners concerned must have knowledge of the partner/trustee's breach of trust, and be liable under general trust principles.[9] However, whilst the liability of individual partners will therefore depend upon their knowledge of the breach of trust, the beneficiaries are left with their proprietary right to trace.

JOINT OR SEVERAL LIABILITY?

In some situations a partner is liable jointly with the other partners, whilst in other cases he is liable severally. Different principles apply depending upon whether the action involving the partnership is one based on contract or tort.

CONTRACT

A partner who creates a contractual responsibility for his firm subjects it to a single joint obligation binding all the partners, including himself. The result is that a partner who has contracted on behalf of his firm is liable only as a member of the firm and therefore jointly with his co-partners, and has no individual separate responsibility.[10]

---

[7] *Keble v Thompson* (1790) 3 Bro CC 112; *Rae v Meek* (1889) 14 App Cas 558; *Brinsden v Williams* [1894] 3 Ch 185; *Mara v Browne* [1896] 1 Ch 199; *Re Bell's Indenture* [1980] 1 WLR 1217.

[8] *Ex p Apsey* (1791) 3 Bro CC 265; *Ex p White* (1871) 6 Ch App 397.

[9] *Smith v Jameson* (1794) 5 Term Rep 601; *Ex p Watson* (1814) 2 Ves & B 414; *Ex p Woodin* (1843) 3 Mont D & De G 399; *Ex p Poulson* (1844) De G 79.

[10] *Ex p Wilson* (1842) 3 Mont D & De G 57; *Ex p Buckley* (1845) 14 M & W 469, De G 153.

Such separate individual authority will only arise if it is separately created, as by holding himself out as the sole member of the firm,[11] or framing the contract so as to bind both himself individually and the firm jointly.[12]

As a result of the general principle, each of the partners is liable for the claim in its entirety in one action, and the release of any one partner from his obligation is the release of all. The position was established by the House of Lords in *Kendall v Hamilton*[13] and is now given effect by the Partnership Act 1890, s 9, which provides that:

> 'every partner in a firm is liable jointly with the other partners . . . for all debts and obligations of the firm incurred while he is a partner; and after his death his estate is also severally liable in a due course of administration for such debts and obligations so far as they remain unsatisfied, but subject . . . to the prior payment of his separate debts.'

It will be observed that s 9 refers to debts and obligations incurred whilst the individual concerned was a partner in the firm, and this almost certainly extends to non-contractual debts such as a judgment debt or taxes which are owed. Further, it should be noted that the section only applies to debts and obligations incurred whilst the individual was a partner. Consequently, if the debt or obligation arose after the individual had ceased to be a partner, he will not be liable in respect of it. This can potentially have a curious effect in transactions involving the sale of goods, as is illustrated by *Bagel v Miller*,[14] where goods were ordered by a firm whilst the individual was a partner, but delivered after he had ceased to occupy that position. Under a contract for sale of goods, the price does not become payable until the goods are delivered, and consequently no debt or obligation was created while the individual was a partner. Had the contract required pre-payment of the price at a date whilst the individual was still a partner (not the usual situation in sale of goods transactions), the decision would inevitably have been otherwise.

The principle of *Kendal v Hamilton*, now incorporated in s 9,

---

11 *De Mautort v Saunders* (1830) 1 B & Ad 398; *Bonfield v Smith* (1844) 12 M & W 405.
12 *Higgins v Senior* (1841) 8 M & W 834; *Ex p Wilson* (1842) 3 Mont D & De G 57; *Ex p Harding* (1879) 12 Ch D 557.
13 (1879) 4 App Cas 504. See also *Wilson Sons & Co Ltd v Balcarres Brook SS Co Ltd* [1893] 1 QB 422.
14 [1903] 2 KB 212.

was capable of working with most unfortunate consequences, as shown by the facts of that case itself. The plaintiff made a loan to the firm in which W and M were partners. When it was not repaid, he sued W and M for it and obtained judgment against them, which remained unsatisfied because of their lack of resources. The plaintiff then discovered that H had been a partner in a firm at the relevant time. H was a person of resources. The plaintiff then brought a second action against H in respect of the same loan, but was confronted with the fact that liability was joint, and the judgment obtained in the previous action therefore extinguished H's obligation. The joint obligation to pay of all the partners had merged in the judgment obtained. Fortunately, the restriction on subsequent proceedings has now been removed by the Civil Liability (Contribution) Act 1978.[15]

LIABILITY OF THE ESTATE OF A DECEASED PARTNER

Section 9 of the 1890 Act expressly preserves the *joint and several liability* of the estate of a deceased partner for debts and obligations of the firm incurred while the deceased was a partner. This exception was in fact long established in equity before the decision in *Kendall v Hamilton*, and therefore was simply recognised by the House of Lords in that case. As a consequence, in this situation, since liability is joint and several, the creditor has concurrent remedies which he can pursue as he chooses, subject to two conditions.[16] First, as s 9 expressly recognises, he is not to be allowed to compete with the deceased's separate creditors, and consequently is postponed to their claims.[17] Second, it is usual for the courts to require the involvement of the surviving partner or partners in some way so that partnership accounts can be taken.[18]

In this the position would be no different if the creditor takes a joint guarantee or covenant as security for the debt.[19] On the other hand, individual responsibility may be negatived by the express

---

[15] Section 3. Points of procedure which also may operate to modify the impact of this are discussed in Chapter 7, p 155, below.

[16] *Ex p Kendall* (1811) 17 Ves Jr 514; *Wilkinson v Henderson* (1833) 1 My & K 582; *Re Doetsch Matheson v Ludwig* [1896] 2 Ch 836; *Re Hodgson, Beckett v Ramsdale* (1885) 31 Ch D 177.

[17] Section 9. See *Re Hodgson, Beckett v Ramsdale* (1885) 31 Ch D 177.

[18] *Re McRae* (1883) 25 Ch D 16.

[19] *Lane v Williams* (1692) 2 Vern 292; *Bishop v Church* (1751) 2 Ves Sen 371; *Devaynes v Noble, Sleech's Case* (1816) 1 Mer 539; *Devaynes v Noble* (1831) 2 Russ & M 495; *Smith v Smith* (1861) 3 Giff 263.

terms of the contract itself or the circumstances in which the obligation was undertaken, and in such circumstances the courts will
impose joint liability only on the estate of the deceased partner.[20]

TORT AND MISAPPLICATION OF MONEY OR PROPERTY

The Partnership Act 1890, s 12 expressly provides that every partner is liable jointly with his co-partners and also severally for
everything for which the firm, while he is a partner, becomes liable
under both ss 10 and 11 of the Act. The consequence of this is that
liability both in tort and in respect of misapplication of money or
property is joint and several.[1]

EVIDENCE AND PROCEDURE

The 1890 Act has express provisions affecting the authority of individual partners in the areas of evidence and procedure. In the field
of evidence the provisions concern admissions and representations
of partners, and in the field of procedure they concern the giving of
notice to partners on behalf of the firm. These will be considered in
turn.

Admissions and representations of partners

The 1890 Act deals with the issue of admissions and representations
made by partners by applying simple agency rules. Section 15 provides that 'an admission or representation made by any partner
concerning the partnership affairs, and in the ordinary course of
business, is evidence against the firm'.[2]

---

[20] *Sumner v Powell* (1816) 2 Mer 30; affd (1823) Turn & R 423; *Rawstone v Parr*
(1827) 3 Russ 539; *Richardson v Horton* (1843) 6 Beav 185; *Clarke v Bickers*
(1845) 14 Sim 639; *Jones v Beach* (1852) 2 De GM & G 886; *Other v Iveson*
(1855) 3 Drew 177.

[1] Section 12 gives effect to the situation evolved by case law. See, eg *Plumer v
Gregory* (1874) LR 18 Eq 621; *Atkinson v Mackreth* (1866) LR 2 Eq 570.

[2] Section 15 enacts pre-existing common law. See *Wood v Braddick* (1808) 1 Taunt
104; *Nicholls v Dowding and Kemp* (1815) 1 Stark 81; *Rapp v Latham and Parry*
(1819) 2 B & Ald 795; *Nottidge v Pritchard* (1834) 2 Cl & Fin 379; *Sangster v
Mazarredo* (1816) 1 Stark 161; *Thwaites v Richardson* (1790) Peake 16; *Grant v
Jackson* (1793) Peake 203; *Wright v Court* (1825) 2 C & P 232; *Blair v Bromley*
(1847) 2 Ph 354.

A number of points should be noted with regard to this provision. First, an admission by one partner is not evidence against his co-partners in relation to transactions arising before the creation of the partnership, unless a joint responsibility attaches to the transactions under the general law.[3] Second, whilst an admission by a partner in the circumstances set out in the section is evidence against the firm, it is certainly not conclusive unless it gives rise to an estoppel.[4] The facts admitted by the individual partner can still be denied by the firm and issue taken. The admission is merely evidence which will be considered in deciding the particular issue.[5] Third, the admission or representation must concern the partnership affairs. Fourth, the admission or representation must be made in the ordinary course of business.

It will be recollected that there are certain things which a partner cannot normally do in the ordinary course of business with the result that he has no apparent authority to bind the firm. It would follow that admissions or representations made by any partner with regard to such a matter would also be made outside the ordinary course of the partnership business, and not be evidence against the firm. Therefore, representations and admissions with regard to the creation of a new partnership involving the existing partners with others in a new business, or with regard to submitting a dispute to arbitration, should not be evidence against the firm.[6] Further, representations by a partner as to the extent of his own authority, or as to the nature of the partnership business, are not evidence against a firm, for to treat them as evidence would enable a partner to bind his firm on fundamental matters by his own assertion.[7]

Notice to partner to be notice to firm

Section 16 of the 1890 Act has an important provision by which notice given to an active partner is constituted notice to the firm as a whole. The section provides that:

---

[3] *Catt v Howard* (1820) 3 Stark 3; *Parker v Morrell* (1848) 2 Ph 453.
[4] *Re Coasters Ltd* [1911] 1 Ch 86.
[5] *Newton v Belcher* (1848) 12 QB 921; *Newton v Liddiard* (1848) 12 QB 925; *Wickham v Wickham* (1855) 2 K & J 478; *Hollis v Burton* [1892] 3 Ch 226. It may thus be shown that the apparent admission was made on the basis of a mistake as in *Hollis v Burton*.
[6] *Stead v Salt* (1825) 3 Bing 101.
[7] *Ex p Agace* (1792) 2 Cox Eq Cas 312; *Armagas Ltd v Mundogas SA, The Ocean Frost* [1986] AC 717; *United Bank of Kuwait v Hammoud* [1988] 1 WLR 1051.

'notice to any partner who habitually acts in a partnership business of any matter relating to partnership affairs operates as notice to the firm, except in the case of a fraud on the firm committed by, or with the consent of, the partner.'

A number of matters should be noted with regard to the provision. First, if a partner commits a fraud on the firm, or is party to such a fraud, his knowledge of his own misconduct does not operate as notice to his co-partners.[8] In *Williamson v Barbour*[9] Jessel MR gave the example of a clerk who accepted deliveries which were deficient in quantity in return for bribes from the trader supplying the goods to his firm. If the clerk is later taken into the firm, his knowledge arising from his own wrongdoing is not to be deemed as notice to the firm.

Second, the section requires that the notice be given to an active partner. Notice received by a dormant partner will not operate as notice to the firm.

1.   INCOMING PARTNERS

This brings us to a third point. Does notice given to someone who is an employee of the firm at the time that the notice is given, but who is subsequently made a partner in the firm, operate as notice to the firm itself? In the example given from *Williamson v Barbour* it will be seen that Jessel MR assumed that it would be. However, the wording of s 16 of the 1890 Act seems to suggest that a recipient of the notice must be an active partner at the time which the notice is received for the firm to be bound. This would seem to be in itself correct, since s 16 is applying basic agency principles to solve the question and, indeed, Jessel MR accepted that agency principles were the applicable area of law to resolve the issue. It is submitted that the following propositions are correct:

(1)   the effect of notice served on an individual within a partnership falls to be determined by the normal principles of agency law;

(2)   in so far as notice is received by a partner, s 16 gives statutory effect to those principles;

---

[8]   This represents the law as stated by Jessel MR in *Williamson v Barbour* (1877) 9 Ch D 529 at 535; *Bignold v Waterhouse* (1813) 1 M & S 255; *Lacey v Hill* (1876) 4 Ch D 537; affd sub nom *Read v Bailey* (1877) 3 App Cas 94; *Re Hampshire Land Co* [1896] 2 Ch 743; *Houghton & Co v Nothard, Lowe & Wills Ltd* [1928] AC 1 at 14, 15, 19.

[9]   (1877) 9 Ch D 529.

(3) where notice is served on an employee who only later becomes a partner in the firm, s 16 does not apply. The position here is to be resolved by the applications of the principles set out in (4) below;

(4) if notice is given to an employee of a firm the effect on the partners is to be determined by normal agency principles. Applying these, if the notice relates to something within the authority of the employee to deal with, he is authorised to receive the notice and the firm is bound. If it is outside such matters, he has no authority to receive it, and the firm is not, without more, bound by it.

2. OUTGOING PARTNERS

A final point to note with regard to the operation of s 16 is that notice given to an active partner with regard to partnership matters binds his fellow partners, including those who are partners by holding out.[10] If, therefore, a partner retires he will, in general, cease to be a partner, and he will not be affected by notice received by the remaining active partners. If, however, he allows himself to be held out as continuing as a partner in the firm, he will be affected by the notice.[11] In any event, an exception to the principle that retirement of a partner leaves him unaffected by notices received by the continuing partners exists in relation to notices of dishonour. It has been held that a notice of dishonour of a bill of exchange, drawn by partners and given to the continuing partner after the dissolution of the firm, does constitute sufficient notice to the retiring partner under s 49(11) of the Bills of Exchange Act 1882, which expressly requires notice to be given to each of several drawers of a bill of exchange who are not partners unless one has authority to receive notice for the rest.[12]

3. FIRMS WITH PARTNERS IN COMMON

Particular problems arise with regard to firms with common partners. Information may be received by the common partner in the course of his activities on behalf of one firm relating to the partnership affairs of the other. It appears that in such circumstances the information that he receives constitutes notice to the partners of the second business, since the requirements of the section are

---

[10] Partnership by holding out is discussed in the next section.
[11] *Adams v Bingley* (1836) 1 M & W 192.
[12] *Goldfarb v Bartlett and Kremer* [1920] 1 KB 639.

satisfied.[13] However, if the information received by the common partner related to the *clients or customers* of the second business and their affairs, this does *not* constitute notice to the partners in the second business, since the information does not relate to the partnership affairs of the first firm.[14] In short, the rule of notice exists to debar a firm from evading a liability of its own by pleading ignorance of facts within the knowledge of one of the partners. It can have no bearing on a situation in which the knowledge relates not to the firm's own affairs, but to the affairs of its clients or customers regarding which the partner to whom the information is confided, far from being bound to disclose it, may well owe a duty to the clients or customers who confided it to him to keep it to himself.

4. CONSEQUENCES OF NOTICE

Two consequences flow from the provisions of s 16 of the 1890 Act. The first is that, where it is necessary to establish that the firm had notice of some fact, it is sufficient to show that the information was received by an active partner. As a corollary to this, where it is necessary to give notice to a partnership in relation to its affairs, all that is needed is that it should be given to an active partner in compliance with the section. The second consequence is rather less obvious. If a firm enters into a transaction with a third party, it cannot use its own ignorance of information given to a partner to secure a more favourable position than that partner would have been able to secure had he entered into the transaction himself.[15]

5. RATIFICATION

As has been noted, partners may ratify the act of an individual partner which falls outside the scope of his actual authority pursuant to s 5 of the 1890 Act. For ratification to bind the partners so acting they must enter into it knowing of the act in issue; one cannot ratify in ignorance of the act in question.[16] The knowledge of the ratifying partners must be actual knowledge possessed by them.

---

[13] *Jacaud v French* (1810) 12 East 317; *Powles v Page* (1846) 3 CB 16; *Re Worcester Corn Exchange Co* (1853) 3 De GM & G 180; *Steele v Stewart* (1866) LR 2 Eq 84.
[14] *Campbell v McCreath* 1975 SLT (notes) 5.
[15] *Collinson v Lister* (1843) 7 De GM & G 634; *Oppenheimer v Frazer & Wyatt* [1907] 2 KB 50.
[16] Per Lord Russell of Killowen CJ in *Marsh v Joseph* [1897] 1 Ch 213 at 246, CA; quoted with approval by Bigham J in *Hambro v Burnand* [1903] 2 KB 399 at 414; decision reversed on other grounds [1904] 2 KB 10; *Lacey v Hill* (1879) 4 Ch D 537; affd sub nom *Read v Bailey* (1877) 3 App Cas 94.

For this purpose they will not be imputed with the knowledge of the partners whose act they are alleged to have ratified by the use of s 16. Section 16 has no application in such circumstances.

LIABILITIES OF INCOMING AND OUTGOING PARTNERS

The basic principle of partnership law is that a partner is liable in respect of partnership liabilities created whilst he is a partner. It follows that prima facie he is not liable for liabilities created at a time when he is not a partner. From this it follows that in principle an individual is not liable as a partner for things done before he entered the firm, or for things done after he had retired from the firm. These basic principles are, however, modified by the Partnership Act 1890, s 17 in respect of incoming and outgoing partners.

INCOMING PARTNERS

A person who is admitted as a partner into an existing firm does not thereby become liable to the creditors of the firm for anything done before he became a partner.[17]

1. NOVATION

The basic principle is clear. However, by novation an incoming partner may take over the liabilities of the existing firm, and thereby make himself liable to the creditors. A novation implies an agreement between the new partners and the creditors, which may be either expressed or inferred from conduct. In the words of *Lindley and Banks on Partnership*:[18]

'In order that one liability may be extinguished by being replaced by another by agreement, it is essential that the person in whom the correlative right resides should be a party to the agreement, or should, at all events, show by some act of his own that he accedes to the substitution.'[19]

---

[17] Section 17(1). This does not make him *automatically* liable. He will only be liable where the application of the normal agency principles already discussed makes him liable.

[18] (16th edn, 1990) p 246.

[19] Quoted with approval by Farwell J in *British Homes Assurance Corpn Ltd v Paterson* [1902] 2 Ch 404 at 409.

For a novation to have occurred, two conditions must be satisfied. First, the new firm must have assumed liability for the pre-existing obligation. Second, the creditor must agree to accept the new firm as his debtor in substitution and discharge for the old firm.[20] Where a novation occurs, the incoming partner and the continuing partners give consideration by undertaking the existing obligations and receive consideration on the release of the old firm from those obligations.

If no novation is achieved, an incoming partner is liable only for new obligations. These, however, may take the form of new debts arising out of a continuing contract made by the firm before he joined it. The point is neatly illustrated by *Dyke v Brewer and Tiddy*,[1] where a continuing contract for the supply of bricks led to deliveries both before and after the admission of the new partner. The court concluded that each delivery constituted performance of a divisible contract where each order for bricks under a general contract created a new contract. Consequently, the incoming partner was liable for deliveries made pursuant to orders given after his admission.

It will be seen that novation can arise from conduct. Whether or not novation has arisen is essentially a question of fact. Despite Lord Eldon's views that 'very little evidence'[2] or 'slight circumstances'[3] will be sufficient to prompt the court to find that novation has been effected, the more modern reality seems to be that the courts make the most logical deductions that they can from the circumstances actually in front of them. Thus, in one case, a banking firm had two partners, A and B. Customers deposited money with the bank. Later, they were advised by means of a circular that X and Y were also joining the firm. A died, as they knew, but the new partners continued to pay interest to them on their deposits. Subsequently, the bank became insolvent, and the customers proved in the bankruptcy of the new partners. When they then attempted also to prove for their debts in A's estate, the court refused to allow them to do so since there had been a novation after A's death, which absolved his estate from liability.[4]

In another case, where a banking firm was being carried on in partnership and a new partner was admitted on the death of an

---

[20] *Rolfe v Flower, Salting and Co* (1865) LR 1 PC 27.

[1] (1849) 2 Car & Kit 828. See also *Helsby v Mears* (1826) 5 B & C 504.

[2] *Shirreff v Wilkes* (1800) 1 East 48; *Ex p Williams* (1817) Buck 13.

[3] *Ex p Peele* (1802) 6 Ves 602 at 604.

[4] *Bilborough v Holmes* (1876) 5 Ch D 255. See also *Evans v Drummond* (1801) 4 Esp 89; *Ex p Peele* (1802) 6 Ves 602; *Ex p Williams* (1817) Buck 13; *Hart v Alexander* (1837) 7 C & P 746; *Rolfe v Flower Salting & Co* (1865) LR 1 PC 27.

existing partner, customer A, knowing of the death, drew out part of a sum due to him on deposit, accepting a new receipt for the reduced balance in the ordinary way of banking business. Another customer went to the bank to draw out the balance of his current account and was persuaded by the surviving partner to transfer the balance on the account to a deposit account. The first customer was held not to have effected a novation, thereby keeping intact his claim on the deceased partner's estate. The second customer was held to have accepted the surviving partner's sole liability in respect of his deposit.[5] Thus the whole question is essentially factual in nature.

2. AGREEMENT BETWEEN PARTIES TO TAKE ON EXISTING DEBTS

It should be noted that for novation to occur there must be an agreement *with the creditors* that the new partner take on the existing debts. For this to occur the creditors must be parties to the agreement. It is perfectly possible for the partners to agree amongst themselves that the new partner will become liable for the existing debts without involving the creditors. In such a case the partners are bound as amongst themselves, but there is no novation and the creditors cannot rely on the agreement since they are not parties to it.[6]

If there is no such agreement between the new partners to take on the existing debts of the firm, and the continuing partners purport to take on obligations in the name of the new firm to discharge the pre-existing debts, this will constitute a fraud on the new partner and he will not be bound by them.[7]

RETIRING PARTNERS

The position arising on partners leaving the partnership is best considered under three separate headings, namely (1) existing obligations, (2) continuing guarantees in respect of transactions of a firm, and (3) future dealings with the firm.

Existing obligations

The basic rule with regard to an outgoing partner's liability for existing liabilities is that a person who retires from a firm does not

---

5 Contrast *Head v Head* [1893] 3 Ch 426 with *Head v Head (No 2)* [1894] 2 Ch 236. See also *Rouse v Bradford Banking Co* [1894] 2 Ch 32.
6 Per Parke J in *Vere v Ashby* (1829) 10 B & C 288 at 298; *Ex p Peele* (1802) 6 Ves 602; *Ex p Williams* (1817) Buck 13.
7 *Shirreff v Wilks* (1800) 1 East 48.

thereby cease to be liable for partnership debts or obligations incurred before his retirement.[8] The obligations for which a retiring partner will be responsible will be executory engagements made during the period of his partnership, and which continue to be performed after his retirement.[9] It makes no difference that the withdrawal of the partner from the practice was caused by his death.[10] However, by his withdrawal from the practice, the outgoing partner is no longer in a position to be able to participate in any re-negotiation of the contract terms between the continuing partners and the third party. Accordingly, he is treated as occupying the position of a surety for the partnership performance of its obligations so that he is discharged if the third parties varies the contract with the continuing partners as by giving more time to them to perform their obligations. Such a variation places the continuing partner/surety in a new situation, thereby exposing him to risks and potential liabilities to which he would not otherwise be liable, and this should not occur without his express agreement.[11] Variation may be effected by the creditor releasing a partner from his obligations[12] or by otherwise varying the terms of payment.[13]

The continuing obligation can be discharged in two other ways, namely payment and novation.

1. PAYMENT

Payment of a debt naturally extinguishes the obligation. However, complications arise in the case of partnerships in two situations. Payment of a partnership debt made by one partner will discharge

---

[8] Partnership Act 1890, s 17(2). This will include continuing obligations under a covenant in a lease: see *Hoby v Roebuck and Palmer* (1816) 7 Taunt 157; *Graham v Whichelo and Hull* (1832) 1 Cr & M 188.

[9] *Oakford v European and American Steam Shipping Company Ltd* (1863) 1 Hem & M 182; *Court v Berlin* [1897] 2 QB 396.

[10] *Phillips v Hull Alhambra Palace Co* [1901] 1 KB 59.

[11] Per Lord Lyndhurst in *Oakley v Pasheller* (1836) 10 Bli NS 548 at 590.

[12] *Mercantile Bank of Sydney v Taylor* [1893] AC 317; *Re EWA* [1901] 2 KB 642. A release by a partner is not the same as a personal covenant not to sue given by him. In the latter situation the other partners may be sued: per Lord Morris in *Commercial Bank of Tasmania v Jones* [1893] AC 313 at 316; *Clayton v Kynaston* (1699) 2 Salk 573; *Walmesley and Nestrop v Cooper* (1839) 11 Ad & El 216; *Price v Barker and Clark* (1855) 4 E & B 760; *Re Wheeler (a Debtor)* [1982] 1 WLR 175. A release which retains the liability of the continuing partners is not a true release, but in reality a covenant not to sue: *Hartley v Manton* (1843) 5 QB 247; *Duck v Mayeu* [1892] 2 QB 511; *Re EWA* [1901] 2 KB 642.

[13] *Oakeley v Pasheller* (1836) 10 Bli NS 548, 4 Cl & F 207; *Wilson v Lloyd* (1873) LR 16 Eq 60; *Rouse v Bradford Banking Co* [1894] 2 Ch 32; affd [1894] AC 586.

all the partners from the debt if *either* that is the intention of the partner,[14] *or* the payment is made out of partnership funds. If, however, the partner pays out of his own funds and intends to keep the debt alive for his own benefit it will not cease to exist, and may be recovered by the partner from the firm in an action in which the creditor sues on his behalf.[15] Similarly, on a change in the firm, if the new partners pay an existing debt on behalf of the old firm the debt is extinguished,[16] but if payment is made to satisfy the creditor on terms that the debt continues, the new partners will be able to sue through the creditor to recover from the old firm.[17]

If a number of debts are owed to a single creditor it may well be important, in resolving the obligations of the partners, to determine which debts continue and which have been discharged. Here the rules with regard to the appropriation of payments may be decisive. The basic rules are that, if a debtor owes several debts to the same creditor, he may appropriate any payment to the particular debt of his choice.[18] If, however, he makes no such appropriation, either expressly or by implication, the creditor may choose to which debt the payment is appropriated, including debts which are otherwise statute-barred under the Limitation Act 1980.[19] To these general principles there exists the exception of the rule in *Baring v Noble, Clayton's Case*,[20] which can have an effect on the responsibility of the partners. Under this, if there is one single current account between two parties on which payments are made, all payments which cannot be attributed to some particular item on the account are taken to be in payment of the earliest items on the account at the time of payment.[1] However, the rule in *Clayton's Case* only applies to payment on a single running account. It has no application to transactions between two parties where separate accounts are maintained.[2]

---

14 *Watters v Smith* (1831) 2 B & Ad 889; *Beaumont v Greathead* (1846) 2 CB 494; *Thorne v Smith* (1851) 10 CB 659.
15 *M'Intyre v Miller* (1845) 13 M & W 725.
16 *Belshaw v Bush* (1851) 11 CB 191; *Kemp v Balls* (1854) 10 Ex Ch 607; *Hirachand Punamchand v Temple* [1911] 2 KB 330; *Jones v Broadhurst* (1850) 9 CB 173.
17 *Lucas v Wilkinson* (1856) 1 H & N 420.
18 *Newmarch v Clay and Lumb* (1811) 14 East 239; *Jones v Maund* (1839) 3 Y & C Ex 347.
19 *Halsbury's Laws of England* (4th edn) paras 505 et seq; *Chitty on Contracts* (26th edn, 1989) paras 1533 et seq.
20 (1816) 1 Mer 572.
1   See, eg *Clayton's Case* itself; *AMKMK v Chettiar* [1955] AC 230; *Re James R Rutherford and Son Ltd* [1964] 1 WLR 1211; *Re Yeovil Glove Company Ltd* [1965] Ch 148; *Hooper v Keay and Draper* [1875] 1 QBD 178. A specific partnership example is *Simson v Ingham* (1823) 2 B & C 65.
2   *Bradford Old Bank v Sutcliffe* [1918] 2 KB 833.

However, it should be noted that these rules apply to payments made by, or on behalf of, the firm. A payment by a partner to a creditor in respect of his own debts may not be allocated by the creditor as a payment in respect of partnership debts owed to the same creditor, and vice versa.[3]

2. NOVATION

To the general principle that a retiring partner is not released from liability for partnership debts and obligations there lies the exception of novation. The Partnership Act 1890 provides that a retiring partner may be discharged from any existing liabilities by an agreement to that effect between himself and the members of the firm as newly constituted and the creditors, and this agreement may be either express or inferred as a fact from the course of dealing between the creditors and the firm as newly constituted.[4] The circumstances in which the courts will conclude that a novation has been effected have already been considered.[5] However, one particular problem arises in the case of retirement. A partner may retire without a new person being taken into the partnership to replace him. If a novation is agreed between himself, the continuing partner and the creditors, is it effective as a novation or does it fail for want of consideration? The issue was raised in *Thompson v Percival*.[6] A and B were in partnership. A wished to retire from the partnership and B wished to continue. It was agreed that B should carry on the business alone, and receive and pay all debts. On this basis, they dissolved the partnership. C was a creditor of the firm. He applied to A for payment of the funds due to him, and was informed that B alone was responsible. C drew a bill on B which was dishonoured. C then sued A. The court held that it was a question of fact for the jury whether C had agreed to accept B as his sole debtor and B's acceptance of the bill of exchange as satisfaction of the debt due from A and B. The fact that B had agreed to meet all the debts of the partnership was evidence that he had A's authority to effect a novation with C.

In reaching this conclusion the court overruled one previous decisions to the contrary[7] and distinguished another.[8] The difficulty

---

[3] *Thompson v Brown and Weston* (1827) Mood & M 40.
[4] Section 17(3).
[5] See p 143, above.
[6] (1834) 5 B & Ad 925.
[7] *David v Ellice* (1826) 5 B & C 196.
[8] *Lodge v Dicas* (1820) 3 B & Ald 611.

with the case is resolving the legal proposition for which the case is authority. The possibilities seem to be as follows:

(1) the court may have found consideration for the novation in the giving of the negotiable security for the new agreement because of its negotiability and easy proof of dishonour. If so, the case turns upon its somewhat special facts, and would only be followed in cases where a negotiable instrument was given by the continuing partners in respect of the obligation. This situation apart, the issue of the need for consideration remains unresolved. Further, it might well be that the decision does not survive the decision of the Court of Appeal in *D & C Builders v Rees*[9] which decided that payment of a smaller amount by cheque in satisfaction of a large debt does not discharge the debt, but leaves the creditor just as free to sue for the balance as he would be if he paid cash;[10]

(2) Lord Chelmsford found consideration in the analysis that the sole liability of one of two debtors might be more beneficial than the joint liability of the two because of factors such as convenience, the position in bankruptcy, survivorship, etc might have that effect. At first sight this argument is plainly less convincing than that in (1) above, but it does receive support from the recent decision of the Court of Appeal in *Williams v Roffey Bros & Nicholls (Contractors) Ltd*,[11] where consideration was deduced from just such pointers in different circumstances;

(3) the case may be authority for the proposition that no consideration is necessary.

Given the doubts attaching to the implications of the decision it is plainly desirable that continuing partners should provide some express consideration to the creditor in respect of the obligation due to him to remove all doubt. One obvious way in which this can be done in respect of outstanding accounts is to agree a slightly earlier date for payment than that which was originally agreed.

It would appear, therefore, that it is possible that the introduction of a new partner is not essential to establish a consideration to make the new arrangement binding. In any event, in all cases the issues will be: (a) whether a new agreement has been created binding the firm as newly constituted; and (b) whether it was also agreed that the old

[9] [1966] 2 QB 617.
[10] Overruling *Goddard v O'Brien* (1882) 9 QBD 37, and distinguishing *Sibree v Tripp* (1846) 15 M & W 23.
[11] [1990] 1 All ER 512.

firm should be discharged from responsibility.[12] If there is an agreement that the new firm should be bound, there will be no discharging novation unless the old firm is also agreed to be released, even if new partners become members of the new firm.[13] The only relevance of the new partners may be that it makes it a more likely inference that the creditor also agreed to the release of the old firm.[14]

Of course, for the old partner to be discharged the creditor must know of him. If, therefore, P1 and P2 are both partners in a firm but P1 is the active partner and P2 a dormant partner, it may well be that the existence of P2 will not be known to creditors of the firm. If P1 enters into arrangements with creditor C, there will be no discharge of P2 if he retires, so that he can still be sued when discovered, unless those arrangements discharge the debt in respect of the old firm including P1 himself.[15]

Continuing guarantees

A continuing guarantee or cautionary obligation given either to a firm or to a third person in respect of the transactions of a firm is, in the absence of agreement to the contrary, revoked as to future transactions by any change in the constitution of the firm to which, or of the firm in respect of the transactions of which, the guarantee or obligation is given.[16] Thus, for a guarantee to continue past a change in the constitution of the partnership there must be an express stipulation or some necessary implication to show that this was what was intended.[17] The implication may, however, arise from the very nature of the guarantee itself.[18]

---

[12] *Lodge v Dicas* (1820) 3 B & Ald 611; *David v Ellice* (1826) 5 B & C 196; *Heath v Percival* (1720) 1 P Wms 682; *Fergusson v Fyffe* (1841) 8 Cl & Fin 121; *Harris v Farwell* (1846) 15 Beav 31; *Rouse v Bradford Banking Co* [1894] AC 586; *Smith v Patrick* [1901] AC 282.

[13] *Gough v Davies* (1817) 4 Price 200; *Kirwan v Kirwan* (1834) 2 Cr & M 617; *Fergusson v Fyffe* (1841) 8 Cl & Fin 121; *Harris v Farwell* (above).

[14] Certainly there seems to be a greater willingness on the part of the court to reach this inference where new partners are admitted to the firm. If a partner retires and his fellow partners merely continue, the outgoing partner will not necessarily be discharged even if the continuing partners give the creditor a new security for the debt: *Swire v Redman* (1876) 1 QBD 536; *Bedford v Deakin* (1818) 2 Stark 178. However, on the former case see the critical comments of the Court of Appeal in *Rouse v Bradford Banking Co* [1894] 2 Ch 32 at 59–60, 69.

[15] *Robinson v Wilkinson* (1817) 3 Price 538.

[16] Partnership Act 1890, s 18 re-enacting the Mercantile Law Amendment Act 1856.

[17] Per Blackburn J in *Backhouse v Hall* (1865) 6 B & S 507 at 520.

[18] *Metcalf v Bruin* (1810) 12 East 400.

Future dealings after dissolution

Where a person deals with a firm after a change in its constitution, he is entitled to treat all apparent members of the old firm as still being members of the firm until he has notice of the change.[19] In *Tower Cabinet Co Ltd v Ingram*[20] it was decided that the word 'apparent' means 'appear to be members to persons dealing with the firm'. Apparent members of the old firm are therefore those who appear to be members whilst the partnership continued. In the *Tower Cabinet Company* case a partnership was dissolved on one partner leaving the partnership, and subsequently the continuing partner located a new trade supplier and obtained supplies from him. In confirming the order the continuing partner used some old headed notepaper, which still contained the name of the outgoing partner and which had not been destroyed when he left. This was the only knowledge which the supplier had of the outgoing partner's connection with the firm with which they were dealing. When they subsequently sought to make the outgoing partner liable for the goods supplied, it was held that they could not succeed. The outgoing partner was not one who appeared to be a member of the company to persons dealing with the firm at the time that the contract for the supply of the goods was made.

The real significance of s 36(1), therefore, appears to be in relation to those who had dealings with the original partnership and continued to deal with the firm after the particular partner has retired. Indeed, if no notice is given, an outgoing partner may be liable on a promissory note given by his former partners after the date of his departure.[1] It follows that actual notice of retirement should be given to all customers of the old firm. On the other hand, an advertisement in the London Gazette is notice to persons who had not had dealings with the firm before the change in its constitution so advertised.[2] Further, in the case of persons dealing with

---

[19] Section 36(1). In fact this merely applies the normal rules of agency.

[20] [1949] 2 KB 397.

[1] *Parkin v Carruthers* (1800) 3 Esp 248; *Williams v Keats and Archer* (1817) 2 Stark 290; *Brown v Leonard* (1816) 2 Chit 120. In the case of a negotiable instrument given to someone who had no previous dealing with a firm an ex-partner will only be liable if he has allowed himself to be held out as a partner since leaving the firm: *Dolman v Orchard* (1825) 2 C & P 104.

[2] Section 36(2). This provides that an advertisement in the London Gazette as to a firm whose principal place of business is in England and Wales, in the Edinburgh Gazette as to a firm whose principal place of business is in Scotland, and in the Belfast Gazette as to a firm whose principal place of business is in Ireland, shall be notice to persons who had no dealings with the business before the date of the dissolution or change so advertised.

the firm to whom the retiring partner was not known as a partner, no notice is necessary.[3] However, *proving* that the third party had no knowledge of the connection of the retiring partner with the firm would clearly be difficult,[4] but it may be possible to show this in the case of a dormant partner.

An important limitation on the potential liability of a retiring partner arises from s 36(3) of the Partnership Act. The estate of a partner who dies or becomes bankrupt, or of a partner who, not having been known to the person dealing with the firm to be a partner, retires from the firm, is not liable for partnership debts contracted after the date of the death, bankruptcy or retirement respectively. The reason for this is that the event (death, bankruptcy, retirement) has terminated the partnership and therefore the *actual* authority of the other partners to act as his agent, prior to the debt being contracted.

The effect of notice

The effect of giving notice in appropriate form of the cessation of a firm or the retirement of a partner is to bring to an end the ostensible authority of the partner and with it his power to bind the firm.[5] To this principle there are three exceptions.

1. EXPRESS AUTHORITY

Express authority continues where the continuing partners have express authority to use the former partner's name.[6]

2. WINDING UP

Under s 38 of the 1890 Act the authority of the partners continues after the dissolution of the partnership in so far as it is necessary to wind up the partnership affairs.[7]

---

[3] Partnership Act 1890, s 36(3); *Evans v Drummond* (1801) 4 Esp 89; *Carter v Whalley* (1830) 1 B & Ad 11; *Heath v Sansom and Evans* (1832) 4 B & Ad 172. The presence or absence of the name of the retired partner in the firm name may be very important when it comes to resolving whether or not the third party dealing with the firm knew of the ex-partner's connection with the firm.

[4] Even those who never had dealings with the firm and knew of its existence only by reputation are entitled to assume that it continues to exist unless and until notice is given to the contrary: *Parkin v Carruthers* (1800) 3 Esp 248.

[5] *Minnit v Whinery* (1721) 5 Bro Parl Cas 489; *Abel v Sutton* (1800) 3 Esp 108; *Paterson v Zachariah* (1815) 1 Stark 71; *Wrightson v Pullan* (1816) 1 Stark 375; *Dolman v Orchard* (1825) 2 C & P 104; *Spenceley v Greenwood* (1858) 1 F & F 297.

[6] *Burton v Issitt* (1821) 5 B & Ald 267; *Smith v Winter* (1838) 4 M & W 454.

[7] This is discussed under dissolution in Chapter 12, p 282, below.

3. LIABILITY FOR HOLDING OUT AS A PARTNER

In spite of his retirement, the outgoing partner may find liability imposed upon him for holding himself out as a partner, or knowingly suffering himself to be represented as a partner.[8] Indeed s 36(1), under which apparent members of the old firm remain liable for its future dealings to third parties until they have notice of change, can be seen as an example of partnership by holding out for which separate statutory provision has been made.

Under the more general concept of partnership by holding out, the issue arises as to whether a partner who retires and allows his name still to be used as part of the firm name thereby holds himself out as a partner. In the case of those who have had dealings with the firm, there is no reason why it should, since, because of the clear provision contained in s 36, s 14 could only be called in aid by a third party who has been given express notice of the retirement. Such a person knows the position and the continued use of the old firm name will have no impact on him. With regard to those who have had no previous dealings with the firm, the use of the old firm name including that of the retired partner has been held not to create a liability on him as a partner by holding out.[9] It makes no difference that the retiring partner has expressly authorised the use of his name.[10]

The word 'knowingly' requires knowledge of the outgoing partner that he is being represented as a partner; mere carelessness is not sufficient. Liability as a partner by holding out was argued in *Tower Cabinet Co Ltd v Ingram*.[11] In that case the outgoing partner had done more than merely allow the continued use of his name as part of the firm name. The old headed paper actually showed him as a partner. However, the most that could be said of him was that he had been careless in not destroying the headed notepaper on the dissolution of the partnership, and the court held that no liability attached to him since he had not 'knowingly' suffered himself to be represented as a partner.

Section 14(2) of the Partnership Act makes express provision applying the principles applicable on the retirement of a partner to the death of a partner. Where, after a partner's death, the partnership business is continued in the old firm name, continued use of that name, or of the deceased partner's name as part thereof, does

---

8 Section 14(1).
9 *Re Fraser, ex p Central Bank of London* [1892] 2 QB 633.
10 *Newsome v Coles* (1811) 2 Camp 617.
11 [1949] 2 KB 397.

not of itself make his executors or administrator's estate or effects liable for any partnership debts contracted after his death.

The importance of the Business Names Act 1985

The requirement that partnerships comply with the Business Names Act 1985 has already been noted.[12] The effect of compliance will often ensure that notice of any change in the firm is given to the customers, since compliance is intended to publicise the membership of the firm.[13] This may often be decisive in resolving whether notice has been given.

---

[12] See Chapter 5, p 90, above.
[13] *Barfoot v Goodall* (1811) 3 Camp 147; *Hart v Alexander* (1837) 2 M & W 484.

CHAPTER 7

LITIGATION INVOLVING THE FIRM

INTRODUCTION

Where partners are involved in litigation with others who have dealt with the firm there are special rules of procedure which need to be borne in mind. These will be examined in this chapter. It will be remembered that the potential liability of partners can be either joint or joint and several. Traditionally where the liability is joint and some only of the partners are sued to judgment, subsequent proceedings cannot be brought against those not included in the original action if those partners who were made defendants turn out to be insolvent.[1] The special rules were intended to ameliorate the potential difficulties of this. The conceptual basis of the special rules is that the firm can be sued in the firm name. Apart from these special provisions the procedural rules for litigation involving the partnership as a firm are the same as those applicable generally.

The procedures for actions brought by or against partners are laid down for High Court actions by RSC Ord 81, and there are comparable rules for the county court.[2]

FIRM'S RIGHTS AND OBLIGATIONS

The procedural rules discussed in this chapter concern the firm's rights and obligations. Therefore, their use demands a continual appreciation of the distinction between, on the one hand, the rights and obligations of the firm, and, on the other, the rights and obligation of the individual partners. Only the former can affect the position of the firm and be the subject of the use of the procedure.

[1] See p 136, above.
[2] CCR Ord 5, r 9(1).

In this respect the position of the individual partner as agent of the firm able to negotiate rights and obligations on behalf of the firm must be remembered. If the right or obligation is negotiated on behalf of the firm and the other party is led to believe that the individual partner negotiates but as agent, the right or obligation is that of the firm.[3] If the third party is led to believe that the individual partner negotiates on his own behalf, the right or obligation is that of the individual partner himself.[4]

Similarly, in tort it is important to resolve whether the tort is one for which the firm rather than the individual partner is liable or, alternatively, where a tort is suffered, whether it was committed against the individual partner or against the firm itself. In this latter connection an important question is: who suffered the loss – the firm or the partner? If the former, the firm can, in principle, sue;[5] if the latter, only the individual partner.[6] If both are damaged by the same tort, two independent causes of action arise, one in favour of the individual partner and one in favour of the firm in relation to the separate damage each has suffered.[7] A technical difficulty arises where a partner or partners collude together with a third party to carry out a fraud on the firm. The innocent partners may maintain an action against the third party, and if the fraudulent partner refuses to be a co-plaintiff he may be joined as a defendant.[8]

Of course, in the case of bills of exchange and promissory notes these general principles are modified by the technical requirements pertaining to these instruments. Unless the only or last endorsement of such an instrument is in blank, the proper parties to any action on the bill are those named as drawers, payees or indorsees.[9]

---

[3]   *Townsend v Neale* (1809) 2 Camp 190; *Garrett and Boldenham v Handley* (1825) 4 B & C 664; *Cothay v Fennell* (1830) 10 B & C 671; *Alexander v Barker* (1831) 2 Cr & J 133; *Sims v Brittain* (1832) 4 B & Ad 375; *Sims v Bond* (1833) 5 B & Ad 389; *Cooke and Farquar v Seeley* (1848) 2 Ex Ch 746.

[4]   *Brand v Boulcott* (1802) 3 Bos and P 253; *Hopkinson v Smith* (1822) 1 Bing 13; *Agacio v Forbes* (1861) 14 Moo PCC 160; *Brandon and Brown v Hubbard and Keys* (1820) 2 Brod & Bing 11.

[5]   *Addison v Overend* (1796) 6 Term Rep 766; *Forster v Lawson* (1826) 3 Bing 452; *Williams v Beaumont* (1833) 10 Bing 260; *Le Fanu and Bull v Malcomson* (1848) 1 HL Cas 637; *South Hetton Coal Co Ltd v North & Eastern News Association Ltd* [1894] 1 QB 133.

[6]   *Solomons v Medex* (1816) 1 Stark 191; *Robinson v Marchant* (1845) 7 QB 918; *Pullman v Walter Hill & Co Ltd* [1891] 1 QB 524.

[7]   *Forster v Lawson* (1826) 3 Bing 452; *Haythorn v Lawson* (1827) 3 C & P 196; *Harrison v Bevington* (1838) 8 C & P 708; *Thomas v Moore* [1918] 1 KB 555.

[8]   Per Jessel MR in *Williamson v Barbour* (1877) 9 Ch D 529 at 536; *Longman v Pole* (1828) Mood & M 223; *Johnson v Stephens & Carter Ltd and Golding* [1923] 2 KB 857; RSC Ord 15, r 4(2).

[9]   *Guidon v Robson* (1809) 2 Camp 302; *Pease v Hirst* (1829) 10 B & C 122.

The fact that the people so named are partners or that the instrument relates to the partnership business is irrelevant, and it is the individual partner named in the bill who should be the party to the action.[10] Similarly, in the case of actions for the recovery of land, the proceedings should be brought in the names of the persons in whom the legal estates is vested.

Set off

The principle that the distinction between the rights and obligations of the firm and those of the individual partners is decisive in disputes between the firm and third parties extends also to set offs. The great principles of set off are twofold, namely (1) debts owed by and to the same person in the same right can be set off and (2) debts not owed by or to the same persons in the same right cannot be set off. Debts owed by or to individual partners in their own right are not owed in the same right as rights and obligations owed to and from the firm.[11] Thus, where the firm has the same bankers as one or more of the individual partners, sums due from the firm on the partnership account cannot be set against sums due to the individual partners, and vice versa.[12] Again, where the third party has had dealings with a single partner it is important to resolve whether the partner was acting on his account or on behalf of the partnership in order to determine whether the obligations created were due to and from him personally or to and from the firm.[13]

There is, however, an exception to the principle in the case of dormant partners which arises through the concept of holding out. Where one partner has been allowed to act as if he were principal, and not merely the agent of the firm, so that the third party was led to believe that he was dealing with him as principal, set off between the firm's obligations and those of the active partner will be allowed so that the third party is not prejudiced.[14]

---

[10]   *Bawden v Howell* (1841) 3 Man & G 638.

[11]   It is therefore important to resolve whether the partner or the firm owe, or are owed, the relevant debts: *Slipper v Stidstone* (1794) 5 Term Rep 493; *French v Andrade* (1796) 6 Term Rep 582; *Addis v Knight* (1817) 2 Mer 117; *MacGillivray v Simson* (1826) 2 C & P 320; *Boswell v Smith* (1833) 6 C & P 60; *Smith v Parkes* (1852) 16 Beav 115; *Powell v Brodhurst* [1901] 2 Ch 160.

[12]   *Watts v Christie* (1849) 11 Beav 546; *Cavendish v Geaves* (1857) 24 Beav 163.

[13]   *Gordon v Ellis* (1844) 2 CB 821; by analogy *Bhogal v Punjab National Bank* [1988] 2 All ER 296.

[14]   *Stacey v Decy* (1789) 7 Term Rep 361n; *George v Clagett* (1797) 7 Term Rep 359; *Teed v Elworthy* (1811) 14 East 210; *De Mautort v Saunders and Saunders* (1830) 1 B & Ad 398.

ACTIONS BY AND AGAINST FIRMS

Given the complications which can arise from partnership joint liability, as noted above, perhaps the most important procedural provision involving partnerships is contained in Ord 81, r 1, which permits proceedings[15] by or against two or more partners who carry on business within the jurisdiction to be commenced in the name under which they carried on business when the cause of action accrued.

Consequently, persons carrying on business together may sue and be sued in their firm name, without the necessity of setting out the names of the individual partners.[16] This may be done even though the firm has changed its partners or been dissolved since the accrual of the cause of action, although there is no great benefit in proceeding in the firm name in such circumstances since each of the original partners will have to be individually served with the proceedings.[17] Where the provision applies it may be used, even though one of the partner may be suffering from a disability but, in such circumstances, any judgment obtained binds only those partners *not* suffering from a disability.[18]

Since, by its own terms, RSC Ord 81, r 1 applies to 'two or more persons claiming to be entitled or alleged to be liable as partners' it envisages that a party may seek to use it when subsequently it is shown that in fact no partnership existed. In such circumstances, provided the party acted in the genuine belief that a partnership

---

[15] Proceedings for these purposes include those commenced by originating summons, RSC Ord 81, r 8.

[16] However, foreign firms cannot sue or be sued under these provisions unless they carry on business within the jurisdiction. If they do carry on business within the jurisdiction it matters not that the partners reside or are domiciled outside the jurisdiction or are not of British nationality: *Worcester City and County Banking Co v Firbank, Pauling and Co* [1894] 1 QB 784; *Hobbs v Australian Press Association* [1933] 1 KB 1. The doubts expressed in *Grant v Anderson & Co* [1892] 1 QB 108 do not seem well founded and overlook the provisions of Ord 81, r 5 (formrly Ord 48, r 8). It follows, however, that where the partners cannot be shown to have been carrying on business within the jurisdiction at the relevant time Ord 81 cannot be relied on. In principle, therefore, proceedings must be brought in the individual names of the partners: *Western National Bank of the City of New York v Perez Triana & Co* [1891] 1 QB 304; *Indigo Co v Ogilvy* [1891] 2 Ch 31; *Dobson v Festi Rasini & Co* [1891] 2 QB 92. Exceptionally, however, proceedings may be brought in the name of the firm if it can be shown that, under the law by which it is constituted, the firm has a separate legal personality: *Von Hellfeld v Rechnitzer and Mayer Freres & Co* [1914] 1 Ch 748.

[17] *Re Wenham* [1900] 2 QB 698.

[18] *Lovell & Christmas v Beauchamp* [1894] AC 607.

existed, the court will allow the action to proceed amongst the correct parties.[19] Usually, when proceedings are brought by a firm in the firm name, they will be brought with the consent of all the partners. Equally, if proceedings are brought against a partnership in the firm name and they become defended, this will be because the partners have agreed that the proceedings should be defended. However, whether the partners are in agreement or not, if proceedings are brought or defended on the instructions of one partner, all are bound, since the power to authorise the initiation or defence of proceedings lies within the apparent authority of any partner.[20] Any individual partner who is not in agreement with proceedings being brought in the firm name is left to protect himself by seeking an indemnity against any costs to which he might be subjected by the use of that name.[1] The authority of one partner to bind another in this respect, therefore, extends to an active partner binding a dormant partner or partners.[2]

When proceedings are brought by the firm in the firm name, all partners become responsible for the costs of the proceedings. One partner has the power to make others responsible for these by acting within his authority in sanctioning the proceedings to be brought, even though the partnership is dissolved while the action was pending. The only requirement is that a cause of action should have accrued during the subsistence of the partnership, as where the proceedings are for a debt due to the firm.[3] In any event, an uncooperative partner, who has disclaimed all benefit in the cause of action, and who is not liable for the costs, may still be made to cooperate in the proceedings as by revealing relevant information.[4] It follows that, if the power to initiate or defend litigation falls within the implied or ostensible authority of a partner, so also does the power to stay proceedings to terminate them.[5]

DISCLOSURE OF PARTNERS' NAMES

From the point of view of the other party to the proceedings the identities of the partners involved in the firm, and whose liability is

---

[19] *Noble Lowndes & Partners (a firm) v Hadfields Ltd* [1939] Ch 569.
[20] *Tomlinson v Broadsmith* [1896] 1 QB 386; *Court v Berlin* [1897] 2 QB 396.
[1] Per Bayley J in *Whitehead v Hughes* (1834) 2 Cr & M 318 at 319.
[2] *Court v Berlin* [1897] 2 QB 396.
[3] Ibid.
[4] *Seal & Edgelow v Kingston* [1908] 2 KB 579.
[5] *Harwood v Edwards* (1739), *Gow on Partnership* p 65n.

therefore tied up in the firm name, are of fundamental importance. It is something which he needs to know, and provision is made to assist him in discovering this information. Any *defendant* to an action brought by partners in the name of a firm may serve on the plaintiffs, or their solicitor, a notice requiring them or him to furnish the defendant with a written statement of the names and places of residence of all the persons who were partners in the firm at the time when the cause of action accrued. If the notice is not complied with, the court may order the plaintiffs or their solicitor to furnish the defendant with such a statement and to verify it on oath, or otherwise, as may be specified in the order, or may order that further proceedings in the action be stayed on such terms as the court may direct.[6]

Further, any *plaintiff* in an action brought against partners in the name of the firm may serve on the defendants, or their solicitor, a notice requiring them or him to furnish the plaintiff with a written statement of the names and places of residence of all the persons who are partners in the firm at the time when the cause of action accrued. If the notice is not complied with, the court may order the defendants, or their solicitor, to furnish the plaintiff with such a statement and to verify it on oath, or otherwise, as may be specified in the order.[7]

When the names of the partners have been declared in compliance with a notice or order, the proceedings are to continue in the name of the firm, but with the same consequences as would have ensued if the persons whose names have been declared had been named as plaintiffs in the writ.[8]

These provisions apply whether or not a firm is within the jurisdiction. It will be seen that they enable both a defendant being sued by a plaintiff firm and a plaintiff suing a defendant firm to obtain disclosure of the names and addresses of all partners within the firm at the time that the cause of action accrued, if necessary, by court order.

SERVICE OF WRIT

Where proceedings are issued against a firm in the firm name, special provisions are made with regard to the service of the writ. This

---

[6] Order 81, r 2(1). The oath is given by affidavit. The court has no jurisdiction to order cross-examination of the maker of the affidavit or trial of the issue: *Abrahams & Co v Dunlop Pneumatic Tyre Co* [1905] 1 KB 46.
[7] Rule 2(3). Again, the oath is given by affidavit and the court lacks jurisdiction to order cross-examination or trial of the issue.
[8] Rule 2(2).

may be served (1) on any one or more of the partners, or (2) at the principal place of business of the partnership within the jurisdiction,[9] or (3) on any person having, at the time of service, the control or management of the partnership business there. Where service of the writ is effected in accordance with these provisions, it is deemed to have been served on the firm, whether or not any member of the firm is out of the jurisdiction.[10]

However, where a partnership has been dissolved, *to the knowledge of the plaintiff*, before an action against the firm has begun, the writ by which the action is begun must be served on every person within the jurisdiction sought to be made liable in the action. This latter provision is an important modification of the basic principle. Where the partnership has been dissolved, and the plaintiff has knowledge of the dissolution, an outgoing partner may only be made liable for the debt if a writ is actually served upon him.[11] It makes no difference that he was a partner when the debt was contracted and therefore liable for it, for the provisions now under consideration are merely procedural provisions dealing with how he might be served.

Every person on whom a writ is served must be given a written notice at the time of service stating whether he is served as a partner, or as a person having the control or management of the partnership business, or both as a partner and as such a person. However, any person on whom a writ is so served, but to whom no such notice is given, is deemed to be served as a partner.[12] It would therefore seem that where a person is served as partner, no written notice is in fact necessary.

---

[9] If the proceedings are sent to the wrong address the service is ineffective. If, however, in such circumstances a copy of the proceedings can be shown to come into the hands of a partner at the correct address it appears that the service then becomes effective: *Austin Rover Group Ltd v Crouch Butler Savage Associates* [1986] 1 WLR 1102.

[10] Rule 3(1); *Meyer v Louis Dreyfus et Cie* [1940] 4 All ER 157. However, in these circumstances complications may arise with regard to enforcement, RSC Ord 81, r 5(3); CCR Ord 25, r 9(2) discussed at p 165, below. To avoid these the proceedings should be brought against any partners out of the jurisdiction *and* the firm, or in the names of the individual partners. In any event leave to serve on the partner(s) out of the jurisdiction should be obtained: *West of England SS Owners Protection and Indemnity Association Ltd v John Holman & Sons* [1957] 1 WLR 1164.

[11] Order 81, r 3(4); *Shepherd v Hirsch Pritchard & Co* (1890) 45 Ch D 231; *Wigram v Cox, Sons, Buckley & Co* [1894] 1 QB 792.

[12] Rule 3(4). There is no equivalent requirement in the County Court Rules.

ACKNOWLEDGEMENT OF SERVICE IN AN ACTION AGAINST A FIRM

Where persons are sued as partners in the name of their firm, service may not be acknowledged in the name of the firm but only by the partners thereof in their own names, but the action shall nevertheless continue in the name of the firm.[13] Consequently, even if one of the partners involved in the firm dies after the service of the writ and the return of the acknowledgment of the service, the proceedings do not continue against the surviving partners alone. They must continue to defend in the name and on behalf of the firm.[14] It also follows that an acknowledgment of service returned by one of several partners where a firm is sued is a sufficient acknowledgment for the whole firm, and, further, it matters not that the acknowledging partner is one of two foreigners, provided that the firm was trading in partnership in England.[15] Further, since normal agency principles apply, a solicitor employed by the active partner of a firm to defend an action which is brought against the firm has authority to acknowledge service in the names of each individual partner even though some of the partners are dormant.[16]

Where, in an action against a firm, the writ by which the action is begun is served on a person as a partner, that person, if he denies that he was a partner or liable as such at any material time, may acknowledge service of the writ in the action, and state that he does so as a person served as a partner in the defendant firm but who denies that he was a partner at any material time. An acknowledgment of service given in accordance with this provision is to be treated as an acknowledgment by the defendant firm.[17] It is therefore good unless and until it is set aside.

Where an acknowledgment of service is so given by a defendant, the *plaintiff* may apply to the court to set it aside on the ground that the defendant was a partner, or liable as such, at a material time, or may leave that question to be determined at a later stage of the proceedings. Equally, the *defendant* may apply to the court to set aside *the service of the writ* on him on the ground that he was not a partner or liable as such at a material time. Alternatively, the defendant may, at a proper time, serve a defence on the plaintiff denying, in

[13] Rule 4(1).
[14] *Ellis v Wadeson* [1899] 1 QB 714.
[15] *Lysaght Ltd v Clark & Co* [1891] 1 QB 552.
[16] *Tomlinson v Broadsmith* [1896] 1 QB 386.
[17] Rule 4(2).

respect of the plaintiff's claim, either his liability as a partner or the liability of the defendant firm, or both.[18] Further, the court, on the application of either the plaintiff or the defendant at any stage of the proceedings in which a defendant has so acknowledged service, may order that any question of the liability of that defendant or the defendant firm be tried in such manner and at such time as it directs.[19] Where the writ by which the action is begun in an action against a firm is served on a person as a person having the control or management of the partnership business, that person may not acknowledge service in the action unless he is in fact a member of the firm sued.[20]

JUDGMENT

If proceedings are brought against the firm in the firm name it follows that any judgment obtained is against the firm (ie those who were partners at the time that the cause of action accrued) and judgment must normally be entered in the firm name.[1] If, however, one of the partners is under a disability (eg infancy) judgment should be entered against the firm other than the affected partner.[2]

Any acknowledgment of service by a partner is given on behalf of the firm. It therefore prevents judgment being taken by default either against the firm as such[3] or any partner who fails to file an acknowledgement as an individual.[4]

ENFORCING JUDGMENT OR ORDER AGAINST FIRM

If a judgment is obtained against a firm and is not satisfied by the firm and its partners, it may be necessary to issue execution to enforce it. Again, the rules of court make special provisions in the case of partnerships.

Where a judgment is given or order made against a firm, execution to enforce the judgment or order may issue against property of the firm within the jurisdiction.[5] Further, where a judgment is

---

[18] Rule 4(3).
[19] Rule 4(4).
[20] Rule 4(5).
[1] *Jackson v John Litchfield & Sons* (1882) 8 QBD 474.
[2] *Lovell & Christmas v Beauchamp* [1894] AC 607.
[3] *Alden v Beckley & Co* (1890) 25 QBD 543.
[4] *Adam v Townend* (1884) 14 QBD 103 at 104.
[5] Rule 5(1).

given, or order made against a firm, execution to enforce the judgment or order may issue against any person who (1) acknowledged service of the writ in the action as a partner, or (2) having been served as a partner with the writ of summons failed to acknowledge service of it in the action, or (3) admitted in his pleading that he was a partner, or (4) was adjudged to be a partner.[6] Thus, in these circumstances, execution may be levied against the property of the individual partners without first levying execution against the partnership property.

Also, where a party who has obtained a judgment or order against a firm claims that a person is liable to satisfy the judgment or order as being a member of the firm and none of these provisions applies in relation to that person, that party may apply to the court for leave to issue execution against that person. The application for leave must be made by a summons served personally on the person against whom it is wished to issue execution and ask the court to determine whether the individual was, or had held himself out to be, a partner.[7] Where the person against whom such an application is made does not dispute his liability, the court hearing the application may give leave to issue execution against that person. On the other hand, where that person disputes his liability, the court may order that the liability of the person be tried and determined in any manner in which any issue or question in an action may be tried and determined.[8]

Partner out of the jurisdiction

These provisions give considerable assistance to those seeking to enforce a judgment or order against a firm. However, exception is made in the case of members of the firm who were out of the jurisdiction when the writ of summons was issued. Here, execution to enforce a judgment or order given or made against a firm may not issue against any member of the firm who was out of the jurisdiction when the writ of summons was issued unless he (1) acknowledged service of the writ in the action as a partner; or (2) was served within the jurisdiction of the writ as a partner; or (3) was, with the leave of the court given under RSC Ord 11, served

---

[6] Rule 5(2).

[7] Rule 5(4). The procedure is a simplifying one. The judgment creditor retains his right to bring an action on the judgment in the previous action against the individual partner and to execute any judgment obtained in the second action, *Clark & Son v Cullen* (1882) 9 QBD 355.

[8] Rule 5(5); *Davis v Hyman & Co* [1903] 1 KB 854.

out of the jurisdiction with the writ, or notice of the writ, as a partner. Further, a judgment or an order given or made against a firm does not affect a member who was out of the jurisdiction when the writ was issued except in so far as the judgment is issued against the property of the firm itself.[9]

Receiver appointed

If the court has appointed a receiver in respect of the partnership property it is necessary to obtain leave to be able to issue execution. The court is likely to direct the receiver to pay the judgment creditor out of money coming into his hands or may give the creditor a charge over property held by the receiver rather than allow execution to be levied if this will see the creditor paid.[10] In such circumstances, allowing the execution to proceed is likely to be viewed as very much the last resort.

Where a judgment has been obtained against the firm, a bankruptcy notice cannot be issued against an individual partner unless execution could be issued against him pursuant to these provisions.[11]

Two firms with common partner(s)

If two firms share a common partner or partners and judgment has been obtained by one against the other, the leave of the court is required before the judgment can be executed. On the application for leave the court may give such directions as may be just, eg for accounts to be taken.[12]

USE OF FIRM NAME

At one time it was unsettled whether the firm name could be used in actions between a firm and any of its own members or, indeed, as has been noted, between firms having a partner or partners in common. Any doubts have now been removed and such actions will

---

[9] Rule 5(3).
[10] *Kewney v Attrill* (1886) 34 Ch D 345. A charge gives the judgment creditor priority over other creditors and the trustee of an insolvent partner: *Re Gershon and Levy* [1915] 2 KB 527; *Newport v Pougher* [1937] Ch 214.
[11] *Re Ide* (1886) 17 QBD 755.
[12] RSC Ord 81, r 6(1); CCR Ord 25, r 10.

lie although the leave of the court is required for execution to be levied on any judgment obtained.[13] However, these provisions may only be relied on where, under the normal rules of partnership law, the effect is not to make a partner both plaintiff and defendant in the action.[14]

DEBTS OWED BY FIRMS WITH NON-RESIDENT PARTNERS

An order for attachment may be made under RSC Ord 49, r 1 in relation to debts due or accruing from a firm carrying on business within the jurisdiction, notwithstanding that one or more members of the firm is not resident within the jurisdiction.[15] An order to show cause under the rule relating to such debts must be served on a member of the firm within the jurisdiction, or on some other person having the control or management of the partnership business.[16] Where an order under the rule requires a firm to appear before the court, an appearance by a member of the firm constitutes a sufficient compliance.[17]

INDIVIDUAL CARRYING ON BUSINESS IN ANOTHER NAME

Special provision is made regarding the application of these rules to a person carrying on business in another name. An individual carrying on business within the jurisdiction in a name or style other than his own name may be sued in that name as if it were the name of his firm.[18] Consequently, the writ may be served in the same manner as previously discussed in this chapter unless the individual is resident outside the jurisdiction. In the latter situation these provisions do not apply, and, if the English courts have jurisdiction in the matter, leave to serve the writ abroad will have to be obtained.[19]

---

[13]   Rule 6. For County Courts see CCR Ord 25, r 10.
[14]   *Meyer & Co v Faber (No 2)* [1923] 2 Ch 421.
[15]   Rule 7(1).
[16]   Rule 7(2).
[17]   Rule 7(3).
[18]   Rule 9.
[19]   *De Bernales v New York Herald* [1893] 2 QB 97n; *St Gobain v Hoyermann's Agency* [1893] 2 QB 96; *Taylor Bros & Co Ltd v A Johnson & Co* [1917] WN 341. A Scot resident in Scotland is a foreigner in relation to these provisions: *MacIver v G & J Burns* [1895] 2 Ch 630. Proceedings against foreign residents must therefore be pursued under Ord 11.

APPLICATIONS FOR ORDERS CHARGING PARTNERS INTEREST IN PARTNERSHIP ASSETS

Section 23 of the Partnership Act 1890 has provisions whereby an individual partner's interest in partnership property may be charged.[20] RSC Ord 81, r 10(1) contains provisions with regard to the applicable procedure.[1] Every application to the court by a judgment creditor of a partner for an order under the Partnership Act 1890, s 23, and every application by a partner of the judgment debtor made in consequence of an application made by such a judgment creditor must be made by summons.[2] Every summons issued by a judgment creditor, and every order made on such summons, must be served on the judgment debtor and on such of his partners as are within the jurisdiction.[3] Every summons issued by a partner of a judgment debtor, and every order made on such a summons, must be served (1) on the judgment creditor, (2) on the judgment debtor, and (3) on such of the other partners of the judgment debtor as do not join in the application and are within the jurisdiction.[4] A summons or order served in accordance with the rules on some of the partners is deemed to have been served on all the partners in the partnership.[5]

---

[20] See p 215, below.
[1] It should be noted that the present County Court Rules make no express provision for the applicable procedure for applications under s 23. It is arguable that the RSC provisions are applicable by analogy by virtue of the County Courts Act 1984, s 76. This appears to be the assumption of the *County Court Practice 1988* at p 529.
[2] Rule 10(1).
[3] Rule 10(3).
[4] Rule 10(4).
[5] Rule 10(5).

CHAPTER 8

THE RIGHTS AND DUTIES OF PARTNERS INTER SE

THE RIGHT TO PARTICIPATE IN MANAGEMENT OF THE PARTNERSHIP

Section 24(5) of the Partnership Act 1890 provides that 'every partner may take part in the management of the partnership business.' This statutory recognition of the right of a partner to participate in the management of the partnership business is subject to any actual or implied agreement between the members of a partnership to the contrary. Thus, a partner may by the terms of the partnership agreement be excluded from such participation. However, in the absence of such a contrary agreement the courts are jealous of inferring or sanctioning the exclusion of a partner from the management of the partnership business through any other cause.[1]

Notwithstanding any agreement between partners which may restrict their respective management functions inter se, in the absence of actual notice of this, third parties may deal with all the members of the partnership as if they all carried equal authority to bind the business.[2]

---

[1] See Lord Eldon in *Peacock v Peacock* (1809) 16 Ves 49 at 51. In *Rowe v Wood* (1822) 2 Jac & W 553 the court prevented a partner who was the mortgagee of his co-partner's share of the partnership from exercising his rights as mortgagee during the continuation of the partnership so as to exclude his co-partner from being involved in the management of the business.

[2] See the Partnership Act 1890, ss 5 and 8. It should be noted that it may be unlawful to exclude a partner from the management of the business solely on grounds of sex or race, see Chapter 5.

168

PARTNERSHIP DECISIONS

A partnership agreement should also provide a mechanism for the resolution of disputes between partners in the absence of unanimous agreement, determining, inter alia, the majority required if a resolution or decision is to be approved by the partnership. In the absence of the partnership agreement providing such a procedure for resolving disputes in general, or a particular dispute, s 24(8) of the Partnership Act provides:

> 'Any difference arising as to ordinary matters connected with the partnership business may be decided by a majority of the partners, but no change may be made in the nature of the partnership business without the consent of all existing partners.'

Thus, changes in the type of business carried out by the partners, the admission of a new partner, changes in the partnership deed or agreement, or changes in the structure of the business by the sale of a substantial part of the partnership assets, will in the absence of contrary agreement require unanimity.[3]

Any fundamental change in the partnership business therefore requires the unanimous agreement of the partners.[4]

All other day-to-day decisions, such as the employment of staff, require the approval of only a majority of the partners. What constitutes such day-to-day, ordinary matters for the purposes of s 24(8) must be a question of fact in each case, although it seems that the status of such matters must be determined by reference to the running of the *actual* business in question, rather than by reference to the running of the business in what may be regarded as the 'usual way'.[5]

Even where a business matter may be resolved by a majority

[3] See the words of Lord Lindley in *A-G v Great Northern Rly* (1860) 1 Drew & Sm 154 at 156 in the following vein: 'no majority, however large, can lawfully engage the partnership in matters outside the partnership business against the will of even one dissentient partner.' See also *Nixon v Wood* (1987) 284 Estates Gazette 1055. Note also s 24(7) of the Partnership Act 1890 which governs the admission of a new partner and s 25 which regulates the expulsion of a partner. On the expulsion of a partner see p 179, below.

[4] In the absence of any contrary provision in the partnership agreement: see the Partnership Act 1890, s 19.

[5] Although the courts should, it is suggested, take notice of what may be regarded as ordinary matters and practice within the relevant trade or profession carried on by the partnership in determining whether a matter is an ordinary matter for the partnership in question. Note the case of *Highley v Walker* (1910) 26 TLR 685, where the taking on of one of the partner's son as an apprentice was regarded as an ordinary matter.

decision, by virtue of an agreement between the partners or by s 24(8), the majority must exercise their power to determine such a matter in good faith. Furthermore, the majority must not, in exercising their decision, deprive the minority of their partnership rights, or gain an unfair advantage in the day-to-day running of the business.[6]

Despite s 24(8), if the partners are equally divided on a business matter requiring a decision, the status quo must be maintained.[7]

Where the partnership agreement requires a quorum for a partners' meeting, at which decisions concerning ordinary matters connected with the partners' business may be determined, the necessity for the prescribed quorum to be present at any such duly convened meeting is absolute. Any decision taken at an unquorate partners' meeting concerning any ordinary business matter connected with the partnership business will be invalid.[8]

FIDUCIARY DUTIES

Partners stand in a fiduciary relationship[9] with one another. Thus a partner is under a fiduciary duty vis-à-vis his co-partners and must display the utmost good faith towards them in respect of all partnership dealings, transactions or matters.[10] This fiduciary duty remains, though the relationship of the partners may be deteriorating, and the partnership is ripe for dissolution.[11] If, however, a partner is made fully aware of an act by one or more of his co-

---

6 See *Highley v Walker* (1910) 26 TLR 685. In the case of *Const v Harris* (1824) Turn & R 496 at 525 Lord Eldon observed the following: 'For a majority of partners to say, We do not care what one partner may say, we, being the majority, will do what we please is, I apprehend, what this Court will not allow.'

7 *Donaldson v Williams* (1833) 1 Cr & M 345; *Clements v Norris* (1878) 8 Ch D 129; *Harris v Black* (1983) 46 P & Cr 366.

8 *Re London and Southern Counties Freehold Land Co* (1885) 31 Ch D 223; *Howbeach Coal Co v Teague* (1860) 5 H & N 151.

9 Such a fiduciary relationship also arises between parties who are negotiating entry into a partnership or where the full terms of the partnership agreement have not been agreed; see *United Dominions Corpn Ltd v Brian Pty Ltd* (1985) 60 ALR 741; *Fraser Edmiston Pty Ltd v AGT (Qld) Pty Ltd* [1988] 2 Qd R 1; *Floydd v Cheney* [1970] Ch 602.

10 *Blissett v Daniel* (1853) 10 Hare 493; *Maddeford v Austwick* (1826) 1 Sim 89; *Law v Law* [1905] 1 Ch 140. The duty extends to honesty in dealings with third parties, in so far as such dealings may affect the partnership: see *Carmichael v Evans* [1904] 1 Ch 486.

11 *Floydd and Cheney* [1970] Ch 602. Although the existence of a partnership was not unambiguously established in the case the duty of good faith, which included the duty not to disclose confidential information, was recognised by the court.

partners which is a breach of the partner(s) fiduciary duty to him, and he nevertheless elects to affirm the partnership, he will be estopped from denying the continued existence of the partnership. Furthermore, the co-partner(s) may treat the partnership agreement as still binding inter se.[12]

The existence of a fiduciary relationship between partners is therefore dependent on the mutual recognition by all the members of a partnership of the obligations such a relationship imposes inter se. Partners must be willing to recognise the continuing existence of this relationship, until a partner repudiates the partnership or refuses to accept the status of his co-partners.[13] From the moment of repudiation a partner cannot demand from his former co-partner(s) the performance of any fiduciary duty in his favour which would have been owed to him during the subsistence of the partnership.[14]

The full nature of a fiduciary relationship, the situations where it may be imposed upon parties, and a consideration of the duties such a relationship engenders are outside the scope of this work. Reference should therefore be made to the standard works on the rules and principles of equity.[15] Nevertheless, the Partnership Act 1890 refers to particular matters which can only be regarded as aspects of the fiduciary duties noted above, and which are imposed upon a partner by virtue of the Act. The first such duty or general obligation is prescribed by s 28 of the Partnership Act 1890, which provides that:

'Partners are bound to render true accounts and full information of all things affecting the partnership to any partner or his legal representatives.'

This provision may be regarded as imposing upon a partner the duty of utmost good faith to make honest and full disclosure of all matters relevant to the partnership business to his co-partners or their representatives.

The fiduciary duty remains imposed upon the partners although the partnership is in dissolution. Thus, in such cases the partners must co-operate to ensure the just and equitable distribution of partnership assets: see *Chan v Zacharia* (1984) 154 CLR 178.

[12] *Law v Law* [1905] 1 Ch 140; *Peyman v Lanjani* [1985] Ch 457.

[13] *Dale v Hamilton* (1847) 2 Ph 266.

[14] *Abbatt v Treasury Solicitor* [1969] 1 WLR 1575; *Const v Harris* (1824) Turn & R 494, per Lord Eldon at 524; *McClure v Ripley* (1850) 2 Mac & G 274; *Reilly v Walsh* (1848) 11 1 Eq R 22; *A Akman & Son (Fla) Inc v Chipman* (1988) 45 DLR (4th) 481.

[15] See Snell *Principles of the Rules of Equity.*

This statutory duty would appear to codify the general duty of good faith considered above, and to apply it to partners as regards their dealings inter se. It must be emphasised that this statutory duty is strict. A partner may therefore breach this duty although his failure to comply with the provision is in no way fraudulent, or even negligent.[16] The section thus recognises that a partnership relationship is one of *uberrimae fidei*. Since the duty applies to 'all things affecting the partnership' it is imposed upon a partner, eg when he seeks to buy and ultimately buys out a co-partner's share in the business.[17]

Accountability of partners for private profits

Section 29 imposes an obligation upon a partner not to derive a personal benefit at the expense of his co-partners and provides that:

> 'Every partner must account to the firm for any benefit derived by him without the consent of the other partners from any transaction concerning the partnership, or from any use by him of the partnership property, name or business connection.
>
> This section applies also to transactions undertaken after a partnership has been dissolved by the death of a partner, and before the affairs thereof have been completely wound up, either by any surviving partner or by the representatives of the deceased partner.'

The rules of equity prohibit a trustee or an office holder, who are both under a fiduciary duty to third parties, from making a profit from their office. Section 29 of the Partnership Act ensures that there is no doubt that an equivalent duty is imposed upon a partner. It would seem that the duty recognised by s 29 is a strict one: any profit obtained, however innocently, by a partner's 'use of the business connection' within the terms of s 29 will render him liable to account for that profit to his co-partners. A partner may only keep such a profit if he has the full consent of his co-partners so to do. Furthermore, in order to do so he must make full and

---

[16] *Winsor v Schroeder* (1979) 129 NLJ 1266.
[17] In the case of *Law v Law* [1905] 1 Ch 140, Cozens Hardy LJ at 157 expressed the law thus: 'Now it is clear law that, in a transaction between copartners for the sale by one to the other of a share in the partnership business, there is a duty resting upon the purchaser who knows, and is aware that he knows, more about the partnership accounts than the vendor, to put the vendor in possession of all material facts with reference to the partnership assets, and not to conceal what he alone knows.'

frank disclosure to his co-partners of all relevant facts relating to the acquisition of the profit before the co-partners can be said to be in a position to give their consent.[18] Thus in *Dunne v English*[19] it was held that an agent for sale who took an interest in a purchase he negotiated on behalf of his principal was bound to disclose to the latter the exact nature of his interest, viz the extent and amount of expenses and fees retained by him in executing the purchase. It was not enough for the agent to disclose that he had an interest in the transaction. It was for the agent to establish that he had made full and frank disclosure.

Secret profit

Section 29 clearly prohibits a partner from obtaining a secret profit from the buying of property from, or the selling of property to, the partnership business. The most celebrated case which illustrates this aspect of s 29, although it predates the Partnership Act, is *Bentley v Craven*.[20] C was a member of a four-partner firm involved in the sugar business. He was the firm's buyer, and could obtain sugar at a discount on the market price. He purchased sugar at a discount, but sold it to the partnership at market price. He retained the difference. The co-partners, on discovering this practice, successfully recovered C's profits from his dealings carried out on behalf of the partnership.

Use of partnership assets by a partner for personal benefit

The unauthorised use of a partnership asset, which includes the partnership business name, by a partner for personal benefit or the realisation of a profit will render that partner liable to account for any such profits made to his co-partners.[1]

An individual may continue to run a business in which he was formerly a partner. If, in doing so, he utilises what was the firm's

[18] See *Dunne v English* (1874) LR 18 Eq 524; *Imperial Mercantile Credit Association v Coleman* (1871) 6 Ch App 558. Even where a partnership asset is sold by a partner on behalf of the partnership at a price greater than that authorised by the partnership, the co-partners are entitled to their respective share of the extra profit gained.
[19] See fn 18, above.
[20] (1853) 18 Beav 75.
[1] *Benson v Heathorn* (1842) 1 Y & C Ch Cas 326; *Burton v Wookey* (1822) 6 Madd 367; *Williamson v Hine* [1891] 1 Ch 390.

assets or business connections in order to realise a profit, he must account for that profit to his former co-partner(s).[2]

Partnership property

The rules of equity have determined that where a trustee holds trust property which includes a lease as part of the trust property and he acquires a renewal of such a lease for his own benefit, he must hold that lease as a constructive trustee, for the benefit of the beneficiaries of the original trust.[3] The same rule has been applied to cases where a partner has obtained the renewal of a lease which was partnership property and where he did so solely in his own name, by the use of his partnership position and in breach of his fiduciary duties.[4]

It is irrelevant whether the partner in such cases seeks to obtain a renewal of the partnership lease for his own benefit in a clandestine manner, or with his giving notice of his intended acquisition to his co-partners. If the obtaining is by the use of his partnership position and in breach of his fiduciary duties, he will be deemed to hold such property for the benefit of his co-partners.[5]

Conversely, where a partner obtains a renewal of a lease owned by the partnership, he cannot compel his co-partners to accept the renewed lease as a partnership asset, unless he acquired the property with their authority, or the co-partners affirm the acquisition.[6]

Whether a partner who obtains the *reversion* of a lease which is partnership property will be regarded as holding such a reversion as

---

[2] In *Pathirana v Pathirana* [1967] 1 AC 233 the partners ran a petrol service business. The partnership was dissolved. Before the expiration of the notice of dissolution, the defendant obtained a *renewal* of a number of petrol supply agreements in his sole name. He then continued in the petrol service business as a sole trader in his own name, and from the former business premises of the partnership. He was held accountable to his former co-partner for a share of the profits which could be attributed to the renewed petrol supply agreements.

[3] See *Keech v Sandford* [1726] Cas temp King 61.

[4] Whether the partner has so obtained the renewal of a lease which was formerly partnership property and whether he is in breach of his fiduciary duties is, of course, a question of fact; see *Re Biss* [1903] 2 Ch 40. See also *Featherstonhaugh v Fenwick* (1810) 17 Ves 298; *Clegg v Fishwick* (1849) 1 Mac & G 294; *Clements v Hall* (1858) 2 De G & J 173; *Burdon v Barkus* (1862) 4 De G F & J 42; *Chan v Zacharia* (1984) 154 CLR 178.

[5] See *Clegg v Edmondson* (1857) 8 De GM & G 787. In this case the partners were denied the relief they sought on the ground of laches. For an outline discussion of the doctrine of laches see Prime and Scanlan *The Modern Law of Limitation* (1993) Chapter 13.

[6] *Clements v Norris* (1878) 8 Ch D 129.

trustee for his co-partners is not entirely clear.[7] In *Bevan v Webb*[8] the partner acquired a reversion of a lease which was partnership property in good faith and honestly, though for his own benefit. The court found that the obtaining of the reversion had not been by virtue of his interest in the lease as a partner *and* that the lease was *not* renewable either by custom or contract. In such circumstances the defendant was not regarded as holding the reversion as a trustee for the benefit of his co-partners.[9]

By way of contrast is *Thompson's Trustee v Heaton*.[10] In this case Pennycuick V-C[11] held that a reversion of a lease, the lease being an undistributed partnership asset after the dissolution of the partnership, could not be acquired by any one partner for his own benefit, without his co-partners being first given the opportunity to acquire the reversion jointly.[12] Accordingly, this case appears to apply a general prohibition upon a partner obtaining a reversion on a lease where the lease is a partnership asset. Although the present situation is not entirely free from doubt, the *Thompson* case probably represents current judicial thought. Furthermore, the case has the merit of consistency of approach with other recent authorities,[13] which concern the unauthorised acquisition of partnership assets, or the making of a secret profit by a partner of a business.

Unauthorised secret profit by the use of information gained as a partner

A partner may gain information and business connections through his involvement in a partnership. If the partner then uses such information or connections for his own benefit, in order to make a secret profit, he may be liable to account for any such profit to his

7 For cases where trustees have obtained the reversion of a lease which is trust property, see *Prothereo v Prothereo* [1968] 1 WLR 519 and cases cited therein.
8 [1905] 1 Ch 620.
9 See also *Brenner v Rose* [1973] 1 WLR 443. The effect of statute, which may empower a lessee to renew a lease, must be considered in this context. See the Landlord and Tenant Act 1954; *Griffith v Owen* [1907] 1 Ch 195.
10 [1974] 1 WLR 605; see also *Wicks v Bennet* (1921) 30 CLR 80; *Protheroe v Protheroe* [1968] 1 WLR 519.
11 Applying *Protheroe v Protheroe* [1968] 1 WLR 519.
12 A partner may, presumably, enjoy an unemcumbered interest in a reversion of a partnership lease where, subsequent to the acquisition, his co-partners in full knowledge of the circumstances of acquisition consent to or affirm the acquisition.
13 *Protheroe v Protheroe* [1968] 1 WLR 519; *Chan v Zacharia* (1984) 154 CLR 178; *Regal (Hastings) Ltd v Gulliver* [1942] 1 All ER 378.

co-partners.[14] It would seem, however, that if the secret profit is generated by the partner's involvement in a transaction which is outside the scope of the partnership business, then the partner may be able to retain any secret profit he has made from that transaction, notwithstanding that he has utilised information or business connections gained from his involvement in the partnership.[15] Thus, in *Aas v Benham*[16] a partner in a firm of shipbrokers used information acquired during his involvement in the partnership business in setting up a ship-building company. He received remuneration from this company and a salaried directorship. A claim by his co-partners for an account of these benefits failed. The basis of the decision was that the company business, and therefore the partner's transactions with the company, were outside the scope of the partnership's business. However, subsequent cases, and in particular *Boardman v Phipps*,[17] determine that persons who hold a fiduciary position and who use information or connections gained from that position in order to make a secret profit, must account for any such profit to the persons to whom the corresponding fiduciary duties are owed. If such authority is applied to partners and their co-partners unreservedly, then the status of *Aas v Benham* would appear to be questionable. It is therefore advisable for a partner who uses any information, or business connection derived from his involvement in the partnership business, in a transaction unrelated to the partnership business and from which he makes a profit, to disclose in full the nature of that transaction to his co-partners and to seek their consent to his actions. Such a disclosure should preferably be made by the partner to his co-partners before the former engages in any transaction of the kind noted above. With such disclosure of and subsequent consent to the transaction by the co-partners, the partner may then retain the profits realised from his involvement in such a transaction. Because disclosure is made, the retention by a partner of profits earned by him in the circumstances noted above will not be dependent upon the questionable and narrowly legalistic issue of whether the transaction which generated the profits was outside or within the scope of the partnership business of which he is or was a member.[18]

---

[14] *Boardman v Phipps* [1967] 2 AC 46; *Regal (Hastings) Ltd v Gulliver* [1942] 1 All ER 378; *Industrial Development Consultants Ltd v Cooley* [1972] 1 WLR 443; *Seagar v Copydex (No 2)* [1969] 1 WLR 809.

[15] *Aas v Benham* [1891] 2 Ch 244; *Re Coffey's Registered Designs* [1982] FSR 227.

[16] See fn 15.

[17] [1967] 2 AC 46. The authorities alluded to in the text have involved trustees, company directors and, as in the case of *Boardman*, a solicitor.

[18] See *Pathirana v Pathirana* [1967] 1 AC 233 and the Partnership Act 1890, s 29(2).

Conflict of duty and interest

A partner must not place himself in a position where his duty to his co-partners conflicts with his own private interests. Section 30 of the Partnership Act 1890 provides that:

'If a partner, without the consent of the other partners, carries on any business of the same nature as and competing with that of the firm, he must account for and pay over to the firm all profits made by him in that business.'

By this provision a partner who, without the fully informed consent of his co-partners, engages in a business which is in *competition* with that of the partnership must account to his co-partners for any profits he derives from that competitive business.[19] Whether such an enterprise is in competition with the partnership business is a question of fact, and will depend upon the scope of the partnership business.[20] Where the business in which the partner is engaged is not in competition with the partnership business he will not in general be liable to account to his co-partners for any profits he has made thereby.[1] However, where a partner is under an obligation by virtue of a provision in the partnership agreement or deed to devote himself full time to the furtherance of the partnership business, his involvement in another enterprise may render him liable to an action by his co-partners for breach of covenant.[2]

As a corollary to the above, where a partner in a business is only able to carry on another *non-competing* business by virtue of his involvement or connection with the partnership, he may be liable to account for any profits he may make from the other business to his co-partners. Such liability to account is founded on the duty of a partner not to carry on an enterprise which is derived from the partnership and arises because of his connection with it. In such

---

[19] *Glassington v Thwaites* (1823) 1 Sim & St 124; *England v Curling* (1844) 8 Beav 129.
[20] See *Aas v Benham* [1891] 2 Ch 244 noted above, for a consideration of the concept of the scope of a business. See also *Dean v Macdowell* (1878) 8 Ch D 345.
[1] See *Aas v Benham* [1891] 2 Ch 244.
[2] *Grimston v Cuningham* [1894] 1 QB 125; *Davis v Foreman* [1894] 3 Ch 654; *Kirchner & Co v Gruban* [1909] 1 Ch 413; *Hill v CA Parsons & Co Ltd* [1972] Ch 305. There is no statutory or common law obligation imposed upon a partner to devote himself full time to the affairs of a partnership. Even when a partner devotes more time to partnership affairs than his co-partners, he is not entitled thereby to a greater reward or remuneration than the other members of the partnership in the absence of a provision to that effect in the partnership agreement: see the Partnership Act 1890, s 24(6).

cases the partner may not be carrying out his duties as a partner in the best interests of the partnership.[3]

INTRODUCTION OF NEW PARTNERS

The introduction of a new partner into a partnership is not regarded by the Partnership Act 1890 as an 'ordinary matter' of business.[4] Accordingly, in the absence of an express provision in the partnership deed or agreement, the introduction of a partner into a partnership cannot be determined by a simple or qualified majority of the existing partners. Section 24(7) of the Partnership Act provides that, in the absence of any such express provision in the partnership deed governing the admission of partners: 'No person may be introduced as a partner without the consent of all existing partners.'

A clause within a partnership deed or agreement may not only prescribe the procedure for the admission of a partner, but it may also restrict the class of persons who may be admitted to the partnership.[5] The partnership agreement may also prescribe conditions upon the entry of a potential partner, which must be satisfied before he can be validly nominated or introduced as a partner to the business.[6] Partners may be given an absolute or qualified veto on the admission of new partners.

A person may, therefore, be nominated as a new partner to a business within the provisions of the relevant partnership deed or agreement by one of the existing partners. If all conditions for entry to the partnership have been complied with, the nominee is regarded as a partner in equity.[7] The nominee may therefore be regarded as a beneficiary under a trust, the partners of the business being the trustees and the business enterprise being the trust property. If a nominee in such a case then finds that his existing partners refuse to recognise him as a partner, or to admit him to the business, he may seek recourse to the equitable remedy of specific performance of the

[3] *Russell v Austwick* (1826) 1 Sim 52.
[4] See s 24(8) of the Partnership Act 1890, which refers to ordinary matters of business and which is considered above.
[5] But see Chapter 5, where the issue of unlawful discrimination is considered within the context of partnerships.
[6] See, eg *Byrne v Reid* [1902] 2 Ch 735. The procedures and conditions governing the admission of partners may thus be a matter entirely for the agreement of the parties as evidenced by provision in the partnership agreement: see the Partnership Act 1890, s 19.
[7] *Page v Cox* (1852) 10 Hare 163.

trust. This will compel his potential co-partners to execute and become parties with him to any deeds or agreements which would formally constitute him a partner in the business, and which may vest in him his share of the partnership assets.

The nominee must in such cases establish that he has been validly nominated by an existing partner, and that the nomination is unconditional, or that any conditions which would apply to the nomination by virtue of the partnership agreement have been satisfied.[8]

Of course, if a nominee is himself a party to a contract admitting him to a partnership, he may, if he has provided consideration, seek specific performance of the agreement on the basis of his contractual rights, and is not reliant on any trust which may exist in his favour.

EXPULSION OF A PARTNER

In the absence of an express clause in the partnership deed or agreement, a partner may not be expelled from the partnership. This principle is enshrined in s 25 of the Partnership Act 1890.[9]

An expulsion of a partner may also involve a dissolution of the partnership;[10] such a consequence is inevitable where a partner expels his sole partner from the business. Although it has been suggested that an express expulsion clause in a partnership deed or agreement cannot stand where the relevant partnership is a partnership at will,[11] this principle would seem to be limited to partnerships at will which consist of only two partners.[12] Such partnerships can in any event be dissolved by notice.

---

[8] For a consideration of what constitues a valid nomination, see *Martin v Thompson* (1962) SC (HL) 28 and *Page v Cox* (1852) 10 Hare 163. For the need to satisfy conditions imposed upon a nomination, see *Re Franklin and Swaythling's Arbitration* [1929] 1 Ch 238. In the latter case the condition was that the introduction of a suitably qualified person as a new partner by an existing partner required that the other partners should consent to the admission. Such consent was not forthcoming. The relevant clause in the partnership agreement provided that such consent should not be unreasonably withheld.

[9] Section 25 provides that no majority of the partners can expel any partner unless a power to do so has been conferred by express agreement between the partners.

[10] For a consideration of the nature of a dissolution of a partnership see Chapter 12.

[11] *Clark v Leach* (1863) 1 De GJ & SM 409.

[12] See *Walters v Bingham* [1988] 1 FTLR 260 where, although the partnership was one at will, it was nevertheless a large partnership. The judge held an express expulsion clause was not inconsistent with such a partnership, as expulsion was (in such a case) fundamentally different from a dissolution.

In considering the effect and application of an expulsion clause in a partnership agreement the courts will have regard to the following matters.

Is the expulsion within the terms of the clause?

An expulsion clause will set out the terms upon which a partner may be expelled from the partnership. Where the partnership is a professional practice, the grounds of expulsion set out in the partnership agreement will frequently be drafted in terms of the professional misconduct of a partner. In such circumstances, misconduct by a partner which is unrelated to the partnership business or practice, and which does not affect the running or standing of the partnership, will generally not constitute grounds for expulsion.[13]

In general, an expulsion clause in a partnership agreement will be construed strictly and literally in any litigation. However, if its adoption in a particular case would lead to manifest and absurd results, a restrictive literal approach will be rejected by the courts.[14]

The need to comply with the rules of natural justice

The expulsion of a partner from a partnership is a procedure which has serious consequences for the expelled partner. On this basis it would be a reasonable requirement that the expulsion procedure prescribed in the partnership agreement should follow the rules of natural justice. The courts have considered the application of the rules of natural justice to the procedure of expulsion principally in the context of supplying the partner to be expelled with the full and precise grounds for the proposed expulsion, together with an opportunity to contest such grounds. In *Barnes v Young*[15] the court held the expulsion of a partner unlawful, on the basis that he had not

---

[13] An expulsion clause in a partnership agreement will be construed against the person relying on it. See *Re a Solicitor's Arbitration* [1962] 1 All ER 772 where the power to expel a partner was given to the *other partners*. The court held that the clause as drafted excluded the interpretation of the term 'partners' as including the singular partner. Accordingly, a partner could not use the clause to expel his partners from the partnership.

[14] In *Hitchman v Crouch Butler Savage Associates* (1983) 127 Sol Jo 441 the expulsion clause required that the signature of the senior partner be appended to the notice of expulsion in order for the expulsion to be valid. Where the other partners sought to expel the senior partner under the aegis of the clause, the courts dispensed with the need for the notice to be so signed.

[15] [1898] 1 Ch 414.

been fully informed of the grounds for his expulsion. However, later authority has substantially rejected this approach. In *Green v Howell*[16] and *Peyton v Mindham*[17] the courts regarded the procedure for expulsion of a partner as administrative, and not judicial or quasi judicial in nature.[18] This aspect of the law is therefore in an uncertain state at present. Clearly the partner(s) seeking expulsion of a co-partner must in exercising such a power act in good faith.[19] It would also be advisable, until the law is conclusively settled, to supply the partner to be expelled with the grounds upon which the expulsion is sought, together with an opportunity to contest such grounds.

The requirement of good faith

A partner, or a majority of partners, in seeking to expel a co-partner(s) must exercise such a power in good faith. Accordingly, in exercising the power of expulsion of a co-partner, partners must do so for the benefit of the partnership as a whole and not for personal benefit. Partners must not place themselves, by the exercise of the power of expulsion, in a position where their duties as partners conflict with their individual interests. The expulsion of a partner must not be sought by the other partners in order that the latter may obtain the expelled partner's share of the business at a discount.[20] Such an expulsion will be invalid since it places the expelled partner in a disadvantageous position in relation to his former partners. The power to expel must be used for its intended purposes, and not to facilitate a gain for the majority partners at the expense of the expelled partner(s).[1]

The courts, however, do not always clearly distinguish between the duty of partners to act in good faith while exercising a power of expulsion from the requirement that they should also in such cases

---

16 [1910] 1 Ch 495.

17 [1972] 1 WLR 8; see also (1969) 35 Conv (NS) 32 B Davies.

18 In *Green v Howell* [1910] 1 Ch 495 the court held that the prescribed expulsion procedure need not observe the rules of natural justice, since the partner seeking expulsion had acted in good faith. It may be submitted that *Green v Howell* and *Peyton v Mindham* may be distinguished from *Barnes v Young* on the basis that the former cases involved two partner firms. Accordingly, the expulsion procedure in each case was a de facto dissolution of the partnership and not a true expulsion.

19 For the requirement of a partner to act in good faith, see fn 18 above.

20 *Bissett v Daniel* (1853) 10 Hare 493.

1 *Walters v Bingham* [1988] 1 FTLR 260.

observe the rules of natural justice. In *Kerr v Morris*[2] Dillon LJ defined the duty of good faith in the following vein:[3]

> 'Prima facie it may be said, therefore, with some force that, if the other partners are giving the defendant notice of expulsion, they must specify a reason for giving it . . . which must prima facie be a reasonable reason . . . So it may well be that, apart from the question whether they were bound to afford him a hearing . . . the question . . . will come down to whether they were justified in their honest belief that the trust necessary between partners had been breached by the defendant.'

Such a judicial view lends considerable force to an argument that, in expelling a partner, the other partners should always seek to apply the rules of natural justice to the expulsion procedure.[4]

Where partners have satisfied the above requirements in seeking the expulsion of a co-partner(s), the courts will endorse any such expulsion.[5]

ASSIGNMENT OF PARTNERSHIP SHARE

An assignment of a partnership *share*, in the absence of contrary agreement between the parties to the assignment and the partners, does not make the assignee a partner in the business. The effect of such an assignment is generally to vest in the assignee the assignor's right to his share of the partnership's assets and the right to partic-ipate in a share of the profits.[6] Assignments may be voluntary, and may be part of a commercial transaction which involves pledging the partnership share as security. Assignments may also be invol-untary where, eg a judgment creditor wishes to levy execution against a partner for the latter's private debts. These two forms of assignment will be considered in turn.

---

[2] [1987] Ch 90.
[3] At 111.
[4] With the possible exception where the partnership is a two-man partnership and the expulsion is tantamount to a dissolution.
[5] See *Carmichael v Evans* [1904] 1 Ch 486.
[6] A partner has a 'beneficial interest' in the *entirety* of the partnership assets and may enforce such an 'interest' against his co-partners to the extent that he can ensure that the partnership assets are used for the benefit of the partnership. Such an interest is in fact a personal right which is inherent in the office of partner. A partner cannot assign this personal right to a third party, *Hadlee & Sydney Bridge Nominees v IRC* [1993] NPC 40. However, he may assign his right to his share in the partnership assets.

Voluntary assignment

The rights of an assignee under a voluntary assignment of a partnership share where the partnership is a going concern are set out in s 31 of the Partnership Act 1890. The section provides that:

'An assignment by any partner of his share in the partnership, either absolute or by way of mortgage or redeemable charge, does not, as against the other partners, entitle the assignee, during the continuance of the partnership, to interfere in the management or administration of the partnership business or affairs, or to require any accounts of the partnership transactions, or to inspect the partnership books, but entitles the assignee only to receive the share of profits to which the assigning partner would otherwise be entitled, and the assignee must accept the account of profits agreed to by the partners.'

The rights of an assignee of a partnership share as regards any involvement in the day-to-day running of the partnership are therefore severely restricted. An assignee has a right to any profits which would have accrued to the assignor; but he has no control over the partnership assets per se. In receiving the share of profits he is obliged to accept the partner's accounts which determine such profits unreservedly.

If partners in good faith alter the profit-sharing ratios of their business, any assignee of a partnership share may receive a lesser share of the profits of the business than he would otherwise have obtained. Although not entirely free from doubt, it seems that such an arrangement – eg by increasing salary payments to partners with a corresponding reduction of profits that would otherwise be available for distribution in respect of each partnership share – cannot be questioned by an assignee of a partnership share.[7] Such an arrangement could, it is suggested, be questioned by an assignee of a partnership share, where the arrangement was improper, fraudulent, or designed solely to reduce the amount of profits otherwise payable to the assignee.

---

[7] In *Re Garwood's Trusts* [1903] 1 Ch 236 the partners received salaries as part of a new arrangement for the partners to take a supervisory role in the business in order to stop pilfering. Such an arrangement may be said to be a management decision based on good faith. It would reduce thefts from the business and, in the long term, increase profits. This appeared to be the basis of the court's decision that the assignee of a partnership share had therefore to accept the reduced profits disclosed by the partner's accounts.

Where the partnership is in dissolution, the position of an assignee of a partnership share is governed by s 31(2) of the Partnership Act 1890 which provides that:

> 'In case of a dissolution of the partnership, whether as respects all the partners or as respects the assigning partner, the assignee is entitled to receive the share of the partnership assets to which the assigning partner is entitled as between himself and the other partners, and, for the purpose of ascertaining that share, to an account as from the date of dissolution.'

Irrespective of whether the assigning partner is leaving the partnership and removing his share of the assets from the business or whether the partnership as a whole is being dissolved, an assignee has certain rights. The assignee retains, in either of the above cases, a right to the assigning partner's share, together with a right to an account quantifying the value of the partnership share vested in him. In the absence of such an account, the partners cannot impose upon the assignee any financial arrangement they may have agreed amongst themselves which purports to place a value on partnership assets. In *Watts v Driscoll*[8] a father advanced a loan to his son in order that the latter could enter into a partnership. The enterprise was not a success, and the son sold his share of the partnership to his co-partner at a mutually agreed price. In essence this action amounted to a dissolution. The father had taken an assignment of his son's partnership share as security for the loan. The Court of Appeal endorsed the father's argument that the agreed sale price between the son and his former partner did not constitute a valuation of the son's share and could not bind the father. The latter was entitled to an account within the terms of s 31(2) so as to ascertain a true valuation of his son's partnership share. It would seem that such an account need only be taken on behalf of an assignee in the normal course of the partnership business in good faith and on the footing that the partnership is a going concern. The account so taken must give due regard to the rights of the party seeking the account, ie the account must be taken in good faith.[9]

---

[8]   [1901] 1 Ch 294.

[9]   See also *Bonnin v Neame* [1910] 1 Ch 732, where the court held that assignees were not bound by an arbitration agreement in the partnership deed which the partners sought to use to resolve disputes as to valuation of partnership assets upon the dissolution of the partnership.

An assignee of a partnership share will not be held responsible for partnership losses.[10]

Involuntary assignments

Section 23(1) of the Partnership Act 1890 provides that a private creditor of a partner may not enforce a judgment for any private debt(s) incurred by such a partner in his personal capacity against partnership property.[11] Execution against partnership assets is a remedy only available to creditors of the partnership. However, s 23(2) provides that:

'The High Court, or a judge thereof . . . (a) or a county court may, on the application by summons of any judgment creditor of a partner, make an order charging that partner's interest in the partnership property and profits with payment of the amount of the judgment debt and interest thereon, and may by the same or a subsequent order appoint a receiver of that partner's share of profits (whether already declared or accruing), and of any other money which may be coming to him in respect of the partnership, and direct all accounts and inquiries, and give all other orders and directions which might have been directed or given if the charge had been made in favour of the judgment creditor by the partner, or which the circumstances of the case may require.'

The effect of this provision is that a private creditor of a partner can, after obtaining judgment in respect of a private debt, ask the court to make him for all practical purposes the assignee of the debtor partner's share in the partnership. Such an assignee may also ask the court to appoint a receiver under and within the terms of the subsection. Such a receiver, however, has no right to involve himself in the running of the partnership. The courts have construed s 23(2) very strictly, and against the interests of the private debt judgment creditor. Thus, there is a clear burden of proof imposed upon the judgment creditor to establish that the assets are partnership assets and not the personal and private assets of a partner, whether the assets are those of the debtor partner or another partner. In such cases the partners must be given a chance to interplead in any proceedings where an order under the subsection is sought, or where a

[10] Subject to being held out as a partner see Chapter 6 and the Partnership Act 1890, s 14. See also *Dodson v Downey* [1901] 2 Ch 620 which suggests the contrary sed quaere?
[11] Section 23(1).

party is seeking execution against the disputed assets. *Only* if the assets are determined as being solely the assets of the debtor partner can execution be levied. Conversely, if the assets are determined as partnership assets, s 23(1) prevents execution against those assets by a judgment creditor seeking enforcement of a judgment against a partner for private debt.[12] If the court, however, finds that the assets are partnership assets it must make an enquiry under s 23(2) to determine, inter alia, the debtor partner's share in such assets. The court can then make an order under s 23(2), charging a debtor partner's interest in the partnership assets with payment of the amount of the private judgment debt and interest thereon. The courts will not, however, automatically make in addition to such an order an order for an account.[13] Such an order will, it appears, only be made in exceptional circumstances.[14]

If the innocent partner(s) wish to object to the imposition of a charge against the partnership assets under s 23(2) they have recourse to two procedures. First, by virtue of s 23(3) they may redeem at any time the interest charged or, in the case of a sale of the assets being directed by the court, they may purchase the same.[15]

The second and more drastic remedy would be to dissolve the partnership under s 33(2) of the Partnership Act 1890. Such a procedure would, however, end a potentially profitable business enterprise and render s 23(2) redundant, which as a provision was intended to enable a thriving partnership to survive the private insolvency or financial embarrassment of a partner.

---

[12] Neither can execution be levied in such cases if the assets are determined as being the sole assets of an innocent partner: see *Peake v Carter* [1916] 1 KB 652.

[13] See *Brown Janson & Co v Hutchinson (No 2)* [1895] 2 QB 126. The justification in denying an involuntary assignee an automatic right to account seems based on the principle that such an assignee is in a similar position to an assignee under a voluntary assignment under s 31(1) of the Act. Such voluntary assignees have no right to demand that the partners make an account in respect of the partnership assets.

[14] See fn 13, above.

[15] If the partners elect to purchase the debtor partner's partnership share they must seek to avoid a conflict of interest. See s 28 of the Partnership Act 1890. Thus, the partners should seek to purchase such assets only after they have obtained an independent valuation of those assets. Furthermore, partnership money should not be used to purchase the share.

CHAPTER 9

PARTNERSHIP PROPERTY

INTRODUCTION

Since the liability of partners for partnership debts and obligations is unlimited, it might be thought that there is little need to identify and consider partnership property as a separate entity. In fact, however, whether or not particular property is or is not partnership property may be of great importance. First, partnership property is the property of the firm, and must be only used for the firm's purposes and in accordance with the underlying partnership agreement. Second, if a firm is dissolved, each individual partner is entitled to have the partnership property applied in payment of the debts and liabilities of the firm, and to have any surplus applied to meet what is due to the individual partners.[1] Third, partnership property and the individual assets of the partners are available to meet the separate claims which may exist against the firm and the individual partners in accordance with set priorities.[2] Fourth, in the absence of an intention that it should be held differently, land owned by the partnership is subject to the doctrine of conversion, although it does not pass by right of survivorship.[3] Fifth, if an asset increases in value, the extra value is owned by the firm if the asset is partnership property, but otherwise the increase will accrue to the individual partner who owns the particular asset. On the other hand, if property is owned by an individual partner, who merely allows the partnership to use it, and the property is sold, the proceeds belong to the partner/owner.[4] Equally, if compensation were

---

[1] Pursuant to s 39. This may have the effect of enriching particular partners at the expense of others: see, eg *Robinson v Ashton* (1875) LR 20 Eq 25.

[2] See Chapter 13, p 321, below.

[3] See p 212, below.

[4] Per Warrington J in *Bevan v Webb* [1905] 1 Ch 620 at 631; *Burdon v Barkus* (1861) 3 Giff 412; affd (1862) 4 De G F & J 42.

payable in respect of the property in such circumstances it would also belong to him alone.[5]

It follows necessarily, therefore, that in any given situation it may be of the utmost importance to identify whether or not particular items of property are in fact partnership property.

PARTNERSHIP PROPERTY AND ASSETS WITHIN THE BUSINESS – AN IMPORTANT DISTINCTION

It might be thought that all assets used by the partnership would be partnership property. This is, however, not the case. First, an individual partner may allow the partnership to have the use of specific property without parting with the ownership of the property concerned. In such a case the partner remains the owner of the property, the partnership having at most the right to use the property for the duration of the partnership.[6] Second, it frequently happens that partners may not draw out all the profits accruing to them in any particular year. The profits left in the business will be part of the assets used by the business, but will not lose their character of undrawn profits unless the partners concerned capitalise them by choosing to add them to the partnership property. In the absence of such a decision the accumulated sums may be withdrawn by the partners concerned at any time as undrawn profits.[7] Finally, the assets within the business may include sums of money lent by a partner to the firm, which will not lose its character as a loan simply because its source was a partner.[8]

In short, whether or not property is or is not partnership property is an issue determined by the intention of the partners and the agreements which they made. The partnership property is the capital which the individual partners have agreed to make available for this purpose.

---

[5] *Campbell v Mullett* (1819) 2 Swan 551.

[6] See Chapter 1, p 18, above.

[7] It may, of course, be commercial disaster for the firm if large sums of undrawn profits have accumulated and are suddenly withdrawn by the partners entitled, since their presence may have disguised the need for further capital.

[8] This of course is a different situation to that which arises when a partner has borrowed money as a means of raising his capital contribution to the partnership. The proceeds of his loan are dedicated by him as partnership property, and no issue arises because of the source of the funds.

Increase and reduction of capital

Since the capital of the firm is its life blood and its size and contribution depends on the agreement of the partners, there is a clear rule that, in the absence of contrary agreement, the capital of the firm can be neither increased nor reduced without the consent of every partner.[9] This is so even where the capital of the business has been exhausted and the firm cannot continue without a further injection of capital. Equally, if no partner can be compelled to contribute to the partnership capital beyond the sum which he has agreed, neither can he withdraw any part of his capital so long as he remains a partner.[10]

Interest on capital

A further point which makes the distinction between partnership property and other assets within the partnership important is that interest may be payable on the capital. While the Partnership Act 1890 provides that a partner is not entitled, before the ascertainment of profits, to interest on the capital subscribed by him,[11] the provision is not mandatory and the partners may agree to the contrary in the partnership articles. If such an agreement is made, it is important that the partnership agreement also be clear and precise as to the value of each partner's capital upon which the interest is to be calculated.

WHAT IS PARTNERSHIP PROPERTY?

The central provisions of the Partnership Act relating to partnership property are contained in ss 20 and 21. These offer useful guidance, but are by no means completely exhaustive authority for the issues which arise.

The major provision is s 20(1). This provides that all property and rights and interests in property originally brought into the partnership stock or acquired, whether by purchase or otherwise, on account of the firm or for the purposes and in the course of the

---

[9] Per Lord Bramwell in *Bouch v Sproole* (1887) 12 App Cas 385 at 405, cited with approval by Lindley LJ in *Re Bridgewater Navigation Co* [1891] 2 Ch 317 at 327; *Heslin v Hay* (1884) 15 LR Ir 431.

[10] For the position of the partners on dissolution of the partnership see Chapter 12, p 261, below.

[11] Section 24(4).

partnership business are called in this Act partnership property, and must be held and applied by the partners exclusively for the purposes of the partnership and in accordance with the partnership agreement.[12] In support of this there is a second important supporting provision (s 21) that, unless the contrary intention appears, property bought with money belonging to the firm is deemed to have been bought on account of the firm.[13] The two provisions operate on a similar basis in that they both apply in the absence of any agreement, whether express or implied, to the contrary. Accordingly, they operate as rebuttable presumptions, which may be displaced on evidence to the contrary. However, whilst in form they operate in similar manner, from a chronological point of view they will usually, but not invariably, operate sequentially. The first provision relates to property brought into the partnership by the partners themselves, and this will usually occur at the inception of the partnership. The second applies to property acquired during the life of the partnership by use of the firm's money to purchase it, which in most cases is how property is subsequently acquired by a firm.

Property brought into the partnership stock or acquired on account of the firm

If the major of the two provisions is considered carefully, it will be found to bring together two distinct but related aspects. On the one hand there is the existence of the partnership property itself and, on the other, the nature of the interest of the partners in the property thus identified.

Under the major provision partnership property can either be brought into the firm at its inception or acquired subsequently on account of a firm. Thus, the major provision deals with both the initial capital brought into the partnership to set it up and subsequent acquisitions whilst the firm is trading. Most usually, however, subsequent acquisitions of capital will arise from purchase with the firm's money and fall within the supporting provision noted above.[14]

---

[12] However, if land which is partnership property is held by legal owners other than the partners it devolves according to the principles of land law, but is beneficially held in trust for the partners: s 20(2).

[13] See p 194, below.

[14] Section 21.

Property brought into the firm at the beginning

Property brought into the firm at the beginning of the partnership will consist of the various contributions of capital made by each partner. Inevitably such contributions constitute partnership property. If the property is partnership property it does not cease to be partnership property merely because it is held in the name of an individual partner rather than by all the partners together.[15] However, from a practical point of view there is much to be said for partnership property being vested in the names of all the partners since this makes clear the reality of the situation, and avoids the difficulty of proving that items of property vested in individual partners were, in fact, partnership property – difficulties which, indeed, may prove to be insurmountable in any particular case.

The most valuable partnership property in the case of most firms is the freehold land and buildings, if any, from which the business is conducted. The vesting of this item in the names of the partners is particularly advantageous, since each will then have an interest in any appreciation in value of the item. There is, however, no reason why this item should be made partnership property. If the partners are simply made owners of the property they can allow the partnership the use of it for partnership purposes. However, they cannot grant a lease *to the firm* to secure the firm's right to use it.[16]

If land is not held in the name of all the partners and clearly identified as being partnership property, it is inevitable that disputes may arise. In the case of such a dispute it may be possible to identify whether or not the property is partnership property by an examination of the partnership accounts. If the property is shown there as partnership property the problem is resolved by the accounts themselves, otherwise it is necessary that the court be persuaded from the surrounding circumstances that there was an implied agreement that the property was brought in as partnership property. These include how the particular item has been treated subsequently. It cannot be pretended that it is easy to persuade the court to draw any such inference.

---

[15] See s 20(2).

[16] The firm is not a separate body, so that the principle enshrined in the House of Lords decision in *Rye v Rye* [1962] AC 496 that a person cannot grant an effective lease to himself is violated. Two obvious means to avoid this difficulty are for the land and buildings to be vested in a company in which the partners are shareholders, or for the land and buildings to be vested in the partners and their spouses. A lease could in either case be granted to the partnership. The preferable alternative will probably be dictated by tax considerations in every individual case.

In particular it must be remembered that, merely because property is used by the partnership, this does not constitute it the property of the partnership. Such a simple approach is made impossible by the express definition of the partnership in s 1 of the Act:[17]

> 'It is not the law that partners in business, who are the owners of the property by means of which the business is carried on, are necessarily partners as regards that property. That conclusion is expressly negated by its sub-section 1 of section 2 of the Act of 1890.'[18]

Consequently, it has been held that the horses used in a coaching business were not partnership property of the firm running the business,[19] and that land belonging to co-owners as tenants in common from which stone was quarried was not partnership property of the firm doing the quarrying in the absence of further evidence to add to that conclusion.[20] Indeed, in the words of Lindley –

> 'it by no means follows that property used by all the partners for partnership purposes is partnership property. For example, the house and land in and upon which the partnership business is carried on often belongs to one of the partners only, either subject to a lease to the firm, or without any lease at all.'[1]

A more modern illustration of this is *Miles v Clarke,*[2] which concerned a partnership at will between two photographers. One, Miles, was a celebrated photographer and had a well-established reputation; the other, Clarke, was the owner of the lease of the studio and the equipment within it. As well as his reputation and experience, Miles also brought with him his existing negatives. Whilst the partners had agreed that profits were to be shared equally, there was nothing to indicate any express agreement with regard to the various items being brought into the business. Subsequently, the partnership was dissolved, and consideration had to be given to the ownership of the various items used within it. There was nothing to indicate that the

[17] Discussed in Chapter 1, p 4, above.
[18] Per North J in *Davis v Davis* [1894] 1 Ch 393 at 401, discussed in Chapter 1, p 18, above.
[19] *Fromont v Coupland* (1824) 2 Bing 170. See also *Ex p Smith* (1819) 3 Madd 63; *Ex p Owen* (1851) 4 De G & Sm 351; *Pilling v Pilling* (1865) 3 De G J & SM 162; it is probable that stock in trade is more likely to be viewed as partnership property than other chattels used by the firm in its business.
[20] *Steward v Blakeway* (1869) 4 Ch App 603; affg (1868) LR 6 Eq 479.
[1] (16th edn) at p 439, quoted with approval by the Privy Council in *Gian Singh & Co v Devraj Nahar* [1965] 1 WLR 412 at 415; *Harrison-Broadley v Smith* [1964] 1 WLR 456; *Barton v Morris* [1985] 1 WLR 1257.
[2] [1953] 1 All ER 779.

parties had agreed any change in the ownership of the lease, the equipment, or the existing negatives. Nor did the court consider that it was necessary to imply any terms with regard to the ownership of these items to give the partnership agreement business efficacy.[3] Consequently, the court concluded that none of these items had become partnership property.

It is unfortunate, but inevitable, that problems of ownership of property used by the partnership often pertain to its most important assets. Thus, in *Harvey v Harvey*[4] the item in question was the farm on which a farming business was based. The farm was in the name of one Harvey. The partnership which did the farming involved himself, his brother, and the sons of that brother. When the partnership was established it was agreed that Harvey should supply the farming stock and equipment. His brother and the nephews brought in nothing, but it was agreed that they would provide labour and skill in farming the land, with profits and expenses being divisible equally. Nothing was agreed with regard to the farm itself except that it should be improved. The partnership was carried on for a period in which improvements were made to the farm, substantially increasing its value. When the partnership was dissolved, Harvey's family, not unnaturally, sought a share in the major asset used for the partnership. However, the court refused to conclude that the farm was partnership property, pointing out that in so far as the claim that it belonged to the partnership depended upon the improvements made to the farm, these merely were the result of the agreement that had been made to improve the farm and explicable by this, and not in themselves an indication that the farm was partnership property.

It is, perhaps, convenient to dispose briefly of one older authority which seems anomalous, wrongly decided, and unlikely to be followed in the light of more modern authorities. That case is *Pocock v Carter*.[5] The litigation concerned a three-partner firm of tailors and outfitters in Salisbury. Under the partnership agreement the lease of the premises used by the firm remained the property of one partner, and the partnership was expressed to run for his lifetime. It was also provided that rents, rates and taxes attributable to the premises were to be paid from business profits. Despite the individual partner's continued ownership of the lease, the court was

---

[3] For an example of a case where the court was prepared to imply a term that at least the partnership should have the right to *use* the property, see *Harrison-Broadley v Smith* [1964] 1 WLR 456.

[4] [1970] ALR 931.

[5] [1912] 1 Ch 663.

prepared to infer that there was in fact a tenancy of the premises in favour of the partnership for the duration of the partnership. It is submitted that this decision is wrong and out of line with the approach of the courts in other cases.[6] The most that could reasonably be inferred from the circumstances was that the partners had agreed that the partnership should have the use of the premises during the subsistence of the partnership. Breach of this by the partner owning the lease would be a simple breach of contract. This is quite different from inferring some form of tenancy with the right to possession associated with that status.

The anomalous nature of the decision in *Pocock v Carter* is emphasised by the narrow construction given by the courts to general provisions concerning partnership property inserted into the partnership deed. Broad descriptions of partnership property using generalised descriptive words such as 'assets' have been construed by the courts in recent years as being insufficiently specific to include major individual items such as valuable leases or freehold land and buildings.[7] The inference seems to be that, if it was really intended to make such valuable items partnership property, they would have been specifically mentioned and not merely left to be covered by the general words.

Property acquired during the continuance of the partnership

The major provision of s 20(1) is applicable also to the situation whereby property is acquired by the firm during the subsistence of the partnership. It designates as partnership property those assets acquired, whether by purchase or otherwise, on account of a firm or for the purposes and in the course of the partnership business. This would appear to be applicable to three separate types of transactions, namely purchases using funds provided by the partnership, purchases using funds provided by the individual partners, and property acquired other than by purchase.

1. PURCHASES BOUGHT WITH PARTNERSHIP MONEY

This is likely to be the most usual cause of further property being acquired by the partnership. It should be remembered that in this

---

[6] It also seems unlikely that a tenancy for the duration of a partnership can be other than void for uncertainty of term: see *Lace v Chantler* [1944] KB 368 ('for the duration of the war').

[7] *Singh v Nahar* [1965] 1 WLR 412; *Eardley v Broad* (1970) 120 NLJ 432.

situation s 21 provides that unless the contrary intention appears, property bought with money belonging to the firm is deemed to have been bought on account of the firm. Consequently, property thus acquired does not *automatically* become partnership property because there may be a contrary intention. It is, however, presumed to be intended to be owned by the partnership. In short, despite the use of the word 'deem' in the provision, it actually raises a rebuttable presumption.[8]

However, it should be born in mind that, while there is no inflexible rule that property bought by partners out of partnership assets for use in the partnership business necessarily becomes partnership property, it has been said that in such circumstances it is 'scarcely possible to conceive a case in which there could be evidence to rebut' the presumption.[9] However, if it can be shown that finance which appeared to be the money of the firm was genuinely lent by the firm to a particular partner to enable him to purchase the asset concerned, the presumption will not come into play at all, and the asset will be that of the partner.[10]

Where the presumption applies and is not rebutted, the asset concerned becomes partnership property, whether the conveyance was taken in the name of the firm or in the name of a specific individual partner.[11] Thus, in one case shares in a company paid for from partnership funds were held to be partnership property, even though in the register of the company they appeared as registered in the name of one partner only, and could not have been registered in the name of more than one person under the terms of the company's constitution.[12] In another case, a policy of insurance effected both on the life of, and in the name of, one of the partners was held to be partnership property on the basis that premiums had been paid by the firm, and the policy used as security for an advance of money to the firm.[13]

---

[8] The provision is based on established case law: see, eg *Morris v Barrett* (1829) 3 Y & J 384; *Robley v Brooke* (1833) 7 Bli NS 90; *Helmore v Smith* (1886) 35 Ch D 436. The mere fact that the assets concerned are shown in the books of the company in the name of a partner does not prevent the assets from being partnership property: *Ex p Hinds* (1850) 3 De G & Sm 613.

[9] Per Knight Bruce LJ in *Ex p M'Kenna* (1861) 3 De GF & J 629 at 658.

[10] *Smith v Smith* (1800) 5 Ves 189; *Walton v Butler* (1861) 29 Beav 428; *Ex p Emly* (1811) 1 Rose 61.

[11] *Forster v Hale* (1800) 5 Ves 308; *Bank of England Case, Re Streatfield Laurence & Co* (1861) 3 De GF & J 629.

[12] *Ex p Connell* (1838) 3 Deac 201.

[13] *Forrester v Robson's Trustees* (1875) 2 R 775.

Whilst the presumption in the circumstances discussed is that the property is partnership property and, further, it appears that this presumption is a strong one, it is rebuttable. It may be rebutted by showing that the funds employed by the partnership to purchase the asset were not intended to be used for the purposes of the firm's business,[14] or by showing that it was intended that the asset purchased was intended for the individual enjoyment of a particular partner.[15] All the circumstances surrounding the acquisition must be considered to determine whether or not the asset was acquired on account of the firm or for the purposes of and in the course of its business. Thus, in one case, a partner applied for the grant of a new tenancy under Pt II of the Landlord and Tenant Act 1954 in respect of the premises from which the firm carried on its business. It was shown that all the partners (including the applicant) regarded the application as made by and on behalf of the firm, as, indeed, had been the situation on a previous occasion. The court concluded that the tenancy was a partnership asset, and that the personal representatives of the by now deceased applicant partner held the tenancy on trust for the benefit of the surviving partners.[16] The mere use of an asset, such as the premises from which the firm's business is carried on, does not in itself constitute the asset partnership property.[17]

In applying these principles, however, the courts adopt considerable subtlety in considering what the property is that has become partnership property, and in this they are much assisted by the fragmentation of property interests possible under English law. A recent illustration is the Court of Appeal decision in *Harwood v Harwood*.[18] The case concerned a husband and wife, and the partnership of the husband with a third party, Storey, to publish a magazine on taxation. The partnership paid the husband a salary and also the rent and outgoings of the property where he was living with his wife and family as a package of remuneration for his services to the partnership. Subsequently, the wife negotiated the purchase of the reversion to the property from the landlords. The purchase price was to be provided by a mortgage of £50,000 and the balance from the partnership. As between husband and partner,

---

[14] As by making a loan to one of the partners as in *Smith v Smith* (1800) 5 Ves 189.
[15] (1819) 2 Swanst 551.
[16] *Hodson v Cashmore* (1972) 226 EG 1203.
[17] *Gian Singh & Co v Devraj Nahar* [1965] 1 WLR 412; *Barton v Morris* [1985] 1 WLR 1257.
[18] [1991] 2 FLR 274.

it was understood that the property was to be partnership property; as between husband and wife, the wife at least understood that she was to get a beneficial half share. The house was conveyed into the joint names of husband and wife who executed the mortgage. The partnership paid the balance of the moneys needed. On the breakdown of the marriage the court concluded that one half of the property was owned by the wife, and the other half by the partnership in which the husband had an interest. Since the husband could assign his partnership interest the court could order him to assign all or part of that interest to the wife as part of the divorce settlement. Thus, the wife had half of the property because the court had declared that she was the owner of it anyway, and could have up to one half of the balance after the partnership debts were paid, thereby enabling her to receive up to three quarters of the equity in the property.

Indeed, the operation of s 21 can be seen as a statutory enactment of the consequences in this situation of the equitable concepts of the resulting trust. Where property is purchased out of joint funds and placed in the name of one person only, then, unless the two people are married, it is presumed that the property is held on resulting trust. The presumption is equally applicable to partners, and in such a situation it is submitted that the property should be viewed as partnership property unless there is clear evidence that the other partners intended to make a gift of their interest to the partner in whose name the property has been placed. It is hardly likely that the presumption could be rebutted in many cases. The presumption of resulting trust has been applied in a modern Australian case.[19] In the particular case a partner took out a policy of insurance on his own life, and in his own name. Subsequently, the firm ran into difficulties and the benefits of the policy were assigned to a creditor to secure payment of the debt due to him. The policy was for a larger sum than the amount of the debt. When the partner died there was a dispute as to whether or not the policy was partnership property. On finding that the premiums on the policy had been paid by the firm and not by the partner individually, the court applied the concept of the resulting trust, and, since there was no evidence to rebut it, concluded that the insurance policy was partnership property.

[19] *Carter Bros v Renouf* (1962) 36 ALJR 67.

2. PROPERTY PURCHASED BY FUNDS PROVIDED BY
INDIVIDUAL PARTNERS

Simply because a presumption is provided in favour of partnership
property in situations in which the purchase moneys are provided
by the partnership itself, it does not follow that there is a presumption against partnership property if the finance is provided by
individual partners. The effect of the drafting of the Partnership Act
is simply to leave the latter position at large. However, the most natural inference in such cases may well be that it is not intended that
property should belong to the partnership.

Nevertheless, two specific matters need to be borne in mind.
Firstly, there is the issue of the good faith owed by partners between
themselves. This has been discussed elsewhere,[20] but the principle
has the potential to have particular impact in the present situation.
Thus, every partner must account to the firm for any benefit
derived by him without the consent of his co-partners from any
transaction concerning the partnership, or any use by him of the
partnership property, name or business connection.[1] This provision
may have the effect of forcing a partner to account for benefits
derived from transactions concerning the partnership, even though
created by himself.[2] Also, any partner who, without the consent of
his co-partners, carries on any business of the same nature as, and
in competition with, that of a firm, must account for and pay over
to the firm all profits made by him in that business.[3] Property
received in pursuance of this provision, even though arising from
finance provided by individual partners, will constitute partnership
property. The underlying principle which it expresses may well be
the explanation for the decision in *Pillans Bros v Pillans*.[4] Here the
partnership in question was between three brothers for the carrying
on of a business trading in rivets, nuts and bolts. One brother
acquired a rival business of a similar nature. He was held to have
acquired the rival business on account of the firm (with which it
would necessarily compete) even though the firm, at that time, had
not commenced trading.

The second consideration in this situation is a statutory provision.
Section 20(3) of the Partnership Act 1890 makes provision for a
specific situation. Where co-owners of an estate or interest in any

---

[20] See Chapter 8, p 170, above.
[1] Partnership Act 1890, s 29(1).
[2] *Pathirana v Pathirana* [1967] 1 AC 233.
[3] Partnership Act 1890, s 30.
[4] (1908) 16 SLT 611.

land, not being itself partnership property, are partners as to profits made by the use of that land or estate, and purchase other land or estate out of the profits to be used in like manner, the land or estate so purchased belongs to them, in the absence of an agreement to the contrary, not as partners, but as co-owners of the same respective estates and interests as are held by them in the land or estate first mentioned at the date of purchase.[5] The provision raises a rebuttable presumption against ownership by the firm in the circumstances to which it applies. Since the original land was not partnership property, it presupposes a distinction between profits generated by the use of the land itself, which will not be partnership property, and profits generated for each partner by the operations of the firm. It is to land purchased by use of the former to which the provision applies. Since in these circumstances the ownership is presumed to be that of the owners of the land, it is possible to bring evidence in rebuttal which satisfies the court that the land acquired was agreed to be partnership property. Whilst the section itself only applies to subsequent purchases, it has been applied by analogy to improvements to the original property paid for out of profits generated by the land. Thus, in *Davis v Davis*[6] North J applied the provision even though the situation before him did not strictly fall within its wording, observing:

'In the present case, the money which was borrowed was not employed in paying for the land which was brought into the business; if it had been the case it would have been exactly within the sub-section; but the case seems to me so like that, that although it is not literally covered by the sub-section, the same law applies to it.'

Consequently, s 20(3) formed part of his reasoning in concluding that the improvements financed from the profits arising from the land remained outside the body of partnership property.

Further, a constructive trust can arise if one person spends money on improving or developing another's property.[7] Consequently, if a

---

5 Section 2(1) ensures that co-ownership of land does not of itself make it a partnership asset. Section 20(3) ensures that, in the absence of contrary agreement, property purchased by the profits generated from land which is not partnership property does not itself become property of the firm.

6 [1894] 1 Ch 393 at 405. The facts are given in Chapter 1, p 18, above.

7 For such a trust to arise, however, it now appears that there must be a direct contribution to the purchase price, either initially or by the making of mortgage payments. Mere contributions to the improvement of the property are not likely to be sufficient: *Lloyds Bank v Rosset* [1991] 1 AC 107. Cases such as *Cooke v Head* [1972] 1 WLR 518 and *Eves v Eves* [1975] 1 WLR 1338 are unlikely to be followed in the future.

firm uses partnership money to improve or develop property owned by one partner, it is possible to argue that a trust arises. Much depends upon the intention to be deduced from the underlying transaction. Whilst it is possible that it may be intended in such circumstances that a beneficial interest should arise to the partnership, a more natural inference will usually be that it was a loan which was intended to be made. If that be so, the money advanced is a loan and will be treated as such by the courts. The final possible inference is that the partnership intended to make a gift to the individual partner, but it is submitted that this is intrinsically so unlikely that it would require the clearest evidence for a court to draw such an inference.

3. ACQUISITIONS OTHER THAN BY PURCHASE

Section 20(1), being a general provision, covers all acquisitions on account of the firm 'whether by purchase or otherwise'. Acquisitions other than by purchase may be of two types: exchanges and gifts. In many ways, an exchange of property is very similar to a purchase in that, in either case, the partnership is losing partnership property (in the case a purchase in the form of money) to acquire further assets. However, s 21 refers specifically to a purchase from partnership money and it cannot therefore be pretended that an exchange falls four square within its terms. Nevertheless, it is submitted that it is likely that s 21 would be applied to the exchange situation by analogy.[8]

In the case of gifts, the question will always be resolved by trying to determine the parties to the gift. Thus, in one case a man carried on a nursery business with the assistance of his sons. There was no partnership between them. On his death, his estate, including the land on which the business was carried on, devolved to his sons as tenants in common. They then formed a partnership between themselves, and carried on the business in this manner. Subsequently, the business expanded and they bought more land for the purposes of the nursery, which they paid for out of the father's estate. One son died and his brothers bought his share of the business. They raised money on the security of the additional land to finance the purchase. Subsequently, matters arose which put in issue the ownership of the additional land. In all the circumstances, including the fact that the new land had been included in the purchase by the surviving partners of their deceased brother's share, the court inferred that the new land had become involved in

---

[8] As s 20(3) was applied by analogy in *Davis v Davis*, see p 199, above.

the partnership business and consequently had become partnership property.[9]

ASSETS TRANSFERRED INTO OR OUT OF PARTNERSHIP

Partnership property is characterised by its dedication to partnership purposes by the common agreement of the partners. It follows that partnership property cannot be removed from the assets of the firm except by common agreement, nor can the capital of the partnership be increased unless all of the partners agree. However, so long as the firm is solvent and all of the partners agree, the capital may be reduced and assets removed from the partnership property.[10] In principle, the creditors have no voice in the matter. It is only if insolvency looms that the freedom of the partners to act without reference to the interests of the creditors is affected.[11] Under the Insolvency Act 1986 dispositions which have the effect of delaying and defeating the claims of creditor, or of preferring one set of creditors at the expense of others, may be set aside.[12]

GOODWILL

One of the major assets of the firm, indeed possibly its only substantial asset, will be its goodwill. Goodwill represents the probability that all existing customers of a firm will wish to continue to deal with it,[13] and is therefore a valuable commodity for which purchasers are willing to pay money. It can, therefore, only be realised in the event of a business being sold as a going concern. In such circumstances the value of the goodwill will be represented by the difference between the total purchase price which the purchaser is prepared to pay and the intrinsic value of the other assets. In the

---

[9] *Waterer v Waterer* (1873) LR 15 Eq 402. There is a useful discussion of the previous cases by North J in *Davis v Davis* [1894] 1 Ch 393.

[10] *Ex p Ruffin* (1801) 6 Ves 119 at 127; *Ex p Williams* (1805) 11 Ves 3; *Ex p Rowlandson* (1811) 1 Rose 416.

[11] The power of the court to intervene to prevent the interests of creditors from being prejudiced by recognising as effective only dispositions of partnership property made in good faith while the partnership was solvent pre-dates the Insolvency Act 1986: see *Ex p Benjamin Mayou* (1865) 4 De G J & SM 664; *Ex p Walker* (1862) 4 De GF & J 509.

[12] See Chapter 13.

[13] Per Lord Eldon in *Cruttwell v Lye* (1810) 17 Ves 335 at 346.

past, goodwill was built up by the gradual spread of the reputation of a firm by the quality of its work and the building up of its connections. In more recent years, in our more image conscious age, it can be generated far more quickly by the large scale payment of money to finance expensive advertising campaigns.[14]

It follows that where a business is carried on in partnership the goodwill generated normally constitutes an asset of the firm. Where, however, a partnership is formed to take over an existing business with an established goodwill, the ownership of the goodwill depends upon the intention of the parties involved.[15] While no doubt in the majority of cases the natural inference will be that the goodwill was intended to be acquired by the firm, this result may not always follow.

Contractual provisions

Because goodwill is such an important item of partnership property it is usual to pay careful regard to it in all agreements entered into by the partners which relate to it. In particular, therefore, it is right that a formal partnership agreement should contain provisions pertaining to the following matters:

(1) the ownership of the goodwill on the sale of the partnership business as a going concern;
(2) the right of an individual partner to be paid for the goodwill in the event that he leaves the firm;[16]
(3) provisions protecting the goodwill by preventing individual partners undertaking actions which will damage the goodwill and, so far as possible, requiring them to undertake activities which will promote the goodwill.

In addition, on the sale of a partnership business as a going concern (or equally the acquisition of an existing business by a partnership) it is usual to include provisions preventing the seller of the business from competing in any way with the business so that the goodwill is protected. However, it must always be borne in mind that, if the

---

[14] A fact recognised as long ago as 1896 by Lord Macnaughten in *Trego v Hunt* [1896] AC 7.
[15] *Jennings v Jennings* [1898] 1 Ch 378.
[16] *Miles v Clarke* [1953] 1 WLR 537. This has an important bearing on the ease with which new, able and dynamic partners can finance the acquisition of a partnership share on the retirement of the old. The right of the individual partner to payment for the goodwill may be at the expense of the capacity of the firm to renew itself.

restrictions imposed are wider than is reasonably necessary to protect the business goodwill, they will be held to be in restraint of trade and struck down by the court.[17]

In the absence of a contractual provision protecting the goodwill on the sale of a business, the purchaser's protection is extremely limited and is protected merely by the tort of passing off and the principle of confidentiality. Thus, in such circumstances, the vendor is free to carry on a similar business which competes with that acquired by the purchaser, provided that he does not do so in any way which represents to the public that he is carrying on his old business at new premises.[18] While he may not directly solicit the custom of his previous clientele, he is free to advertise the new business generally.[19]

Finally, it should be remembered that when the partnership enters into contracts of employment with employees whose activities may have an effect on the goodwill of the business, a provision should be inserted in the contract to protect the goodwill.[20]

Non-contractual protection

The goodwill of the business may, of course, be threatened by strangers who have no contractual relationship with that business. Here protection of the goodwill by contractual provision is not possible, and any protection must rest on tort or property rights effective against such a stranger. Under English law protection may be derived in both ways, and the protection may be that of the goodwill of the partnership name in general, or merely to individual brands of goods marketed by it. The remedy available in tort is that of passing off; the possible remedy available for invasion of a property right derives from registration under the Trade Marks Act 1994,[1] for the effect of effective registration is the conferral of a property right valid against all the world in respect of the rights registered. In one important respect the two remedies differ. The tort of passing off is available only to protect a goodwill built up by a period of trading with the public. By contrast, a mark (which can be a name) may be registered by a business prior to any trading under

---

[17] *Maxim Nordenfelt Guns and Ammunition Co v Nordenfelt* [1894] AC 535.
[18] *Trego v Hunt* [1896] AC 7; *Curl Bros Ltd v Webster* [1904] 1 Ch 685.
[19] *Trego v Hunt.*
[20] As examples see Forms 10 and 14 in the *Encyclopaedia of Forms and Precedents* (5th edn) vol 14.
[1] At the time of writing the new Act has not, in fact, been brought into force. Until it is in force the old Trade Marks Act 1938 can be relied on, although its provisions are somewhat different.

the mark being commenced. The distinction is important as it corresponds to a practicality. Goodwill can be created over a substantial period of time through trading with the public so that they associate particular goods or services with the name or the mark. On the other hand, the association can be created almost overnight by an intensive and effective advertising campaign. Both registration and passing off will protect goodwill once created, but only registration in advance will prevent the mark owner preventing competitors from riding on his advertising campaign prior to reputation being established. In practice, registration tends to be used by larger businesses because it is comparatively expensive, and is, therefore, less known by partnerships, which tend to be of modest size, than the passing off action. The ever increasing size of professional partnerships which has characterised the past 20 years or so may well rapidly change this.

Passing off

There have been two recent major decisions on the subject of passing off, in each of which the House of Lords was given the opportunity to consider the ingredients of this important tort namely *Erven Warnink v Townend*[2] and *Reckitt & Coleman v Borden*.[3] A book of this nature is not one in which a complex discussion of the differing articulations of the factors necessary for the tort to be made out can be attempted. Perhaps the best and most reliable statement of them is that of Lord Diplock in *Erven Warnink v Townend*, who stated the ingredients as:

'(1) a misrepresentation (2) made by a trader in the course of trade, (3) to prospective customers of his or ultimate consumers of goods or services supplied by him, (4) which is calculated to injure the business or goodwill of another trader (in the sense that this is a reasonably foreseeable consequence) and (5) which causes damage to a business or goodwill of the trader by whom the action is brought or (in a quia timet action) will probably do so.'[4]

It will be seen that the heart of the matter is injury to an existing goodwill of the injured trader as a result of the misrepresentation by

---

2 [1980] RPC 31.
3 [1991] RPC 428.
4 At 93. These words were quoted with approval by Lord Jauncey in one of the two leading judgments in the *Reckitt and Coleman Products* case [1991] RPC 428.

the other trader. The misrepresentation will be that the goods or services of the second trader are in fact those of the first, when they are not. The trader inflicting the passing off will be causing confusion in the minds of the public as to the source of goods supplied by him. Thus, the tort cannot be used as a means of suppressing possibly unfair competition, when no such misrepresentation is made. In *Cadbury-Schweppes v Pub Squash*[5] the plaintiff brought a passing off action against the defendant. The plaintiff had run an advertising campaign promoting lemon squash. The defendant had jumped on the bandwagon thus started by running a very similarly styled advertising campaign. However, the defendant had been careful not to confuse its products with those of the plaintiff, so that the public were not confused with regard to the origin of the products. In effect, all that it was doing was to divert the interest created by the plaintiff's advertising campaign to its own product. This might be unfair competition, but in the view of the Judicial Committee of the Privy Council it did not constitute passing off.

Registered trade marks

The Trade Marks Act 1994 allows registration of any sign capable of being represented graphically which is capable of distinguishing goods or services of one undertaking from those of other undertakings. In particular it may consist of words (including personal names), designs, letters, numerals, or the shape of goods or their packaging.[6] The effect of registration is that the proprietor of the mark obtains a property right which is infringed if the mark is used in particular ways in the United Kingdom without his consent.[7] There are two principle ways in which unauthorised use will amount to infringement.[8] First, a person infringes a registered trade mark if he uses in the course of trade a sign where there exists a likelihood of confusion on the part of the public because the sign is identical or similar to the trade mark and is used in relation to goods or services identical with or similar to those for which the trade mark is registered. This creates a principle of infringement very similar to that which is created by passing off, since the infringement occurs only when the trade mark used is sufficiently similar to, and also used in circumstance sufficiently similar to, that of the registered trade mark.

[5] [1981] RPC 429.
[6] Section 1.
[7] Section 9.
[8] Section 10.

The second form of infringement tackles a different area. A person also infringes a registered trade mark if he uses in the course of trade a sign, which (1) is identical with or similar to the trade mark, and (2) is used in relation to goods or services which are not similar to those for which the trade mark is registered in the following circumstances. First, the trade mark must have a reputation in the United Kingdom and the use of the sign, being without due cause, takes unfair advantage of, or is detrimental to, the distinctive character or repute of the trade mark. This provision is addressed to what is called the dilution problem. A well-known name or mark (say Coca Cola) is used by some aggressive entrepreneur for an entirely different product (eg Coca Cola Amusement Arcade, Nethersea). It is not likely that the general public will be confused into believing that the local amusement arcade is in any way connected with the international company, but the latter may nevertheless well find that to allow its up-market name to be associated with a rather seedy operation will detract from its name and image, thereby reducing the value of its brand name. The second form of infringement comes in here.

The reforms to UK law produced by the 1994 Act are important in replacing a badly drafted piece of legislation with one which is more clearly set out and worded, and which is inevitably also much better designed for modern conditions. What prompted the change was a European Directive adopted as a result of the single market initiative.[9] Even greater change is in the pipe-line. Over and above the reform of the UK trade mark law there is an unstoppable momentum towards the creation of a European trade mark, one under which registration creates a trade mark operating throughout the whole of the European Community.[10] Part II of the new legislation allows it to be adapted in the new European regime as the need arises.

OTHER INTELLECTUAL PROPERTY RIGHTS

In addition to the goodwill of the partnership in its name and that of its products, if any, there may be other intellectual property rights which it owns which are protected by other means. Thus, it may have industrial designs protected by either of the twin systems of protection, one of which requires registration under the Registered

---

[9] First Council Directive 89/104, 21 December 1988 to approximate the laws relating to trademarks [1989] OJ L40/1.
[10] Council Regulation No 40/94/EEC.

Designs Act 1949, and the other which gives protection by a system of unregistered design right created by the Copyright, Designs and Patents Act 1988.[11] It may have inventions which are protectable by registration under the Patents Act 1977,[12] music, literary works (including letters and business forms), computer programmes in which copyright exists under the Copyright, Designs and Patents Act 1988, and information which it has shared in confidence with employees and others and to which common law rights of confidence attach which the courts will protect.[13] Intellectual property rights are of ever increasing importance in the modern world, and many small to medium size businesses, including those conducted through the medium of partnership, are insufficiently aware of them, thereby often failing to obtain adequate protection of their own rights and too often invading the intellectual property rights of others through a combination of negligence and even wilful ignorance.

Intellectual property rights give rise to specific problems for partnerships. While other intellectual property rights largely depend on registration, copyright does not, and arises automatically if certain conditions are satisfied. It vests automatically in the creator of the work. If there are two or more creators they will own it jointly. Those who own it will be able to prevent others from infringing their rights (in common with other intellectual property rights it is a *property* right). The following points therefore arise:

(1) intellectual property rights, like other property rights, may belong to either the partnership or some only of the partners. If the intellectual property right was created before the partnership was entered into, by some only of the partners, it will not become partnership property unless there is clear agreement of the creators that it was to do so.[14] In the case of copyright establishing who created the work and whether there was such an agreement is a matter to be established by the evidence as a whole.[15] In the case of intellectual property rights requiring registration the register shows in whom the legal title is vested. An agreement to transfer will not be easily inferred. In the case of a registered intellectual property right it will be shown by changes in the registration particulars;

---

[11] Design rights are discussd in Total *The Law of Industrial Design* (1990).
[12] On patents see *Terrell on the Law of Patents* (13th edn, 1982).
[13] Both the modern law of copyright and the action for breach of confidence are discussed in Prime *The Law of Copyright* (1992).
[14] *Stuart v Barrett* [1992] 8 EIPRD162.
[15] Ibid.

(2)   where the intellectual property was the creation of all the partners prior to the partnership slightly different considerations apply in the case of copyright. Here, the courts may be a little more prepared to infer that there was an agreement that the work should become partnership property.[16] Forms of intellectual property requiring registration would still require a change in the registration particulars;

(3)   where a copyright work is created after the formation of the partnership by some only of the partners its ownership will depend on whether or not it was agreed that it should be partnership property. In the absence of clear agreement it will be the property of the partners who created it;

(4)   where a copyright work is created after the formation of the partnership by all of the partners for the furtherance of the business in the absence of agreement to the contrary the work will be that of the partnership. If the work were not for the purposes of the business the rights would be those of the partners as individuals;

(5)   intellectual property rights are enforceable against third parties by those in whom the legal rights are vested, whether by creation, registration or assignment;

(6)   an assignment may be in the form of general words. Thus, a sale or disposal of all the partnership assets will assign all copyrights belonging to the partnership;[17]

(7)   if one partner assigns his rights to another, the other becomes the sole property owner and can bring proceedings if subsequently the assigning partner infringes the rights.[18]

THE NATURE OF A PARTNER'S INTEREST

Section 20(1) is central not only to a discussion of what constitutes partnership property but also to consideration of the nature of the partners' interests in it, for it requires that it be held exclusively for partnership purposes and in accordance with the partnership agreement. This has consequences for both the legal and beneficial interests in the property.

---

[16]   Ibid.
[17]   *Murray v King* [1986] FSR 116 (Federal Court of Australia).
[18]   Ibid.

The legal interest

The property may be vested in some or all of the partners.[19] In particular, if land is conveyed to numerous partners then under the Law of Property Act 1925, s 34(2) the legal estate will vest in the first four named in the conveyance as joint tenants. The legal estate will, however, be held as trustees for the partners as a whole, and the beneficial interests will accrue as tenants in common so that no right of survivorship will arise in respect of the beneficial interests. Whether any particular partner has any interest in any particular piece of partnership property and, if so, the extent of the interest, will be determined by the partnership agreement itself. Thus, for instance, it may provide that particular partners have no interest in the goodwill of the business.

The beneficial interests

Whilst the beneficial interests of the partners arise from the partnership itself, subject to the terms of the agreement, an issue arises as to when it falls into possession. As has been noted, the property is held exclusively for the purposes of the partnership and in accordance with the partnership agreement. During the subsistence of the partnership, therefore, each partner is entitled to require that the partnership assets be used for the purposes of the partnership, and no partner is entitled to exclusive use or enjoyment of an asset individually.[20] Further, on determination of the partnership the partnership property is held for the payment of the firm's debts with only the surplus being available for division amongst the partners, and any individual partner may require that the property be dealt with in this way.[1] It follows, therefore, in the classic words of Lindley:

'What is meant by the share of a partner is his proportionate interest in the partnership assets after they have been all realised and converted into money, and all the partnership debts and

---

[19] A recent example of this is the Scots case of *Gordon v IRC* [1991] STC 174 where some of the land farmed by the partnership was vested in one partner only, namely AG, and the remainder in a third party from whom AG had the personal rights to demand its conveyance. The partner was held to hold both the land and the personal right as trustee for the firm.

[20] *Lingen v Simpson* (1824) 1 Sim & St 600 at 603; *Cockle v Whiting* (1829) Taml 55; *Marshall v Maclure* (1885) 10 App Cas 325; *Re Bainbridge* (1878) 8 Ch D 218.

[1] Partnership Act 1890, ss 9 and 44.

liabilities have been paid and discharged. This it is, and this only, which on the death of a partner passes to his representatives or to a legatee of his share . . . and which on his bankruptcy passes to his trustee.'[2]

It is clear, therefore, that the nature of the partner's beneficial interest in partnership property may depend on whether the partnership is continuing, or has been dissolved. When it is remembered that the death, retirement, or expulsion of an individual partner may, or may not, result in the dissolution of a partnership[3] it is seen that a discussion of the beneficial interests of individual partners in partnership property might best be conducted under three heads, namely, where the partnership continues, when it is dissolved, and the death, retirement or expulsion of an individual partner.

1. CONTINUING PARTNERSHIP

So long as the partnership continues, its property is held for the purposes of the firm and for the payment of any debts created by the firm, with the consequence that the partners' beneficial interest cannot give them a vested beneficial interest in the trust. What, therefore, is the precise nature of a partner's interest until his beneficial interest does vest? Is it a purely personal right, or does it have proprietary connotations? It is the Australian courts which have wrestled with this particular problem. In *Canny Gabriel Castle Jackson Pty Ltd v Volume Sales (Finance) Pty Ltd*[4] the court concluded that the interest of the partner was an equitable interest and therefore capable of taking priority over subsequent equitable interests including an equitable charge. More support for this can also be gathered from both English and Australian cases.[5] In this it differs from the position which arises for the beneficiary under the will of

---

[2] (16th edn, 1990) at 455, citing *Rodriguez v Speyer Bros* [1919] AC 59 at 68 per Finlay LC; *Re Ritson* [1899] 1 Ch 128; *Burdett-Coutts v IRC* [1960] 1 WLR 1027; *Livingston v Comr of Stamp Duties* [1961] ALR 534; *Dimov v Dimov* [1971] WAR 113; *Doddington v Hallett* [1750] 1 Ves Sen 497; *Croft v Pyke* (1733) 3 P Wms 180; *West v Skip* (1749) 1 Ves Sen 239; *Taylor v Fields* (1799) 4 Ves 396; *Crawshay v Collins* (1808) 15 Ves 218; *Featherstonhaugh v Fenwick* (1810) 17 Ves 298; *Richardson v Bank of England* (1838) 4 My & Cr 165; *Darby v Darby* (1856) 3 Drew 495; *Re Rhagg* [1938] Ch 828; *Re Betts* [1949] WN 91; *Re White* [1958] Ch 762; *Farquhar v Hadden* (1871) 7 Ch App 1; *Ekins v Brown* (1854) 1 Spinks, Ecc & Ad 400; *A-G v Higgins* (1857) 2 H & N 339; *Smith v Stokes* (1801) 1 East 363.

[3] See Chapter 12, p 261, below.

[4] (1974) 131 CLR 321.

[5] *Re Fuller's Contract* [1933] Ch 652; *Comr of Taxation v Everett* (1980) 54 AJLR 196.

a deceased, where the assets of the estate are held for the payment of the debts and the administration of the estate, and where it has been held that pending completion of the administration a beneficiary has no proprietary interest, but merely the right to have the estate properly administered.[6]

2. DISSOLUTION OF THE PARTNERSHIP

If the partnership is dissolved, each individual partner is entitled to require that the partnership assets be used to pay any debts or liabilities of the firm and any surplus divided amongst the partners in accordance with the partnership agreement.[7] Until the debts are paid it is difficult to see how the beneficial interests of the individual partners can vest, and it is submitted that the beneficial interests remain unvested. On the other hand, once any claims of the creditors have been met it is submitted that no further purposes of the firm remain, and that being so the beneficial interests of partners may vest.

3. DEATH, RETIREMENT OR EXPULSION OF A PARTNER

The effect of the death, retirement or expulsion of a partner depends on the terms of the partnership agreement.[8] If it causes a general dissolution of the partnership the consequences with regard to the interests of the outgoing partner in the partnership property will be as outlined in the previous paragraph. Otherwise, the partnership continuing, the partner will have no vested beneficial rights in the partnership property, and his right will be a personal right. Consequently, if the partnership agreement sets out the manner in which the outgoing partner's entitlement is to be calculated and paid for, his share will constitute a debt payable on the date on which he ceased to be a partner.

Where there is no such clear provision, the outgoing partner's rights are rights to participate in the surplus after the assets of the partnership have been sold and the debts paid. However, a sale is unlikely to meet the practicalities of the aspirations of either the outgoing or the continuing partners. Consequently, if the outgoing partner impliedly accepts that the continuing partners will continue the business, they are entitled to acquire his share at a valuation and, if necessary, the court will direct that accounts be

---

[6] *Stamp Duties Comr (Queensland) v Livingston* [1965] AC 694.
[7] Partnership Act 1890, ss 39 and 44.
[8] See Chapter 12.

taken and any necessary enquiries carried out for the value to be fixed.[9] If the outgoing partner does not impliedly accept that the partnership will continue, but the other parties wish to continue it and are prepared to pay the outgoing partner the market value of his share, the court may, as a matter of discretion, refuse to order the sale of the partnership property, and instead require that the outgoing partner's share be valued and the outgoing partners pay the sum so ascertained.[10]

Doctrine of conversion and partnership land

Since the future beneficial interest of a partner in the partnership assets is a right to participate after they have been liquidated to pay any partnership debts it follows that the underlying trust on which the property is held is a trust for sale. It further follows from the imposition of the trust for sale that the doctrine of conversion applies to any land which is held as partnership property. Section 22 of the Partnership Act 1890 is specific on the latter point:

'Where land or any heritable interest therein has become partnership property, it shall, unless the contrary intention appears, be treated as between the partners (including the representatives of a deceased partner) and also as between the heirs of a deceased partner and his executors and administrators, as personal or moveable and not real or heritable estate.'[11]

This provision operates the doctrine of conversion except where there is a contrary intention. However, it is supported by two provisions in the Law of Property Act 1925, ss 34 and 36, which are to the effect that, in the absence of an express trust for sale, partnership land vested in one or more partners is held on a statutory

---

[9] *Sobell v Boston* [1975] 1 WLR 1587. The value is that of the share at the date the outgoing partner ceased to be a partner, Partnership Act 1890, s 43; *Sobell v Boston*. For the almost inevitable delay in payment the outgoing partner is entitled to be compensated by the payment of either interest or a share of profits: Partnership Act 1890, s 42.

[10] *Syers v Syers* (1876) 1 App Cas 174; *Rivett v Rivett* (1966) 200 Estates Gazette 858. In this case the date with reference to which the value of the share is fixed is the date on which the valuation is carried out, *Syers v Syers*.

[11] The legislation gives effect to the position achieved at common law, see, eg *Ripley v Waterworth* (1802) 7 Ves 425; *Tamstend v Devaynes* (1808) 1 Mont Part, note 2 Appx p 96; *Phillips v Phillips* (1832) 1 My & K 649; *Broom v Broom* (1834) 3 My & K 443; *Morris v Kearsley* (1836) 2 Y & C Ex 139; *Essex v Essex* (1855) 20 Beav 442. However, the cases were not uniform: see, eg *Bell v Phyn* (1802) 7 Ves 453; *Cookson v Cookson* (1837) 8 Sim 529.

trust for sale, with the result that all beneficial interests in it are converted into personal property. These latter provisions are entirely mandatory. The two sets of provisions, the one in the Partnership Act and the other in the 1925 legislation, do not sit well side by side. The reason is essentially historical. The earlier provision represents the position achieved by the case law on partnership itself, which permitted the operation of the doctrine of conversion to be prevented by the contrary intention of the parties.[12] By contrast, the 1925 legislation is mandatory because it is effecting a total change of the principles of English land law applicable to co-ownership of land. As the 1925 legislation is the later legislation it imposes a mandatory requirement of the application of the doctrine of conversion to land held as partnership property. Nevertheless, despite both sets of provisions, it appears that a sale of a partner's interest in land is a sale of an interest in land requiring a written contract.[13]

THE EXTENT OF EACH PARTNER'S SHARE

The extent of each partner's share as a proportion of the partnership assets depends on the terms of the partnership agreement. In the absence of agreement the position is governed by the Partnership Act 1890, s 24(1) which provides:

'The interests of the partners in partnership property and the rights and duties in relation to the partnership shall be determined, subject to any agreement express or implied between the partners by the following rules:
(1) All partners are entitled to share equally in the capital and profits of the business, and must contribute equally towards the losses whether of capital or otherwise sustained by the firm.'

As Lindley concluded from the case law which gave rise to the statutory provision:[14]

'Whether, therefore, partners have contributed money equally or unequally, whether or not they are on a par as regards skill,

---

12 *Steward v Blakeway* (1869) 4 Ch App 603; *Re Wilson* [1893] 2 Ch 340.
13 *Cooper v Critchley* [1955] Ch 431.
14 See, eg *Steward v Forbes* (1849) 1 Mac & G 137; *Webster v Bray* (1849) 7 Hare 159; *Copland v Toulmin* (1840) 7 Cl & Fin 349; *Robinson v Anderson* (1855) 20 Beav 98; affd 7 De GM & G 239; *Peacock v Peacock* (1809) 16 Ves 49; *Farrar v Beswick* (1836) 1 Mood & Rob 527.

connection, or character, whether they have or have not laboured equally for the benefit of the firm, their shares will be considered as equal, unless some agreement to the contrary can be shown to have been entered into.'[15]

However, the presumption of equality has been displaced in some situations. In one case the court was prepared to infer that the partners agreed that the property was held in unequal shares from the way in which the partners dealt with each other, and from the contents of the firm's books showing how capital was first provided for the partnership.[16] If the customs according to which a particular trade or business is carried on generally provide for the holding of property on unequal terms then no doubt this would be an implied term of the particular partnership agreement, but practical examples of this principle have not evidenced themselves. Logically, too, if partners agree to share profits in unequal shares they are to be presumed to have agreed to hold partnership property in the same proportions in the absence of agreement to the contrary.[17]

If it is established that partnership property is held unequally at a particular point in a firm's existence, the *subsequent* retirement of a partner will not be taken to have altered the capital-sharing arrangements in the absence of agreement to the contrary, so that the share of the retiring member will be held by the continuing partners in the shares which they held relative to each other prior to the retirement.[18]

EXECUTION IN RESPECT OF A PARTNER'S SEPARATE DEBTS

Since a partnership is not in law a legal person it is in the nature of this particular type of business organisation that a distinction between the partnership property and the individual property of the partners should be difficult to maintain in all respects. Whilst the individual partners are denied exclusive use of the partnership property so long as the partnership continues and the property was used for partnership purposes, the fact remains that the partnership property is owned by the partners. In principle, therefore, if a part-

---

[15] (16th edn, 1990) p 462. In fact the litigation in *Peacock v Peacock* was settled and the case is little authority for any proposition.
[16] *Robley v Brooke* (1833) 7 Bli NS 90.
[17] *Lindley* (16th edn) p 463.
[18] Ibid.

ner owes an individual debt there is no reason why his creditor should not be able to levy execution both against the partner's individual property and that of the partnership itself. This indeed was the position under the case law established prior to the 1890 Act. Inevitably, the practical application of the principle was capable of giving rise to great commercial complications and difficulties for partnerships which was, to some extent inevitably, detrimental to the efficacy of partnership as a business organisation.[19]

The 1890 Act introduced a new procedure whereby a judgment against an individual partner could be executed against his partnership share rather than the partnership property as a whole. The procedure is set out in s 23. Under this a writ of execution may not be issued against any partnership property except on a judgment against the firm.[20] In return, by s 23(2) the High Court, or a judge thereof or a county court may, on the application of any judgment creditor of a partner, make an order charging that partner's interest in the partnership property and profits with payment of the amount of the judgment debt and interest thereon, and may by the same or subsequent order appoint a receiver of the partner's share of profits (whether already declared or accruing), and of any other money which may be coming to him in respect of the partnership, and direct all accounts and enquiries, and give all other orders and directions which might have been directed or given if the charge had been made in favour of the judgment creditor by the partner, or which the circumstances of the case may require.[1] The provisions apply in the case of a cost book company as if the company were a partnership within the meaning of the 1890 Act.[2] Where orders are made under the provisions the other partner or partners are at liberty at any time to redeem the interest charged or, in the case of a sale being directed, to purchase the same.[3] The provisions apply to a foreign firm with a branch office in England.[4] Whilst a charging order may be made under s 23 against the partnership share of a mentally disordered partner,[5] no order can be made in respect of the share of a deceased partner.[6]

---

[19] See *Lindley* (4th edn) vol 1 at p 687 et seq.
[20] Section 23(1).
[1] Section 23(2).
[2] Section 23(4).
[3] Section 23(3).
[4] *Brown Janson & Co v A Hutchinson & Co* [1895] 1 QB 737.
[5] *Re Sir F Seager Hunt* [1900] 2 Ch 54n; *Horne v Pountain* (1889) 23 QBD 264; *Re Leavesley* [1891] 2 Ch 1.
[6] *Stewart v Rhodes* [1900] 1 Ch 386.

The procedure for obtaining an order under the section is governed by RSC Ord 81, r 10. The rules are discussed elsewhere.[7] Since the process of charging a partner's share in the partnership involves either the appointment of a receiver to receive the profits or, alternatively, the ordering of a sale of the partnership share, the procedure is comparatively rarely used because of the complexity involved.

The effect of an order under s 23 is to charge the whole of the debtor's share in favour of the creditor, but gives the creditor no greater right in the partnership property than the debtor-partner himself enjoyed.[8] Consequently, the application of the creditor can be outflanked if the debtor assigns his share prior to the order being made,[9] although if the creditor hears of an attempt to assign before the assignment has been effected he may obtain an interlocutory injunction to prevent assignment taking place. Further, the charging order cannot prevent bona fide arrangements between the partners which may have an adverse effect on the share charged, such as increasing salaries of partners, thereby reducing profits.[10] Clearly, however, if such an arrangement were made with the deliberate intention of prejudicing the creditor it would be open to attack by him.

A charging order operates subject to the insolvency provisions, and would not be regarded as a completed execution allowing the creditor to retain the property charged.[11] Further, if the insolvent's partners have paid a sum of money into court to redeem or purchase the insolvent debtor's share, it is the insolvent partner's trustee who will be entitled to the sum, the execution only being completed by the payment of the money by the court to the creditor.

TRANSFER OF A PARTNERSHIP SHARE

If a partnership share is regarded as a separate item for the purpose of an external creditor seeking to enforce a debt, it follows that it should also constitute a separate item of property in the hands of

---

[7] See Chapter 7, p 167, above.
[8] *Cooper v Griffin* [1892] 1 QB 740; *Howard v Sadler* [1893] 1 QB 1; *Sutton v English and Colonial Produce Co* [1902] 2 Ch 502.
[9] *Brearcliff v Dorrington* (1850) 4 De G & Sm 122; *Scott v Lord Hastings* (1858) 4 K & J 633.
[10] Per Lord Alverstone CJ in *Watts v Driscoll* [1901] 1 Ch 294 at 306; *Re Garwood's Trusts* [1903] 1 Ch 236.
[11] Within the Insolvency Act 1986, s 183.

the individual partner. Statutory effect is given to this principle by the Partnership Act 1898, s 31. An assignment by any partner of his share in the partnership, either absolute or by way of mortgage or redeemable charge, does not, as against the other partners, entitle the assignee during the continuance of the partnership to interfere in the management or administration of the partnership business or affairs, or to require any accounts of the partnership transactions, or to inspect the partnership books, but entitles the assignee only to receive the share of profits to which the assigning partner would otherwise be entitled, and the assignee must accept the account of profits agreed to by the partners.[12]

In the case of a dissolution of the partnership, whether in respect of all the partners or in respect of the assigning partner, the assignee is entitled to receive the share of the partnership assets to which the assigning partner is entitled as between himself and the other partners and, for the purpose of ascertaining that share, to an account as from the date of dissolution.[13]

The statutory provisions give effect to the position reached by the case law.[14] The assignee is not entitled to participate in the management of the firm, nor to inspect the partnership books or require the taking of accounts while the firm continues. However, if the partnership is dissolved it will be seen that under the statutory provisions the assignee has a statutory right to an account as from the date of dissolution, and the partners may not deliberately act so as to prejudice that right once they know of the assignment.[15] However, they are of course free to exercise the existing terms of the partnership agreement and the various management powers bona fide for the purposes of the partnership even if the position of the assignee is adversely affected.[16]

---

12 Section 31(1).
13 Section 31(2). Despite the apparently clear wording of the provision in *Public Trustee v Elder* [1926] Ch 776 at 790, Sargent LJ expressed the opinion that the provisions of the section should apply by analogy to the assignment of a share in a partnership which has been already dissolved. The opinion is clearly obiter, but may well be correct since in most respects the 1890 Act is merely declaratory of existing law. The section does not apply directly to assignment of a part share, but again may well be applied by analogy to fill the vacuum.
14 See, eg *Smith v Parkes* (1852) 16 Beav 115; *Whetham v Davey* (1885) 30 Ch D 574; by analogy *Bergmann v McMillan* (1881) 17 Ch D 423.
15 *Watts v Driscoll* [1901] 1 Ch 294.
16 Per Vaughan Williams LJ in *Watts v Driscoll* [1901] 1 Ch 294 at 311; *Re Garwood's Trusts* [1903] 1 Ch 236.

Indemnity for losses

Whilst the assignee is entitled to the profits attributable to the share he is not a partner and, consequently, he is not *directly* liable for any losses which arise in the partnership trading. Nevertheless, by agreeing to be the recipient of the assigning partner's share the assignee has effectively agreed to stand in his shoes, and accordingly he is bound to indemnify the assignor in respect of the proportion of any trading losses falling to the assignor.[17]

---

[17] *Dodson v Downey* [1901] 2 Ch 620.

CHAPTER 10

ACTIONS BETWEEN PARTNERS

INTRODUCTION

Whatever the historical restrictions that were once placed upon litigation between a partner and his partnership[1] the right of a partner to institute proceedings against his co-partner(s) is now generally recognised. This chapter will consider the types of action that may be instituted between partners, and the incidents that may be attached to such proceedings.[2] It will also review the situations in which the courts will not interfere in partnership disputes, and will conclude with a consideration of the defences available to a partner where a co-partner seeks to maintain an action against him in equity.

Actions between partners which involve the taking of an account will be considered first.

ACTION FOR ACCOUNT WITHOUT DISSOLUTION

This is a most common action instituted between partners.[3] It is the only procedure which will enable a partner to claim his share of any profits made by his co-partner(s).[4] Although an account is generally

---

[1] See *Ellis v Kerr* [1910] 1 Ch 529; *Meyer & Co v Faber (No 2)* [1923] 2 Ch 421. The restrictions were based on the objection to a party being both a plaintiff and a defendant.

[2] It should be noted that proceedings may be commenced by or against a partnership in the firm name. See RSC Ord 81. This ability is purely procedural and does not alter the fact that the parties to any action remain individuals.

[3] The right to an account is authorised by the Partnership Act 1890, s 28. See also Chapter 11.

[4] *Green v Hertzog* [1954] 1 WLR 1309.

sought as an ancillary remedy by a partner who is seeking a dissolution of his partnership, the action is not limited to such circumstances.[5] It may therefore be sought by a partner as a principal action against his co-partners in a number of circumstances, without seeking the dissolution of the partnership, although a dissolution of the partnership may subsequently take place. Generally, in such cases all partners must be joined to the action.[6] The cases where a partner may maintain an action for account against a co-partner without seeking an immediate dissolution of the partnership are:

(1)   where a co-partner seek(s) to withhold profits earned by him in which the partner seeking an account is interested;[7]

(2)   where the partnership is a fixed term partnership, and a co-partner seeks, or has sought, to exclude or expel a partner from that partnership, or otherwise drive the latter to contemplate or seek a dissolution of the partnership;[8]

(3)   closely related to the above case is the situation where a party derives a profit from his involvement with another individual in a business enterprise, and the association could amount to a partnership between that party and that individual, but the latter seeks to deny the existence of a partnership and his relationship of partner with the other party. If the existence of a partnership is subsequently established by the other party he may seek an account of the past dealings and transactions undertaken by the 'partnership'[9] from his 'co-partner';

(4)   in exceptional cases a limited account may be sought by a partner where the partnership venture has failed, the partners are too numerous to be made parties to the action, and such an account is necessary to do justice between the

---

[5]   *Forman v Homfray* (1813) 2 Ves & B 329; *Loscombe v Russell* (1830) 4 Sim 8.

[6]   *Dean v MacDowell* (1878) 8 Ch D 345; *Fuller v Duncan* (1891) 7 TLR 305; *Trimble v Goldberg* [1906] AC 494.

[7]   *Hichens v Congreve* (1828) 1 Russ & M 150; *Fawcett v Whitehouse* (1829) 1 Russ & M 132. Of course, a dissolution may follow such an action or may be sought: *Clegg v Fishwick* (1849) 1 Mac & G 294; *Aas v Benham* [1891] 2 Ch 244.

[8]   See *Harrison v Armitage* (1819) 4 Madd 143; *Fairthorne v Weston* (1844) 3 Hare 387. In *Richards v Davies* (1831) 2 Russ & M 347, Sir John Leach MR ordered an account on the basis that the plaintiff would otherwise be left without a remedy. Such an action may be maintained each time a partner is excluded from the partnership or he is deprived of his right to a share of any profits made by the partnership. For a case involving expulsion see *Blisset v Daniel* (1853) 10 Hare 493.

[9]   *Knowles v Haughton* (1805) 11 Ves 168.

partners.[10] It has been noted[11] that partnership size is in general restricted. However, in the case of an account ordered in the circumstances noted above, the partner seeking the account may resort to representative proceedings.

Representative proceedings

Although in general there is a statutory restriction on the maximum size of a partnership, certain professional partnerships are permitted to exceed such statutory restrictions on membership.[12] Where proceedings are contemplated between the partners of such a large partnership, the number of potential plaintiffs and defendants constitute a formidable administrative and judicial obstacle and it may be advisable to join partners to any action as representative plaintiffs and/or defendants.[13] However, representative proceedings will not be appropriate, where the interests of a partner are distinct from, and in conflict with, that of *all* his co-partners. In such cases, *all* the partners must be joined as parties to any action instituted by that partner against the partnership, irrespective of the number of partners. Only where partners share a distinct interest, and their interests do not conflict inter se, can a single partner from such a group be joined to an action as a representative of those other partners, who share the common or same interest.[14] Any subsequent judgment or order made in the course of representative proceedings will bind those partners so represented, but it cannot be enforced against a partner who was not made a party to the proceedings, without the leave of the court.[15]

---

10 See *Wallworth v Holt* (1841) 4 My & Cr 619, which involved an insolvent joint stock banking company. The account was sought against the officers of the company and shareholders who were not fully paid up, for the purpose of having the assets of the company applied to the payment of its debts. Such an account may also be sought to obtain a division of surplus assets and profits.

11 See Chapter 2.

12 See Chapter 2, p 40, above on the maximum size of partnerships and exceptions to this rule.

13 See RSC Ord 15, r 12; CCR Ord 5, r 5.

14 See RSC Ord 15, r 12(1); CCR Ord 5, r 5(1); *Van Sandau v Moore* (1826) 1 Russ 441; *Mcmahon v Upton* (1829) 2 Sim 473; *Prudential Assurance Co Ltd v Newman Industries Ltd* [1981] Ch 229; *Roche v Sherrington* [1982] 1 WLR 599; *Irish Shipping Ltd v Commercial Union Assurance Co plc, The Irish Rowan* [1991] 2 QB 206 and authorities cited therein.

15 The failure to join a partner is thus in general not fatal to the action: see RSC Ord 15, r 6(11); CCR Ord 5, r 4. For obtaining leave of the court to enforce a judgment or order see RSC Ord 15, r 12(3); CCR Ord 5, r 5(5). A partner may be appointed a representative of his co-partners in any action irrespective of whether he consents to such an action or not: RSC Ord 15, r 12(2); CCR Ord 5, r 5(2)(b); *Wood v McCarthy* [1893] 1 QB 775.

Actions for account that do not require the joining of all partners to the action

Where an account is sought by a party as against a partner to a business enterprise, but the account does not involve the partnership business per se, that partner's co-partners should not be joined as parties to the relevant action.[16] Although an individual partner may not be a necessary party to an action for account involving his co-partners, he may be joined to such an action if some form of relief other than an account is sought against him, by the party seeking the account, and that relief is connected with the action for account, and is sought in those proceedings.[17]

The nature of an order for account

The account which a partner may seek may be a general account of the dealings and transactions of the partnership business. Generally, such an account will be sought with a view to the winding up of the partnership. In addition, and as an alternative to the above form of account, a partner may seek a limited account, confined to a particular transaction which is, or set of transactions which are, the subject of dispute between the partners.

An account sought by a partner in respect of partnership matters may be refused by the court on the ground that it would serve no useful purpose. Such an action is, however, usually granted whenever it is alleged by a partner that he is entitled to recover money from a co-partner or co-partners which is derived from any business dealing carried out by the firm, or which is the firm's property. An action for account will also usually be granted to a partner if he can establish that the money claimed is his own, or that it is he who is owed the money and not the partnership.

---

[16] *Brown v De Tastet* (1819) Jac 284; *Bray v Fromont* (1821) 6 Madd 5. Note also where an assignee seeks an account of a partner's share during the continuance of a partnership. Note also where partners act as personal representatives in respect of a deceased partner's share and misuse that share to accrue profits to themselves as executors. In such a case the other partners are not necessarily partners to an action for account: *Simpson v Chapman* (1853) 4 De GM & G 154.

[17] *Bevan v Lewis* (1827) 1 Sim 376.

Summary order for account and inquiries

An action for account by a partner against his co-partners may be commenced by writ endorsed with a claim for account. If the only issue in dispute between the parties to the action is the fact of the account,[18] the court may make a summary order for accounts and inquiries to be made at any time after (1) the defendant has acknowledged service; *or* (2) after the time prescribed for acknowledgement of service has expired.[19] The application for the account is made by summons.[20] In making the order, the court will generally give directions as to how the account is to be conducted or the inquiry made.[1] A summary order for an account and inquiry can, it seems, still be made although fraudulent conduct is alleged.[2] Consideration must now be given to matters which are ancillary to the taking of a partnership account.

1. PAYMENT INTO COURT

Where proceedings for an account are pending, and a partner admits or is found to have, or to have had, partnership money in his hands, he may be ordered to make a payment into court.[3] Such an order is more likely to be made if the partner concerned admits,[4] or it is established from the partner's previous conduct or statements, that he obtained the money the subject of the action for account improperly or in breach of his fiduciary duties.[5] To the above principles there is a proviso. As a general rule, a partner will not be ordered to make a payment into court unless the other partners are

---

[18] And not further issues, eg the existence of the partnership. The court may also find that there is no matter in dispute between the parties, other than the claim for an account.

[19] RSC Ord 43, rr 1 and 2. A summary order for an account on inquiries may also be obtained where the writ is endorsed with a claim which necessarily involves taking an account, CCR Ord 13, r 7(1)(h); *Turquand v Wilson* (1875) 1 Ch D 85. A similar order may be obtained on any counter-claim: see RSC Ord 43, r 1(1a).

[20] The application should generally be supported by affidavit, which should set out the transactions which are the subject of the dispute: RSC Ord 43, r 1(2).

[1] RSC Ord 43, r 3.

[2] *Newton Chemical Ltd v Arsensis* [1989] 1 WLR 1297 at 1303, 1307.

[3] Such an order may be made irrespective of the fact that the relevant partner no longer has control or possession of such moneys, if the court is of the opinion that that partner should still have possession or control of that money. See *Freeman v Cox* (1878) 8 Ch D 148.

[4] Such an admission must be made by the partner concerned. Such an admission may be oral: *Re Beeny* (1894) 1 Ch 499. An inadvertent admission may with leave of the court be withdrawn.

[5] *Foster v Donald* (1820) 1 Jac & W 252.

also prepared to do so.[6] Furthermore, where a partner holds moneys in his hand, he cannot be ordered to make payment into court before the hearing of the action for account, if he claims, that on the taking of the account, an overall balance will be found to be due to him.[7] Neither will a partner be ordered to make payment into court of a sum which constitutes a debt owed to the partnership if the debt is not admitted and cannot be fully quantified.[8]

A court may, where it cannot compel a partner to make payment into court pending the outcome of an action for an account, nevertheless grant a Mareva injunction against him to prevent the distribution and dissipation of his assets, until the determination of the action for account.

A partner who is a defendant to an action for account, and who is ordered to make a payment into court, may still find that he is liable to be sued by the partnership's creditors on any unpaid partnership debts. In such a case he may seek a provision in the order, directing that he may apply for payment of any such debts, to be made out of any sums that he has paid into court.[9]

2. DISCOVERY

An order for an account and inquiry may be of little use to a partner unless, in seeking such an order, he is able to discover from his co-partners all relevant aspects of the transactions and dealings which form the subject matter of the dispute between the partners, and for which an order for an account is sought. Accordingly, a partner seeking an order for account is also entitled to an order for discovery against his co-partner(s).[10] Where discovery is sought in such circumstances against a former partner in a legal practice, the former partner cannot refuse to make available for discovery any relevant documents in his possession on the grounds of legal professional privilege.[11] Furthermore, a partner who fails to

---

6 See *Foster v Donald* (1820) 1 Jac & W 252.
7 *Richardson v Bank of England* (1838) 4 My & Cr 165. However, where a partner has withdrawn more from the partnership than he ought to have done he may be ordered to make payment in respect of the excess.
8 *Mills v Hanson* (1802) 8 Ves 68; *Wanklyn v Wilson* (1887) 35 Ch D 180. Where such a debt can be quantified and there is no claim by the partner concerned that there is an overall balance due to him, an order for payment may be made.
9 *Toulmin v Copland* (1836) 3 Y & C Ex 625 at 643 but see *Toulmin v Copeland* (1819) 6 Price 405; *Piddocke v Burt* [1894] Ch 343.
10 See the Partnership Act 1890, ss 24(9) and 28: see also rights to discovery under RSC Ord 24 and CCR Ord 14. Note, however, the restrictions upon inspection of partnership books by an agent: *Bevan v Webb* [1901] 2 Ch 59 at 76.
11 *Lewthwaite v Stimson* (1966) 110 Sol Jo 188.

separate any private or other business records from any relevant partnership records in his possession may, on an order for discovery, be forced to produce all such records, unless those private or non-partnership records can be entirely physically separated from any relevant partnership records. In such a case the partnership records produced must constitute a complete and independent record.[12]

3. ANCILLARY ASPECTS TO DISCOVERY

A partner may, in order to increase the effectiveness of an order for discovery in cases where he is seeking an account, make an application for an Anton Piller order.[13] Such an order, although it seeks to protect vital evidence (such as partnership books) from possible loss or destruction is not readily granted by the courts, and must be regarded as an extraordinary remedy.[14]

Where, as an adjunct to the action for an account, interrogatories are permitted to be administered by the partner seeking the account to his co-partners,[15] an interrogated partner is generally only bound to provide information in his possession or obtainable by him, which would enable the partner seeking to administer the interrogatories to utilise the information so obtained for his benefit. A prime example of such a benefit would be for the partner administering the interrogatories to have the partnership books produced thereby for his inspection.[16] However, where a particular interrogatory is of a specific nature which cannot be answered, eg by a general reference to partnership books or accounts, the interrogatory must specify the particular information or source of information which is required.[17] The purpose of interrogatories, and the other ancillary remedies noted above, is to facilitate the production and inspection of documents relevant to the partnership, and in particular the partnership books, matters which are essential to a successful action for account.

Where the existence of a partnership is in dispute, the court

---

12 *Pickering v Pickering* (1883) 25 Ch D 247.
13 *Anton Piller K G v Manufacturing Processes Ltd* [1976] Ch 55.
14 *Yousif v Salama* [1980] 1 WLR 1540; *Emanuel v Emanuel* [1982] 1 WLR 669; *Distributori Automatici Italian SpA v Holford General Trading Co Ltd* [1985] 1 WLR 1066; *Lock International plc v Beswick* [1989] 1 WLR 1268 at 1281; *Tate Access Floors Inc v Boswell* [1991] Ch 512; *Colombia Pictures Industries Inc v Robinson* [1987] Ch 38.
15 RSC Ord 26, r 1(3); CCR Ord 14, r 11.
16 *Christian v Taylor* (1841) 11 Sim 401; *Seeley v Boehm* (1817) 2 Madd 176.
17 *Drake v Symes* (1859) John 647; *Taylor v Rundell (No 1)* (1841) Cr & Ph 104; *Earl of Glengall v Frazer* (1842) 2 Hare 99; *Taylor v Rundell (No 2)* (1843) 1 Ph 222: *Alliott v Smith* [1895] 2 Ch 111.

cannot compel a party to produce any potentially relevant books or documents in any action for an account unless all the alleged partners are joined as parties to the action.[18] This is but a particular example of the general principle that a party cannot be compelled to produce the books or documents of a business which belong not only to him, but also to persons who are not a party to any action in which the production of such documents or books is sought.[19]

On the obtaining of an order for the production and inspection of partnership books and documents, a partner may authorise such inspection to be carried out by his agent be it, eg a solicitor or an accountant.[20] The co-partners may prevent such an inspection if they can show that their objection to inspection by the nominated agent is not unreasonable.[1]

Any information obtained as a result of an inspection of partnership documents cannot lawfully be used by the partner who has carried out such an inspection, except in relation to the partnership business or the relevant action. The disclosure of any such information by a partner to third parties may therefore be restrained by the co-partners by resort to an injunction.[2]

Where partnership documents such as partnership books are in continuous use at a partnership's place(s) of business, production and inspection of any books or documents may be ordered to take place in situ.[3] As an alternative, production and inspection of verified copies of such documents may be ordered by the court if it considers such a procedure as sufficient. Only in exceptional circumstances will the documents be ordered to be deposited in court.[4]

---

[18] Trustees may, however, be compelled to produce documents of business affairs (even if they relate to a partnership with other persons who are not parties to the action) at the behest of the beneficiaries, where the trustees have used trust moneys in carrying on that business. Where defendant partners are joined to the action as representative defendants the interests of all parties affected by such representation must not conflict as regards disclosure of partners' records or documents: *Murray v Walter* (1839) Cr & Ph 114. A party cannot be joined to an action if the only reason for so doing would be to obtain inspection of a partnership document, *Douihech v Findley* [1990] 1 WLR 269.

[19] *Stuart v Lord Bute* (1841) 11 Sim 442, (1842) 12 Sim 460; *Vyse v Foster* (1872) LR 13 Eq 602; see also *Bovill v Cowan* (1870) 5 Ch App 495; RSC Ord 24, rr 12, 13(1), Ord 29, r 2, Ord 38, r 13; CCR Ord 14, rr 7, 8; *Re Smith* [1891] 1 Ch 323.

[20] *Wilhams v Prince of Wales Life Co* (1857) 23 Beav 338; *Bevan v Webb* [1901] 2 Ch 59; see Partnership Act 1890, s 24(9) and Chapter 11.

[1] *Draper v Manchester & Sheffield Rly* (1861) 7 Jur NS 86.

[2] Information obtained pursuant to s 24(9) may not be subject to such restraint: *Crest Holmes plc v Marks* [1987] AC 829.

[3] RSC Ord 24, r 14.

[4] *Mertens v Haigh* (1860) John 735.

Consideration must now be given to the defences that may be raised by a partner(s) who seeks to defend a claim by a co-partner to a partnership account.

4. LIMITATION[5]

Actions for account between partners will not become time-barred during the subsistence of the partnership. Only where the partnership is dissolved, or a partner is expelled from the partnership, will any such action maintained by a partner against his former partners be subject to the provisions of the Limitation Act 1980.[6] The Limitation Act[7] provides that an action for account will be governed by the same limitation period which governs the claim which forms the basis of the account. It must be noted, however, in accordance with Pt II of the Limitation Act 1980[8] that fraud on the part of the defendant partners, or the disability of the plaintiff partner, may postpone the accrual of the limitation period that would otherwise govern the action for an account.

Closely related to the concept of limitation are the equitable doctrines of laches and acquiescence.[9] Where a partner fails by negligent inactivity to instigate an action for account against his co-partners, he may indicate by such an omission, that he has acquiesced in his claim. Such acquiescence may lead to the court refusing to grant the equitable relief of taking an account, through the application of the doctrine of laches.

5. DENIAL OF PARTNERSHIP

A party who is a defendant to an action for a partnership account may resist the action by denying that a partnership actually exists, or ever existed, between him and the plaintiff. Such a denial[10] may also

---

[5] For a review of the defence of limitation see McGee *Limitations Periods* (1994) and Prime and Scanlan *The Modern Law of Limitation* (1993).

[6] See *Betjemann v Betjemann* [1895] 2 Ch 474. Furthermore time will run in any action between partners and a *former* partner: see *Knox v Gye* (1872) LR 5 HL 656. See also Partnership Act 1890, s 43. Even a time-barred action may be effectively revived by an act of acknowledgment. Such an act results in the accrual of a fresh cause of action. Any sum that could have been claimed under an action for account that has expired may be revived by part payment of the relevant debt or liquidated pecuniary claim: see *Whitley v Lowe* (1858) 2 De G & J 704.

[7] Section 23.

[8] Sections 28 and 32 of the 1980 Act; *Rawlins v Wickham* (1858) 3 De G & J 304; *Betjemann v Betjemann* [1895] 2 Ch 474.

[9] See Prime and Scanlan *The Modern Law of Limitations*, Chapter 13 and p 43, above.

[10] Which should be made on oath.

be used as a ground for refusing to answer interrogatories, and in resisting an order for discovery of any business documents.[11]

Nevertheless, despite the denial of the existence of a partnership by a defendant to an action for account the courts may still order discovery of documents in the possession of the defendant which the court considers are relevant to the issue of whether a partnership actually exists or has existed between the parties to the action. In *Mansell v Feeney*[12] the court, though ordering that inspection of business documents in the possession of the defendant should take place, also prevented the plaintiff from inspecting parts of certain business books in the possession of the defendant which the latter had sworn did not bear upon the issues in the action. Furthermore, the courts will not permit the administering of interrogatories to the defendant in an action for account which are not directly pertinent to the issues raised by the action.[13]

It is advisable, therefore, where a defendant to an action for a partnership account denies the existence of a partnership between himself and the plaintiff, to have the issue of the existence of the partnership determined as a preliminary issue.[14]

6. SETTLED ACCOUNT

An account which has been agreed between partners may subsequently constitute a defence for any partner who is a defendant to an action for a partnership account, but only in so far as such an action seeks an account of transactions and matters already covered by the agreed account.[15] Such an agreed or 'settled' account should, in order to constitute a defence to an action for account, have the following characteristics:

(1)   the account should be in writing, although it need not be prepared in any particular prescribed form;
(2)   although it is desirable that the settled account be signed by all

---

[11] *Sanders v King* (1821) 6 Madd 61; *Harris v Harris* (1844) 3 Hare 450.
[12] (1861) 2 John & H 313.
[13] Thus in *Kennedy v Dodson* [1895] 1 Ch 334 the plaintiff sought to establish a partnership in respect of certain land transactions. He was not permitted to administer interrogatories to the defendant in respect of matters which related to the existence of several partnership relationships with the defendant which were unrelated to the transaction in issue in the action.
[14] See RSC Ord 33, r 3; CCR Ord 17, r 1. Such a practice would establish at the outset the documents in the possession of the defendant which are relevant to the action as well as the nature of the interrogatories that can be administered: see also *Re Leigh* (1877) 6 Ch D 256.
[15] *Taylor v Shaw* (1824) 2 Sim & St 12.

the partners, it is only necessary for all the partners to have received and acquiesed in the account;[16]

(3) the acquiesence of a partner in the settled account must relate not only to the principles which governed the taking and preparation of the account, but also to the particular items included in the account;

(4) a settled account remains for the above purposes a settled account despite the omission of a few items which are not unambiguously relevant to the account.

A court may set aside a settled partnership account if it has been tainted in its preparation in whole or in part by the fraud or misrepresentation of a partner. In such cases a new account will be directed.[17] There would appear to be no time limit upon a court making such a direction, especially in cases where fraud on the part of a partner can be established in respect of the preparation of the relevant account.

Where the whole of a settled account is affected by error, however, a new account will be directed by the court, unless the settled account has been left to stand for a considerable time.[18] Where an account is left to stand, the only remedy available to an aggrieved partner is to seek leave to surcharge and falsify the settled account, where both errors of fact and law in respect of any partnership account may be corrected. Both parties to an action for account may seek such leave.[19] The court may, as an alternative to the granting of the above remedies, merely rectify particular items in the settled account. Any errors in a settled account must be separately identified and established by the partner seeking to contest the account. This remains the case even where the account was originally settled on an errors excepted basis. Where an item has been omitted from a partnership account as a result of a mutual mistake on the part of the partners, the account will normally be subject to correction by the court. In the absence of fraud or undue influence, improper omissions from a settled account, which are known to the partners, will however be regarded as having been dealt with in an

---

[16] Thus, merely rendering an account to a partner will not prevent a partner seeking to have the account taken again under the direction of the court: *Clements v Bowes* (1853) 1 Drew 684 at 692. Although the settled account should thus be agreed between all the partners, an account agreed between a majority of the partners may rarely bind all, but this latter view remains doubtful. See *Carmichael v Carmichael* (1846) 2 Ph 101.

[17] *Vernon v Vawdry* (1740) 2 Atk 119; *Clarke v Tipping* (1846) 9 Beav 284.

[18] *Williamson v Barbour* (1877) 9 Ch D 529; *Gething v Keighley* (1878) 9 Ch D 547.

[19] *Brownell v Brownell* (1786) 2 Bro CC 61.

agreed manner, and accordingly the settled partnership account will not be subject to correction by the court.[20]

A settled account which has been prepared following the retirement, death or expulsion of a partner may involve the partners, former partners or personal representatives of a deceased partner giving mutual releases. In such cases the settled account cannot be set aside and a new account ordered by the court until the mutual releases are themselves set aside.[1]

7. ARBITRATION AWARD

An action for account instituted by a partner against his co-partners may be resisted by a defendant partner, on the ground that the matters the subject of the dispute which have provoked the action have, prior to the instigation of the action for account, been settled by an arbitration award binding on the plaintiff partner. An agreement to *refer* such disputed matters to arbitration will not constitute a defence to an action for account, but may constitute a ground for the staying of the action.[2]

Other defences to an action for account

Where a sum of money is paid by one partner to a co-partner which the latter accepts in lieu of all demands that he may have made against the former in respect of any dispute connected with the partnership, then such an action will amount to an accord and satisfaction, and will constitute a good defence to an action for an account.[3]

---

[20] *Laing v Campbell* (1865) 36 Beav 3.

[1] *Fowler v Wyatt* (1857) 24 Beav 232.

[2] *Routh v Peach* (1795) 2 Anst 519; affd 3 Anst 637; *Thompson v Charnock* (1799) 8 Term Rep 139. Cf the position where the arbitration award relates to matters other than those the subject matter of the action for account, see *Spencer v Spencer* (1828) 2 Y & J 249. Many partnership agreements contain a provision providing for the referral of partnership disputes to arbitration. A partner seeking to bring an action concerning the partnership to the courts where the partnership agreement contains such a provision may find the action stayed on the application of his co-partners, under the Arbitration Act 1950, s 4. In such a case a stay will be granted so that arbitration may be continued unless the court is satisfied that the matter could be resolved more satisfactorily by court action and that the partners seeking to stay court proceedings are doing so purely to delay, see *Russell v Russell* (1880) 14 Ch D 471. Arbitration is generally unsuitable for resolving partnership disputes where there are allegations of fraud or gross professional incompetence made between the partners: *Turner v Fenton* [1982] 1 WLR 52.

[3] *Brown v Perkins* (1842) 1 Hare 564.

If a partner has agreed to waive all rights to seek an action for an account and such an agreement is untainted by fraud or undue influence and, furthermore, the agreement is supported by sufficient consideration, no party to that agreement will be permitted to maintain any action for account in respect of any partnership accounts which are the subject of such an agreement.[4]

As has been noted above, a release will be a defence to an action for account. However, a release can be set aside, and a new account ordered, if the account the subject of the release is subsequently found by the court to be erroneous. Nevertheless, in such cases the relevant account may be permitted to stand, if evidence can establish that the partners intended without condition and unambiguously to abide by that account. A release can always be set aside if there has been fraud or misrepresentation exercised by a partner in securing the release.[5] A release, if it is not to be regarded as merely a form of settled account, must be effected by deed.[6]

1. JUDGMENT FOR A PARTNERSHIP ACCOUNT

The judgment for an account should require the account to be taken of all partners' dealings and transactions between the plaintiff partner(s) and the defendant co-partner(s) from a specified date. The judgment should also provide that, upon the taking of the account, the account should be certified to be due from either of the parties to the other. The judgment may also provide that payment by one party to the other should be made in accordance with that certified to be due from one party to the other party.[7]

The judgment for an account may make supplementary provision for the taking of the account in chambers[8] or leave such directions to the master or district judge. The costs of such an action (being an account sought without a dissolution) will usually follow the event. The costs incurred in taking an account will usually be paid out of partnership assets, and where such assets are insufficient by a contribution between the partners. The costs of the action, if payable out of partnership assets, will nevertheless rank in order of priority

[4] *Sewell v Bridge* (1749) 1 Ves Sen 297.
[5] *Brooks v Sutton* (1868) LR 5 Eq 361.
[6] *Millar v Craig* (1843) 6 Beav 433.
[7] For appropriate precedents of such an order see *Atkins Court Forms* (2nd edn) vol 30 (1987 issue) p 123ff.
[8] RSC Ord 44, r 3(a); Ord 43, r 3; CCR Ord 13, r 7(1) and Ord 23, r 2(3). County Courts Act 1984, s 65(1)(b); CCR Ord 19, Pt II.

after partnership debts and liabilities, and any sums due to partners in respect of advances.[9]

2.   TAKING THE ACCOUNT

In the taking of a partnership account[10] under a judgment, regard should be had to the financial standing both between partners and non-partners, and partners inter se. In the latter case, particular regard should be had to advances made by partners to the partnership. Furthermore, any profits and losses of the partnership should be apportioned between the partners in accordance with the terms of the partnership agreement[11] in order that cross claims can be settled. In taking the partnership account, the personal property of the partners must be distinguished from partnership property. To this end, regard must also be had to the joint and separate debts of the partners, and the profits and losses which are to be credited or debited to a particular partner or partners, or to all the partners. Allowances which are regarded as just and reasonable between the partners will be made in taking the account. What is just and reasonable will be determined by the terms of the partnership agreement and by the principles of the law of partnership.[12]

An account ordered by the court will be taken, as a general rule, from the date of the last settled account of the partnership, unless the latter is reopened.[13] In all other cases the account of the partnership dealings and transactions will, as a general principle, be taken from the date of the commencement of the partnership.[14] Where the partners have had dealings prior to the formation of the partnership, which however are nevertheless pertinent to the setting up of the partnership, an account can also be taken of such dealings.[15]

In taking an account the partnership books and documents are of paramount importance. Unless entries in the partnership books have been made by a partner without the knowledge and authority of his co-partners, such entries are prima facie evidence of the

---

[9]   *Austin v Jackson* (1879) 11 Ch D 942n; *Butcher v Pooler* (1883) 24 Ch D 273.

[10]   Which may be taken by a professional accountant or the official referee, RSC Ord 32, r 16, Ord 40. See also County Courts Act 1984, s 39; *Hill v King* (1863) New Rep 341; RSC Ord 36, r 1; County Courts Act 1984, s 65(1)(b); CCR Ord 19, Pt II.

[11]   *West v Skip* (1749) 1 Ves Sen 239.

[12]   See Chapter 1.

[13]   See fn 11, above and *Beak v Beak* (1675) Cas temp Finch 190; *Cook v Collingridge* (1823) Jac 607.

[14]   See fn 7, above.

[15]   *Cruickshank v McVicar* (1844) 8 Beav 106.

relevant transactions.[16] Although a judgment for an account may direct that all the partners will produce on oath all relevant partnership books and documents in their possession, in the absence of such a direction a partner may seek from his co-partners any relevant partnership books and documents by way of discovery.[17]

THE ACTION FOR AN ACCOUNT AS AN ADJUNCT TO THE DISSOLUTION OF A PARTNERSHIP

The above rules and principles concerning the action for an account are also generally applicable to such an action where it is ancilliary to the dissolution of a partnership.

The particular rules and principles applicable to the taking of a partnership account, where such an account is an adjunct to a dissolution, are considered in the chapter which considers the grounds upon which a partnership may be dissolved.[18]

Actions for fraud and misrepresentation

A partner may have been induced by either the fraud or fraudulent misrepresentation of a co-partner(s) to enter into a partnership agreement. In such a case he may, on discovering the fraud, either affirm or rescind the partnership agreement. In either event he may *also* claim damages for any loss sustained by him as a consequence of the fraud or fraudulent misrepresentation of his co-partner(s).[19]

However, where the representation of a co-partner which induces a partner to enter into the partnership is either negligent or innocent, the partner who has suffered loss as a consequence may find that the courts will only award him damages but not grant him recission of the partnership agreement. Where damages are awarded to a partner in lieu of rescission of the

---

[16] *Lodge v Prichard* (1853) 3 De GM & G 906; *Gething v Keighley* (1878) 9 Ch D 547.

[17] See p 224 above for a consideration of the law relating to the production of partnership documents upon discovery.

[18] See Chapter 12.

[19] *Archer v Brown* [1985] QB 401; *Redgrave v Hurd* (1881) 20 Ch D 1; *Derry v Peak* (1889) 14 App Cas 337. Cf where the fraudulent action is that of a third party, which cannot be attributed to a co-partner. See also recovery for a negligent misrepresentation by a third party: *Hedley Byrne & Co Ltd v Heller & Partners Ltd* [1964] AC 465.

partnership agreement under the Misrepresentation Act 1967 the measure of damages will be those recoverable under the laws of contract.[20]

Notwithstanding the above, any misrepresentation – be it innocent, negligent or fraudulent – by one partner to another partner, which induces the latter to enter into a partnership agreement, will give rise to a right to rescind such an agreement.[1] This right does not seem to be lost, even where, before entering into the partnership agreement, the innocent partner could have discovered but did not discover the true facts.[2]

The principal rights of a partner where a partnership has been dissolved for fraud or misrepresentation are now encapsulated in s 41 of the Partnership Act 1890 which provides that:

'Where a partnership contract is rescinded on the ground of the fraud or misrepresentation of one of the parties thereto, the party entitled to rescind is, without prejudice to any other right, entitled

(a)   to a lien on, or right of retention of, the surplus of the partnership assets, after satisfying the partnership liabilities, for any sum of money paid by him for the purchase of a share in the partnership and for any capital contributed by him, and is

(b)   to stand in the place of the creditors of the firm for any payments made by him in respect of the partnership liabilities, and

(c)   to be indemnified by the person guilty of the fraud or making the representation against all the debts and liabilities of the firm.'

Section 41 is not intended to be exhaustive in prescribing the rights which a partner may exercise following the rescission of a partnership agreement. As has been noted above, a partner may in such cases also seek damages from his co-partner(s) for any consequential loss arising from his co-partner's fraud or misrepresentation. It would also seem that, in addition to recovering the price paid for his partnership share and interest thereon, a partner rescinding a partnership agreement may also recover any capital he has contributed to the partnership with interest. Further, he retains a lien on any

---

[20] See under the Misrepresentation Act 1967, s 2(1).

[1] *Redgrave v Hurd* (1881) 20 Ch D1; *Museprime Properties v Adhill Properties* (1990) 61 P & Cr 111.

[2] *Rawlins v Wickham* (1858) 1 Giff 355.

surplus partnership assets pending payment of such interest and the costs of any action.[3] Where the partnership has been dissolved for fraud or misrepresentation a partner may also be able to claim interest on payments made by him in satisfying partnership debts and liabilities. Conversely, he must in such cases give credit to his co-partners, with interest, for any sums received by him during the subsistence of the partnership which constitute his share of any partnership profits.[4]

An agreement to dissolve a partnership may itself be subject to rescission. The principal ground justifying a party seeking to rescind a dissolution agreement is that he was induced to enter into the agreement as a consequence of fraud or misrepresentation.

Injunctions

A partner may act in such a way that he effectively and wilfully disregards the terms of the partnership agreement. He may also act in breach of the implied duty of good faith that he owes to his co-partner(s). In such cases the courts may be prepared, at the instigation of his co-partners, to grant an injunction against the offending partner so as to restrain his miscreant and potentially destructive behaviour. However, an injunction, being an equitable remedy, will not be granted without sufficient or suitable cause.

Accordingly, temporary or minor squabbles and disagreements between partners will not constitute sufficient or suitable grounds for the granting of equitable relief. However, a partner may seek an injunction so as to prevent his co-partner(s) from excluding him from involvement in the partnership business.[5] A partner may also seek an injunction so as to prevent his co-partner(s) from using partnership assets otherwise than in the course of the partnership enterprise.[6] The prevention of a partner by his co-partner(s) from enjoying the benefit of partnership assets[7] will also constitute sufficient and suitable grounds for the granting of an injunction by the courts.

The courts have also seen fit to grant an injunction where a partner retired from a fixed term partnership and, before the expiration of that partnership, he sought to carry on an enterprise in direct

---

[3] Or costs incurred in the action.

[4] *Adam v Newbigging* (1888) 13 App Cas 308; *Rawlins v Wickham* (1858) 1 Giff 355.

[5] *Hall v Hall* (1855) 20 Beav 139.

[6] See Chapter 8.

[7] *Doe d Warn v Horn* (1838) 3 M & W 333; *Hawkins v Hawkins* (1858) 4 Jur NS 1044.

competition with his former partners. Furthermore, in conjunction with his new partners he assumed the name of the old partnership and interfered in the latter's affairs. The injunction granted by the courts in favour of the former partners not only restrained the defendant ex-partner from carrying on his new business, but also prevented his new partners from engaging in that business with him.[8]

The above is an example of gross misconduct on the part of an ex-partner which was restrained by an injunction. The misconduct of a partner within a subsisting partnership, which renders the continuance of the partnership virtually and practically impossible, will also justify the co-partners in seeking an injunction restraining such conduct. Where the misconduct which is the subject of complaint is carried out by a partner who has been appointed by the partnership agreement as the managing partner, an injunction restraining that partner's conduct will generally only be granted by the courts in the most obvious situations, where the case against the miscreant partner is particularly strong.[9] The courts will not grant an injunction in such cases if the partner(s) seeking the injunction can only establish that the misconduct of the managing partner is merely affecting or may affect the public's confidence in the business enterprise.[10]

Since an injunction is an equitable remedy, a partner seeking this relief must show that he is not in breach of any of the obligations imposed upon him by the partnership agreement, or by the Partnership Act 1890. Such a partner must therefore be able and willing to perform his own partnership obligations before he seeks to restrain any co-partner[11] from any breach of his equivalent obligations. A partner's own misconduct may, therefore, constitute a complete bar to a successful application for an injunction, irrespective of the behaviour of a miscreant co-partner.[12]

It has been argued[13] that an injunction will not be granted in favour of a partner and against a co-partner, restraining the latter from breaching his partnership obligations, where the partnership is a partnership at will. The supposed rationale behind this rule was that an injunction would be rendered a nullity by a partner giving

---

[8] See *England v Curling* (1844) 8 Beav 129; see also *Aas v Benham* [1891] 2 Ch 244.
[9] *Waters v Taylor* (1808) 15 Ves 10; *Walker v Hirsch* (1884) 27 Ch D 460.
[10] *Anon* (1856) 2 K & J 441.
[11] Or in appropriate cases a former partner: see *England v Curling* (1844) 8 Beav 129.
[12] *Smith v Fromont* (1818) 2 Swan 330; *Littlewood v Caldwell* (1822) 11 Price 97.
[13] See *Lindley & Banks on Partnership* (16th edn) para 23–133.

notice of dissolution of the partnership. Modern authority would seem however to suggest such a view is unfounded.[14]

Injunctions granted in respect of and as an adjunct to a dissolution action are considered in outline in the chapter on dissolution of partnerships.[15]

Appointment of a receiver

An injunction is not the only remedy available to a partner[16] who seeks to prevent a co-partner from ignoring the terms of the partnership agreement, or from being in breach of his obligations as a partner. The courts may in such cases, on the application of a partner, appoint a receiver or receiver and manager to manage the partnership and its affairs. Such a remedy may be granted in conjunction with an injunction.[17] The appointment of a receiver is a draconian remedy, which affects all the members of the partnership including the partner(s) who sought the appointment. The difference between a receiver and a manager were set out succinctly by Lord Lindley:

'The object of having a receiver appointed by the Court is to place the partnership assets under the protection of the Court, and to prevent everybody, except the officer of the court, from in any way intermeddling with them. The object of having a manager is to have the partnership business carried on under the direction of the Court, a receiver, unless he is also appointed manager, has no power to carry on the business.'[18]

The courts are most reluctant to appoint a receiver otherwise than with a view to a dissolution of a partnership. Furthermore, without a partnership being in dissolution the courts have never appointed a receiver and manager.[19] There would appear to be three instances, however, where the courts have been willing to appoint a receiver

14 See *Floydd v Cheney* [1970] Ch 602.
15 See Chapter 13.
16 It seems that an employee who is entitled to a share of the firm's profits may seek such a remedy: *Walker v Hirsch* (1884) 27 Ch D 460; *Katsch v Schenck* (1849) 18 LJ Ch 386. But note *Sobell v Boston* [1975] 1 WLR 1587. The remedy is, however, available to a party who claims he is a partner to an enterprise if he can establish a prima facie case of the existence of the partnership and his membership of that enterprise: *Floydd v Cheney* [1970] Ch 602.
17 *Evans v Coventry* (1854) 3 Drew 75.
18 See *Lindley* (16th edn) para 23-143.
19 See *Lindley* (16th edn) para 23-143.

without a dissolution of the partnership.[20] These cases are as follows:

(1)   where the misconduct of a partner has produced a situation of jeopardy to the partnership assets.[1] Such misconduct must be of so grave a nature that it destroys immediately the relationship of mutual trust that must subsist between the members of the partnership;[2]
(2)   where a party has fraudulently induced another party to enter into a partnership;[3]
(3)   where a partner wrongfully excludes a co-partner from the management of the partnership business,[4] or prevents the co-partner from enjoying his interests in the partnership assets.[5]

In considering whether to appoint a receiver, the court will have regard to various matters. Thus, the larger the firm, the less likely will the court be ready to appoint a receiver, the courts in such cases are more willing to grant a remedy to an aggrieved partner by way of injunctive relief.

Furthermore, since the appointment of a receiver is a matter of discretion, the courts are most reluctant to do so where the partnership consists of a professional practice. In such cases the court is cognisant of the possibility that the appointment of a receiver will damage the professional standing both of individual partners and the partnership as a whole. This matter was considered by Megarry J in *Floydd v Cheney*, and he concluded:[6]

'I do not think that it can be denied that news that a receiver of a business or a professional practice has been appointed is news that may well cause members of the general public to hesitate in resorting to that business or practice. It may well indeed be that some of the inferences that the public would draw from the

---

[20]   *Rowe v Wood* (1822) 2 Jac & W 553.
[1]   See *Const v Harris* (1824) Turn & R 496.
[2]   Such misconduct includes: (i) misappropriation of assets (see *Evans v Coventry* (1854) 5 De G M & G 911; *Sheppard v Oxenford* (1855) 1 K & J 491); (ii) collusion with debtors (*Estwick v Conningsby* (1682) 1 Vern 118); (iii) the improper use of partnership assets and mismanagement of partnership affairs so as to endanger the whole enterprise, *Harding v Glover* (1810) 18 Ves 281.
[3]   *Ex p Broome* (1811) 1 Rose 69.
[4]   Examples of such conduct include cases where a partner maintains that his co-partner is not a partner, or that no partnership exists: see *Tate v Barry* (1928) 28 SRNSW 380.
[5]   See fn 7, p 235, above.
[6]   [1970] 2 WLR 314 at 320; see also *Sobell v Boston* [1975] 1 WLR 1587 at 1593–1594.

appointment of a receiver would be quite wrong; but one cannot expect the public to have a precise appreciation of every aspect of the institution of receivership. One must remember that a professional man's reputation is a delicate blossom, which, once injured, can never be fully restored.'

It follows that where the existence of a partnership is in dispute, and the appointment of a receiver is sought within interlocutory proceedings relating to the disputed partnership, the courts will be most unwilling to make such an appointment if it would be likely to damage the defendant's business or professional reputation.[7]

A defendant partner in any action concerning the partnership may seek the appointment of a receiver by way of a summons or motion or by way of counter-claim to a plaintiff partner's action.[8] Where a defendant denies the existence of a partnership which the plaintiff claims exists between the parties, the defendant in that action cannot seek the appointment of a receiver by way of summons or motion but only by way of counter-claim.[9]

The appointment, remuneration and powers and duties of a receiver are considered in the chapter on dissolution of a partnership.[10]

Actions for specific performance

In accordance with the general principles governing the granting of the remedy of specific performance, the courts will not as a matter of course order the specific performance of an agreement for a partnership.[11] Not only do the courts usually regard damages as an adequate remedy for the breach of such an agreement, but there is the recognition by the courts that a partnership agreement which is specifically enforced could still be immediately dissolved by one of the partners if it is one at will. Even a partnership agreement for a fixed term partnership might, if it was specifically enforced, subsequently require the court to supervise the partnership

---

[7] See cases cited in fn 6, above and *Chapman v Beach* (1820) 1 Jac & W 594; *Hardy v Hardy* (1917) 62 Sol Jo 142. Note also the problems that may arise if subsequently the partnership is found to be illegal: see *Sheppard v Oxenford* (1855) 1 K & J 491.

[8] See RSC Ord 15, r 2, Ord 30, r 1; CCR Ord 9, r 2(1)(d), Ord 32, r 1; *Sargant v Read* (1876) 1 Ch D 600.

[9] Equally, where the plaintiff's action is not based on the existence of a partnership: see *Floydd v Cheney* [1970] Ch 602.

[10] See Chapter 12.

[11] *Hercy v Birch* (1804) 9 Ves 357; *Sichel v Mosenthal* (1862) 30 Beav 371.

throughout its existence. This latter difficulty may not, however, constitute an unsurmountable obstacle to the granting of an order for specific performance of a partnership agreement,[12] and the courts have in a limited number of cases been prepared to grant to a party the remedy of specific performance of a partnership agreement. Thus, they have ordered a party, once he has become a member of a partnership, to execute a formal agreement which sets out the terms of that partnership. Such an order may confer rights upon the members of a partnership which can only be enforced inter se when a formal agreement has been executed. The court will make an order in the above circumstances notwithstanding that the relevant partnership may be subject to immediate dissolution.[13]

Where a plaintiff claims in an action that there is a partnership in existence between him and the defendant which the latter denies, the courts may declare and order that any partnership agreement made between the parties shall be specifically enforced. In general, such an order may then provide the basis for an action for account to enable a party to recover his share of the profits of a business transaction or enterprise to which he has contributed.[14]

The courts may also grant an order for the specific performance of an agreement for the dissolution of a partnership. Such an order will be granted where the court considers it just and equitable to do so.

Declarations and ancillary relief

The courts will, in exceptional cases, grant declaratory relief as to the rights and duties of partners under a partnership agreement.[15] Any such declaration must relate to a dispute existing between the partners which is more than merely trivial, or which gives rise to issues between the partners which are of more than academic or theoretical importance.

---

[12] See *Shiloh Spinners Ltd v Harding* [1973] AC 691 at 724 per Lord Wilberforce; *Tito v Waddell (No 2)* [1977] Ch 106 at 321–323, per Megarry V-C.

[13] *Buxton v Lister* (1746) 3 Atk 383; *Sichel v Mosenthal* (1862) 30 Beav 371 at 376.

[14] *Dale v Hamilton* (1846) 5 Hare 369; on appeal (1847) 2 Ph 266.

[15] See RSC Ord 15, r 16. Under the County Court Rules such a declaration may only be granted as ancilliary to a claim which the court has jurisdiction to hear and determine. See County Courts Act 1984.

Actions for damages

Although not strictly a matter involving partners, an action for damages may be maintained by one party against another for a breach by the latter of a mutual agreement to enter into a partnership. If a party, after becoming a party to a partnership agreement, refuses to carry out that agreement, he may be sued by the other parties to that agreement for damages. As an ancillary matter to such actions a court may order that any premiums paid by one party to another in contemplation of entering into a partnership may also be recovered.[16]

Despite the historical restrictions imposed upon partners in respect of an action for damages inter se,[17] it would seem that a partner may now seek such a remedy where his co-partner or co-partners have by their conduct breached the *express* terms of the partnership agreement.[18] Any damages awarded to a partner in an action against his co-partners may be recovered by way of a partnership account, though recovery of such damages is not dependent on the courts granting this remedy.[19] It is likely that a breach of the terms of the partnership agreement by a partner which is regarded by a co-partner to be so grave as to merit the latter instituting an action for damages against the former will generally lead to a dissolution of the partnership and the claim for damages being pursued and recovered in conjunction with an action for a partnership account. However, an action for damages for breach of the partnership agreement instituted by a partner against his co-partner(s) where the latter is, or are, in breach of any term(s) of the partnership agreement is not dependent on the plaintiff partner seeking an order for the dissolution of the partnership.[20]

[16] *Walker v Harris* (1793) 1 Anst 245; *Gale v Leckie* (1817) 2 Stark 107; *Andrewes v Garstin* (1861) 10 CBNS 444.
[17] See *Lindley* (16th edn) para 23-189 onwards for a consideration of the historical restrictions on the ability of a partner to maintain an action against a co-partner in respect of partnership matters.
[18] It remains unclear whether an action for damages can be maintained by a partner against a co-partner in respect of a breach of an implied duty of the latter to act in good faith: see Chapter 8. For an action for damages by a partner against a co-partner for breach of an express term of a partnership agreement, see *Hitchman v Crouch Butler Savage Associates* (1983) 80 LS Gaz R 554.
[19] A loss incurred by the partnership, as opposed to a loss sustained by an individual partner, may require the taking of an account before recovery of such loss can be maintained.
[20] See RSC Ord 81, r 6(1)(a); CCR Ord 25, r 10(1)(a).

Execution between partners

Although execution of a judgment against a partnership will gener-ally follow the normal procedures, special consideration must be given to the execution of judgments relating to actions between partners. Where a partner has maintained an action against his partnership, the latter being sued in the firm's name or, conversely, where a partner is sued by his partnership which pursues the action in the firm's name, any resulting judgment or order can only be enforced with leave of the court.[1] In giving such leave, the court may also make any direction it sees fit, and may direct the taking of accounts and enquiries.[2]

CASES IN WHICH THE COURT WILL NOT INTERFERE IN DISPUTES BETWEEN PARTNERS

Notwithstanding the general recognition of the rights of a partner to maintain an action against his co-partners in respect of partnership matters, the courts, acting in their equitable jurisdiction, may under certain circumstances refuse to grant any equitable relief sought by a partner against his co-partners. The grounds upon which the courts may refuse to interfere in partnership affairs are more restricted than formerly. In the past, the courts were particularly unwilling to allow a partner to maintain an action for account against his co-partners, otherwise than with a view to the dissolution of the partnership. A similar reluctance on the part of the courts was also prevalent where a partner sought an injunction against his co-partner(s). Although the granting of the forms of relief noted above no longer depends on a partner seeking the dissolution of the part-nership, the courts remain reluctant to appoint a receiver and manager unless dissolution of the firm is also sought.[3]

Trivial disputes

The courts will not permit themselves to become the forum for the airing of disputes between partners which are trivial in nature. In such circumstances, the courts will invariably decline to grant any

---

[1]   RSC Ord 81, r 6(1)(a); CCR Ord 25, r 10(1)(a).
[2]   RSC Ord 81, r 6(2); CCR Ord 25, r 10(2).
[3]   For the appointment of a receiver without the dissolution of a partnership see p 237, above. For the appointment of a receiver and manager as an adjunct to the dissolution or winding up of a partnership see Chapter 12.

equitable relief which is sought by a partner against a co-partner. The courts therefore expect partners to be flexible in the day-to-day running of the business and to exercise tolerance and forbearance, and to exhibit goodwill inter se. Squabbles and minor disagreements between partners are not therefore generally to be the subject of judicial scrutiny or interference.[4] Allied to this principle is the fact that the courts will not readily grant equitable relief to a partner in respect of the conduct of a co-partner where the latter is thereby carrying out the functions of the managing partner[5] unless that conduct constitutes an improper exercise of his management powers.[6]

Laches and acquiesence

Where a partner seeks equitable relief against a co-partner, he may find that his claim to such relief is defeated by the equitable doctrines of acquiesence and laches.[7] Thus, where a partner has delayed in seeking equitable relief against a co-partner, he may be regarded as having acquiesced or agreed to the alleged wrongdoing of his co-partner. In such cases equity may regard it as inequitable that he should therefore be permitted to enforce his claim. Furthermore, delay on the part of a partner to enforce a claim to equitable relief against a co-partner may render the claim stale and unenforceable; this is the application of the doctrine of laches. Both of the above defences may be denied to a defendant co-partner where he has himself acted improperly, eg by fraudulent or other improper conduct, which has contributed to the plaintiff partner's delay in seeking equitable relief. The defences of acquiescence and laches are especially pertinent to cases where a partner brings proceedings for a partnership account.[8]

The courts have shown a particular reluctance to grant a plaintiff the remedy of an order for specific performance of a partnership agreement where he has delayed entering into the relevant partnership. Such behaviour on the part of a plaintiff may frequently be explained on the ground that he hoped thereby to avoid the responsibility and liabilities of the partnership venture if the venture failed, but by subsequently bringing an action for specific performance he

---

[4] *Lawson v Morgan* (1815) 1 Price 303; *Anderson v Anderson* (1857) 25 Beav 190.
[5] And where the co-partner has been so appointed.
[6] *Lawson v Morgan* (1815) 1 Price 303.
[7] For the nature of these defences see Prime and Scanlan *The Modern Law of Limitations*, Chapter 12.
[8] See p 227, above and *Sherman v Sherman* (1692) 2 Vern 276; *Stupart v Arrowsmith* (1856) 3 Sm & G 176; *Thornton v Proctor* (1792) 1 Anst 94.

hopes to ensure a share of the profits and benefits of the partnership on its proving to be successful. Such conduct is inequitable on the partners involved in the venture from its inception who have been led to believe by such conduct that the plaintiff has abandoned the venture.[9] It would seem, however, that a defence of laches can be successfully raised in an action for specific performance of a partnership agreement even where the defendant cannot positively prove that the plaintiff has abandoned his rights in the proposed business venture.[10] Nevertheless, conduct on the part of a defendant partner(s) which expressly or impliedly recognises the continuing equitable rights of the plaintiff in the partnership or business will be fatal to the successful raising of the defence of laches.[11] Where a plaintiff can be proved to have abandoned his interest or involvement in a business venture he may be estopped from seeking to enforce such a claim against the parties who remain involved in that enterprise. Alternatively, such abandonment may be evidence from which the courts may infer that the plaintiff has agreed to release his rights in the venture to the other parties.[12]

It would appear that a defence of laches, where raised by a defendant, is most likely to succeed where a plaintiff has delayed instituting proceedings for specific performance of a partnership agreement and the relevant business venture involves high risk or is a speculative enterprise. The presence of such factors, however, can never be conclusive.[13] It has been mooted[14] that there are two authorities which seem to conflict with the general statements of principle considered above. The cases are *Clarke v Hart*[15] and *Clements v Hall*.[16] In the first case the plaintiff was a shareholder in a mining company. He also had a legal interest in the principal business asset, a mining lease which he had retained up to the time of the action. The plaintiff had failed to provide his share of the finance required to continue mining operations. His co-shareholders sought to exclude him (although without lawful authority) from

[9]   *Cowell v Watts* (1850) 2 H & Tw 224; cf *Blunden v Storm* (1971) 20 DLR (3d) 413.

[10]   See *Clegg v Edmondson* (1857) 8 De GM & G 787; *Reilly v Walsh* (1848) 11 1 Eq R 22.

[11]   *Penny v Pickwick* (1852) 16 Beav 246.

[12]   *M'Lure v Ripley* (1850) 2 Mac & G 274; *Palmer v Moore* [1900] AC 293; *Garden Gully United Quartz Mining Co v McLister* (1875) 1 App Cas 39.

[13]   *Norway v Rowe* (1812) 19 Ves 144; cf *Clegg v Edmondson* (1856) 8 De GM & G 787 where the venture was self-financing.

[14]   See *Lindley* (16th edn) para 23–26 onwards.

[15]   (1858) 6 HL Cas 633.

[16]   (1857) 24 Beav 333; on appeal (1858) 2 De G & J 173.

the venture, and to deny him any share of the profits realised by the business. In the circumstances of the case the court was not prepared to hold the plaintiff a trustee of his share of the mining lease for the benefit of his co-shareholders. The court, therefore, had no alternative but to hold that he retained a beneficial interest in the mining lease and accordingly granted the plaintiff his share of the profits of the enterprise realised on that asset. *Clements v Hall*, another mining lease venture, can be explained, inter alia, on the improper conduct on the part of the sole surviving partner of the business. It was this conduct which had delayed the instigation of proceedings against him. Furthermore, the plaintiff who sought to enforce his rights, both in respect of the business and in respect of his rights in the principal business asset (the mining lease), was an assignee of such rights. The assignor had obtained the relevant share of the mining lease under the will of one of the original partners of the venture. This beneficiary had also sought by action to ascertain his rights. The beneficiary was held on the facts of the case to have commenced his action promptly. The plaintiff was also held to have commenced his action without unreasonable delay. Accordingly, there had been no laches on the part of either, and the plaintiff was entitled to the relief he claimed so as to secure his interest in the mining lease.

Both of the above cases, therefore, can be explained within the context of their special circumstances, and do not displace the general proposition that the courts are unwilling to grant relief to a party who, by an action, seeks to claim an interest in a business venture as a partner, where he has delayed in seeking to enforce his claim.

CHAPTER 11

PARTNERSHIP ACCOUNTS

INTRODUCTION

Partnership is a business carried on in common with a view to profit.[1] It follows from this definition that a basic concept within partnership law is that of profit.[2] Profit is a matter of calculation, since all businesses have income and overheads, and the profit element is the difference between the two.[3] In any business it is desirable that its financial position be ascertained at regular intervals since businesses can make both profits and losses, and large losses can quickly lead to business annihilation if not curtailed. In the case of partnership there is a further reason for the regular calculation of profit, since, if the business becomes loss-making, and the losses can be shown to be endemic and unlikely to be reversed, the business can no longer be said to be carried on with a view to profit, and any of the partners may bring it to an end on that ground before the firm's capital has been wiped out.

Full accounts will be drawn and agreed between the partners on a yearly basis. In practice, it is likely that interim balances and calculations of profit or loss will take place on a regular basis within the year, probably on a monthly or quarterly basis, so that any adjustments necessary to the business practices or direction of the firm can be achieved when the need for them can be first identified.

Consideration of partnership accounts involves consideration of three separate topics, namely: the obligation to keep accounts; profit and loss; and the manner in which the accounts should be kept. These will now be considered in turn.

---

[1] See Chapter 1.
[2] Discussed at p 12, above.
[3] For a fuller discussion of the profit concept see p 253, below.

OBLIGATION TO KEEP ACCOUNTS

In general there is no specific requirement of partnership law that accounts be kept. To this broad general principle there is an exception in the case of partnerships, whether limited or ordinary, all of whose participants having unlimited liability are limited companies, thereby limiting their liability through the limited liability of the company (the limited company exception).[4] This exceptional situation is discussed later, and derives from the requirements of the Partnerships and Unlimited Companies (Accounts) Regulations 1993.[5]

It follows that such requirements as exist for most partnerships to keep accounts arise from general partnership law. General partnership law supports the account-drawing process in two respects. First, it presumes that accurate books of accounts will be kept and be available for inspection by any of the partners.[6] Thus, the partnership is obliged to keep detailed books containing the minutiae of information of the firm's financial dealings from which the accounts can be drawn at regular intervals. Further, s 28 of the Partnership Act imposes on members of a partnership an obligation 'to render true accounts and full information of all things affecting the partnership'. This obligation, of course, is one created in favour of the partners themselves, but the law recognises the interests of third parties in such accounts[7] and the Inland Revenue will calculate the tax responsibilities of the partnership from the books and accounts which are kept.

The significance attached to the keeping of accounts by the Partnership Act itself is, however, only part of the picture. The statutory provisions merely, however, arise from deeper duties recognised at common law. The right to have proper accounts kept of the financial transactions entered into by, and on behalf of, the firm is one of the fundamental incidents of a partnership which will be upheld and supported by the courts.[8] Thus, where proper accounts have not been kept, or where proper accounts have been kept but have been destroyed or falsified, any innocent partner who has not been involved in the impropriety can sue for an account to be taken and, where it finds it has no firm foundation on which to

---

[4] Discussed p 248, below.
[5] SI 1993/1820.
[6] Section 24.
[7] Such as prospective new lender to or participants in the firm.
[8] Per Lord Eldon in *Rowe v Wood* (1822) 2 Jac & W 553 at 559; per Lord Davey in *Trego v Hunt* [1896] AC 7 at 26. For a fuller discussion of a partner's rights of access to such accounts see Chapter 8.

base the account, the court will draw presumptions against the interests of those who have failed in their duty to maintain the proper accounts.[9]

The right of access to the accounts

The right of access to the financial information on which knowledge of the partnership's affairs must be based, contained in s 24(9), is clearly important. This subsection provides that, subject to any agreement, express or implied, to the contrary, the partnership books are to be kept 'at the place of business of the partnership (or the principal place if there is more than one) and every partner may, when he thinks fit, have access to and inspect and copy any of them.' Three aspects of this right need to be noted.

First, unless the right of inspection is expressly limited to personal inspection by the partners themselves, the right may be exercised through an agent, such as an accountant.[10] However, the use of an agent must be reasonable in the particular circumstances,[11] and the agent selected must be someone to whom the other members of the firm can raise no reasonable objection.[12]

Second, any inspection, whether carried out personally or through an agent, may only be used to obtain information legitimately required by the inspecting partner as partner and not for other purposes. Any information obtained by such an inspection may not be put to use for other purposes.[13]

Third, the right is subject to agreement to the contrary and a partner may agree to rely on statements prepared by his co-partners of the firm's financial position, thereby giving up his right to inspect the books on which the statements are based.[14]

THE LIMITED COMPANY EXEMPTION

In respect of some partnerships the keeping of accounts is compulsory due to the obligations imposed by the Partnerships and

---

[9] Per Lord Deas in *Cameron v McMurray* (1855) 17 D 1143–1144; *Bevan v Webb* [1901] 2 Ch 59.
[10] However the agent need not necessarily be a professional person.
[11] *Dodd v Almagamated Marine Workers Union* [1924] 1 Ch 116.
[12] *Dadswell v Jacobs* (1887) 34 Ch D 278.
[13] *Trego v Hunt* [1896] AC 7; *Bevan v Webb* [1901] 2 Ch 59; *Duché v Duché* (1920) 149 LT Jo 308.
[14] *Turney v Bayley* (1864) 4 De GJ & SM 332.

Unlimited Companies (Accounts) Regulations 1993,[15] which came into effect on 21 July of that year, and which were introduced to implement a European Community initiative.[16]

Application

In relation to partnerships[17] the regulations apply to those partnerships, whether limited partnerships or general partnerships, in which all those members who bear unlimited liability are themselves limited companies. The rationale is that the limited liability nature of the partners bearing unlimited liability within the partnership means that in reality that liability is limited, and no partner remains whose liability in practice is unlimited. Thus, the regulations govern a partnership which is governed by the laws of any part of Great Britain if each of its members is *either* a limited company *or* an unlimited company or a Scottish firm, each of whose members is a limited company.[18] Such partnerships are referred to as qualifying partnerships. In support of this where the members of a qualifying partnership include *either* (1) an unlimited company, or a Scottish firm, each of whose members is a limited company or (2) a member of another partnership each of whose members is (a) a limited company, or (b) an unlimited company, or a Scottish firm (each of whose members is a limited company) references in the regulations to members of the qualifying partnership includes references to the members of that company, firm or other partnership.[19]

Further, references to an unlimited company, a Scottish firm or another partnership or limited company include a reference to any comparable undertaking in or formed under the law of another country or territory outside Great Britain.[20]

The requirement imposed by the regulations apply without regard to any change in the members of a qualifying partnership which does not result in its ceasing to be such a partnership.[1]

[15] SI 1993/1820.
[16] They implement Council Directive 90/605/EEC (OJ L317 16.11.90 pp 60–62) which amends Directive 78/660/EEC on annual accounts (OJ L222 14.8.78 pp 11–31) (the fourth EC Company Law Directive) and Directive 83/349/EEC on consolidated accounts (OJ L193 18.7.83 pp 1–17) (the Seventh EC Company Law Directive) in relation to the scope of those directives.
[17] The regulations also apply to unlimited companies.
[18] Regulation 3(1).
[19] Regulation 3(2).
[20] Regulation 3(4).
[1] Regulation 3(3).

Contents of the accounts

The members of a qualifying partnership (in the case of limited partnership the general members)[2] who are members of a qualifying partnership at the end of the financial year of the partnership are required to prepare annual accounts and an auditor's report in respect of that year in the form required of a under Pt VII of the Companies Act 1985, subject to detailed modifications set out in the Schedule. The effect of the Schedule is to apply those requirements of Pt VII which do not derive from the European directives on accounts.[3] The accounts must be prepared within a period of ten months beginning immediately after the end of the financial year.[4]

Failure to comply with the accounting requirements has criminal sanctions. Every person who is a member of the partnership or a director of such a member at the end of the year is guilty of a summary offence punishable with a fine. However, it is a defence for a person to show that he took all reasonable steps for securing that the requirements in questions would be complied with.[5]

Delivery of accounts to the Registrar of Companies

An obligation is imposed on a limited company which is a member[6] at the end of any financial year of the partnership to append to the copy of its own annual accounts which is next delivered to the Registrar of Companies[7] a copy of the partnership accounts prepared for that year.[8] Further, a limited company which is a member of a qualifying partnership must supply to any person on request the name of each member which is to deliver, or has delivered, a copy of the latest accounts of the partnership to the Registrar. It must also, on request, supply the name of each member incorporated in a member state of the European Community other than the United Kingdom, which is to publish, or has published, the latest accounts

---

[2] Regulation 2(2).
[3] Regulation 4(1).
[4] Regulation 4(2). They must also state that they are made under the regulations. However, the members of a qualifying partnership need not prepare accounts for a financial year commencing before 23 December 1994 (reg 12(1)).
[5] Regulation 8(1), (4).
[6] In the case of a limited partnership the members are the general members: reg 2(2).
[7] Pursuant to s 242 of the Companies Act 1985.
[8] Regulation 5(1).

of the partnership.[9] Additionally, companies which are members of qualifying partnerships are subject to additional disclosure requirements in the notes to their accounts. The requirements are too detailed for a work which is a book on partnership rather than company law.[10]

If the accounts of a qualifying partnership, a copy of which is delivered to the Registrar under these provisions or which are made available for inspection under the provisions discussed in the next section, do not comply with the regulations a criminal offence is committed. Every person who, at the time when the copy was so delivered or (as the case may be) the accounts were first made available for inspection, was a member of the partnership or a director of such a member is guilty of a summary offence punishable with a fine.[11] Further, if a member of a qualifying partnership fails to comply with the requirements as to delivery to the Registrar or making the accounts available for inspection under the provisions discussed in the next section, that member and any director of that member is guilty of a summary offence and liable to a fine.[12] It is a defence for any person charged with any of these offences to show that he took all reasonable steps to secure that the requirements in question would be complied with.[13]

Publication of accounts at head office for partnerships composed of members

An obligation is imposed on qualifying partnerships to publish their accounts by making them available at their head office. This obligation applies where the qualifying partnership's head office is in the United Kingdom and each of its members falls into one or other of two categories. The first category is that of undertakings comparable to a limited company which are incorporated in a country or territory outside the UK. The second is that of undertakings comparable to an unlimited company or partnership which is incorporated or formed under the law of such a country or territory, *and* each of whose members are undertakings within the first category.[14]

---

[9] In accordance with the provisions of the Fourth or Seventh Directives on company accounts.
[10] They are set out in reg 11.
[11] Regulation 8(2).
[12] Regulation 8(3).
[13] Regulation 8(4).
[14] Regulation 6(1).

Clearly, this regulation has no impact on domestic partnerships and is aimed at partnerships composed of foreign entities, but whose head office is situated in the UK. Such a body will have no member obliged to file copies of the annual accounts with the Registrar of Companies pursuant to the obligation discussed in the previous section. Since the accounts will not be publicised in that way, this regulation imposes publication by making the accounts available for inspection at the head office of the partnership. However, it may be that one or other of the foreign members will be under an obligation to publish the accounts under the law of another member state of the European Community. If so, the partnership is exempted from publication at its head office.[15]

The consequences of breach of these requirements are discussed at the end of the previous section.

Consolidated accounts exemption

An exemption from the regulations is created where the partnership has been dealt with in consolidated group accounts. The members of a qualifying partnership are exempt from the obligations to produce and publicise partnership accounts if the partnership is dealt with on a consolidated basis in group accounts prepared by *either* (1) a member of the partnership which is established under the law of a member state of the European Community, *or* (2) a parent undertaking of such a member which is so established.[16] However, for the exemption to be applicable the group accounts must be prepared and audited under the law of the member state concerned in accordance with the provisions of the Seventh Directive[17] which requires the method of full or proportional consolidation on the equity method of accounting.[18]

---

[15] Regulation 6(2).
[16] Regulation 7(1).
[17] Seventh Council Directive (83/349/EEC) of 13 June 1983 on consolidated accounts as amended.
[18] Regulation 7(2). The notes to the accounts must also disclose that advatage has been taken of the exemption (ibid). Where advantage is taken of the exemption, any member of the qualifying partnership which is a limited company must disclose on request the name of at least one member or parent undertaking in whose group accounts the partnership has been or is being dealt with on a consolidated basis: reg 7(3).

PROFIT AND LOSS

The major purpose of keeping books of account is to enable the financial position of the firm to be overviewed and controlled, and the financial position of the partners arising from their dealings with the firm verified, both for the purposes of the individual partners in assessing their accumulations of personal wealth and, coincidentally, for the purposes of the Inland Revenue in raising tax assessments upon the participants. Both these aspects are directly dependent on the profitability of the firm, since it is those profits which will contribute to the accumulation of the wealth of the individual partners and on which they will pay tax.

However, whilst profit is at the heart of English partnership law, the 1890 Act attempts no definition. It has been left to the judges to attempt this. At a basic level the words of Atkinson J point a distinction which, although obvious, is often not drawn by the uninitiated, and all too often forgotten by the neglectful:

'Profits, as it seems to me, must not be confused with receipts. Profits consist of a sum arrived at by adding up the receipts of a business and by deducting all the expenses and losses, including depreciation and the like, incurred in carrying on the business.'[19]

The most thorough exposition and definition is that of Fletcher-Moulton LJ in *Re Spanish Prospecting Co Ltd*:[20]

'The word "profit" has in my opinion a well-defined legal meaning, and this meaning coincides with the fundamental conception of profits in general parlance, although in mercantile phraseology the word may at times bear meanings indicated by the special context which deviate in some respects from this fundamental signification. "Profits" implies a comparison between the state of a business at two specific dates usually separated by an interval of a year. The fundamental meaning is the amount of gain made by the business during the year. This can only be ascertained by a comparison of the assets of the business at the two dates . . . We start therefore with this fundamental definition of profits, namely, if the total assets of the business at the two dates be compared, the increase which they show at the later date as compared with the earlier date (due allowance of course being made for any capital introduced into or taken out of the business in the meanwhile) represents in strictness the profits of the business during

---

[19] *Rushden Heel Co Ltd v Keene* [1946] 2 All ER 141 at 144.
[20] [1911] 1 Ch 92.

the period in question. But the periodical ascertainment of profits in a business is an operation of such practical importance as to be essential to the safe conduct of the business itself. To follow out the strict consequences of the legal conception in making out the accounts of the year would often be very difficult in practice. Hence the strict meaning of the word "profits" is rarely observed in drawing up the accounts of firms or companies . . .'[1]

Translated into bookkeeping and accounting terms, the principles applicable to the calculation of profit and loss in accordance with these principles were set out by Clyde LP in *Whimster v IRC*.[2] He said:

'In computing the balance of profits and gains . . . two general and fundamental commonplaces must always be kept in mind. In the first place, the profits of any particular year . . . must be taken to consist of the difference between the receipts . . . and the expenditure laid out to earn those receipts. In the second place, the account of profit and loss to be made up for the purpose of ascertaining that difference must be framed consistently with the ordinary principles of commercial accounting . . .'

It will be seen from this that profits are calculated by taking a snapshot at the end of the year and measuring the receipts against the expenditure (overheads) expended to earn those receipts. If the receipts are greater than the expenditure there is a profit; if less there is a loss. Secondly, in sorting out the respective receipts and expenditures to go into either side of the balance, ordinary principles of commercial accounting must be applied. The ordinary principles of commercial accounting give rise to numerous issues relevant to the manner in which partnership accounts should be kept.

MANNER IN WHICH ACCOUNTS SHOULD BE KEPT

The ordinary bases of commercial accounting impose some requirements as to how the accounts should be kept. However, in some cases the requirements are not clear-cut, and leave some degree of choice to be exercised.

---

[1] At 98–99.
[2] 1926 SC 20.

Accounting basis

For many businesses there is a delay between sending out an invoice for work which has been done or goods supplied, and the receipt of payment in respect of the invoice. An issue arises, therefore, as to whether the receipts of a business should merely be the cash actually received, or be based on completed work for which accounts have been delivered and which are therefore payable. In any particular tax year the manner in which the accounts are dealt with in this respect will determine whether or not invoices sent but not yet paid will form part of the receipts of the business.

Further, in respect of partnerships providing services rather than supplying goods, a decision must be made as to whether receipts should include a figure for work in hand but not yet completed because, in a professional partnership, a lot of hours will be expended in any particular year on work which is not completed at the end of the year and in respect of which invoices have not been sent.

A further decision which it is necessary to make in relation to a firm which carries substantial stock is whether the value of stock bought in the year but unsold at the end of it should also be included in the accounts. In general, it is probable that the most accurate picture of a firm's financial position will be achieved by taking the receipts on an invoice basis, adding a figure for any work in hand and stock purchased but not yet sold, but making a deduction of an estimated figure for bad debts being accounts rendered which turn out to be irrecoverable. A correct estimate in respect of the latter can only be achieved from trading experience, or by drawing on the general experience of the particular trade or profession.

Perhaps more important than the choice of the accounting basis on which the accounts are prepared is the commonsense point that the same basis should be carried from year to year, since to move from one accounting base to another will inevitably cause distortions making it difficult to see just how well or how badly the firm is doing.

Receipts

The receipts to be included are not necessarily all the sums actually received by the firm and paid into its bank account. The firm's profit or loss is its trading profit or loss, and only its trading receipts are relevant to this. These are the sums received for the goods or services supplied by the firm in the course of its business. Other receipts are irrelevant and should not be included. Thus, sums received as compensation,[3] or as a gift in appreciation for past services which are not continued,[4] are not trading receipts and should not be included in the trading accounts, since they are not part of the income of the partners giving rise to taxation. Capital items belonging to the firm such as its plant and equipment are part of the partnership property, and if an item of partnership property is sold, the proceeds are also partnership property forming part of the firm's capital.

Payments

Under normal accounting principles all payments attributable to the earning of the receipts are the firm's expenditure, and should be brought into account in calculating its profits and losses. However, not all such items will necessarily be deductible for tax purposes, and to this extent a distinction may have to be made between the calculation of profits in respect of the partners dealings between themselves, and the calculation of profits for the purposes of payment of tax.[5]

Valuations of stock and work in progress

Stock and work in progress will require valuation since its value has not been fixed by an actual sale. The generally accepted basis of such valuation assumes that the stock acquired first is used first.[6]

The same principles apply to the valuation of work in progress, although here further problems may arise. In *Ostime v Duple Motor Bodies*[7] the value of the work in progress of a motor body manufacturer was in dispute between the manufacturer and the Revenue. The manufacturer valued the work in progress by reference to the costs of the materials used plus that of the labour directly involved in the manufacture. The Inland Revenue argued that, in addition, a proportion of the general overheads of the business should be included. It was shown that there was no established accounting

3   *IRC v Brander and Cruickshank* [1971] 1 WLR 212.
4   *Simpson v John Reynolds & Co Ltd* [1975] STC 271, followed in *Murray v Goodhews* [1978] 2 All ER 40.
5   Tax considerations are discussed in Chapter 15.
6   This is the basis which is acceptable for tax purposes, see *BSC (Footwear) Ltd v Ridgeway* [1972] AC 544.
7   (1961) 39 TC 537.

practice to determine the matter. Against that background the House of Lords held that, since the Revenue had failed to show that the manufacturer's method was wrong, the manufacturer was free to adopt it.

Thus, it seems that, in general, where there is no firmly established general commercial accounting practice, the taxpayer is free to adopt a practice of his choice, provided that it is reasonable to the needs and nature of his own particular business.

Division of profits

The calculation of the profits of the firm is only the beginning of the story of how the profits should be dealt with in the accounts. The second part of the story is that of the allocation of the profit or loss to the individual partners. Fundamentally, this depends upon the terms under which the profits are to be shared. These terms will be contained in the partnership agreement. If, by any chance, the partners have omitted to agree specifically as to the division of the profits and losses prior to trading, s 24(1) of the Partnership Act provides that all the partners are entitled to share equally in the capital and profits of the business and must contribute equally towards the losses, whether of capital or otherwise, sustained by the firm.

Capital and current accounts

The original capital of the firm is the amount contributed by the partners to establish the firm, and agreed between them to be its capital. Amounts cannot be withdrawn from this without the agreement of all partners, and it is desirable that it should be shown as a separate item. As a partnership trades, profits will be earned. The partners have to live as the profits are being earned, and it should be agreed between them that certain sums should be drawn each month on account of profits to enable them to live. Such sums should be significantly less than the estimated profits, so that inroads are not made on the capital of the firm. It is desirable that a current account also be opened showing the drawings of each partner throughout the year, and the profits attributable to each partner at the end of the year. Assuming that each partner's profits are indeed greater than his drawings, the difference will represent his undrawn profits. Such undrawn profits are withdrawable by a partner at any time, except to the extent that all partners subsequently agree that undrawn profits should be capitalised to increase the capital of the firm. If a partner's drawings are in excess of the profits earned at the end of the accounting period, he will have overdrawn, and will be responsible to repay the amount by which he is overdrawn.

Since each partner's capital will be shown as a sum of money, any revaluation of assets used within the partnership, or a sale of such property producing a profit, will improve the current and not the capital position of the partners, unless the partners agree that such profits be taken to capital account. For this reason it is sensible that any freehold land or buildings belonging to the partnership should remain on the partnership books at cost, until a change in the personnel of the partnership takes place necessitating revaluation. On such an event, the new partnership should be completely re-capitalised.

A partner's personal position in relation to the firm will be shown from the capital and current accounts. It is the effect of these two accounts combined which shows his individual position.

These different accounts merely represent accountancy implementation of the legal structures of partnership law.

Other internal accounts

As well as capital and current accounts to reflect the financial consequences of the partnership trading it is possible for the firm to maintain other accounts to reflect other aspects of its legal position. Thus, a retention may be made out of each partner's profit share each year on account of income tax and shown as a special tax reserve account. Also, to overcome potential problems arising from profits generated by revaluation of capital assets, a special revaluation reserve may be opened in respect of such profits, against which no drawings may be made. This has the effect of showing the capital profits separately from the original capital of the business, but at the same time preserving the integrity of the increased value within the firm so that the position of the business is not prejudiced.

Interest

Despite the provision of s 24(4) that in the absence of agreement no partner is entitled to interest on his capital to the ascertainment of profits, in practice it is frequently agreed between partners that interest should be payable, at least where the capital has been contributed in proportions different from those in which profits are to be shared. Where it is agreed between the partners that interest at an agreed rate is to be credited to the partner's current account, the appropriate amounts are credited to the current accounts and the profits reduced by the total of such credits prior to division between the partners. Any loans made by partners to the firm on which interest is payable would be similarly dealt with.

Salaries

Similarly, despite the provision of s 24(6) of the Partnership Act that, in the absence of agreement, no partner shall be entitled to remuneration for acting in the partnership business, it is by no means uncommon that a salary for one or more of the partners should be agreed between them. This usually occurs in a partnership where some of the partners are active and others are passive, and the salary is agreed in favour of the active partners to pay them for their activity. Where such a salary is payable, it is credited to the current account of the partners entitled to it, and the total of such salaries deducted from the profits of the firm prior to division between the partners.

Final division of profits

It is only after all expenditure has been met, and any allocations of interest or salaries to partners have been made, that a figure is arrived at by way of profits, which can be divided between the partners in their agreed shares.

Accumulation of profits

As noted, each partner's position vis-à-vis the firm is ascertained by looking at the combined totals due to him on the capital and current accounts.

If the partnership trades for a number of years, making profits annually, and each partner draws less each year than the amount of the profits generated, each partner's current account will grow every year. It will only be reduced if either (1) a partner draws on his accumulated profits, or (2) a decision is made by the partners to capitalise some of the undrawn profits in their current accounts. If the trading position of a firm is adverse losses are accumulated in a similar way.

The result of this is to constitute each partner a notional creditor of the firm to the extent that there is a net credit balance on his accounts, or as a debtor to the firm to the extent that there is a net debit balance. A partner's account to the firm can therefore be closed and settled by the payment of any balance due to or from him.

From a financial point of view, the analysis clarifies the position and helps to understand the accounting situation achieved. However, from a legal point of view the analysis should not be relied upon, for it has shortcomings. As Lord Cottenham made clear in *Richardson v Bank of England*:[8]

> 'Though these terms "debtor" and "creditor" are so used, and sufficiently explain what is meant by the use of them, nothing can be more inconsistent with the known law of partnership, than to consider the situation of either party as in any degree resembling the situation of those whose appellation has been so borrowed. The supposed creditor has no means of compelling payment of his debt; and the supposed debtor is liable to no proceedings either of law or in equity – assuming always that no separate security has been taken or given. The supposed creditor's debt is due from the firm of which he is partner; and the supposed debtor owes the money to himself in common with his partners.'

FINALITY OF ACCOUNTS

When the annual accounts have been prepared they will be signed by all the partners. The signature of the partners to the prepared accounts is significant because it shows the partners' acceptance of the accounts as drawn. Even if they do not sign the accounts, they may verbally accept them. In any event, if partners are presented with the accounts to which they do not object they will be taken, after the lapse of a reasonable time, to have accepted the accounts by implication. Once the accounts have been accepted by a partner, he cannot thereafter challenge them, except in very restricted circumstances.[9]

[8] (1838) 4 My & Cr 165 at 171–72.
[9] See Chapter 10.

CHAPTER 12

DISSOLUTION AND WINDING UP OF PARTNERSHIPS

INTRODUCTION

The term 'dissolution' is not defined within the Partnership Act 1890. A partnership may, however, be said to be dissolved, or in dissolution, when the relationship between the partners is effectively terminated. Nevertheless, such a dissolution does not prevent the creation of a new partnership between any of the partners of a dissolved partnership, nor does it automatically follow that a dissolution of a partnership will inexorably lead to that partnership being wound up.

Technical dissolution

A purely technical dissolution may occur where there is a change in the constituent members of the partnership. In such cases the firm may continue post-dissolution, carrying out the same business enterprise, with substantially the same assets and liabilities as before, although with a difference in the membership of the partnership.[1] This form of dissolution will be referred to in this chapter as a 'technical dissolution'.

Dissolution

A dissolution may, however, constitute a stage in the ultimate winding up of the partnership and its affairs.[2] This chapter is principally concerned with this form of dissolution.

---

[1] A technical dissolution may take place by operation of law or by agreement between the partners see, eg Partnership Act 1890, s 34.

[2] For the winding up of a partnership see p 283, below.

Grounds of dissolution

Dissolution may be brought about in the following circumstances:

(1)   by the agreement of all the partners. Though a partnership may be a fixed term partnership, it can still be terminated at any time prior to the expiration of the agreed term or the occurrence of a prescribed event by the unanimous agreement of the partners.[3] Note, however, that in the absence of an enabling provision in the partnership agreement, a fixed term partnership cannot be prematurely dissolved otherwise than by such unanimous agreement of the partners,[4] or by order of the court, or by the operation of provisions of the Partnership Act;[5]

(2)   a partnership may be dissolved in accordance with the terms of an express power as contained in the partnership agreement;

(3)   a partnership may be dissolved where a party has been induced to enter into the partnership by the fraud or misrepresentation of his co-partner(s). He may in such cases seek to rescind the partnership agreement;[6]

(4)   a partnership may be dissolved by an innocent partner who finds that he is the victim of a repudiatory breach of the partnership agreement by his co-partner(s).[7]

Dissolution by statutory provision

A partnership may be dissolved by the operation of the express provisions of the Partnership Act 1890. These provisions are as follows.

---

[3]   See Chapter 3 and Partnership Act 1890, s 19. For the dissolution by law of a fixed term partnership or one formed to execute a particular transaction see Partnership Act 1890, s 32 and Chapter 2. See also *Lindern Trawler Managers v WHJ Trawlers* (1949) 83 Ll L Rep 131; *J & J Cunningham v Lucas* [1957] 1 Lloyd's Rep 416; *Mann v D'Arcy* [1968] 1 WLR 893. A partnership at will may be terminated by notice, see p 265, below and Chapter 3.

[4]   See Chapter 3; Partnership Act 1890, s 19; and below.

[5]   Ibid.

[6]   See Chapter 10 for a consideration of the power to rescind a partnership agreement.

[7]   See *Hitchman v Crouch Butler Savage Associates* (1983) 80 LS Gaz 554; *Fulwell v Bragg* (1983) 127 Sol Jo 171.

1. THE DEATH OR BANKRUPTCY OF A PARTNER

Section 33(1) of the Partnership Act provides that:

'Subject to any agreement between the partners, every partnership is dissolved as regards all the partners by the death or bankruptcy of any partner.'

Death

It should be noted that this provision takes effect subject to contrary agreement. It would therefore generally be advisable for the partnership agreement to provide that the death of a partner would constitute only a technical dissolution of the partnership,[8] or even to prevent such an event from amounting to any form of dissolution.[9] In the absence of such a contrary agreement the death of a partner will prematurely dissolve even a fixed term partnership. In such cases dissolution of the partnership is from the date of death of the deceased partner.[10]

Bankruptcy

The bankruptcy[11] of a partner will also dissolve a partnership, unless there is contrary provision in the partnership agreement. An express power in the partnership agreement to expel a bankrupt partner from the partnership should, it is suggested, always be included in a partnership agreement, as it is a more suitable alternative to dissolution of the firm. Such a provision would also constitute a contrary agreement within the terms of s 33(1), thus excluding the operation of that provision in cases where a partner is made bankrupt. It would appear that where a partnership is dissolved by the bankruptcy of a partner, the date of dissolution runs from the making of the bankruptcy order.[12]

---

[8] See p 261, above for a consideration of what may be regarded as a technical dissolution. A technical dissolution may not be a practical consideration if the deceased partner is essential to the continuance of the partnership.

[9] By providing that the amount due to the representatives of a deceased partner as the share of the partnership assets be satisfied from the proceeds of an insurance policy covering the death of any partner.

[10] See *McLeod v Dowling* (1927) 43 TLR 655; *IRC v Graham's Trustees* 1971 SLT 46. For the procedure of winding up a partnership on the death of a partner see p 292, below.

[11] For a consideration of the circumstances in which a partner can be made the subject of a bankruptcy order see Chapter 13.

[12] Note that where a partnership is ordered to be wound up as an unregistered company the date of dissolution of the partnership may predate any bankruptcy order made against any partner.

A corporate partner may be the subject of a winding up order; it remains unclear whether the effect of such an order is to dissolve the relevant partnership. There would appear to be no authority on this point, but it is suggested that a corporate partner which is insolvent should be regarded as being in the same position as an individual partner who is the subject of a bankruptcy order.[13] Clearly, this should be the case where a corporate partner is dissolved. Such a procedure ensures the ending of the company and is the equivalent of the death of an individual partner.

2. CHARGING ORDER ON A PARTNER'S SHARE

Section 33(2) of the Partnership Act 1890 provides that:

> 'A partnership may, at the option of the other partners, be dissolved if any partner suffers his share of the partnership property to be charged under this Act for his separate debt.'

The effect of the subsection is clear. The circumstances in which a partnership share may be made subject to a charging order is considered elsewhere in the book.[14] The provision takes effect subject to the contrary agreement of the partners. The only matters to consider are how and under what circumstances the option to dissolve the partnership can be exercised under the subsection. It would appear that, by virtue of the subsection, the option to dissolve the partnership must be exercised by the unanimous consent of the partners, excluding, of course, the partner whose partnership share is the subject of the charging order.[15] The option, it is suggested, must be exercised within a reasonable time after the relevant partnership share has been charged. The option would also appear to be incapable of being withdrawn, once it is communicated to the partner whose partnership share is charged.[16] The dissolution of the partnership take place on the date the option is exercised.

3. ILLEGALITY

Section 34 of the Partnership Act 1890 provides that a partnership is in every case dissolved by the happening of any event which

---

[13] Note in Chapter 4, where consideration is given to the desirability of making provision for the situation where a petition for a winding up order is made against a corporate partner.

[14] See Chapter 9.

[15] Cf the wording of ss 26(1) and 32(c): see also *Re a Solicitor's Arbitration* [1962] 1 WLR 353.

[16] *Scarf v Jardine* (1882) 7 App Cas 345; *Clough v London and North Western Rly Co* (1871) LR 7 Ex Ch 26; *Re Longlands Farm* [1968] 3 All ER 552.

makes it unlawful for the business of the firm to be carried on or for the members of the firm to carry it on in partnership. A partnership will be automatically dissolved if it has been formed to carry on an enterprise which is subsequently prescribed as illegal.[17] Although the above section is silent on the matter, it would seem that a partnership might not be dissolved under the section if only one of its enterprises, albeit not a major aspect of the partnership business, was subsequently prescribed as illegal.

In the case of certain professional partnerships, statute may prohibit such a partnership between professionally qualified persons and a party who is not so qualified.[18] Where a partner of such a partnership, although professionally qualified at commencement, subsequently ceases to be professionally qualified, it is advisable that the partnership agreement should provide that such a partner is deemed to have retired from the partnership from the date of dissolution.[19]

Since the terms of s 34 cannot be excluded by any contrary provision in the partnership agreement, a partnership caught by s 34 is automatically dissolved. In the case of dissolution of a professional partnership because a partner ceases to be professionally qualified, a provision in the partnership agreement retiring that partner from the partnership at the point of dissolution would not prevent the remaining partners from forming themselves into a new partnership.

Notice of dissolution

A partnership may be dissolved by the serving of a notice of dissolution between the partners.

The notice may be served in accordance with the terms of the partnership agreement or any provisions in the Partnership Act 1890. The partnership agreement will usually prescribe that the matters noted above are grounds for service of a notice of dissolution.

The giving of notice of dissolution where the partnership is a

---

[17] For a consideration of the nature of illegity see Chapter 2. A partnership cannot be formed for an illegal purpose.

[18] See Chapter 2.

[19] See Chapter 2 and *Hudgell Yeates & Co v Watson* [1978] QB 451. Unlike the above statutory grounds, the partnership agreement cannot nullify the effects of s 34.

partnership at will is principally considered elsewhere.[20] The remaining aspects of the law governing the giving of a notice of dissolution are equally applicable to both fixed term partnerships and partnerships at will and are considered below.

A notice of dissolution may be served upon a partner, although he may be suffering from a mental disorder.[1] There is no duty imposed upon a partner to exercise restraint, or to be reasonable in his decision to serve a notice of dissolution.[2] Nevertheless, the serving of the notice must not be a fraudulent action or carried out in bad faith, so as to secure a personal advantage for one partner at the expense of his co-partners; in such cases such a notice will not be upheld by the courts.[3]

A notice of dissolution must be unequivocal in its intent. A notice may, however, be inferred from the conduct of a partner, thus a writ issued by a partner initiating a court action which seeks to dissolve a partnership will constitute a notice of dissolution.[4] A notice which seeks to dissolve the partnership on terms which are not accepted by the partners is not an effective notice.[5] The notice must seek to dissolve the partnership between all the partners.[6] It may, however, be a prospective notice. To be effective, a notice must be communicated to all the partners.[7] Once given, a notice can only be withdrawn with the consent of all the partners.[8] A prospective notice to dissolve may, however, be superseded by an event which dissolves the partnership before the notice takes effect.

A partnership will be dissolved by a notice of dissolution from the date when the notice has been communicated to all the partners or,

---

[20] See Chapter 2. Note that a notice of dissolution of a partnership at will may be given by a partner at any time: see *Firth v Amslake* (1964) 108 Sol Jo 198. Furthermore, a partnership at will may be terminated by inference, without the serving of a notice: *Pearce v Lindsay* (1860) 3 De GJ & SM 139. Although it appears that a notice issued under s 26(1) can be in writing, s 32(c) does not require a notice of dissolution issued under its aegis to be in writing. Although such a notice may therefore be given orally, prudence would recommend the giving of written notice in all cases.

[1] *Mellersh v Keen* (1859) 27 Beav 236.

[2] *Russell v Russell* (1880) 14 Ch D 471.

[3] *Walters v Bingham* [1988] 1 FTLR 260; *Neilson v Mossend Iron Co* (1886) 11 App Cas 298; *Daw v Herring* [1892] 1 Ch 284.

[4] *Unsworth v Jordan* [1896] WN 2.

[5] *Hall v Hall* (1855) 20 Beav 139.

[6] *Clarke v Hart* (1858) 6 HL Cas 633; *Sobell v Boston* [1975] 1 WLR 1587.

[7] *Walters v Bingham* [1988] 1 FTLR 260.

[8] *Jones v Lloyd* (1874) LR 18 Eq 265; *Glossop v Glossop* [1907] 2 Ch 370.

in the alternative, from the date prescribed in the notice, if that date is subsequent to communication.[9]

Dissolution by order of the court

A partnership may be dissolved by order of the court, under s 35 of the Partnership Act 1890. The grounds upon which a court may order a dissolution under s 35 are:

(1) permanent incapacity of a partner other than the partner suing under the section;

(2) conduct on the part of a partner, other than the partner suing, which is calculated prejudicially to effect the running of the business;

(3) wilful or persistent breach of the partnership agreement or other conduct on the part of a partner other than the partner suing which renders the continuance of the partnership impractible;

(4) when the partnership can only be carried on at a loss;

(5) that the dissolution of the partnership is just and equitable.

1. SECTION 35(B): PERMANENT INCAPACITY

A partner may be suffering from a mental or physical incapacity which renders his further involvement in the running of a partnership either impractical or impossible. If such an incapacity can be established as permanent[10] in nature by his co-partner(s), the latter may apply to the court under s 35(b) of the Partnership Act 1890 for the partnership to be dissolved. Although a partial incapacity of a partner may, if permanent in nature, constitute sufficient grounds for a court ordering a dissolution under s 35(b), such a partial incapacity must render the affected partner incapable of substantially performing his part of the partnership contract. Thus, an incapacity which merely reduces the overall efficiency of a partner to perform his partnership duties satisfactorily would not constitute sufficient grounds for a court to order a dissolution of a partnership under s 35(b).[11] Where a partner has become a patient[12] under the

---

[9] See Partnership Act 1890, s 32; *Jones v Lloyd* (1874) LR 18 Eq 265.

[10] Cf *Whitwell v Arthur* (1865) 35 Beav 140.

[11] *Sadler v Lee* (1843) 6 Beav 324.

[12] See the Mental Health Act 1983, which defines a patient as: 'A person incapable, by reason of mental disorder, of managing and administering his property and affairs; and a person as to whom the judge is so satisfied is referred to in this Part of this Act as a patient.'

Mental Health Act 1983, the Court of Protection has jurisdiction to dissolve a partnership of which the patient is a member.[13] This power of the Court of Protection is considered below.

2. SECTION 35(C): CONDUCT INJURIOUS TO PARTNERSHIP BUSINESS

The court, in considering whether to grant an application for dissolution of a partnership under this provision, must have regard to a number of factors. Thus, the nature and size of the business, the position of the recalcitrant partner within the business, and the nature of the latter's conduct are all pertinent and interrelated factors. In determining whether the conduct of a partner has been injurious to the partnership business, the court must have regard to the viewpoint of the partners seeking the dissolution of the partnership. The court must, therefore, take an essentially subjective viewpoint in determining this matter, and in considering whether to dissolve the partnership under the subsection. It is therefore difficult to be precise as to the circumstances in which the relevant conduct will be held sufficient to dissolve the partnership.

Nevertheless, it is suggested that criminal conduct on the part of a partner involving fraudulent or dishonest conduct will almost certainly constitute conduct injurious to the partnership for the purposes of s 35(c), as will offences involving allegations of serious assault. Immoral behaviour, per se, would not, it is suggested, constitute such injurious conduct, unless the partnership was a professional practice, and the behaviour reflected on the professional standing of the offending partner, and by implication the partnership.[14]

It is clear from the words of the provision that the offending conduct need not be carried out by the offending partner within the context of, or on behalf of, the partnership business.[15] However, it is crucial that the partner(s) seeking dissolution establish that the offending partner is 'guilty' of that conduct. This would appear to suggest that the offending conduct must be both voluntary and intentional.[16] Furthermore, the conduct of the offending partner must be 'calculated' to injure the partnership business. In the absence of direct authority, such a requirement

---

[13] See ss 95 and 96, Mental Health Act 1983.

[14] *Essell v Hayward* (1860) 30 Beav 158; *Carmichael v Evans* [1904] 1 Ch 486.

[15] *Pearce v Foster* (1886) 17 QBD 536. Although the case concerned an employee, the principle remains sound.

[16] Ie not carried out while the partner was suffering from insanity: *R v Davison* [1972] 1 WLR 1540; *British Vacuum Cleaner Co Ltd v New Vacuum Cleaner Co Ltd* [1907] 2 Ch 312.

may well be interpreted as requiring the offending partner only to be aware of the fact that his conduct is likely to injure the partnership business. It is submitted, however, that there is no ground for excluding the possibility that the term 'calculated' within s 35(c) may be interpreted as merely requiring an offending partner to be recklessly indifferent as to whether his conduct is injurious to the partnership.

A partner can only seek a dissolution of a partnership under the authority of the subsection, if he is himself innocent of any conduct which would be injurious to the partnership.

3. SECTION 35(D): BREACH OF PARTNERSHIP AGREEMENT AND DESTRUCTION OF MUTUAL CONFIDENCE

This provision constitutes two separate grounds upon which a dissolution of a partnership may be sought. The first requires a partner to be wilfully or persistently in breach of the partnership agreement. The second requires misconduct on the part of a partner which renders the continuation of the partnership impractical. In the latter case the mutual confidence that must subsist between partners must have been destroyed by such misconduct. The continuance of the partnership is therefore rendered impracticable.[17] The courts will be most reluctant to dissolve a partnership under this provision where the partnership is facing only minor and temporary difficulties, which have exacerbated the personal relationships between the partners, even though such difficulties have arisen through the misconduct of one or more of the partners. However, the deliberate ignoring of the provisions of the partnership agreement by a partner is likely to persuade a court to invoke this provision, and to dissolve a partnership of which that partner is a member, at the behest of his co-partner(s).

Clearly, assaults upon a partner by another partner would justify a dissolution of the partnership under this provision, as would the making of serious, though unfounded, allegations of professional misconduct or fraud by a partner in respect of another.[18] However, any misconduct of a partner even of a minor nature could, if it continues to destroy and eat away at the mutual confidence that must exist between partners, ultimately justify a dissolution of a partnership under s 35(d). A partner who is deliberately conducting himself with a view to forcing the dissolution of a partnership

---

[17] *Re Yenidje Tobacco Co Ltd* [1916] 2 Ch 426; *Harrison v Tennant* (1856) 21 Beav 482.

[18] *Greenaway v Greenaway* (1939) 84 Sol Jo 43; *Cheesman v Price* (1865) 35 Beav 142.

cannot invoke this provision on his own behalf. However, the misconduct of a partner in such a case where there is no express power in the partnership agreement to expel him, may compel his co-partners to invoke s 35(d) on their own behalf, though such a course of action may well provide the miscreant partner with the very consequence he desires.

4. SECTION 35(E): PARTNERSHIP CARRIED ON AT A LOSS

The dissolution of a partnership on such a ground would appear to be self-evident. The essence of a partnership is the carrying on of a business with a view to profit. A business carried on at a loss is the very negation of a partnership. However, this provision cannot be invoked merely because the partnership is running temporarily at a loss. The partnership must be practically incapable of ever running at a profit. This may arise because the firm's capital is exhausted, and to continue the business would require further injections of capital by the partners, some of whom may be unwilling or incapable of supplying further capital.[19] However, any partnership which is structured or organised in such a way that it is practically impossible for it ever to run at a profit will be ripe for dissolution under s 35(e).[20]

Notwithstanding the above, it is unnecessary for a partner to prove the insolvency of the partnership in order to seek its dissolution under s 35(e).[1] In cases of a partnership insolvency a winding up order is a more appropriate procedure.[2] If a partner cannot present a winding up petition in respect of an insolvent partnership, the court may be prepared to intervene on motion, and appoint a person to sell the business and wind up the affairs of the partnership.[3]

5. SECTION 35(F): THE JUST AND EQUITABLE GROUND

This provision may be regarded as the general purpose ground authorising a court to dissolve a partnership at the instigation of a partner. This provision is in no way restricted in its ambit by the previous provisions of s 35, noted above, and should be construed

---

[19] See *Jennings v Baddeley* (1856) 3 K & J 78.
[20] *Handyside v Campbell* (1901) 17 TLR 623.
[1] Note the sanction of a possible disqualification order made against a partner carrying on a partnership knowing it to be insolvent: Insolvency Act 1986, s 214; Company Directors Disqualification Act 1986, s 10; Insolvent Partnership Order 1994, SI 1994/2421.
[2] See Chapter 13.
[3] *Heywood v BDC Properties* [1963] 1 WLR 975.

sui generis. The courts are not prepared to interpret the provision so as to restrict its future application.[4] It would seem, therefore, that a court will make an order for dissolution of a partnership under this provision if, from whatever cause, the objects of the partnership can no longer be achieved, or at least achieved in the manner contemplated by the partners. However, the dissolution of a partnership should only be sought under this particular provision if the other provisions of s 35 cannot be applied to the instant case.[5] Furthermore, there is no bar on a partner guilty of misconduct seeking dissolution of a partnership under this provision, although it is unlikely that an order would be made in such a partner's favour.[6] It must be borne in mind that, in all cases where an order for dissolution of a partnership is sought under s 35, the court, in granting or refusing to grant such an order, is exercising a discretion and remains unfettered by the provisions of the section.[7]

Where a court orders the dissolution of a partnership under s 35 the date of such a dissolution will as a general rule run from the date of the judgment ordering the dissolution, or from a date expressly stated in the judgment.

Grounds for dissolution outside the Partnership Act 1890

1. MENTAL DISORDER

By s 96(1)(g) of the Mental Health Act 1983 a nominated judge[8] may direct, order, or authorise the dissolution of a partnership where a patient[9] is a member of that partnership. This statutory power, like the power vested in the court under s 35 of the Partnership Act 1890 is a discretionary power. However, the prime considerations to which a judge should give weight when exercising the discretion to dissolve a partnership under the Mental Health Act are the interests and requirements of the patient. It would also appear that an order for dissolution under the above Act will only be ordered where a receiver has already been appointed to administer the affairs of the patient, and there are no outstanding disputes between the partners under any of the provisions contained in the

---

4 *Re Amalgamated Syndicate* [1897] 2 Ch 600; *Ebrahimi v Westbourne Galleries Ltd* [1973] AC 360.
5 *Harrison v Tennant* (1856) 21 Beav 482.
6 *Re American Pioneer Leather Co Ltd* [1918] 1 Ch 556.
7 See note 12 above.
8 See the Mental Health Act 1983, s 93(1).
9 See fn 12, p 267 above and the Mental Health Act 1983, s 94(2).

partnership agreement.[10] Where a patient is a dormant partner, an order for the dissolution of the partnership under the Mental Health Act should only be ordered so as to free the patient from his obligations as a partner, or to realise his share of the partnership assets.

An order for a dissolution of a partnership under the above provisions will usually provide that the date of dissolution runs from the date the judgment is delivered.[11] The costs of any such action are generally to be paid out of the partnership assets.[12]

2. THE INSOLVENCY ACT 1986

It should be noted that an insolvent partnership may be dissolved under the provisions of the Insolvency Act 1986.[13] This aspect of partnership law is, however, considered in detail elsewhere.[14]

JURISDICTION AND PROCEDURAL MATTERS

Jurisdiction to dissolve a partnership

1. ARBITRATION

An arbitrator conducting an arbitration between partners in respect of a partnership dispute may be given jurisdiction to order the dissolution of the partnership.[15]

2. HIGH COURT

Although all causes or matters involving the dissolution of partnerships, or the taking of a partnership account, are normally assigned to the Chancery Division of the High Court, it is not necessary to transfer to that division any dissolution action or action for account commenced in another division of the High Court.[16]

---

[10] See Heywood and Massey *Court of Protection Practice* (11th edn) p 221.
[11] *Besch v Frolich* (1842) 1 Ph 172.
[12] *Jones v Welch* (1855) 1 K & J 765.
[13] See the Insolvency Act 1986, s 221.
[14] See Chapter 13.
[15] See Chapter 10, fn 2, p 230, above.
[16] See the Supreme Court Act 1981, s 61(1). Where the partners are husband and wife and are involved in matrimonial proceedings, the dissolution of the partnership may be within proceedings in the Family Division: see *Williams v Williams* [1976] Ch 278.

3. CASES WHERE COUNTY COURT JURISDICTION IS LIMITED
BY VALUE

The county court's equitable jurisdiction, including its jurisdiction
to hear and determine proceedings for the dissolution of a partnership, is restricted to cases of partnerships with assets which do not
exceed £30,000.[17] The jurisdiction of the county court can, however, be extended by agreement between the partners in writing.[18]

Transfer of proceedings

Where dissolution proceedings which are commenced in the county
court are outside the court's jurisdiction, the action may be struck
out or transferred to the High Court unless the parties agree to the
extension of jurisdiction.[19] Even where the county court has jurisdiction to hear a dissolution action, a transfer to the High Court
may be ordered by the county court if important matters of law or
fact may or are likely to arise during the trial or in any other appropriate case.[20]

Conversely, dissolution proceedings commenced in the High
Court can be transferred to the county court if the parties to the
action agree. Such a transfer may also be ordered if the High Court
is satisfied that the value of the partnership assets does not exceed
£30,000, or it considers that no important matters of law and fact
are likely to arise during the trial.[1] Such an order for transfer may be
made by the High Court of its own motion, or on the application of
a party to the relevant action.

Procedural matters

All partners should, as a general principle, be joined as parties to an
action seeking to dissolve a partnership.[2] However, a party who is
only nominated as a partner, but who cannot otherwise maintain or
assert the rights of a partner, need not be joined to such an action.[3]

[17] County Courts Act 1984, s 23(f); County Court Jurisdiction Order 1981, SI
1984/1123.
[18] Such an agreement in writing can also be made on behalf of the partners by their
legal advisers. See County Courts Act 1984, s 24.
[19] See the County Courts Act 1984, s 34.
[20] See the County Courts Act 1984, ss 42(1)(a) and 41.
[1] See the County Courts Act 1984, s 40(1).
[2] *Richardson v Hastings* (1844) 7 Beav 301. The personal representatives of a
deceased partner should also be joined as parties to an action dissolving a partnership, if they are interested parties in the accounts taken in the winding up of
the partnership.
[3] *Ehrmann v Ehrmann* (1894) 72 LT 17.

Furthermore, an assignor of a partnership share needs to be added as a party to any proceedings for a partnership account initiated by the assignee of that share.[4]

There would seem to be no objection to the use of representative proceedings in a dissolution action where the number of partners is large. The grounds upon which representative proceedings may be undertaken have been considered in Chapter 8.[5] The principle requirement for such proceedings is that the partners within a partnership can be divided into classes of individuals, each class having respective interests. A partner of each such class can then be joined as a party to a dissolution action as a representative of the co-partners of that particular class.

A dissolution action in the High Court should normally be commenced by writ,[6] although where the facts are not in dispute between the parties, the action may be commenced by originating summons.

In the county court a dissolution action may be commenced by plaint procedure.

The remedies and relief that may be sought as an adjunct to dissolution proceedings are considered elsewhere.[7]

In particular, it should be noted that, as an adjunct to a dissolution action, a partner may seek an action for an account of partnership profits both pre- and post-dissolution. The grounds upon which the court may grant such a remedy have been considered in Chapter 10, where the action for a partnership account was discussed, though chiefly in the context of an action in its own right without recourse to a dissolution of a partnership. The grounds upon which an action for a partnership account may be granted and enforced remain the same whether the action is pursued by a partner as a sole remedy or in conjunction with an action for the dissolution of a partnership.

Dissolution agreements

The partners may agree to dissolve the partnership. A dissolution agreement like all agreements may be set aside or rescinded.[8] Such

---

[4] *Public Trustee v Elder* [1926] Ch 776.
[5] *Irish Shipping Ltd v Commerical Union Assurance Co plc, The Irish Rowan* [1991] 2 QB 206. Note that five partners are not for the above purposes numerous:*Re Braybrook* (1916) WN 74.
[6] RSC Ord 81, r 3.
[7] See Chapters 10 and 12 below.
[8] *Knight v Marjoribanks* (1848) 11 Beav 322; *Saunders v Anglia Building Society* [1971] AC 1004.

an agreement will not, however, be subject to rescission merely because one of the parties to the agreement subsequently finds the agreement is disadvantageous to him. The principal grounds upon which a court may rescind a dissolution agreement are fraud, misrepresentation or wilful concealment on the part of one of the parties to the agreement which induced the party seeking rescission to enter into the agreement.[9]

Injunctions in dissolution actions

An injunction will be granted to a party to dissolution proceedings if such relief is specifically sought in order to restrain a fellow partner or partners from acting so as to impede the ultimate winding up of the partnership.[10] Thus, an injunction may be granted within dissolution proceedings to restrain either a breach of a provision in a partnership agreement or a provision in any agreement relating to the dissolution of the partnership. This would include agreements enforcing any provision regulating or prohibiting any professional or business competition between ex-partners, the use by ex-partners of trade secrets of the partnership, or the collecting of partnership debts otherwise than on behalf of the partnership.[11] A partner will be prevented by injunction from carrying on the partnership business except for the purposes of winding up the enterprise.[12] Furthermore, any action by a partner which may damage the goodwill of the partnership, if it is to be sold as part of the partnership assets during the winding up of the business, can be restrained by an injunction.[13]

The courts will also be prepared specifically to enforce any terms in a dissolution agreement against a partner where it is just and equitable to do so.[14]

---

[9] Ibid.

[10] See Chapter 10.

[11] An injunction will also be granted to prevent the acquisition and misappropration of partnership assets by a partner or the use of partnership funds by a partner for purposes outside the partnership business. See *Alder v Fouracre* (1818) 3 Swan 489; *Hood v Aston* (1826) 1 Russ 442; *Eastern Trust Co v McKenzie, Mann & Co Ltd* [1915] AC 750. An injunction will be granted to prevent a partner from withholding partnership books or documents from inspection: *Taylor v Davis* (1842) cited at 3 Beav 388n.

[12] *De Tastet v Bordenave* (1822) Jac 516.

[13] *Re David v Matthews* [1899] 1 Ch 378.

[14] For the grounds upon which a court will grant specific performance of agreements made between partners, see Chapter 10; see also *Re Flavell* (1883) 25 Ch D 89.

THE RIGHT TO RETIRE

A partner retiring from a partnership at will will bring about the dissolution of that partnership. However, such a dissolution will not be deemed to take place if the other partners can establish that the former partner has forfeited his right to compel a sale of the partnership assets. In such cases the retirement of the partner will merely cause a technical dissolution of the partnership.[15]

The right of a partner to retire from the partnership may be contained in the partnership agreement, or may be achieved with the consent of all the partners. In the case where there is no such right to retire from the partnership or the unanimous consent of the partners cannot be obtained, a partner seeking to retire from a fixed term partnership must seek to dissolve the partnership under s 35 of the Partnership Act 1890, with all the attendant consequences. Conversely, where a partner in such cases unilaterally seeks to retire prematurely from a fixed term partnership without the unanimous consent of his co-partners[16] and either does not pursue, or is unable to obtain, a dissolution of the partnership, the other partners may, inter alia, seek injunctive relief against the recalcitrant partner preventing him from disrupting the partnership. They may also continue to treat him as a partner,[17] pending a negotiated settlement between the parties.[18] The partners in such cases may also wish to exercise an option to expel the recalcitrant partner from the partnership under any power of expulsion contained in the partnership agreement. The latter course of action may, inter alia, compel the recalcitrant partner to accept reasonable terms as regards the disposal of his partnership share.

A partner may retire from an insolvent partnership. He may in such cases sell his share of the partnership assets to his co-partners. Such a sale cannot be impeached under the insolvency legislation, in the absence of fraud.[19] However, in retiring from a partnership which is insolvent, a partner must not seek to remove partnership assets from the partnership business as his partnership share. Such

---

[15] See p 261, above for a definition of this term.

[16] And there is no power in the partnership agreement for him to retire.

[17] Thus making the individual liable for the debts of the partnership and under an obligation to account for any profits. The partners may also seek damages for any breaches of the partnership agreement by the recalcitrant partner.

[18] The partners may, of course, treat such actions of their co-partner as a repudiatory breach of the partnership agreement or themselves apply for dissolution of the partnership: see *Hitchman v Crouch Butler Savage Associates* (1983) 80 LS Gaz R 554.

[19] For a consideration of the insolvency legislation see Chapter 13.

an action may be regarded as a fraud on the partnership creditors.[20]. In cases where a partner becomes personally insolvent, his own creditors will be in competition with the partnership creditors.

THE RIGHT TO EXPEL A PARTNER

The right to expel a partner from a partnership can only be achieved where there is an express power of expulsion in the partnership agreement. Accordingly, in the absence of such a power, partners seeking to remove a partner from the firm can only seek a dissolution of the partnership.[1] Even where a partner has, by his conduct, acted to the detriment of the partnership, the court cannot, in the absence of an express power of expulsion in the partnership agreement, order the expulsion of that partner from the firm.[2]

It is suggested that a partnership agreement for a partnership at will can still contain an express power of expulsion.[3] Nevertheless, where a fixed term partnership expires, but the partnership continues though as a partnership at will, any express power of expulsion contained in the original partnership agreement will not, as a general principle, be regarded as an implied term applying to the new partnership.[4]

Appointment of receiver and manager

Where an action is brought by a partner seeking a dissolution of a partnership[5] the court may appoint to the partnership a receiver or receiver and manager.[6] In most cases the appointment of a receiver

---

[20] See the Insolvency Act 1986, ss 238–339, 423. In such cases the retired partner will be liable as a contributory if the firm is wound up as an unregistered company: see Chapter 13.

[1] See Chapter 10 for a consideration of the exercise of an express power to expel a partner; see also the Partnership Act 1890, s 25; *Clarke v Harte* (1858) 6 HL Cas 633.

[2] *Fairthorne v Weston* (1844) 3 Hare 387.

[3] Although a contrary view has apparently been expressed by Brown-Wilkinson V-C in *Walters v Bingham* [1988] 1 FTLR 260 at 268-269, it is suggested that the learned Vice-Chancellor was referring to a partnership at will which consists of only two partners. In such cases an expulsion or a notice to terminate would for all practical purposes have the same effect.

[4] See the Partnership Act 1890, s 27; *Campbell v Campbell* (1893) 6 R 137.

[5] Or its winding up. See p 283, below for a consideration of the procedure for the winding up of a partnership.

[6] For the appointment of a receiver see p 279, below and Chapter 10.

or receiver and manager is for the ultimate purpose of winding up the partnership's affairs. The appointment of a receiver will more readily be made by the court where a dissolution of the partnership is sought or has already taken place, pending the winding up of the affairs of the partnership.[7]

The appointment of a receiver to a partnership by the court has the effect of placing partnership *assets* under the aegis and protection of the court. From the date of appointment all individuals and bodies, except the court or the receiver, are prevented from interfering or intermeddling with the partnership assets. A manager, by way of contrast, is appointed by the court to carry on the partnership business (though under the direction of the court) and with the ultimate winding up of the partnership as the usual objective. A receiver, per se, has no such power. The appointment of a receiver and/or manager to a partnership, however, affects the position of *all* the partners. Where the appointment of a receiver to a partnership is sought by a partner or partners as a means of controlling the conduct of a co-partner the court must find special grounds for granting the application, such as the co-partner by his conduct placing the partnership business in jeopardy.[8] However, where the order to appoint a receiver/manager is sought by a partner(s) against the personal representatives of a deceased partner or the trustee in bankruptcy or liquidator of an insolvent partner, following a dissolution of the partnership, the court will make such an order without the need to establish any such special grounds.[9]

There remains one further situation which would justify a court granting an order appointing a receiver and/or manager to a partnership. Where a partner or partners act in breach of any dissolution agreement, and the agreement has divested all of the partners of their right to wind up the affairs of the partnership, a

---

[7] It seems that the courts have never appointed a receiver and manager to a partnership without the partnership being in dissolution. For the situations where the courts are prepared to appoint a receiver (but not a manager) in cases where a dissolution is not sought see Chapter 10 and *Sobell v Boston* [1975] 1 WLR 1587; *Phoenix v Pope* [1974] 1 WLR 719.

[8] Such grounds are discussed in Chapter 10, where the appointment of a receiver without the dissolution of the partnership is considered. The effect of such an order will be to exclude all partners from interfering in the business.

[9] The same situation will occur where all the partners are dead and the application for the appointment of a receiver/manager is made by the personal representatives of a partnership: see *Philips v Atkinson* (1787) 2 Bro CC 272; *Fraser v Kershaw* (1856) 2 K & J 496.

receiver/manager may be appointed by the court to complete the winding up of the partnership's affairs.[10]

Appointment of receiver/manager

The application to appoint a receiver/manager to a partnership may be made by motion in the High Court, followed by the appointment of a named receiver/manager. However, the naming of an actual receiver/manager can be adjourned and referred to a master or district judge. Such a practice may give time for the partners to resolve their difficulties prior to the appointment of the receiver/manager, and to avoid such an appointment, which clearly remains a draconian measure. The receiver/manager may, however, be appointed from amongst the partners. In such cases the partner must not have been responsible for any misconduct in running the partnership business. He must therefore be a trustworthy individual. The court will usually require such a receiver/manager to give security to manage properly the partnership affairs,[11] and to account for money received by him on behalf of the partnership. A partner appointed as a receiver/manager may be appointed without the right to remuneration although in such circumstances he may be permitted remuneration on a quantum meruit basis for any services he renders which are beyond the scope of his duties, and which are beneficial to the partnership enterprise.[12]

Where a receiver/manager appointed by the court is not a partner, he may be empowered by the court to employ a partner of the firm as a manager. A non-partner receiver/manager is normally remunerated on a quantum meruit basis,[13] as is a partner receiver/manager if the court provides that he is to be remunerated for his services.

The order appointing a receiver/manager should direct the partners to deliver up to the receiver/manager all the effects and securities of the partnership, together with the partnership books and documents.[14] The receiver/manager should be directed to get in the partnership debts. To this end the receiver/manager should also

---

[10] Even, it seems, at the instance of the representative of a deceased or insolvent partner: see *Davis v Amer* (1854) 3 Drew 64; *Turner v Major* (1862) 3 Giff 442.

[11] *Collins v Barker* [1893] 1 Ch 578.

[12] *Harris v Sleep* [1897] 2 Ch 80.

[13] *Davy v Scarth* [1906] 1 Ch 55.

[14] This aspect of an order will not be made if it is unncessary or unduly inconvenient: *Dacie v John* (1824) M'Cle 206.

be directed by the court to pay any partnership debts, and to provide accounts, and to pay any balances thereto to the court.[15]

The powers and liabilities of a receiver/manager

A receiver/manager can only be vested with the same powers of a partner who is a member of the relevant partnership.[16] Once the receiver/manager ceases to hold his position he cannot be prevented from dealing with the partnership's former customers and clients, unless the receiver/manager is a former partner.[17]

A receiver/manager is, prima facie, personally liable for all contracts which he enters into on behalf of the partnership in his capacity as a receiver/manager. However, such personal liability may be excluded by express terms in the contract, or may be implied by virtue of all the circumstances surrounding the contract.[18] Where the receiver/manager is held personally liable on any contracts made on behalf of the partnership, he has a right to be indemnified out of the partnership assets which are in his possession. This right of indemnity takes priority over the claims of the business creditors of the partnership.[19] There is no right, however, for the receiver/manager to be indemnified by the partners.[20]

Interference with receiver/manager

Any interference by a third party with the exercise by a receiver/manager of his powers, or any interference by such individuals with any partnership assets in the possession of the receiver/manager, is a contempt of court.[1] Any such activities can be restrained by injunction.[2]

---

[15] *Wilson v Greenwood* (1818) 1 Swan 471; *Whitley v Lowe* (1858) 4 Jur NS 197; *Collins v Barker* [1893] 1 Ch 578.

[16] The receiver/manager can be vested with the powers of a partner so far as the latter does not exclude the former as provided for by statute and the relevant partnership agreement.

[17] In such cases the ex-partner may be prevented from dealing with such customers by virtue of the partnership agreement.

[18] *Re Boynton Ltd* [1910] 1 Ch 519.

[19] *Batten v Wedgwood Coal Co* (1884) 28 Ch D 317; *Re Glasdir Copper Mines* [1906] 1 Ch 365.

[20] Even if he was appointed with the consent of the partners: *Evans v Clayhope Properties Ltd* [1988] 1 WLR 358.

[1] *Helmore v Smith (No 2)* (1886) 35 Ch D 449.

[2] *Dixon v Dixon* [1904] 1 Ch 161.

Orders for sale of partnership property

Where a general dissolution of a partnership has taken place, every partner can insist that all partnership assets be sold, irrespective of whether the firm's liabilities and debts could be discharged without such an action.[3] Thus, where on the dissolution of a partnership the assets of the partnership (principally stock in trade) could not be effectively and physically divided as per the partnership agreement, an order for the sale of the assets and division of the proceeds was ordered by the court.[4]

Notwithstanding the above, following a dissolution of a partnership the courts will not generally order the sale of partnership assets, if such an order would conflict with the express provisions of the partnership agreement. The presumption in favour of the sale of partnership assets will also be reversed where the conduct of a partner so dictates. Thus, a retiring partner who, on leaving the partnership, recognises the continuation of that enterprise, may be regarded as having relinquished his right to insist on the sale of the partnership assets. Any order for sale would in such a case be contrary to the spirit of the partner's actions and intentions.[5] It can therefore be said that the presumption that an order for sale of partnership assets should take place subsequent to the dissolution of the partnership may be displaced, despite the insistence of a partner to the contrary, if the court is of the opinion that such an order is not in the interests of the partnership and its members as a whole, and that there are more appropriate alternatives to the protection of the interests of all parties.[6] Where, for example, a partner's share in a firm is small, and the other partner(s) wish to carry on the enterprise, the courts may order that the partner with the minority share sells that share to the other partners.[7] The courts will be unlikely, however, to make such an order if the firm is a saleable commodity as a going concern.

There may be partnership assets which are held upon trust for sale for the benefit of the firm, or which are held in undivided shares. The courts can in their discretion authorise the division of

---

[3] *Hugh Stevenson & Sons v Aktiengesellschaft fur Cartonnagen-Industrie* [1918] AC 239.

[4] See *Cook v Collingridge* (1823) Jac 607. A sale has also been ordered where continuing partners have an option in the partnership agreement to acquire an outgoing partner's share, but fail to exercise it.

[5] *Sobell v Boston* [1975] 1 WLR 1587 at 1591.

[6] However, the presumption is a strong one and is not easily displaced: see *Wild v Milne* (1859) 26 Beav 504.

[7] See *Syers v Syers* (1876) 1 App Cas 174.

such property or, as is most likely in the case of the dissolution of the relevant partnership, order the sale of such assets and a division of the proceeds.[8]

Partnership assets may be of considerable value to the partnership, although the assets have no tangible existence, eg goodwill. However, the sale of such assets does not in general give rise to any special problems as regards the partners inter se.[9]

Where partnerships assets are of value to the partnership or even to a particular partner, but the nature of the assets prevents their effective realisation on the winding up of the partnership,[10] the courts can only debit each or the relevant partner with the value of such an asset or assets. This is the only method by which assets of this nature can be dealt with on a dissolution of a partnership.[11]

In effecting a sale of partnership assets during the winding up of a partnership, the court has a discretion as to the manner in which any such sale will be conducted. The discretion is to be exercised with a view to doing justice to all the partners. Thus, a sale of partnership assets may be by way of sale to the highest bidder. The court may, however, defer an immediate sale, and direct an inquiry as to the ultimate mode of sale. During such an inquiry, a manager and receiver may be appointed to carry on the partnership business under the aegis of the court. Partners may in such circumstances be given liberty to bid to purchase partnership assets.[12] Where a partner has sought the order for the sale of partnership assets he may be given the power to conduct the sale. Such a power is, however, unlikely to be granted to a partner who seeks liberty to bid for such assets on his own behalf. In such cases, the power to conduct the sale should be vested in a third party.[13] A party vested with the power to conduct a sale of partnership assets cannot be subject to interference from third parties.[14] An interim order for the sale of a

---

[8] See the Law of Property Act 1925, ss 28(3) and 188.

[9] Although the purchaser, for reasons of valuation, should be informed if any of the partners of the enterprise intend to continue in business and in potential competition with the purchaser.

[10] Eg an office held by a partner on behalf of the firm and for which he must account for any profits or remuneration; *Ambler v Bolton* (1871) LR 14 Eq 427.

[11] For particular difficulties in the application of this principle to medical practices carried on within the National Health Service and therefore possessing National Health Service goodwill and unassignable tenancies, see *Lindley on Partnership* (16th edn) paras 23 and 183-184.

[12] See *Burdon v Barkus* (1862) 4 De GF & J 42; *Wilson v Greenwood* (1818) 1 Swan 471; *Pawsey v Armstrong* (1881) 18 Ch D 698; *Taylor v Neate* (1888) 39 Ch D 538.

[13] A receiver is also likely to be refused liberty to bid for the purchase of partnership assets.

[14] *Dean v Wilson* (1878) 10 Ch D 136.

particular partnership asset may be made in appropriate cases.[15] However, as in all interlocutory cases, such an order will only be made in the most exceptional cases.

Where a contract entered into by the partnership has not been executed at the time of the dissolution of the partnership, the court may order the benefit of that contract to be sold. However, as an alternative, the court may order each partner's share of the benefit of the contract to be valued, or leave the partners to complete the execution of the contract. In the latter case, the ultimate partnership account will be postponed pending completion of the contract.[16]

Declarations and ancillary relief

The High Court may make a declaration as to the rights and duties of the members of a partnership under a dissolution agreement.[17] In the county courts, however, such relief may only be granted as ancillary to a remedy which the court has jurisdiction to grant.[18] A court will not make a declaration as to the rights and duties of partners under a dissolution agreement where there is merely a trivial or theoretical dispute between the partners as to the dissolution of the partnership.[19]

Winding up a partnership

Although a partnership has been dissolved, the authority of the partners continues, but only for the purposes of winding up the affairs of the firm. New contracts and business should not therefore be undertaken by the partners, unless such activities are necessary to the winding up of the partnership, by aiding or easing the sale of the business as a going concern.

There are a number of problems which arise following a general dissolution of a partnership. The position of persons employed under a contract of employment by the partners is one of the most important. It would appear that, in the absence of contrary provision in such a contract, the dissolution of the partnership will terminate the contract.[20] In such cases the employee may be

---

[15] More rarely such an order may be made in respect of the sale of the entire enterprise.
[16] *McClean v Kennard* (1874) 9 Ch App 336.
[17] *Smith v Gale* [1974] 1 WLR 9 and RSC Ord 15, r 16.
[18] See County Courts Act 1984, s 22.
[19] *Mellstrom v Garner* [1970] 1 WLR 603.
[20] See, however, *Lindley* (16th edn) para 25–02, who suggests that such termination for practical purposes only occurs at the conclusion of the winding up of the partnership.

regarded as having been made redundant. This position should be contrasted with a purely technical dissolution[1] of a partnership where contracts of employment will continue if the firm continues to exist.

Post-dissolution profits

One major matter in dealing with the winding up of a partnership is the treatment of post-dissolution profits. An account of post-dissolution transactions must be kept by the partnership, since the partners are authorised to continue partnership affairs until the business is wound up.[2] Partners who have been engaged in such post-dissolution activities pending winding up of the partnership are entitled to share in any profits earned, in accordance with any agreed profit-sharing scheme. This principle is, however, subject to any contrary provision made by order of the court.[3] Such an order of the court may arise in the case where a deceased partner's estate, or an outgoing partner, does not receive a share of such profits or a share of the partnership assets on the due date.

The Partnership Act 1890 makes particular provision for the treatment of post-dissolution profits where a party has died, or otherwise ceased to be a partner for whatever reason, and surviving and continuing partners carry on that business without a final settlement of accounts. The Act provides that[4] in any of the above circumstances and in the absence of any agreement to the contrary, that the outgoing partner or his estate is entitled at the option of himself or his representatives to such share of the profits made since the dissolution as the court may find to be attributable to the use of his share of the partnership assets. As an alternative the outgoing partner, or the personal representatives of a deceased partner may claim interest at the rate of five per cent per annum on the amount of the share of the partnership assets.

Where, however, the partnership contract gives an option to surviving or continuing partners to purchase the interest of a deceased or outgoing partner, and that option is duly exercised,

---

[1] Technical dissolution is considered above.

[2] See Chapter 11 for a consideration of partnership accounts. Partners are only authorised to carry on the partnership's affairs for the purposes of winding up the business: see p 283, above and the Partnership Act 1890, s 38.

[3] See Chapter 10 for a consideration of the position where a partner is excluded from the participation in the running of the partnership business.

[4] See the Partnership Act 1890, s 42 (1) and (2).

the estate of the deceased partner, or the outgoing partner or his estate, as the case may be, is not entitled to any further or other share of post-dissolution profits; where any partner assuming to act in the exercise of the option does not strictly comply with the terms of the option, he is liable to account for any post-dissolution profits he has received but which are attributable to others.

When the terms of the above provision are satisfied, and a former partner or his estate has not received a due entitlement to post-dissolution profits, a former partner or his personal representative[5] may seek a share of those profits *or* the prescribed annual rate of interest on the former partner's share of the partnership assets. However, such a claim is dependent on the post-dissolution profits arising in part from the use by the continuing or surviving partners of the former partner's share of the partnership assets.[6] The courts must therefore consider how the post-dissolution profits have been earned. Thus, a partner or his personal representative cannot invoke the option under s 42(1) if the post-dissolution profits have been earned solely by the skill and assiduity of the continuing or surviving partners or by the goodwill generated by their efforts and reputation and without the use of the former partner's partnership share. The courts will thus make an enquiry so as to determine the principal source or sources of such post-dissolution profits. It must be accepted that it is not generally possible to determine precisely the source of post-dissolution profits. Nevertheless, the principle remains that if, having regard to the nature of the business and the circumstances of the case, the post-dissolution profits cannot rightfully be attributed to the use of a former partner's share of the partnership assets, then there is no right for a former partner or his personal representatives to exercise the option under s 42.[7]

Section 42 of the Partnership Act 1890 cannot be invoked by a former partner or his personal representative where the profits realised by a partnership post-dissolution are of a *capital* nature and not income. Thus, a partner or his personal representative cannot under the authority of s 42 claim a share of the profits realised by a partnership on the sale of the firm's capital assets[8] as part of the

---

[5] Or where the personal representatives of a deceased partner cannot enforce their rights under s 42, the person beneficially interested in the estate may do so.

[6] This will include a share of the goodwill of the business: see *Manley v Sartori* [1927] 1 Ch 157.

[7] *Featherstonhaugh v Turner* (1858) 25 Beav 382; *Page v Ratcliffe (No 2)* (1896) 75 LT 371; *Simpson v Chapman* (1853) 4 De GM & G 154.

[8] Eg business premises or land.

winding up of the business.[9] However, post-dissolution profits arising from the sale of partnership assets which, though normally of a
capital nature, are no more than part of the stock in trade of the relevant firm are potentially within the ambit of s 42. In such a case a
claim to a share of any such profits may be made by a former partner or his personal representatives.[10] Furthermore, s 42 cannot be
invoked by a former partner or a personal representative in order to
claim a share in the increase in value of a capital partnership asset
between the dissolution of the partnership and the sale of such an
asset. The rights of such parties to claim a share of any increase in
the value of any partnership asset depend on their general rights
under partnership law.[11]

Where a claim to a share of post-dissolution profits may not be
sustainable under s 42, a former partner or personal representative
is entitled to the prescribed rate of interest on his share of the partnership assets.

In calculating post-dissolution profits, continuing or surviving
partners who have particularly exerted themselves in earning such
profits are entitled to remuneration for their services. Remuneration
for the profits earned will only be denied to a partner where he is
regarded as a trustee of such profits, and he is in breach of that
trust.[12]

The right to post-dissolution profits under s 42 may be excluded
by the express or implied agreement of the partners and former
partner(s). Such agreement may be inferred from the provisions of
the partnership deed.[13]

Section 42(2), excludes the right of a former partner, or his personal representative, to claim a share in any post-dissolution
profits earned by the partnership where the continuing or surviving partners have an option to acquire the former partner's
partnership share, and that option is duly exercised, and its terms
carried out strictly and precisely.[14] This situation must be contrasted with an executed contract, by which the continuing or

---

[9] See *Barclays Bank Trust Co Ltd v Bluff* [1982] Ch 172. This case should be contrasted with *Meagher v Meagher* [1961] IR 96, which must, in the light of the
above case, now be of doubtful authority. *Meagher* was distinguished in the
Barclays case.

[10] *Barclays Bank Trust Co Ltd v Bluff* [1982] Ch 172 at 183.

[11] *Barclays Bank Trust Co Ltd v Bluff* [1982] Ch 172. See also *Chandroutie v
Gajadhar* [1987] AC 147.

[12] *Brown v De Tastet* (1819) Jac 284; *Mellersh v Keen* (1859) 27 Beav 236.

[13] Eg by an agreement that an outgoing partner's share automatically accrues to the
continuing partners.

[14] *Vyse v Foster* (1874) LR 7 HL 318 at 329; *Willett v Blanford* (1842) 1 Hare 253.

surviving partners have already acquired the former partner's partnership share. There is no right in such a case for a former partner or personal representative to seek to claim a share of any post-dissolution profits unless the continuing or surviving partners have acted fraudulently in securing or completing the contract, or through negligence or otherwise they subsequently fail or have failed to carry out all of the terms of the contract. In any such case, the agreement may be rescinded, and the former partner or his personal representative may seek to claim post-dissolution profits under the terms of s 42.[15] It would seem, however, that until an option to purchase the former partner's partnership share is exercised, a claim under s 42(1) for a share of post-dissolution profits or interest may be made by a former partner or his personal representative without any restriction.[16]

Where the surviving or continuing partners are also the personal representatives of a deceased partner, any rights that may be claimed under s 42 are reserved to the deceased partner's legatees or next of kin.[17] The partners as personal representatives will, however, only be held to account for any post-dissolution profits that they have received.[18] Where the deceased partner's legatees or next of kin instigate an action against the surviving or continuing partners under the terms of s 42, all partners who were partners at the time of death should be joined as parties to any such action. Partners who have been admitted to the partnership after the date of death should, as a general rule, not be joined as parties to any action. These post-death partners should only be joined as parties in any proceedings under the aegis of s 42 where they have been party to, or privy to, any misconduct on the part of the personal representative/partners.[19] In such cases, the action for any share of post-dissolution profits could be framed either within the ambit of s 42, or as an action based upon principles of equity or breach of trust.[20]

Where the personal representatives of a deceased partner are also the surviving partners of the partnership, they may not in general acquire the deceased partner's share, unless there is an express power to do so in the partnership agreement.[1] Even in such cases,

[15] *Vyse v Foster* (1872) 8 Ch App 309.
[16] *Heathcote v Hulme* (1819) 1 Jac & W 122.
[17] *Jones v Foxall* (1852) 15 Beav 388.
[18] *Vyse v Foster* (1874) LR 7 HL 318 at 333-334.
[19] *Flockton v Bunning* (1868) 8 Ch App 323n.
[20] *Vyse v Foster* (1874) LR 7 HL 318.
[1] The rationale behind this principle is that there is a conflict of interest and duty: see *Cook v Collingridge* (1823) Jac 607.

the acquisition of the deceased partner's share must not be capable of being impugned on the grounds of sharp practice or impropriety.

However, by way of contrast, the surviving partners may obtain a deceased partner's share of the partnership where the personal representatives are not partners in the firm unless there is fraud or collusion between the personal representatives and the surviving partners.[2] In such cases, the acquisition may be set aside by those interested in the deceased partner's estate. It must be noted that, if the personal representatives do not obtain a fair value for the deceased partner's share, they may be held liable for devastavit.

DISTRIBUTION OF PARTNERSHIP ASSETS AND ADJUSTMENT OF PARTNERSHIP ACCOUNTS

Before the winding up of a partnership can take place, the partnership accounts must be settled and completed, so as to reflect in toto the rights, entitlements, and obligations of all the partners.[3]

In settling accounts between the partners after a dissolution of partnership, the Partnership Act 1890, s 44 provides the following rules, subject to contrary agreement:

(a) losses, including losses and deficiencies of capital, shall be paid first out of profits, next out of capital, and lastly, if necessary, by the partners individually in the proportion in which they were entitled to share profits;

(b) the assets of the firm, including the sums, if any contributed by the partners to make up losses or deficiencies of capital, shall be applied in the following manner and order:
   1. in paying the debts and liabilities of the firm to persons who are not partners;
   2. in paying to each partner rateably what is due from the firm to him for advances as distinguished from capital;
   3. in paying to each partner rateably what is due from the firm to him in respect of capital;
   4. the ultimate residue, if any, shall be divided among the partners in the proportion in which profits are divisible.

---

[2] See the Trustee Act 1925, s 15; *Davies v Davies* (1837) 2 Keen 534 at 539; *Beningfield v Baxter* (1886) 12 App Cas 167.

[3] As in most cases involving a partnership the courts, in determining whether any accounts are fair to all interested parties, must have regard to the partnership agreement and the conduct of the partners.

Lindley[4] suggests that every partner's capital entitlement should be taken into account before there is any determination of how the costs of dissolution proceedings are to be borne.[5]

Section 44(a) determines that losses, as defined in the subsection, are ultimately to be borne by the partners in the same proportion as they were entitled to share the profits of the business as determined by the partnership agreement. By s 44(b) the partners must, in coming to a final account, discharge the partnership assets in satisfying the obligations set out in the first three stages of the subsection and in the order prescribed. If, at any of these first three stages, there are insufficient partnership assets to satisfy the burdens so prescribed, any deficiency must be treated as a loss as in s 44(a), and must therefore be borne by the partners in accordance with that provision. Each partner must therefore make a rateable contribution, so as to discharge these burdens. Clearly, where the insufficiency arises at the debts and liabilities to non-partners stage, the partners will bear any losses, together with rateable losses as regards advances and capital which would otherwise have been due to them. Where the partnership assets at least are sufficient to discharge the debts and liabilities owed to non-partners under s 44(b)1 any losses borne by the partners will relate only to partnership advances or capital collectively, depending on the degree to which partnership assets exceed the debts and liabilities to non-partners. Any excess once the debts and liabilities to non-partners have been satisfied will first go to the rateable discharge of advances and only subsequently to capital.

If after discharging the burdens imposed by s 44(b)1, 2 and 3 there is a residue of partnership assets, the residue should be divided between the partners in accordance with the terms of s 44(b)4. The division of any residue between the partners is calculated by reference to the right of each partner to share the profits of the partnership. Receipts of an income nature accruing to a partner, such as the right to a partnership salary,[6] since a right to a partnership salary is not a share in profits are, however, to be ignored in determining the division of the residue of partnership assets.

The situation is more complicated where the partners have not

---

4 *Lindley on Partnership* (16th edn) para 25–27.
5 As is the case with the debts of the partnership and any advances made by a partner, it has always been accepted that such liabilities of the partnerships have priority over the costs of dissolution proceedings.
6 Other examples include the provision during the continuance of the partnership business of bonus shares or incentive profit shares, or any provisions which are dependent on the generation of income.

contributed capital to the partnership in equal shares, but they have nevertheless conducted the business on the basis of the equal sharing of profits and losses. In those cases any *loss* relating to capital must, as a general principle, be shared between the partners equally, as with any other loss. Furthermore, any assets must be distributed so as to ensure that capital losses are equally shared between all the partners.[7]

It must be stressed that s 44 is subject to the contrary agreement of the partners. Thus, the partnership agreement may provide that surplus partnership assets are to be distributed in accordance with the capital contribution of each partner or with the agreed profit-sharing ratios prescribed in the partnership agreement. In these cases losses will be borne on any agreed basis.[8]

Garner v Murray

The discussions above have assumed that, in the winding up of the partnership and in the final distribution of partnership assets, all partners are solvent. Furthermore, the text has generally proceeded on the basis that profits and losses are to be shared equally between the partners, irrespective of capital contribution. The distribution of residual partnership assets under s 44(b)4 is rendered more difficult to resolve when a partner is insolvent. In cases where a partner is insolvent he is unable to contribute so as to make good any lost capital. In the case of *Garner v Murray*[9] the court determined that in cases where s 44 applied to the final settlement of a partnership account, it did not follow that where a partner was insolvent the solvent partners were compelled to make good any shortfall in capital resulting from the inability of the insolvent partner to make contribution in respect of the final account. In such cases it is inevitable that there will be a deficiency in capital available for final distribution to the partners. The *solvent* partners will nevertheless contribute *their* share of any capital losses in accordance with the prescribed profit-sharing ratio and, ultimately, they will receive any capital thus accumulated, rateable in accordance with their original *capital* contributions. Any deficiencies in capital are therefore borne by all the partners, pro rata, in relation to their capital contributions

---

[7] See the Partnership Act 1890, s 24(1); *Ex p Maude* (1870) 6 Ch App 51; *Re Weymouth Steam Packet Co* [1891] 1 Ch 66; *Re Wakefield Rolling Stock Co* [1892] 3 Ch 165.

[8] *Wood v Scoles* (1866) 1 Ch App 369.

[9] [1904] 1 Ch 57.

to the partnership and not in equal shares. This remains the case even if the partnership provided that profits and losses were to be shared equally, since the profit and loss ratios agreed between the partners only determine the contribution each partner must make in order to make good any capital losses, and do not determine the share of the accumulated capital they ultimately receive. The seeming rationale behind this principle, sometimes called the rule in *Garner v Murray*, is that the insolvent partner must be regarded as having already received his share of the lost capital. There is therefore no justification in requiring the solvent partners to make good such a loss.[10] It only remains to observe that, where there is no dispute between the partners, a partnership may be wound up without court intervention.[11]

Premiums

The payment of premiums as a condition of entry into a partnership is now a rare event.[12] The return of a premium or part thereof in the cases of fixed term partnerships which are dissolved is governed by s 40 of the Partnership Act which provides[13] that a partner who has paid a premium on entering into a partnership for a fixed term, where the partnership is dissolved before the expiration of that term otherwise than by the death of a partner, may, on the order of the court, be repaid in whole or in part the premium originally paid. In

[10] An example of the application of the principles of *Garner v Murray* to a partnership is given here. Partner A supplied £10,000 capital to the partnership, partners B and C £5,000 each. The partners were to share profits and losses equally. On the winding up of the partnership C is insolvent. After satisfying all obligations the residual capital is £10,000, ie there is a £10,000 shortfall. A and B do not make up the shortfall in entirety, they each supply a third of that amount. C, being insolvent, cannot contribute to the shortfall in capital. A and B have contributed on the basis of the profit-sharing ratio of the partnership. They each supply a third of the shortfall. The capital sum then accumulated is distributed to A and B in accordance with their *capital* contributions. The effect is that A receives net £6,666 and B £3,333, the ratio in which the capital is shared between A and B is 2:1 as is the overall loss. A therefore loses £3,333 capital and B, £1,667. C is deemed to have received his share of the residual capital and to have borne his share of the shortfall in capital. These are the same sums as B. C therefore is deemed to have received £3,333 and to have suffered a loss on his capital of £1,667.

[11] See the Partnership Act 1890, s 39; *Lyon v Haynes* (1843) 5 Man & G 505.

[12] Even in professional partnerships.

[13] Note that a premium which has been induced through fraud may be returned. As a general principle premiums paid in respect of entering into a partnership at will which is then determined are generally not recoverable. See *Tattersall v Groote* (1800) 2 Bos & P 131 at 134.

making an order under s 40 the court will act as it thinks just and will have regard to the terms of the partnership contract and to the length of time during which the partnership has continued. Where, however, the dissolution is, in the judgment of the court, wholly or chiefly due to the misconduct of the partner who paid the premium, or if the partnership has been dissolved by an agreement containing no provision for a return of any part of the premium, then the court will make no order under s 40.

The section clearly provides the court with a wide discretion, though within prescribed limits, to order the return of a premium or part thereof paid by one partner to another as consideration for entry into a fixed term partnership. The courts will clearly have regard to the duration of the partnership and the degree to which the partnership has been prematurely terminated in assessing the amount of premium that may be ordered to be repaid.[14] The situations where the court is precluded from making an order under the section should be noted. Any order made by a court under the section must, of course, be made prior to the winding up of the partnership.

THE DEATH OF A PARTNER

The death of a partner will, subject to contrary provision in the partnership agreement, bring about a general dissolution of the partnership.[15] If the partnership is then wound up, the personal representatives of a deceased partner, unless they are also surviving partners or the partnership agreement provides otherwise, have no right to interfere in the business or to become partners.[16] The personal representatives may, however, unless the partnership deed provides otherwise, bring an action to have the partnership wound up.[17] Since the surviving partners have no general right in law to acquire the deceased partner's share at a valuation, a winding up may be the only way in which the personal representatives can recover the value of the deceased partner's share for the latter's estate.[18] The situations in which the surviving partners may acquire

---

[14] *Bury v Allen* (1845) 1 Coll 589.

[15] For a consideration of the nature of a general dissolution see above. See also the Partnership Act 1890, s 33(1).

[16] Such an agreement may be implied by the conduct of the partners.

[17] See the Partnership Act 1890, s 39.

[18] See also the Partnership Act 1890, s 43, which provides: 'Subject to any agreement between the partners, the amount due from surviving or continuing partners to an outgoing partner or the representatives of a deceased partner in respect of the outgoing or deceased partner's share is a debt accruing at the date of the dissolution or death.'

the deceased partner's share, and so continue the partnership, have been discussed above. If this option is not practicable in a given case and the personal representatives do not seek a winding up of the partnership, the only remaining course of action is for the personal representatives to allow the deceased partner's share to remain in the business, and to allow the business to continue. The problems that arise from this course of conduct are twofold. First, the personal representatives would need to obtain the full and free consent of the beneficiaries of the deceased partner's estate to this course of action. Second, notwithstanding such consent, the personal representatives would run a risk of being constituted partners in the business or being held out as partners to third parties who deal with the partnership.[19] The fact that the personal representatives of a deceased partner's estate are also trustees will not prevent them being held personally liable for any debts incurred by a partnership in which the law determines that they have become partners.[20] Such an inherently dangerous situation may well force the personal representatives of a deceased partner to seek a winding up of the partnership. It follows that it is generally inadvisable for a partner to be constituted an executor under a fellow partner's will. This practice should in general be avoided, since it will place a partner in a position, should the testator partner die, where the former's duties as partner conflict with the duties he owes to the beneficiaries under the will. Such a situation may well arise, and perhaps be inevitable where the partners carry on the business as a family enterprise, and the partners are generally, if not exclusively, the intended beneficiaries to one another's estates.

Although, as a general rule, the personal representatives of a deceased partner cannot interfere in the running of the partnership business, they nevertheless have an interest in the debts owed to, and liabilities of, the partnership.[1] Any debts paid to the partnership by a third party pending the winding up of the partnership are clearly sums in which the deceased partner's estate has an interest. Conversely, in so far as the surviving partners pay the deceased partner's share of any partnership debts, they have a right of reimbursement against the deceased partner's estate.

---

[19] For the situations in which a party may be constituted a partner or be held out as a partner and for the consequences of being constituted or held out as a partner see Chapter 6.

[20] See *Muir v City of Glasgow Bank* (1879) 4 App Cas 337.

[1] The personal representative may, in certain circumstances, between dissolution and the winding up of the partnership seek a share of any post-dissolution profits or interest on the deceased partner's share under the Partnership Act 1890, s 42: see p 284, above.

A surviving partner may institute proceedings against the estate of a deceased partner in two capacities. He may, as a creditor of the deceased partner's estate, institute proceedings in that capacity and seek an administration order against the deceased's estate.[2] As an alternative, a surviving partner may institute proceedings against the deceased partner's estate qua partner and seek a partnership account[3] together with an administration order in that capacity. The personal representatives must be joined as parties to any action instituted against the deceased partner's estate.[4] Where an administration order is subsequently made in respect of a deceased partner's estate, the personal representative will, if they have acted properly in the administration of the estate, be personally exempt and protected from all the consequences that flow from the making of the order.[5]

It would seem that, unless the goodwill of the partnership is sold in the winding up, the surviving partners can reconstitute a new partnership, and carry out their former business under the former partnership name.[6]

The creditors of a partnership

A deceased partner's estate remains, as a general principle, liable for debts incurred by the partnership before his death. His estate also remains liable for any obligations[7] incurred by the partnership prior to his death which arise through any tortious or fraudulent act, including a breach of trust committed by a partner on behalf of the partnership. The liability for debt remains, notwithstanding any arrangements or dealings made between creditors,[8] unless their actions extinguish any liability or their conduct indicates that they

---

[2] *Musson v May* (1814) 3 Ves & B 194.
[3] For the remedy of a partnership account see Chapter 10; RSC Ord 15, r 4; CCR Ord 5, r 2. Such proceedings can be framed in the alternative; *Addis v Knight* (1817) 2 Mer 117; *Robinson v Alexander* (1834) 2 Ch & F 717.
[4] *Rawlings v Lambert* (1860) 1 John & H 458. Such an action may be commenced although no probate or letters of administration has been obtained: see RSC Ord 15, r 6A; CCR Ord 5, r 8; *Re Amirteymour* [1979] 1 WLR 63.
[5] A court will order assets to be set aside to meet future liabilities. Note also the possibility of an indemnity for the personal representatives afforded by the court, for the legatees or next of kin to deal with remote and improbable contingencies.
[6] *Hill v Fearis* [1905] 1 Ch 466.
[7] *Devaynes v Noble* (1816) 1 Mer 529.
[8] Or parties having rights against the partnership by virtue of any fraudulent, tortious act or breach of trust.

have abandoned or lost their rights against the deceased partner's estate.[9]

A particularly important point to note is that of the limitation of any action. Although an action against a deceased partner's estate in respect of a liability incurred by the partnership may become statute-barred,[10] an act of acknowledgment or part payment by the surviving partners may revive such an action, even against the deceased partner's estate.[11]

A creditor of the partnership may proceed against a deceased partner's estate in respect of any liability incurred by the partnership prior to the death, without proceeding against the surviving partners.[12] To this end the state of the account between the deceased partner's estate and the surviving partners is irrelevant to the creditor.[13] Although it may be advisable for a creditor instigating an action against the deceased partner's estate for a liability incurred by the partnership to add the surviving partners as parties to the action, this is not a necessity.[14] The advantages of adding the surviving partners to the action is that the creditor may then proceed against the entirety of the partnership assets in satisfying any judgment obtained. In addition, it must be noted that a creditor of a partnership proceeding solely against the deceased partner's estate does not rank equally with the deceased partner's separate creditors as regards the deceased partner's separate estate, ie his estate excluding his partnership share.[15] The separate creditors, ie the personal creditors of the deceased partner, have priority over the deceased partner's joint creditors, ie the partnership creditors in respect of the deceased partner's separate estate. However, it must be stated that the separate creditors have no rights against the deceased partner's *share* of the partnership assets until the debts of the partnership have been satisfied.[16]

An administration order made against a deceased partner's estate

---

[9] For a review of relevant authorities on this point see *Lindley on Partnership* (16th edn) para 26-15.

[10] See Prime and Scanlan *The Modern Law of Limitation* (1993).

[11] See Prime and Scanlan, ibid.

[12] *Wilkinson v Henderson* (1833) 1 My & K 582; *Re Hodgson* (1885) 31 Ch D 177.

[13] But see *Brett v Beckwith* (1856) 3 Jur NS 31 where the court ordered the taking of accounts between the deceased partner's representatives and the representatives of the bankrupt partner. The court held that the order was appropriate since the partnership creditor had a right to have the estate fully and properly administered.

[14] See RSC Ord 15, r 6(1); CCR Ord 5, r 4.

[15] See the Partnership Act 1890, s 9.

[16] *Hills v M'Rae* (1851) 9 Hare 297; *Re Ritson* [1899] 1 Ch 128.

will vary in its form, depending on whether the creditor is proceeding against the estate as a joint creditor of the partnership or if he is seeking an order as a separate creditor of the deceased partner's estate. Where the creditor is seeking an administration order as a joint creditor of the deceased partner's estate, the order will generally seek to distribute the estate so as to ensure a fair distribution of the assets of the estate between the joint and separate creditors.[17] Where, however, the creditor is seeking to recover debts as both a joint and separate creditor, he will be entitled to the usual form of administration order against the deceased's estate.[18]

It has already been noted that it may be advisable for a joint creditor of a partnership who instigates an action for recovery of the debt against a deceased partner's estate to join the surviving partners as parties to the action. The joining of the surviving parties to the action is necessary if accounts are to be taken of the partnership's dealings so as to determine the composition and extent of the deceased's joint estate. However, the court will order an enquiry into the affairs of the partnership in order to determine the full extent of the liability of the deceased partner's estate. Thus, the court may enquire as to whether partnership creditors have dealt with the surviving partners subsequent to the death. In these cases the deceased partner's estate cannot be held liable for any liabilities that have arisen as a result of the posthumous dealings.

The principle of distinguishing between the deceased partner's joint estate and his personal or separate estate is generally only of importance when the deceased's estate is insolvent. The rules governing the priority for payment of the joint and separate creditors of a partner's insolvent estate are considered in Chapter 13.

Debts incurred by a partnership after a partner's death

As a general principle, a deceased partner's estate is not liable to third parties in respect of any transactions entered into between those parties and the surviving partners of the partnership after the death of the deceased partner.[19] Neither will the deceased's estate be liable for any tortious or fraudulent act, or breach of trust committed by the surviving partners after the deceased's death. However, the deceased partner's estate remains liable in respect of

---

[17] *Hills v M'Rae* (1851) 9 Hare 297; *Moore v Knight* [1891] 1 Ch 547; *Re Hodgson* (1885) 31 Ch D 177. Such an order should it appears be obtained by writ and not originating summons.
[18] See *Heward's Chancery Orders* p 66.
[19] *Bagel v Miller* [1903] 2 KB 212.

liabilities incurred by the surviving partners which have been necessarily and properly entered into in order to effect the winding up of the partnership.

Personal representative admitted as partners

Where the personal representatives of a deceased partner are admitted as partners to the enterprise, they will from the point of admission be rendered personally liable for any liabilities incurred by the partnership. They do not, however, in such cases automatically impose any such liability on the deceased's estate. Where executors of a deceased partner's estate, without the express authority of the testator leave the deceased's partnership assets within the business,[20] and by implication carry on or permit the surviving partners to carry on the business, they may render that part of the deceased's estate subject to any liabilities subsequently incurred by the partnership.[1] This drastic consequence for a deceased's estate ensures that executors should not act in this way, unless that action has been specifically and expressly authorised by the deceased partner in his will.[2] However, a deceased partner's partnership share will not incur liability subsequent to his death if the relevant assets are retained in the business for a short period, and the personal representatives are admitted to the partnership solely with the purpose of realising those assets.[3] Furthermore, the testator may have directed that his partnership share be left within the business only as a loan to the surviving partners. Such an implication will be rebutted where the executors are also empowered to carry on the business and seek to enforce this power.[4]

The situations where a deceased partner's partnership share may be subject to the debts and liabilities incurred by the partnership after his death due to the actions of his personal representatives have been considered above. Where, however, a surviving partner, who is appointed the executor of a deceased partner's estate subsequently carries on the business, the deceased partner's estate will remain

---

[20] *Wightman v Townroe* (1813) 1 M & S 412. For the purposes of this part of the text personal representative includes both an administrator and an executor.

[1] For which the beneficiaries may have a remedy against the personal representatives.

[2] *Kirkman v Booth* (1848) 11 Beav 273. Such an express power must be unambiguous in its intent.

[3] *Marshall v Broadhurst* (1831) 1 Cr & J 403; *Dowse v Gorton* [1891] AC 190 at 199.

[4] See Chapter 1.

liable for debts or obligations which the partnership has incurred post-death. A similar situation occurs where the assets of a deceased partner are with lawful authority properly utilised within the business.[5] The assets are thus rendered available to discharge liabilities incurred by the partnership which are subsequent to death.[6]

Where the personal representatives of a deceased partner carry on the partnership business in accordance with an express power given by the deceased,[7] or in order to realise the relevant assets, or with the full consent of the beneficiaries, they will be entitled to an indemnity from the estate for any personal liability they may so incur. The liability of the estate will not, as a general rule, exceed the amount authorised by the deceased to be employed in the partnership business.[8] Although the personal representatives are given a right of indemnity[9] in the above cases, their creditors remain the creditors of the personal representatives, and are not constituted the creditors of the deceased's estate. Accordingly, those creditors only have a right of action against the personal representatives.[10] The creditors of the deceased partner's estate will have priority over the creditors of the personal representatives unless the former, knowing that the partnership is being carried on for their benefit, consent to the continuation of the business.[11]

The separate creditors of the deceased's estate and beneficiaries

The separate creditors of the deceased partner's estate and those beneficially entitled to the estate must seek their rights and dues out of the assets of the estate, and therefore their avenue of recourse is to the personal representatives. In determining the size of this estate, it will usually be necessary to determine how far the deceased partner's partnership share[12] will eventually contribute to this estate.

---

[5] Such lawful authority may arise through a provision in the deceased partner's will; cf if the assets are used without such authority: see *Ex p Garland* (1804) 10 Ves 110.
[6] Ibid.
[7] Or in accordance with a statutory power to postpone the sale.
[8] *Cutbush v Cutbush* (1839) 1 Beav 184; *Re Johnson* (1880) 15 Ch D 548.
[9] Each personal representative is given a separate right of indemnity, *Re Frith* [1902] 1 Ch 342.
[10] Cf the situation where the deceased's estate has been constituted a trust fund created specifically for the purpose of carrying on the partnership: *Strickland v Symons* (1884) 26 Ch D 245; *Re Evans* (1887) 34 Ch 597.
[11] *Dowse v Gorton* [1891] AC 190; *Re Oxley* [1914] 1 Ch 604.
[12] Unless specifically bequeathed.

Although, as a general principle, only the personal representatives can seek an account from the surviving partners, an account can also be taken in proceedings for an administration order of the deceased's estate, instituted against the personal representatives, by the deceased's separate creditors, legatees or next of kin. It seems the courts in an action instituted by the separate creditors or the beneficiaries of the deceased partner can direct an enquiry as to the value of the partnership share due to the estate. Any enquiry so ordered[13] will clearly require a full account of the entire estate of the deceased partner. Such an enquiry and account cannot be completed without an account and enquiry as to the deceased partner's partnership share.[14] It would seem, however, that the surviving partners cannot be compelled to pay any sum that the enquiry may find is due to the estate. Payment could, however, be enforced by third party proceedings taken by the personal representatives.[15]

Where a personal representative has been guilty of wilful default in realising the partnership share[16] so as to cause loss to those entitled to the deceased partner's estate, the personal representative may be held liable to account for any consequential loss.[17]

There are exceptional circumstances when those beneficially entitled or interested in the deceased partner's estate may institute proceedings directly against the partnership and the surviving partners, as well as the personal representatives. The circumstances which would justify an action of this sort is where the personal representatives have in some way acted improperly[18] so as to deprive those entitled or interested in the deceased partner's estate from obtaining their rights and dues under the estate. Where an action brought by a deceased partner's separate creditors against the surviving partners is successful and an order for costs is made, the costs are paid in priority to any claim of the deceased partner's joint creditors.[19]

---

[13] See *Lindley* (16th edn) para 26–39 although the position is not entirely free from doubt.

[14] *Paynter v Houston* (1817) 3 Mer 297.

[15] RSC Ord 16, rr 1(1)(b); CCR Ord 12, rr 1(1)(b).

[16] But note the powers of the personal representatives to postpone the conversion of a partnership share.

[17] *Kirkman v Booth* (1848) 11 Beav 273; *Grayburn v Clarkson* (1868) 3 Ch App 605.

[18] Thus such actions have been permitted: (1) where the personal representatives and the surving partners are in collusion (see *Alsager v Rowley* (1802) 6 Ves 748); (2) where the personal representatives have refused to seek an account from the surviving partners, or by their conduct have precluded themselves from seeking an account (see *Burroughs v Elton* (1805) 11 Ves 29); (3) where the personal representatives are also partners (*Beningfield v Baxter* (1886) 12 App Cas 167).

[19] *Re McRea* (1886) 32 Ch D 613.

The separate creditors, or those entitled under the deceased partner's estate, have no remedy or right to impeach a bona fide account settled between the personal representatives and the surviving partners.

It should be noted that no account settled between the personal representatives of a deceased partner and the surviving partners can bind those entitled or interested in the deceased's estate if the personal representatives and surviving partners are the same persons. Furthermore, in those cases no account can be regarded as settled.[20]

A deceased partner's partnership share may, in accordance with the terms of the will, be left in the partnership business as a loan, bearing interest.[1] In such a case, the personal representatives can only claim the agreed interest and not a share of the profits derived from the use of the loan by the partnership.[2] However, the personal representatives will not be held personally liable for any loss to the deceased partner's estate if they have acted properly, and within the terms of the powers given to them by the deceased's will. The separate creditors, legatees or next of kin cannot enjoy any effective rights in the partnership share while it is outstanding as a loan. This remains the case even if the partnership share has been loaned to the partnership in breach of trust, unless the surviving partners are aware of the breach of trust.[3]

Where a personal representative, who is also a surviving partner, uses the deceased partner's share in the partnership business without any lawful authority to do so, he commits a breach of trust. He is then liable to account to those beneficially entitled to the deceased partner's estate for the value of the partnership share, together with interest at a rate of 5%. As an alternative, the parties entitled under the deceased partner's estate may claim any profits which can be established as being attributable to the use of that share.[4] It is advisable that any action by the persons beneficially entitled in the deceased partner's estate, which contains a claim to profits attributable to the deceased partner's partnership

---

[20] *Wedderburn v Wedderburn* (1836) 2 Keen 722; affd (1838) 4 My & Cr 41.

[1] See p 297, above and Chapter 1.

[2] *Vyse v Foster* (1872) 8 Ch App 309. This will remain the case even if the surviving partners do not repay the loan on the agreed date.

[3] *Stroud v Gwyer* (1860) 28 Beav 130.

[4] Remedies based upon the equitable doctrine of breach of trust mirror and complement the remedies available to ex-partners, the personal representatives of deceased partners, and those interested in the estate of a deceased partner where a partnership share is used by a partnership following dissolution, without a settlement of an account under the Partnership Act 1890, s 42.

share, should involve the joining of all the surviving partners as parties to the action.[5]

Where surviving partners, who are not the personal representatives of the deceased partner, are aware that a deceased partner's share has been left in the business, they may be held liable to those beneficially interested in the estate under the terms of s 42 of the Partnership Act 1890. It would seem, by analogy with the situation regarding personal representative partners noted above, that partners who are not the personal representatives of a deceased partner, but who are aware that a partnership share has been left in the partnership in breach of trust, will be liable for any loss sustained by those entitled to or interested in the deceased partner's estate. Proof of knowledge of the breach of trust on the part of the surviving partners will be borne by the parties bringing the action. The standard of proof, however, remains the civil standard of proof.[6]

The remedy of account which will in general be available to parties interested in or entitled to the deceased partner's estate[7] has been considered elsewhere in this book.[8]

It must be emphasised that where a personal representative is admitted to a partnership, not in any representative capacity but as a partner in his own right, any profits which accrue to him are his personal property, and are not to be regarded as the assets of the deceased partner's estate.[9]

Bequest of partnership share[10]

Although a partner may, subject to the terms of the partnership deed or the provisions of the Partnership Act,[11] dispose of his

---

[5] Such an action is advisable, since not all the relevant profits may be in the hands of the personal representatives. A claim for mixed profits and interest will succeed only in exceptional cases: *Heathcote v Hulme* (1819) 1 Jac & W 122. A claim for compound interest is more readily acceded to by the courts: see *Vyse v Forster* (1874) LR 7 HL 318 at 346.

[6] *Booth v Booth* (1838) 1 Beav 125; *Travis v Milne* (1851) 9 Hare 141.

[7] *Verrell's Contract* [1903] 1 Ch 65.

[8] See Chapter 10.

[9] *Simpson v Chapman* (1853) 4 De GM & G 154.

[10] A bequest does not constitute a nomination, admitting the beneficiary to the partnership. Subject to any provision in the partnership deed, admission to a partnership requires the consent of all the partners: see Chapter 8. The bequest of a partnership share entitles the beneficiary to the amount due to the partner at the time of his death, and subject to the will and/or the partnership deed a share of the profits made by the partnership since the death of the partner/testator.

[11] See s 44 of the Act.

partnership share, he may make a disposition of something less than his outright interest in that share to an individual.[12]

Thus, a bequest by a deceased partner of his capital in the partnership will nevertheless include all that was due to him in respect of advances. It is suggested by Lindley[13] that such a bequest would include undrawn profits credited to the deceased partner's capital account, but restricted to such profits which were withdrawable at will and which would not form part of the partnership's fixed capital. A bequest by a deceased partner of the net profits of his partnership share will only include profits accruing during the continuation of the partnership business.[14] Furthermore, a bequest by a deceased partner of his partnership share of the goodwill does not carry a right for the beneficiary to compel the surviving partners to sell the goodwill of the business, and distribute the proceeds among the partners.[15]

A partnership share does not attach to a particular partnership asset or assets. A bequest therefore cannot be made in respect of a particular partnership asset.[16] However, where in his will a deceased partner has also provided legacies for the surviving partners, the latter may be put to their election either to permit the particular partnership asset the subject of the bequest to go to the beneficiary, or to provide compensation out of their legacies.[17]

A beneficiary of a deceased partner, who is also a debtor of the latter's estate, may not receive any benefit from the bequest until he has discharged any debts which he owes to the estate.[18]

Where a partner makes a bequest of his partnership share, but subsequently leaves the partnership and is fully compensated by his former partners, his bequest will at his death be subject to the equitable doctrine of ademption. This requires that a specific legacy, such as a partnership share, must exist at the time of the testator's death. In so far as the property the subject of the bequest has been lost, destroyed, exchanged or sold prior to the testator's death, the bequest is regarded as revoked. However, the doctrine of ademption

---

[12] Such a situation may arise through the clearly expressed intention of the deceased partner, or because the bequest is ambiguous and is so construed by the courts: see *Re Rhagg* [1938] Ch 828.

[13] At para 26–56.

[14] *Re Lawes-Wittewronge* [1915] 1 Ch 408.

[15] *Robertson v Quiddington* (1860) 28 Beav 529.

[16] Although it is not improbable that subject to payment of the partnership debts out of the partnership assets effect may be given to such a bequest, as a concession by the surviving partners: see *Re Holland* [1907] 2 Ch 88; *Re Rhagg* [1938] Ch 828.

[17] *Re Gordon's Wills Trusts* [1978] Ch 145 under the doctrine of election.

[18] This principle does not apply to a beneficiary who is a partner in an enterprise which itself is indebted to the estate of the deceased: *Turner v Turner* [1911] 1 Ch 716.

cannot apply to a partnership share while the testator remains a partner, and so remains at the time of his death, irrespective of the degree to which his partnership interests or the nature of his partnership share has been transformed since the date of his will.[19]

A partner may by his will settle his partnership share on life interest trusts. The rules of equity provide that personal property, such as a partnership share in the circumstances noted above, is subject to the doctrine of conversion. This doctrine determines that the property the subject of the life interest should be sold and the life tenant should receive the income from the proceeds of sale which should be invested by the personal representatives/trustees.[20] Such a rule is subject to a clear contrary intention expressed in the will. Only such an unambiguous contrary testamentary intent will entitle the life tenant to seek to prevent the conversion of the partnership share.[1] This doctrine of conversion, as encapsulated in the case of *Howe v Lord Dartmouth*,[2] does not apply to a life interest arising in a partnership share *under the rules of intestacy*. In such cases the personal representatives can distribute the income arising from the *partnership share* to the life tenant.[3] Any trading losses arising from the continuation of the business by the surviving partners and which are borne rateably by the deceased partner's partnership share must not automatically be thrown on the capital. Such a practice would unduly favour the current life tenant, at the expense of the remaindermen.[4] Unless the will of the deceased partner clearly expresses the contrary,[5] the life tenant of an unconverted partnership share is not entitled to profits attributable to the partnership share prior to the testator's death.[6] Nor, under the same principle, will the life tenant of an unconverted partnership share be entitled to profits attributed to the share and declared after the testator's death, but which were earned, and which should have been declared, before the testator's death. Such profits should fall into the deceased partner's general estate.[7]

---

[19] *Backwell v Child* (1755) Amb 260.

[20] *Howe v Lord Dartmouth* (1802) 7 Ves 137a.

[1] *Re Trollope's Will Trusts* [1927] 1 Ch 596; *Re Chancellor* (1884) 26 Ch D 42; *Re Crowther* [1895] 2 Ch 56. An express power to postpone the sale will not for example be sufficient to entitle the life tenant to insist that the partnership share remains unconverted.

[2] See fn 20, above.

[3] *Re Fisher* [1943] Ch 377; Administration of Estates Act 1925, s 33(5) and (7).

[4] *Upton v Brown* (1884) 26 Ch D 588.

[5] *Re Betts* [1949] WN 91; *Re White* [1958] Ch 762.

[6] See *Ibbotson v Elam* (1865) LR 1 Eq 188.

[7] *Browne v Collins* (1871) LR 12 Eq 586.

CHAPTER 13

INSOLVENCY OF PARTNERSHIPS

The law of insolvency of both individuals and business enterprises, as contained in the Insolvency Act 1986, is an area of some complexity. This chapter will therefore seek only to outline the law of insolvency as it applies to partnerships. The chapter is not intended to be comprehensive in its coverage. There are a number of ways in which a partnership may be subject to the insolvency legislation. The first situation to consider is where an insolvent partnership is wound up as an unregistered company.[1]

INSOLVENT PARTNERSHIP WOUND UP AS UNREGISTERED COMPANY

Where an insolvent partnership is wound up as an unregistered company, it is subject to the legislation governing company insolvencies.[2] Such a winding up may be obtained against a partnership either with or without concurrent petitions against one, several, or all of the partners or former partners. The procedure and consequences in each case differ, depending on which type of winding up order is sought. Consideration will first be given to the winding up of an insolvent partnership without concurrent petitions.

---

[1] The provisions of Pt V of the Insolvency Act 1986 which govern the winding up of an unregistered company apply to partnerships by virtue of the Insolvent Partnerships Order 1994, SI 1994/2421. This order came into force on 1 December 1994 and provides a code for the winding up of insolvent partnerships. This order supersedes an earlier order, the Insolvent Partnerships Order 1986, SI 1986/2142, which governs insolvency proceedings commenced against partnership prior to 1 December 1994. The changes wrought by the 1994 Order will be noted in the text.

[2] See fn 1, above. It should be noted that the Insolvent Partnerships Order 1994 modifies some of the provisions of the 1986 Act so that it may apply to partners and partnerships. These modified provisions are reproduced in the Schedules to the Order.

Winding up an insolvent partnership without concurrent petitions

The *procedure* for the winding up of an insolvent partnership as an unregistered company without concurrent petitions against partners or former partners is governed by the Insolvent Partnerships Order.[3] The *grounds* are, however, restricted to the following situations:[4]

(1) where the partnership is dissolved, or has ceased to carry on business or is carrying on business only for the purpose of winding up its affairs. This provision requires no comment;

(2) where the partnership is unable to pay its debts. Under the Insolvency Act 1986 this occurs in the following situations:[5]

   (a) if a creditor by assignment or otherwise has served a written demand in the prescribed form on the partnership for a sum which exceeds £750[6] to which the partnership is indebted to him, and the sum has neither been paid, secured nor compounded within three weeks;

   (b) if proceedings have been instituted against a partner for a debt or demand due to, or claimed to be due from, the partnership (or from the partner in his character as a member of the partnership), notice in writing of such proceedings has been served on the partnership, and the partnership has not within three weeks paid, secured nor compounded the debt or demand, or had the proceedings stayed, or satisfactorily indemnified the defendant partner against the action or proceedings;[7]

   (c) if any execution or process issued in respect of any judgment obtained either against the partnership or any partner in his capacity as partner is returned unsatisfied;[8]

   (d) if it can be proved to the satisfaction of the court that the partnership is unable to pay its debts as and when they fall due;[9]

---

[3] See SI 1994/2421, arts 7 and 9 and Schs 3 and 5 amending Pt V of the 1986 Act.

[4] See the Insolvency Act 1986, s 222, as amended by Sch 3 to the 1994 Order. No insolvent partnership shall be wound up under these provisions voluntarily: s 221(4).

[5] See the Insolvency Act 1986, ss 222–24, as amended by Sch 3 to the 1994 Order.

[6] Insolvency Act 1986, s 222, as amended by Sch 3 to the 1994 Order. By s 222(2) the sum prescribed may be increased.

[7] Insolvency Act 1986, s 223, as modified by Sch 3 to the 1994 Order: whether or not a partner has a right to an indemnity he will still have to bear his share of any costs, damages or expenses incurred; cf the position of a salaried partner.

[8] Insolvency Act 1986, s 224(1).

[9] Ibid.

(e) if it can be proved to the satisfaction of the court that the liabilities of the partnership, whether such liabilities are actual, contingent, or prospective, exceed the value of the partnership assets;[10]

(3) where the court is of the opinion that it is just and equitable that the partnership should be wound up.

A winding up order made under ground (3) is similar to the making of a winding up order against a partnership on the just and equitable ground under s 35(f) of the Partnership Act 1890. Reference should be made to Chapter 10 for a consideration of the circumstances in which this ground would apply. It is suggested that the court will not grant a winding up order under the above ground where the petition is an unreasonable course of action, and where the petitioner could obtain redress by way of other less drastic remedies.[11]

There would be no distinction in the application of these provisions to an insolvent group or sub-partnership.

Consideration must now be given to the parties who may present a petition under the above provisions.

Clearly, a creditor of the partnership, whether he be a contingent or prospective creditor or creditor by assignment, may present a petition for winding up an insolvent partnership on any of the above grounds.[12] Other parties who may present such a petition include:

(1) the liquidator or administrator of a present or former corporate partner;[13]

(2) the administrator of the partnership;[14]

(3) the trustee of a present or former partner's estate;[15]

(4) the supervisor of a voluntary arrangement approved under Pt I of the Insolvency Act 1986 in relation to a corporate partner, or under Pt VIII of the 1986 Act in relation to an individual member.[16] The individuals noted within (1)–(4) above are on the presentation of the petition defined as a 'petitioning insolvency practitioner';[17]

(5) the Secretary of State.[18]

---

[10] Insolvency Act 1986, s 224(2).
[11] *King v Henderson* [1899] AC 720.
[12] Insolvency Act 1986, ss 124, 222(1).
[13] See the Insolvency Act 1986, s 221A(1) and Sch 3 to the 1994 Order.
[14] Ibid.
[15] Ibid.
[16] Company voluntary arrangements are applied to insolvent partnership for the first time by the 1994 Order: see p 337, below.
[17] Schedule 3 to the 1994 Order.
[18] Ibid.

A partner may also present a petition under the above provisions where the partnership consists of not less than eight partners.[1] A winding up petition should be in a prescribed form.[2] An affidavit must accompany the petition and verify its contents, and contain the names and addresses of all the partners.[3] The petition may be presented at the High Court if the partnership has, at any time, had in England or Wales either a principal place *or* a place of business.[4] In the case of a petition presented to the county court the place or principal place of business of the partnership must be within the insolvency district of that court. In the case of a member's petition the courts may hear the petition only if the partnership has its principal place of business within the territorial jurisdiction of the relevant court.[5] Service of such a petition may be effected at the relevant place of business.

Presentation of petition

A winding up of a partnership as an unregistered company is deemed to commence on the presentation of the petition. From that point any disposition of partnership assets or change of partners is of no effect, unless approved by the court.[6]

Once the petition to wind up has been presented, the partnership or any partner or creditor may apply, prior to the winding up of the partnership, to the court, to stay any proceedings pending against the partnership or any partner.[7]

The court may, following the presentation of the winding up petition, appoint the petitioning insolvency practitioner as provisional liquidator of the partnership.[8] Although the court has a wide

---

[1] Insolvency Act 1986, s 221(a), as modified by Sch 5 to the 1994 Order. A partner may also present a petition under the above provision with leave of the court following service on the firm of a written demand in respect of a joint debt exceeding £750 which has been paid by the petitioning partner from non-partnership assets. In such cases the petitioning partner must also have obtained a judgment, decree or order of any court against the partnership for reimbursement of the amount of the joint debt. Furthermore he must have taken all reasonable steps (other than insolvency proceedings) to enforce any such judgment, order or decree.

[2] See Sch 9 to the 1994 Order.

[3] Ibid.

[4] Insolvency Act 1986, ss 221, 117, as modified by Sch 3, paras 3 and 6 and Sch 5, paras 1 and 2 to the 1994 Order.

[5] Ibid.

[6] Insolvency Act 1986, s 127.

[7] Insolvency Act 1986, ss 126, 227.

[8] Insolvency Act 1986, s 135(1) and (2) and Sch 3 to the 1994 Order.

discretion in determining whether a winding up order should be made,[9] the order will generally mirror the types of order made against a company.[10]

The making of a winding up order prevents the continuance or commencement of any other proceedings for debt against the partnership or a partner without leave of the court.[11] There is an express prohibition on any form of execution against partnership assets.[12] It would also seem that leave would be required in the above circumstances to levy execution on the partner's separate estates.[13]

Where a winding up order is made against an insolvent partnership, after the presentation of a winding up petition, the court may appoint the petitioning insolvency practitioner[14] as liquidator of the partnership.[15]

An insolvent partnership shall not be wound up under the above provisions if the business of the partnership has not been carried on in England and Wales at any time within the period of three years, ending with the day on which the winding up petition was presented.[16]

Winding up order against insolvent partnership with concurrent petitions

Consideration must now be given to the winding up of a partnership as an unregistered company with *concurrent* petitions against a member or members of the partnership.[17] On a creditor's petition a minimum of one partner needs to be the subject of a petition concurrently with the partnership.[18]

A court may only exercise its jurisdiction within the ambit of the

---

9   Insolvency Act 1986, s 125(1), but note s 125(2), where a partner petitions on the just and equitable ground noted above.
10   Insolvency Rules 1986, SI 1986/1925 as amended Sch 4, Form 4.11.
11   See the Insolvency Act 1986, ss 130(2) and 228.
12   Section 128. But see *The Constellation* [1966] 1 WLR 272.
13   See *Lindley* (16th edn) para 27—9 and the authorities cited therein.
14   For a definition of this term see fn 17, p 306, above and accompanying text.
15   See also s 140(3) of the 1986 Act.
16   Insolvency Act 1986, s 221(2), as modified by Sch 3 to the 1994 Order.
17   Or former member or members: see the Insolvent Partnerships Order 1994, arts 8 and 10 and Schs 4 and 6, which applies with modifications the provisions of Pt V of the Insolvency Act 1986, which governs the winding up of unregistered companies to the winding up of an insolvent partnership.
18   See art 8(1) of the 1994 Order. Under the previous 1986 Order (SI 1986/2142) a minimum of two partners had to be the subject of concurrent petitions.

provisions noted above if the partnership has carried on business in England or Wales within a period of three years of the presentation of the petition.[19]

1. THE GROUND UPON WHICH A CONCURRENT PETITION MAY BE PRESENTED

The sole ground upon which an insolvent partnership may be wound up where a concurrent petition is or concurrent petitions are presented is that the partnership is unable to pay its debts.[20] This ground may be established by reference to any number of situations where the debt remains unpaid, but will be deemed to occur *only* when a creditor, by assignment or otherwise, has served a written demand in the prescribed form on the partnership *and* on one or more of the partners in respect of a sum owed to him exceeding £750, and that sum has not been paid, secured or compounded to the reasonable satisfaction of the creditor within three weeks of the date on which the demand or last demand was served.[1]

2. CONCURRENT PETITION: CORPORATE PARTNERS

In winding up a partnership under the above provisions, the court may have to consider the position of a corporate partner who may be subject to a concurrent petition. A corporate partner may be simultaneously wound up with the partnership.[2] A concurrent petition to wind up a corporate partner can only be presented on a single ground, namely that the corporate partner is unable to pay the partnership debts.[3] A corporate partner will be deemed unable to pay these debts in the following circumstances.[4] If a creditor by assignment or otherwise to whom the partnership is indebted in a sum exceeding £750[5] then due for which a corporate member or former corporate member of the partnership is liable and:

(1) the creditor has served a written demand in the prescribed form[6] requiring the partnership and any corporate member as noted above to pay the sum due; and

[19] Insolvency Act 1986, s 117, as modified by Schs 4 and 6 to the 1994 Order.
[20] Insolvency Act 1986, s 221(5), as modified by Schs 4 and 6 to the 1994 Order.
[1] Note the sum of £750 may be increased: see the Insolvency Act 1986, s 222, as modified by Sch 4 to the 1994 Order. For service of such a demand see above and ibid.
[2] Insolvency Act 1986, s 117, as modified by Sch 4 to the 1994 Order or former member.
[3] Insolvency Act 1986, s 122, as modified by Sch 4 to the 1994 Order.
[4] Insolvency Act 1986, s 123, as modified by Sch 4, Pt II to the 1994 Order.
[5] This sum may be increased by order: see fn 1, above.
[6] Ibid.

(2) the partnership or corporate member have for three weeks after the service of the demands or last demand if they have been served at different times, neglected to pay, secure or compound the sum to the satisfaction of the creditor.

Service of a demand is effected by leaving it at a place or principal place of the partnership business, or by delivery to an officer of the partnership, or by delivery in accordance with the direction, or approval of the court.[7]

3. CONCURRENT PETITION: PARTNER PRIVATE INDIVIDUAL

A concurrent petition for bankruptcy may be presented against a private partner or former partner as well as against the partnership. Such a concurrent petition may be presented by a partnership creditor against the individual partner or former partner in respect of partnership debts where the individual partner is unable to pay the partnership debt and the debt is liquidated, and totals more than £750.[8]

The individual partner or former partner will be regarded as unable to pay a partnership debt if the relevant debt has despite the serving of a written demand in the prescribed form not been paid, secured or compounded to the satisfaction of the creditor.[9]

The principal parties who may present a petition against a partnership, concurrently with a petition against a corporate or individual partner or former partner within the terms of the above provisions, are the creditors of the partnership. However, a partner, be it a corporate or private individual, may also under the authority of these provisions present a petition against the partnership together with concurrent petitions against the members of the partnership on the ground that the partnership is unable to pay its debts. In this case concurrent petitions must be presented by the petitioner partner against the partnership and *all* the other partners, including himself or itself, all of whom must be willing to have insolvency orders made against them.[10]

---

[7] Ibid or by delivery to the corporate partner's place of business.
[8] See the Insolvency Act 1986, s 222, as substituted by the Insolvent Partnerships Order 1994, Sch 4, Pt I. Note the prescribed sum noted in the text above may be increased by the above provision.
[9] See fn 1, p 309, above. Such a petition may, it is suggested, be presented against a foreign partner. Also, note that personal representatives carrying on the business on behalf of a deceased partner will not be subject to insolvency proceedings in respect of debts incurred by the partnership, unless they have taken on the responsibilities of a partner: see *Re Fisher* [1912] 2 KB 491.
[10] See the Insolvency Act 1986, s 124(2), as substituted by the Insolvent Partnerships Order 1994, art 10 and Sch 6; but note s 124(3) of the 1986 Act. See also Insolvency Act 1986, ss 264, 272, as substituted by the 1994 Order.

The concurrent petitions must be presented simultaneously and to the same court.[11] Where the presentation of petitions against the partnership and all the partners is impracticable, the court may direct that petitions may be presented against the partnership and such member or members as it may specify.[12]

The consequences that follow the presentation of a winding up petition against a partnership have been considered at p 307, above. The same consequences follow the presentation of such a petition against a corporate partner. An individual partner who is the subject of a winding up petition will, of course, be subject to the restrictions imposed upon an individual's right to dispose of his assets as provided by the Insolvency Act 1986.[13]

Although it has been noted that the concurrent petitions against the partnership and the partners must be presented simultaneously, the court must *hear* the petition against the partnership first.[14] The court has a discretion as to whether or not to make a winding up order.[15]

However, where the court makes a winding up order against the partnership, it *may* make the same order against any corporate partner. Furthermore, it is not compelled to make a consequential bankruptcy order against a private partner. If no winding up or bankruptcy order is made against the members of the partnership within 28 days of the making of a winding up order against the partnership, the proceedings against the partnership shall be conducted as a winding up of an insolvent partnership as an unregistered company where no concurrent petition is presented against a member.[16] Where a court refuses or declines to make a winding up order against a partnership, it may also dismiss any concurrent petitions against any partner, be it a private or a corporate partner.[17]

---

[11] Insolvency Act 1986, s 124(4), as substituted by art 10, Sch 6, of the 1994 Order. The court must have jurisdiction to make a winding up order or a bankruptcy order in respect of each of the parties. For a consideration of such jurisdiction see p 307, above and s 117 and s 265 of the 1986 Act.

[12] Insolvency Act 1986, s 124(3), as substitued by art 10, Sch 6 of the 1994 Order.

[13] Insolvency Act 1986, s 284 as amended by art 11, Sch 7 of the 1994 Order.

[14] Insolvency Act 1986, s 124(6), as modified by art 10, Sch 6 of the 1994 Order; see also *Re Marr* [1990] 2 WLR 1264 at 1271.

[15] Insolvency Act 1986, s 125, as modified by art 10, Sch 6 of the 1994 Order. The court may make directions as to the future conduct of any insolvency proceedings in existence against any of the partners. See s 125(2) of the 1986 Acty as substitued by art 10, Sch 6 of the 1994 Order.

[16] See the Insolvency Act 1986, ss 125A(4) and 271, as modified by art 10, Sch 6 of the 1994 Order; *Re Marr* [1990] Ch 773; and s 271 of the 1986 Act.

[17] Insolvency Act 1986, ss 125A(4) and 271, as modified by art 10, Sch 6 of the 1994 Order.

Once a winding up order has been made in respect of the partnership, within the terms of the above provisions all existing proceedings both against the partnership and its partners are stayed, as are all future proceedings or executions.[18] Where the court is made aware after the presentation of a winding up or bankruptcy petition against a partnership or a partner that the latter is a member of an insolvent partnership, the court may make an order as to the future conduct of the insolvency proceedings, and may apply the provisions of the Insolvent Partnership Order 1994 with any necessary modifications.[19]

The jurisdictional rules governing the making of any orders under the above provisions are the same as the jurisdictional rules governing the making of a winding up order against a partnership wound up as an unregistered company without concurrent petitions which has been noted above.

A joint petition by all the partners to wind up the partnership

The final procedure whereby a partnership may be wound up under the Insolvent Partnerships Order 1994 must now be considered. This procedure involves *all* the partners presenting a joint debtor's petition against the partnership, but the latter is *not* wound up as an unregistered company. Nevertheless, the Insolvency Act 1986 applies to such a procedure.[20] All the partners, who must be individuals and who must not be limited partners, must concur with such an action.[1] The only ground for such a petition is that the partnership is unable to pay its debts.[2]

The petition should request the partner's trustees to wind up the partnership business and administer its assets without the partnership being wound up as an unregistered company.[3] The

---

[18] See the Insolvency Act 1986, ss 130(2), 183, 228, 285, 346, 347.
[19] Art 14(1) of the 1994 Order, amending ss 168 and 303 of the Insolvency Act 1986.
[20] See the Insolvent Partnerships Order 1994, art 11 Sch 7 applying the Insolvency Act 1986, s 264, as modified.
[1] See fn 10, p 310, above.
[2] Insolvency Act 1986, s 272 as modified by art 11, Sch 7 of the 1994 Order. The *fact* that the partnership cannot pay its debts must be established.
[3] Insolvency Act 1986, s 264, as modified by art 11, Sch 7 of the 1994 Order. Note the possible application of art 14(1) of the 1994 Order where a winding up order has previously been made against the partnerships. The above procedure would seem to be available to the partners even where one of them is a foreigner.

jurisdiction rules applicable to the court in making such an order are the same jurisdiction rules where a court makes an order winding up a partnership as an unregistered company on a member's petition without concurrent petitions, and has been considered at p 307, above.

PETITION FOR BANKRUPTCY OR WINDING UP ORDER PRESENTED AGAINST ONE OR MORE PARTNERS BUT WITH NO ATTEMPT TO WIND UP THE PARTNERSHIP

The final procedure whereby a partnership, or at least some of its members, may be subject to the insolvency legislation must now be considered. Where a partnership debt remains unpaid, a creditor has an option to present a petition for bankruptcy or a winding up order against one, but not necessarily all, the partners (be they individual or corporate), without seeking to have the partnership wound up as an unregistered company. Subject to the possible application of art 14(2) of the Insolvent Partnership Order 1994,[4] the 1994 Order is inapplicable to such a procedure. The proceedings will therefore be governed by the provisions of the Insolvency Act 1986.[5] This procedure may also be used by one partner against a co-partner, dependent on the former acting in the capacity as a creditor of the partnership.[6] Where a claim is dependent upon the taking of an account, the petition cannot be presented until the account has been completed, and the sum due ordered to be paid.[7]

Regard must be had to the possible application of art 14(2) of the Insolvent Partnership Order 1986 to the insolvency procedure noted above.[8] Where a bankruptcy petition has been presented to the court against any person, including a partner, and the court is made aware that the party the subject of the petition is a member of an insolvent partnership, the court may apply the provisions of the Insolvent Partnerships Order 1994, and make any order under the ambit of that order with any necessary modifications.[9]

---

[4] See also fn 3, above.
[5] See the Insolvency Act 1986, s 254.
[6] See *Ex p Notley* (1833) 1 Mont & A 46; *Ex p Richardson* (1818) Buck 202; *Hope v Meek* (1855) 10 Ex Ch 829.
[7] For the taking of a partnership account see Chapter 10 and *Debtor v Brown* [1986] CLY 131.
[8] See preceding paragraph. This provision reproduces art 14(1) of the 1994 Order.
[9] See also art 14(1) of the 1994 Order.

Consideration must now be given to the procedures that follow the winding up of an insolvent partnership.

PROCEDURES SUBSEQUENT TO THE WINDING UP OF AN INSOLVENT PARTNERSHIP

Where a partnership has been wound up as an unregistered company without concurrent petitions[10] the official receiver may be appointed to act as liquidator,[11] until another party is so appointed. It should be noted that if the petition against the partnership was presented by the liquidator or administrator of a corporate partner or former corporate partner, or the administrator of the partnership[12] or the trustee of a bankrupt partner or former partner, the court may appoint the petitioner as liquidator.[13]

Where a corporate partner has been wound up, the official receiver may also be appointed the liquidator in respect of an insolvent partnership of which the corporate partner was a member.

Where the official receiver is acting as the liquidator of a partnership which has been wound up without concurrent petitions, he *may* call a joint meeting of the creditors and contributories with a view to seeking the appointment of another party as liquidator, ie a responsible insolvency practitioner. The position is now the same if the winding up order was made with concurrent petitions against one or more partners.[14] The liquidator so appointed will, of course, act in that capacity in respect of the partnership, as well as for any corporate partner and/or as trustee for any individual partner.[15]

---

[10] See p 305, above for a consideration of this form of insolvency proceeding.

[11] This is usually the position where the partnership is wound up as an unregistered company with concurrent petitions: see p 308, above for a consideration of this form of insolvency proceedings. See the Insolvency Act 1986, s 136(2).

[12] See p 339, below for a consideration of the making of an administration order in relation to an insolvent partnership.

[13] Such a petitioner is defined as the petitioning insolvency practitioner: Insolvency Act 1986, s 221A(5) as modified by art 7, Sch 3 of the 1994 Order; see also s 221 1A(A) of the 1986 Act. For the appointment of a petitioning insolvency practitioner as provisional liquidator, see also s 140(3) of the 1986 Act.

[14] The 1994 Order removes the *mandatory* requirement under s 136 of the 1986 Act as modified by the revoked Insolvent Partnerships Order 1986, for the official receiver to summon a meeting of creditors to choose a responsible insolvency practitioner in his place. The official receiver is, however, under a duty to consider the exercise of that discretion under s 136A, as modified by Sch 4, para 12 of the 1994 Order.

[15] Insolvency Act 1986, s 136, as modified by Sch 4, para 12 of the 1994 Order. See also s 137(1) and (2) of the 1986 Act.

The official receiver may act as the receiver and manager of a bankrupt partner who was the subject of a petition presented under the ambit of the Insolvency Act 1986 until the appointment of a trustee.[16] Where the bankruptcy order made against an insolvent partner was not made as part of a concurrent petition, the trustee should be appointed during a meeting of the partner's creditors called by the official receiver, although the official receiver may decide to act as trustee.[17] On the making of a bankruptcy order against an individual partner the official receiver does not become receiver and manager pending the appointment of a trustee, but he himself becomes trustee until the appointment of a responsible insolvency practitioner, the appointment being made during a meeting of creditors and contributories called by him.[18]

In any case where such a meeting fails to appoint a trustee the official receiver must consider whether to apply to the Secretary of State for such an appointment to be made.[19]

The Insolvency Act 1986[20] provides for the replacement of a liquidator/trustee or for the latter to seek directions from the court, if a conflict of interest arises in their attempt to carry out their duties.

THE POSITION OF PARTNERS IN THE WINDING UP OF THE PARTNERSHIP

Where a partnership is wound up as an unregistered company[1] each of the partners will be regarded in two capacities:

(1) as a contributory, ie a person liable to contribute to the assets of the partnership in the event of a winding up;[2] and
(2) as an officer of the partnership.[3]

It would appear that a contributory for the above purposes would include:

---

[16] Insolvency Act 1986, s 287(1).
[17] Insolvency Act 1986, s 293.
[18] See art 2 and Sch 4, para 12 of the 1994 Order.
[19] Insolvency Act 1986, ss 295, 296, as modified by Sch 7 to the 1994 Order.
[20] Insolvency Act 1986, s 230, as modified by Sch 4, Pt II, para 26 of the 1994 Order.
[1] For a consideration of this form of insolvency proceeding see p 305, above.
[2] See the Insolvency Act 1986, s 226.
[3] Insolvency Act 1986 as modified by Sch 4 of the 1994 Order, but see 221(7). See art 16 of and Sch 8 to the 1994 Order. Such a partner may be subject to the provisions of the Company Directors (Disqualification) Act 1986 as modified by Sch 8 of the 1994 Order.

(a) a person held out as a partner;[4] and
(b) any outgoing partner who remains directly liable to the creditors of the partnership; or
(c) an outgoing partner who has agreed to bear a proportion of a particular ongoing liability which continues to be incurred by his former partners.

It is suggested that a former partner can be regarded as an officer of the enterprise.[5]

Furthermore, it may be argued[6] that a person held out as a partner, but who has not participated in the control or management of a partnership, could not be regarded as an officer of the partnership under the scope of the above provisions. It is doubtful whether the above provisions would as a general principle result in a salaried partner being held to be an officer of the partnership.[7]

The partner as contributory

As has been noted above, a partner who is solvent may be held liable as a contributory to the insolvent partnership of which he is or was a member and which has been wound up as an unregistered company and therefore must meet calls made by the liquidator.[8]

Whether or not a partner has been placed on the list of contributories, he (or his estate should he die) remains liable to make contributions to the insolvent partnership estate for a prescribed limitation period. The same situation occurs if he is declared bankrupt.[9]

The liability of a partner contributory is unlimited, although there may be adjustments vis-à-vis any contribution made by that partner as between the various members of the partnership in order to ensure that any contribution made by a partner reflects the terms of the partnership agreement, and the agreed ratio of the sharing of

---

[4] For the doctrine of holding out see Chapter 6.
[5] Under art 16 of and Sch 8 to the 1994 Order.
[6] See *Lindley* (16th edn) at para 27–57.
[7] For a consideration of the status of a salaried partner see Chapter 6. Neither s 226 of the Insolvency Act 1986, nor art 16 of and Sch 8 to the 1994 Order can apply where a partnership is wound up but not as an unregistered company for such insolvency proceedings: see p 312, above.
[8] This liability constitutes a speciality debt accruing when the liability commenced. The limitation period is thus 12 years: see the Insolvency Act 1986, s 80 and the Limitation Act 1980, s 8(1). For a consideration of limitation in this context see Prime and Scanlan *The Modern Law of Limitation* (1993).
[9] Insolvency Act 1986, ss 81 and 82.

profits and losses of the business between the members of the partnership.[10] Former partners will be held liable to contribute in respect of debts incurred by the partnership whilst they were partners.[11]

It is for the liquidator to draw up the list of the partnership's contributories and to make calls upon them to settle the partnership's debts and liabilities.[12] The liquidator is also responsible for the adjustment of contributions between the contributory partners.[13] Enforcement of any payment required by a call is by order of the court.[14]

Where a partnership is wound up as an unregistered company, each partner is deemed to be an officer of the partnership. This renders the partners subject to certain provisions of both the Insolvency Act 1986 and the Company Directors (Disqualification) Act 1986.[15] Thus, a partner could be subject to a disqualification order if the liquidator could establish that he had been guilty of, inter alia, misfeasance or breach of any fiduciary or other duty, whereby he would be prevented, without leave of the court, from becoming involved in the management of a company during the prescribed period of disqualification.[16] There would seem to be no objection to making such an order in respect of a former partner.

Once a winding up order is made against a partnership as an unregistered company, the authority of *all* partners to bind the partnership in respect of any transaction, or to dispose of partnership assets, is revoked. All partners are under an obligation to deliver up to the liquidator any partnership assets in their possession.[17] This

---

[10] Insolvency Act 1986, s 226(1) and (2).

[11] Or in respect of a person who was held out as a partner. For the doctrine of holding out see Chapter 6. A party so liable may have a right of indemnity from the current partners.

[12] Insolvency Act 1986, s 160(b) and (d); Insolvency Rules, 1986, rr 4.195, 4.202; Insolvency Act 1986 s 148; Insolvency Rules 1986, rr 4. 196–198; Insolvency Act 1986, s 150; Insolvency Rules 1986, r 4.202.

[13] Including former partners and those held out as partners, see also the Insolvency Act 1986, s 154 and the Insolvency Rules 1986, rr 4.221-2.

[14] Although leave of the court would seem to be required: Insolvency Rules 1986, r 4.205(2); Insolvency Act 1986, s 228 concerning a partnership wound up as an unregistered company; *Williams v Harding* (1866) LR 1 HL 9.

[15] See art 16 of and Sch 8 to the 1994 Order, which applies ss 6–10, 15, 19(c), 20 of and Sch 1 to the Company Directors (Disqualification) Act 1986 to partners in the circumstances noted in the text.

[16] An order could also be made on similar lines by the Secretary of State if he is satisfied that a partner's conduct renders him unfit to be concerned in the management of a partnership. See the Company Directors (Disqualification) Act 1986, s 7, as modified by the Insolvent Partnerships Order 1994, art 16, Sch 8.

[17] See the Partnership Act 1890, s 20; s 234 of the 1986 Act, as modified by art 7 of and Sch 3 to the 1994 Order.

obligation is also imposed on former partners. Any partnership assets in the hands of third parties, including the spouses of partners, can be recovered by the liquidator, following an application by him to the court for an order for delivery up of such assets.[18] Where a winding up order has been made, or a provisional liquidator appointed, the official receiver may require any partner or former partner to submit a statement relating to the partnership's affairs. This will include details of the partnership assets, debts and liabilities.[19] Where the partner is a corporate partner[20] the relevant statement must show its interests in the partnership assets, and make specific reference to the debts and liabilities attributed to the partnership and to its separate estate.[1]

The purpose behind the above provisions is to establish the assets and liabilities of the partner's separate and joint estates, since it is only the partnership assets which vest in the liquidator or trustee.

Consideration must now be given to the case where a partner becomes insolvent, but the partnership of which he is a member remains solvent.

Where a partner is bankrupted, or a corporate partner is wound up and dissolved, the relevant partnership is itself dissolved and the remaining partners have authority to wind up the partnership.[2] The liquidator or trustee of the insolvent partner has no general or unrestricted right to interfere in the winding up or management of the partnership.[3] Unless there has been misconduct on the part of

---

[18] Ibid. Where bankruptcy orders are made against individual partners on a joint debtor's petition, the partners will be under the same obligations as noted above but to the trustee in bankruptcy.

[19] Insolvency Act 1986, s 131(1) as modified by art 7 of and Sch 3 to the 1994 Order.

[20] And the winding up order has been made on concurrent petitions.

[1] Insolvency Act 1986, s 131(1)(a), as modified by art 8 of and Sch 4 to the 1994 Order. Statements in similiar form should be prepared by a partner who has been bankrupted on a concurrent petition, or on a joint debtor's petition: see the Insolvency Act 1986, s 288(2)(a).

[2] See Chapter 12 and the Partnership Act 1890, ss 33(1), 38. However, the partnership agreement may make alternative provision: see Chapters 2 and 12.

[3] He may so interfere if he can establish that the partners are guilty of misconduct or they are all dead or abroad: see *Barker v Goodair* (1805) 11 Ves 78; *Dutton v Morrison* (1810) 17 Ves 193. Neither a liquidator nor a trustee of an insolvent partner can compel the solvent partners to deliver up possession of the partnership books. He can, however, apply to the court to have the partners bought before the court for examination. In such a case the partners may be ordered to produce the partnership books. See the Insolvency Act 1986, ss 236, 336; Insolvency Rules 1986, r 9.1; *Cloverbay Ltd v Bank of Credit and Commerical International SA* [1991] Ch 90.

the solvent partners the court will generally appoint one of them to be the receiver of the partnership assets.[4] The only property that will vest in a liquidator or trustee is the insolvent partner's partnership share, which is itself subject to the liens or rights of the solvent partners.[5] The liquidator or trustee cannot recover any share of the insolvent partner's partnership share until the partnership account is settled and all partnership debts are paid.[6] It should be noted, however, that where the partnership agreement so provides, the solvent partners may buy out the insolvent partner's share at a valuation.[7]

Where accounts are settled between the solvent partners and the liquidator or trustee, the latter will be entitled to share both in any capital profits arising from partnership assets, or income profits which have arisen from the utilisation of the insolvent partner's partnership share, and which have occurred or been earned since the dissolution of the partnership.[8]

It has been noted[9] that the partnership agreement may provide that a partner may be expelled from the partnership where he or it becomes insolvent, but before he or it is subject to an order of bankruptcy or winding up. The agreement may thus provide for an automatic right of acquisition of the insolvent partner's share, or it may provide for automatic accrual of that share to the solvent partners.[10]

SET OFF

The insolvency legislation recognises the possible application of the equitable doctrine of set off in counter-claims against respective estates or parties in the following cases:

(1) in the bankruptcy of an individual partner;[11]
(2) where a corporate partner is wound up;[12]

---

[4] It seems that the liquidator or trustee would not take the place of the insolvent partner even as a joint tenant in any of the partnership assets which consisted of land.

[5] See the Partnership Act 1890, s 39; *Bolton v Puller* (1796) 1 Bos & P 539.

[6] *Taylor v Fields* (1799) 4 Ves 396; *Holderness v Shackels* (1828) 8 B & C 612.

[7] See the Partnership Act 1890, s 44. The conditions upon which such a buy out may take place have been considered in outline in Chapter 12.

[8] See the Partnership Act 1890, s 42; *Barclays Bank Trust Co Ltd v Bluff* [1982] Ch 172.

[9] See Chapter 2.

[10] For the legality and effect of such a provision in a partnership agreement see Chapter 2.

[11] Insolvency Act 1986, s 323 and Insolvent Partnerships Order 1994, art 11.

[12] Insolvency Rules 1986, r 4.90.

(3)   where the partnership is wound up as an unregistered company, whether or not there has been concurrent petitions.

However, it would appear that the circumstances in which cross-demands between respective estates or parties can, and in fact must, be set off against each other requires the satisfaction of the following circumstances:

(1)   that both demands are money demands.[13] Furthermore, the sum sought to be set off against either a trustee or liquidator acting on behalf of an insolvent partner's estate must be provable in the bankruptcy or liquidation;
(2)   the demands have to be mutual;[14]
(3)   the demands must have arisen before the creditor had notice of the presentation of the petition.[15]

The principle of mutuality is the key to an understanding of the application of set off in respect of bankrupt or insolvent partners and partnerships and their estates. As a general principle, a demand against a partnership by a third party cannot be set off against a cross demand of one or more partners against that third party and vice versa.[16] This principle is equally applicable to a debt owed to a partnership by a third party which the partnership seeks to set off against a debt owed to that party which has been incurred by a sole partner, irrespective of the solvency of that partner, or the fact that the partnership succeeded to the partnership business subsequent to a dissolution.[17]

It follows from the above that a joint debt owed by a partnership to a third party cannot be apportioned and set off against several debts owed to the partners in their separate capacities by that third party.[18]

[13]   Insolvency Act 1986, s 323; Insolvency Rules 1986, r 4.90; *Re Charge Card Services Ltd* [1989] Ch 497.
[14]   *National Westminster Bank Ltd v Halesowen Presswork & Assemblies Ltd* [1972] AC 785. A debt accruing after a bankruptcy or winding up order cannot be set off: *Re A Debtor* [1956] 1 WLR 1226.
[15]   Insolvency Act 1986, s 323(3); Insolvency Rules 1986, r 4.90(3).
[16]   *Watts v Christie* (1849) 11 Beav 546; *Re Pennington and Owen Ltd* [1925] Ch 825. A possible exception to this rule is postulated by *Lindley* (16th edn) para 27-78, where a partner in his personal capacity might be able to set off any sum due to him against the partnership where the latter has been wound up, and the courts are prepared to treat the partnership as an unlimited company for the purposes of the Insolvency Act 1986, s 149(2)(a).
[17]   *Ex p Ross* (1817) Buck 125; *Re Jane* (1914) 110 LT 556.
[18]   *Ex p Christie* (1804) 10 Ves 105. An agreement in good faith between partners to set off a joint and separate debt is valid, but cannot affect the application of the insolvency legislation. See *National Westminster Bank Ltd v Halesowen Presswork & Assemblies Ltd* [1972] AC 785.

ADMINISTRATION OF PARTNERS AND PARTNERSHIP ESTATES

A key aspect in the application of the insolvency legislation to insolvent partnership and partners is the continued recognition of the separation of the partnership estate and debts, ie the joint estate and debts, from the separate estates and debts of the individual partners. The basic principle applied in cases of the insolvency of a partnership and the members of that partnership is that the joint creditors should be paid first out of the joint (ie the partnership) estate, and the separate creditors of each partner should first be paid out of the separate estate of each partner. If, after the satisfying of all the creditor's claims in respect of the joint estate, there is a surplus of assets over liabilities, any surplus can be used to satisfy the claims of the creditors of the respective separate estates in so far as any claims remain unsatisfied and vice versa.[19] The detailed workings of this principle are set out in the schedules to the Insolvent Partnership Order 1994. These provisions are clear and require no comment. Nevertheless, they are in part set out below for the purposes of reference.[20] Reference is first made to the issue of expenses incurred by the responsible insolvency practitioner in executing an insolvency order against a partnership or a member of a partnership.

Expenses incurred by responsible insolvency practitioner

The provisions of the 1986 Act as modified by the 1994 Order apply[1] as regards priority of expenses incurred by a responsible insolvency practitioner of an insolvent partnership and of an insolvent member of that partnership against whom an insolvency order has been made in the following manner.

The joint estate of the partnership shall be applicable in the first

---

[19] See *Ex p Elton* (1796) 3 Ves 238; *Ex p Cook* (1728) 2 P Wms 500; *Re Rudd & Son Ltd* [1984] Ch 237.

[20] The Schedule applies ss 175 and 328(1)–(3) and (6) of the Insolvency Act 1986, although modified by the Schedule.

[1] These provisions apply in modified form in the cases of a winding up of a partnership with concurrent petitions by either a creditor or member under arts 8 and 10 of the 1994 Order, and in cases of a joint bankruptcy petition of the partners not involving the winding up of the partnership as an unregistered company under art 11 of the 1994 Order. See Sch 4, Pt II, para 23 and Sch 7, para 21 to the 1994 Order applying in a modified form: ss 175 and 328 (1) – (3) and (6) of the Insolvency Act 1986. In essence the provisions are the same for all three insolvency procedures noted above. The reproduction of the provisions in the text can be used for reference in respect of any of these three forms of insolvency procedure.

instance in payment of the joint expenses and the separate estate of each insolvent member shall be applicable in the first instance in payment of the separate expenses relating to that member.

Where the joint estate is insufficient for the payment in full of the joint expenses, the unpaid balance shall be apportioned equally between the separate estates of the insolvent members against whom insolvency orders have been made and shall form part of the expenses to be paid out of those estates.

Where any separate estate of an insolvent member is insufficient for the payment in full of the separate expenses to be paid out of that estate, the unpaid balance shall form part of the expenses to be paid out of the joint estate.

Where after the transfer of any unpaid balance in accordance with the above provisions any estate is insufficient for the payment in full of the expenses to be paid out of that estate, the balance then remaining unpaid shall be apportioned equally between the other estates.

Where after an apportionment under the above provision one or more estates are insufficient for the payment in full of the expenses to be paid out of those estates, the total of the unpaid balances of the expenses to be paid out of those estates shall continue to be apportioned equally between all the other estates until provision is made for the payment in full of the expenses or there is no estate available for the payment of the balance finally remaining unpaid, in which case it abates in equal proportions between all the estates.

Without prejudice to the above provisions the responsible insolvency practitioner may, with the sanction of any creditor's committee (established under s 141 of the Insolvency Act 1986) or with leave of the court obtained on application:

(a)   pay out of the joint estate as part of the expenses to be paid out of that estate any expenses incurred for any separate estate of an insolvent member, or

(b)   pay out of any separate estate of an insolvent member any part of the expenses incurred for the joint estate which affects that separate estate.

1. PRIORITY OF DEBTS IN JOINT ESTATE

The 1986 Act, as modified by the 1994 Order, applies with regard to priority of debts, where insolvency orders are made against an insolvent partnership and an insolvent member in the following manner.

After payment of expenses in accordance with ss 175 and 328A and subject to ss 175 C and 328(2) of the Insolvency Act 1986 the joint debts of the partnership shall be paid out of its joint estate in the following order of priority:

(a) the preferential debts;
(b) the debts which are neither preferential debts nor postponed debts;
(c) interest under s 189 of the Insolvency Act 1986 on the joint debts (other than postponed debts);
(d) the postponed debts;
(e) interest under s 189 of the Insolvency Act 1986 on the postponed debts.

The responsible insolvency practitioner must adjust the rights among themselves of the members of the partnership as contributories and distribute any surplus to the members or, where applicable, to the separate estates of the members, according to their respective rights and interests in it.

The debts referred to in (a) and (b) above and which are known as the joint debts rank equally between themselves, and in each case, if the joint estate is insufficient for meeting them, they abate in equal proportions between themselves.

Where the joint estate is not sufficient for the payment of the joint debts in accordance with the above paragraphs, the responsible insolvency practitioner shall aggregate the value of those debts to the extent that they have not been satisfied, or are not capable of being satisfied, and that aggregate amount shall be a claim against the separate estate of each member of the partnership against whom an insolvency order has been made which—

(a) shall be a debt provable by the responsible insolvency practitioner in each such estate, and
(b) shall rank equally with the debts of the member referred to in ss 175B(1)(b) and 328B(1)(b) of the Insolvency Act 1986, ie the non-preferential and non-postponed debts.

The debts referred to as preferential include matters such as national insurance payments, debts not defined as preferential but which are not postponed include the usual partnership debts. Interest on such debts, or the payment of postponed debts[2] or interest on such postponed debts, is also subject to aggregation.[3] Where

---

[2] Postponed debts are debts subject to s 3 of the Partnership Act 1890, see Chapter 1.
[3] As noted above, with respect to non-preferential debts which are neither preferential nor postponed.

the joint estate is insufficient to satisfy the debts noted above and in the prescribed order of priority, and where aggregation in respect of any of these liabilities takes place, the aggregated amount shall be a claim against the separate estate of each member of the partnership against whom an insolvency order has been made, and shall be a debt provable by the responsible insolvency practitioner in respect of each such estate. Furthermore, these claims shall rank equally with the equivalent claims of the respective separate estates of the insolvent partners.[4]

Where the responsible insolvency practitioner receives any distribution from the separate estate of a partner in respect of any of the debts and liabilities noted above, such sums become part of the joint estate and shall be distributed in accordance with the order of priority noted above.[5]

2. PRIORITY OF DEBTS IN SEPARATE ESTATES

The order of priority of debts in respect of the separate estate of a partner is as follows.

The separate estate of each member of the partnership against whom an insolvency order has been made shall be applicable, after payment of expenses in accordance with ss 175 and 328 of the Insolvency Act 1986 and subject to ss 175C(2) and 328C(2) in payment of the separate debts of that member in the following order of priority –

(a) the preferential debts;
(b) the debts which are neither preferential debts nor postponed debts;
(c) interest under s 189 of the Insolvency Act 1986 on the separate debts and under ss 175A(6) and 328A(b);
(d) the postponed debts of the member;
(e) interest under s 189 of the Insolvency Act 1986 on the postponed debts of the member and under ss 175A(8) and 328A(8).

The debts referred to in each of the above paragraphs (a) and (b) of s 175 B rank equally between themselves, and in each case if the separate estate is insufficient for meeting them, they abate in equal proportions between themselves.

Where the responsible insolvency practitioner receives any distribution from the joint estate, or from the separate estate of any

---

[4] See Sch 4, para 23 and Sch 7, para 21 of the 1994 Order.
[5] Ibid.

partner against whom an insolvency order has been made, that distribution becomes part of the relevant separate estate, and shall be distributed in accordance with the order of priority noted above. Distinct accounts shall be kept of the joint estate and of the separate estate or estates.

Neither the official receiver, the Secretary of State, nor a responsible insolvency practitioner shall be entitled to remuneration or fees under the Insolvency Rules 1986,[6] the Insolvency Regulations 1986[7] or the Insolvency Fees Order 1986[8] for his services in connection with the transfer of a surplus from a separate estate of an insolvent member to the joint estate or from the joint estate to a separate estate.

If any two or more members of an insolvent partnership constitute a separate partnership, the creditors of such separate partnership shall be deemed to be a separate set of creditors and subject to the same statutory provisions as the separate creditors of any member of the insolvent partnership.[9]

Where any surplus remains after the administration of the estate of a separate partnership, the surplus shall be distributed to the members or where applicable to the separate estates of the members of that partnership according to their respective rights and interests in it.

The above provisions, as has been noted, will apply where an insolvency order has been made against a partnership together with at least a single partner or where an order has been made on a joint debtor's petition presented by *all* of the partners.[10]

The above provisions will also apply[11] as against an insolvent corporate partner which is the subject of an insolvency petition, in cases where it is involved in any of the insolvency proceedings noted above.[12]

Joint and separate creditors

The creditors of a partnership, ie the joint creditors, may also be the creditors of an individual partner. In the latter case the creditor is a separate creditor of the partner, and the partner remains solely liable

---

[6] SI 1986/1925 as amended.
[7] SI 1986/1994 as amended.
[8] SI 1986/2030 as amended.
[9] See Sch 4 and 7 of the 1994 Order.
[10] See the Insolvent Partnerships Order, arts 8, 10 and 11.
[11] With modifications.
[12] See the provisions of the 1994 Order noted on pp 309 and 311, above.

for any such indebtedness. There are a number of cases, however, where a partner may be held severally liable as well as jointly liable for a debt incurred by the partnership.[13] The principle examples where such joint and several responsibility will arise may be listed as follows:

(1)   where the partner has agreed to be severally liable for a partnership debt;[14]

(2)   in the case of a two partner partnership where one of the partners is either dormant or held out as a partner, a creditor may, it appears, regard any partnership debt also as a separate debt of the active partner;[15]

(3)   where a fraud or breach of trust has been committed by or can be imputed to a partnership, the liability of the partners will be joint and several;[16]

(4)   a creditor of the separate estate of a partner may accept a partnership bill of exchange in settlement of the debt, which if given with the authority of all the partners will give rise to a joint obligation.[17]

It must be noted that a joint creditor will lose his rights against the joint estate if he releases one of the joint debtors from his obligation.[18] Furthermore, if a higher security such as a bond is taken by the joint creditor from one partner to secure the joint debt, the creditor will find that he will become entitled to recover the debt solely as a separate debt from that individual partner, his rights as a joint creditor being destroyed.[19] The same situation will occur where a separate creditor of an individual partner accepts a higher security for the separate debt from the partnership. The creditor in such a case becomes entitled solely as a joint creditor.[20] Where,

---

13   With the consequence that the creditor may elect to proceed against either the partner's separate or joint estates. Each will be equally liable to satisfy the debt without any question of priority which arises between the creditors of the respective estates when creditors are solely joint or separate creditors (see p 321, above).

14   For the joint nature of a partner's liability see the Partnership Act 1890, s 9. See also *Ex p Dobinson* (1837) 2 Deac 341; *Ex p Appleby* (1837) 2 Deac 482.

15   *Ex p Hodgkinson* (1815) 19 Ves 291; *Scarf v Jardine* (1882) 7 App Cas 345.

16   *Ex p Adamson* (1878) 8 Ch D 807.

17   Partnership Act 1890, s 7; *Ex p Thorpe* (1836) 3 Mont & A 716.

18   *Ex p Slater* (1801) 6 Ves Jr 146; *Re Darwen and Pearce* [1927] 1 Ch 176. Note by way of contrast s 3 of the Civil Liability (Contribution) Act 1978, which provides that a judgment obtained against one joint debtor does not bar proceedings against fellow joint debtors.

19   Under the so-called doctrine of merger: *Ex p Hernaman* (1848) 12 Jur 643.

20   It also seems that obtaining a joint judgment in respect of a joint and several debt will create a joint debt: *Ex p Christie* (1832) Mont & B 352; but see *Re Davison* (1884) 13 QBD 50.

however, a creditor (be he a joint or separate creditor) merely obtains an *additional* security from either an individual partner or the partnership, for an existing joint or separate debt, he may still prove for his original debt against the relevant estate if the security becomes unavailable.[1]

If, following dissolution of a partnership, the business is continued by a single former partner, who takes responsibility for payment of the former partnership debts, the joint creditors of the original partnership do not become the separate creditors of the former single partner, except in two instances. The first instance is where they concur with the new arrangement; the second is where, with knowledge of the new arrangement, they deal with the single former partner so as to prejudice the rights of the other former partners, the effect of which is to discharge them from their former joint liabilities.[2] Conversely, a debt owed by an individual to a creditor does not become a partnership debt solely because the individual subsequently becomes a member of a partnership, and the members agree between themselves to treat the debt as a partnership debt without the agreement of the creditor.[3]

Joint and separate estates

What constitutes the joint and separate estates of the partners is principally determined by the Partnership Act 1890, and the agreement of the partners. Such agreement may be express, ie contained in the partnership agreement, or implied by the conduct of the partners.[4]

An agreement made in good faith between the partners to convert all or any part of the joint estate into the assets of individual partners will be valid up until the presentation of a petition either winding up the partnership, or winding up a corporate partner, or

---

[1] See *Ex p Meinertzhagen* (1838) 3 Deac 101. Thus, a separate creditor of an individual partner who accepts as an additional security for his debt, a joint bill from the individual partner's partnership may, if the security proves worthless, prove for his debt against the individual partner's separate estate.

[2] Partnership Act 1890, s 17(2) and (3); *Ex p Gurney* (1842) 2 Mont D & De G 541; *Rouse v Bradford Banking Co* [1894] AC 586.

[3] Partnership Act 1890, s 17(1); *Ex p Hitchcock* (1839) 3 Deac 507; *Scarf v Jardine* (1882) 7 App Cas 345.

[4] Partnership Act 1890, s 20. It would appear that a joint estate cannot be created between persons where one of them is merely held out as a partner. The effect of the doctrine of holding out is to render a person *liable as if* he were a partner: see Chapter 6. It cannot, per se, constitute any of his assets, the assets of the partnership.

the presentation of a petition of bankruptcy against an individual partner.[5] Such an agreement would still be valid if entered into by the partners in good faith, even if at the time of the agreement the partnership assets were exceeded by the partnership liabilities.[6]

Notwithstanding the above, an agreement to convert partnership assets into the assets of individual partners as part of their separate assets will not stand in the following cases:

(1)   in cases of fraud, irrespective of whether the fraud is exercised, or perpetrated upon creditors, or other members of the partnership;[7]

(2)   where the agreement has not been executed;[8]

(3)   where the property which forms the subject matter of the agreement is still subject to a lien in favour of one or more of the partners.[9]

Where the agreement is an agreement to convert joint into separate property, the agreement *may* be set aside by the court, if it was made within two years of the presentation of an insolvency petition, if the agreement was either unsupported by consideration or was at an undervalue.[10]

An agreement to convert separate into joint property *may* also be set aside by a court on the grounds noted above, but only if the agreement was made within five years of the presentation of the insolvency petition.[11]

It should be noted that the dissolution of a two-man partnership, or the retirement of a partner from such a partnership, does not lead to an inference that there has been an agreement between the parties to convert the former joint estate into the separate assets of the party who continues the business. The assets may in such cases be vested in the continuing 'partner' solely for the purpose of winding up the affairs of the business.[12]

The situations where a party may act as both the liquidator of the partnership and a corporate partner, and as the trustee in bankruptcy of an individual partner have been considered above.[13] The

---

[5]   *Ex p Ruffin* (1801) 6 Ves 119; *Re Simpson* (1874) App 9 Ch 572.

[6]   *Ex p Walker* (1862) 4 De GF & J 509; cf where there is bad faith, *Re Kemptner* (1869) LR 8 Eq 286.

[7]   *Re Kemptner* (1869) LR 8 Eq 286; Insolvency Act 1986, ss 206–7.

[8]   *Ex p Gurney* (1842) 2 Mont D & De G 541; *Ex p Wood* (1879) 10 Ch D 554.

[9]   *Ex p Dear* (1876) 1 Ch D 514; *Ex p Manchester Bank* (1879) 12 Ch D 917.

[10]   Insolvency Act 1986, ss 240(1)(a), 238(2), 339(4), and (3)(a)–(c), 423.

[11]   Insolvency Act 1986, s 341(1)(a) (individual partner); s 240(1)(a) (corporate partner). A similar power will be exercised in the case of preferences to creditors.

[12]   *Ex p Williams* (1805) 11 Ves 3; *Ex p Cooper* (1840) 1 Mont D & De G 358.

[13]   See p 314, above.

liquidator/trustee must keep separate and distinct accounts in respect of each separate estate and the joint estate.[14] The expenses of the insolvency proceedings in respect of each estate should be first paid out of the respective estates. In so far as the expenses of the insolvency proceedings of the joint estate cannot be satisfied the liquidator/trustee may seek to have the balance of the expenses satisfied out of the separate estates of the partners.[15] However, if expenses have been incurred prior to the appointment of a liquidator,[16] and these expenses are to be met out of an individual's partner's separate estate, but the estate is insufficient to satisfy such expenses, then the balance is to be treated as an expense of the joint estate.[17] If the joint estate then proves insufficient, resort must be had to the separate estates of the other partners, on the basis of apportionment.[18] Where the joint and separate estates are administered independently, apportionment of the expenses of insolvency proceedings cannot arise.

Priority of debts

Consideration has already been given to the principle that the joint estates and debts and the separate estates and debts are administered in insolvency proceedings in accordance with strict rules of priority.[19] Joint debts are first satisfied out of the joint estate. All joint debts will rank equally, except for preferential debts.[20] Debts under s 3 of the Partnership Act are postponed.[1] Any surplus assets of the joint estate may be utilised to satisfy the separate creditors of the individual partners. The separate estates of each individual partner must first satisfy the respective separate creditors; any balance may then be used to satisfy joint creditors. It must be noted that there can be no transfer of any balance of the assets of a *separate* estate of one partner to satisfy the unmet liabilities of the *separate* estate of another partner. If debts or expenses are inadvertently paid out of the wrong estate, any sum so expended must be

---

[14] *Re Wait* (1820) 1 J & W 605.
[15] See p 321, above.
[16] See p 321, above.
[17] Insolvency Act 1986, ss 175(4), 328(4), as modified by the Insolvent Partnerships Order 1994, Sch 4, para 23 and Sch 7, para 21.
[18] Insolvency Act 1986, ss 175(5) and 328(5), as modified by the 1994 Order, Sch 4, para 23 and Sch 7, para 21.
[19] See pp 322 and 324 above.
[20] See the Insolvency Act 1986, s 386 and Sch 6, which lists such debts.
[1] See Chapter 1 for a consideration of the Partnership Act 1890, s 3.

refunded to that estate by the estate that should have borne those debts or expenses.[2]

It would seem that, where there is a group partnership, the creditors of a constituent partnership will be treated as separate creditors as regards the group partnership. The consequences that follow from this have been considered above with respect to the separate creditors of an individual member of a partnership.[3]

Proof against the joint estate

1. RIGHTS OF JOINT CREDITORS

The rights of the joint creditors to prove against the joint estate have been considered above.[4] Where a joint creditor is also a secured creditor he must, as a general rule, *either* realise that security and prove for any balance of the joint debt against the partnership estate, *or* surrender the security, and prove for the entirely of the debt.[5] A joint creditor cannot, therefore, maintain his rights as a secured creditor and prove for the whole of the joint debt. It would appear, however, as a general exception to the above rule, that in the case of partnerships a creditor can maintain his rights in any security *and* prove for the joint debt in whole if the security is not derived from the joint estate.[6]

2. RIGHTS OF THE PARTNERS TO PROVE AGAINST THE JOINT ESTATE

As a general rule, a partner in an insolvent partnership cannot prove for a joint debt owed to him in competition with the joint creditors of the partnership.[7] The rationale behind this principle is manifest: a partner who could prove for a joint debt against the joint estate would be competing with the joint creditors of the

---

[2] *Re Hind & Sons* (1890) 62 LT 327.

[3] Cf the situation between a partnership and a sub-partnership and a creditor of the latter, where it seems any surplus assets transferred from the head partnership will fall into the joint estate of the sub-partnership.

[4] See p 321, above. Note also Chapter 2, which considers the postponing of a debt due to a bankrupt partner's spouse in the administration of their separate estates.

[5] Insolvency Rules 1986, SI 1986/1925, rr 4.88, 4–95 onwards, 6.109, 6.115 onwards; Insolvency Act 1986, ss 269(1) and 383(2).

[6] *Re Debtor (No 5 of 1967)* [1972] Ch 197; *Ex p Cocks Biddulph & Co* [1894] 2 QB 256; *Hind & Sons* (1890) 62 LT 327. Cf p 326, above, where the security is given against an estate other than the estate which is liable for the debt.

[7] *Ex p Williams* (1843) Mont D & De G 433; Sch 4 and 7, Insolvent Partnerships Order 1994 and the Insolvency Act, s 175(c)2.

partnership, who are also *his* creditors in his capacity as partner. Even a party who is held out as a partner[8] will be in no better position to prove against the joint estate than a true partner in respect of the liabilities incurred by the partnership in connection with and as a consequence of the holding out.

The personal representative of a deceased partner's estate may not prove against the joint estate of the surviving partners until either the partnership debts for which the deceased partner's estate is liable[9] are paid, or the estate is freed from such liability. Where the personal representatives have left in the partnership business part or all of the deceased's partnership capital, they will be prevented from proving for the monetary value of those assets until all the partnership debts contracted both before and *after* the deceased's death have been paid.[10]

The general principle forbidding proof of a joint debt by a partner against a partnership until the joint creditors have been satisfied may also be applicable where a partner in one partnership seeks to prove a debt against the joint estate of another partnership, and both partnerships share a common partner.[11]

There are circumstances, however, where a partner may compete with the joint creditors of the partnership of which he is a member. These circumstances are as follows.

Fraud

A partner may have been induced to enter into a partnership by a fraudulent misrepresentation and to provide capital for the partnership. A partner may also find that his separate property has been fraudulently converted for the use of the partnership. In both of these cases the partner the victim of the fraud may prove for such sums on behalf of his separate estate against the joint estate, and in competition with the joint creditors of the partnership.[12]

---

[8] For the doctrine of holding out see Chapter 6.

[9] Partnership Act 1890, s 9; *Ex p Blythe* (1881) 16 Ch D 620; *Ex p Executors of James Douglas* [1930] 1 Ch 342.

[10] *Ex p Butterfield* (1847) De G 570; *Ex p Corbridge* (1876) 4 Ch D 246. Cf where the money or assets has been brought into the partnership business in breach of trust, where the property will not constitute part of the joint estate and may be proved by the personal representatives: *Ex p Garland* (1804) 10 Ves Jr 110. See, however, where the money or assets are merely improperly left in the partnership business, where it seems proof will only be permitted after the partnership debts contracted during the deceased's lifetime have been paid.

[11] *Ex p Brown* (1842) 2 Mont D & De G 718.

[12] *Ex p Sillitoe* (1824) 1 GL & J 374 at 382; Sch 4 and 7, Insolvent Partnerships Order 1994 and the Insolvency Act 1986, s 175(c)2.

Distinct trades

The general inability of a partner to prove for a joint debt against the joint estate of a partnership even against a partnership of which he is not a member, but where the respective partnerships share a common partner has been considered above. However, it should be noted that even where two partnerships share common partners each *partnership* may rank as a *joint* creditor of the other.[13]

Furthermore, it has been determined that where two partnerships, though sharing common partners, carry on *distinct trades* and one of those partnerships becomes the creditor of the other in the ordinary course of business, the creditor partnership may prove against the joint estate of the debtor partnership.[14] It is necessary, however, if the debt is to be provable along with the other joint debts that the two partnerships carry on distinct trades.[15] Furthermore, for the creditor partnership to prove the debt as a joint creditor, the debt must arise by virtue of both partnerships carrying on their own respective trade or business in the regular way. Finally, it would appear that no proof will be allowed, even if the above conditions are satisfied, unless it can be shown that partnership accounts have been taken and a balance is due to the creditor partnership.[16]

Discharge of bankrupt partner

Where a partner is discharged from bankruptcy, or otherwise discharged from the joint debts of the partnership, he may subsequently become a creditor of the partnership. In such a case he may prove for any debt so incurred against the joint estate, because he is no longer a debtor with regard to the joint creditors of the partnership and is therefore not competing with his own creditors.[17]

Finally, where the person proving a debt against the joint estate of a partnership is only a prospective partner, he may prove the debt against the partnership as any other joint creditor, unless he has been held out as a partner.[18] In the latter case, he will be held liable

---

[13] *Ex p Thompson* (1834) 3 Deac & Ch 612.
[14] *Ex p Cook* (1831) Mont 228.
[15] Where the creditor partnership is the smaller partnership, proof of the debt against the larger debtor partnership will not be permitted if the smaller partnership is shown to be merely a branch of the larger partnership and is carrying on part of the latter's business: see *Ex p Hargreaves* (1788) 1 Cox Eq Cas 440.
[16] *Ex p Maude* (1867) 2 Ch App 550.
[17] *Ex p Smith* (1884) 14 QBD 394.
[18] See the Partnership Act, s 14 for the doctrine of holding out.

for the joint debts of the partnership incurred as a consequence of the holding out and, as has been noted above, will not be permitted to prove the debt owing to him from the joint estate until those liabilities have been settled or he has otherwise been discharged from them.[19]

3. RIGHTS OF SEPARATE CREDITORS AS AGAINST THE JOINT ESTATE

A partner may prove for a debt against the partnership's joint estate although he may be in competition with the *separate* creditors of his co-partners. In such cases, the partner's rights of priority are equal with the rights of the separate creditors of his co-partners. Their respective debts may be satisfied out of any surplus of the joint estate, which is available after satisfaction of the joint debts. The surplus should be carried to the partner's separate estates, in proportion to the rights and interests of each partner in the joint estate.[20] Furthermore, any lien which a partner has upon partnership assets must also be satisfied and discharged out of the joint estate, before any part of that estate can be made available to satisfy the debts owing to the separate creditors of the partners.[1] Clearly, where a lien is exercised in favour of a partner it may amount in effect to a preference being given to *his* separate creditors over the separate creditors of the other partner(s) who do not have a right to exercise a lien.[2] However, in so far as the joint estate is insufficient to satisfy and discharge any partner's lien, the balance may be provided against the separate estates of the other partners.[3] Where a joint estate is prematurely divided, and carried into the separate estates of the partners, the joint estate must be restored by those who have received the prematurely divided joint estate.

Proof against the separate estates of the partners

1. RIGHTS OF THE SEPARATE CREDITORS

The priority afforded to the separate creditors of the individual partners to prove debts against the respective separate estates of the partners has already been noted. A partner's separate debts

[19] See p 331, above and *Ex p Turquand* (1841) 2 Mont D & De G 339.

[20] *Ex p King* (1810) 17 Ves 115; see also the Insolvent Partnerships Order 1994.

[1] It must be noted that a partner's lien will be unenforceable against a liquidator, see above.

[2] Or to a preference being given to a partner seeking to prove a debt against the joint estate: *Ex p King* (1810) 17 Ves 115.

[3] *Ex p Terrell* (1819) Buck 345.

generally rank equally, subject to preferential debts,[4] or debts which are postponed to other separate debts such as those which are subject to s 3 of the Partnership Act 1890.[5]

The rights of the separate creditor where he is also a secured creditor are the same as a joint secured creditor and have been considered above.

2. RIGHTS OF JOINT CREDITORS AGAINST THE SEPARATE ESTATES OF THE PARTNERS

The joint creditors of a partnership may not, as a general rule, prove their joint debts against the respective separate estates of the partners in competition with the separate creditors of those partners.[6]

Notwithstanding the above, a joint creditor may compete with separate creditors, and prove a joint debt against the separate estates of the partners in the following circumstances.

The first case is where there is no joint estate. In such a circumstance the joint creditors are entitled to rank as separate creditors equally with the separate creditors of the respective partners.[7] However, this exception cannot apply if there is a joint estate, irrespective of the minuscule nature of that estate.[8] Where a joint creditor or creditors prove against the separate estate of the partner on this ground, but the joint estate is subsequently realised, any sums they have received from the separate estate of a partner must be repaid to that estate.[9]

A joint creditor may effectively compete with the separate creditors of the partners where the partnership is wound up as an

---

[4] See the Insolvency Act 1986, ss 175 and 189, as modified by the Insolvent Partnerships Order 1994, Sch 4, Pt II and s 328 of the 1986 Act as modified by Sch 7 to the 1984 Order; see also the Insolvency Act 1986, s 215(4).

[5] See Chapter 6. Note also the position of debts owed to a partner's spouse considered in Chapter 2.

[6] *Lindley* (16th edn) para 27-130 suggests that where the joint and separate estates are administered independently a joint creditor may prove against both estates.

[7] *Re Budgett* [1894] 2 Ch 557.

[8] *Ex p Kennedy* (1852) 2 De GM & G 228. Joint property pledged for more than its actual value or which cannot be made available for the benefit of the joint creditors will be ignored in determining whether there is a joint estate or not, *Ex p Geller* (1817) 2 Madd 262. However, where a joint creditor holds the joint property on such a pledge he must dispose of it or have it valued before he can rank as a separate creditor: *Ex p Smith* (1813) 2 Rose 63; see also *Ex p Hill* (1802) 2 Bos & P NR 191.

[9] *Ex p Willock* (1816) 2 Rose 392.

unregistered company. This is because the liquidator, in making calls on the partners as contributories, will constitute from such calls a joint estate, though none may have previously existed. The creation of such an estate from the separate resources of the partners naturally diminishes their respective separate estates.[10]

Where the joint creditors pay in full the provable separate debts of the partners to the separate creditors they may then prove both against the joint estate, and the separate estates of the partners, for the sums owing to them.[11]

Where a partner converts partnership property for his own use, he diminishes the joint estate. Nevertheless, the converted property cannot be regarded as part of his separate estate. Accordingly, the joint creditors may prove for partnership debts owing to them against that partner's separate estate. If the other partners condone such conversion of partnership assets the joint estate will be unable to prove against the fraudulent partner's separate estate for the sums converted by him.[12]

The joint estate will be permitted to prove against the separate estate of an individual partner for a debt owed to it by that partner if that partner became indebted to the partnership while he was carrying on a trade or business distinct from that of the partnership. In such a case the debt must have arisen in the ordinary course of carrying on that distinct trade or business.[13]

3. RIGHTS OF PARTNERS TO PROVE AGAINST THE SEPARATE ESTATE OF CO-PARTNER

A partner will not, in general, be permitted to prove for a debt against the separate estate of a co-partner.[14] The reason for this rule is that by so doing he is ultimately reducing the assets that could be made available to the *joint* estate to satisfy any joint liabilities that have not been satisfied by the joint estate. The same rationale also prevents the partnership proving for a debt against any individual partner's estate.[15] There are, however, a number of cases which constitute exceptions to this rule.[16]

---

[10] See p 305, above for a consideration of the winding up of a partnership as an unregistered company.

[11] *Ex p Taitt* (1809) 16 Ves 193.

[12] *Ex p De Tastet* (1810) 17 Ves 247.

[13] See p 332, above for a consideration of the concept of distinct trade in the context of partnership sharing common partners: see also *Ex p Gliddon* (1884) 13 QBD 43.

[14] *Ex p Collinge* (1863) 4 De GJ & SM 533.

[15] *Ex p Turner* (1833) 4 Deac & Ch 169.

[16] See p 336, below.

Thus, proof by a partner for a debt against the separate estate of a co-partner will be permitted if such proof will not involve competition with the joint creditors. There will, of course, be competition with the separate creditors of the co-partner. There will be no competition between a creditor partner and the joint creditors of the partnership where the former proves for a debt against the separate estate of a co-partner in the following circumstances:[17]

(1)   where there are no joint debts;
(2)   where the assets of the co-partner's separate estate is (excluding the debt owed to the creditor partner) insufficient to satisfy in full the separate debts of the co-partner;[18]
(3)   where the creditor partner has paid the joint debts of an insolvent co-partner he may prove against the co-partner's separate estate for the sum the latter should have contributed to the satisfaction of the joint debt.
      In the above cases a partnership account should be taken before proof of any debt is permitted;
(4)   where the co-partner has fraudulently converted partnership property. A partner who has been induced to enter into a partnership and provide the partnership with assets may prove as a creditor for such sum against any co-partner who practised the fraud upon him;
(5)   where the debt owed to the creditor partner has been contracted by the co-partner in the course of his carrying on a trade distinct from that of the partnership of which they are both members;[19]
(6)   where a partnership, though intended to be entered into, has never been forged between two parties, and one of those parties has advanced sums to the other party in contemplation of entering into partnership he may prove for such sums against the other's separate estate;
(7)   where the separate assets of the co-partner is more than sufficient to satisfy in full all the separate creditors, a creditor partner may prove against the separate estate for any debt owed to him by the co-partner.

---

[17]   *Ex p Andrews* (1884) 25 Ch D 505. The absence of joint debts can arise because they have ceased to exist, been paid, become statute barred, or converted to separate debts.
[18]   *Ex p Head* [1894] 1 QB 638.
[19]   *Ex p Maude* (1867) 2 Ch App 550.

4. PROOF AGAINST JOINT AND SEPARATE ESTATES

A party to whom the partners are liable jointly and severally[20] may not, as a general rule, rank as a creditor both of the joint estate and against the separate estates of the partners or a separate estate of a single partner. A party in those circumstances must generally elect whether he will rank as a joint or a separate creditor, with the attendant consequences.[1] Before making an election the creditor has a right to know the respective values of the joint and separate estate(s).[2]

However, the above rule now appears to be subject to a vast number of exceptions, and may perhaps only be applied in cases where the joint and several liability has arisen through the fraudulent conduct, a breach of trust, or tortious conduct by the members of a partnership.[3]

Where the general rule forbidding 'double proof' applies to a creditor who nevertheless enjoys a security for his debt, he may take one of two courses of action:

(1) he may prove for the entire debt against the estate for which he does not hold a security and retain and use the security;[4] *or*

(2) he may surrender the security, prove for the entirety of the debt against the estate which granted the security and prove for any balance owing to him against the other estate.[5]

Voluntary arrangements

The ability of insolvent parties, be they companies or individuals, to enter into voluntary arrangements with their creditors, either before or after insolvency orders are made, should be noted. The detailed procedures to be followed in such cases fall outside this book.[6] However, since 1 December 1994 it has been possible for a partnership to enter into a voluntary arrangement with its creditors.[7]

---

[20] See p 326, above for a consideration of the circumstances in which partners will be regarded as having both joint and several liability to the creditors of the partnership.

[1] See pp 322 and 324 above for such consequences as to priority of debts between the joint and separate estate(s) and *Ex p Bevan* (1804) 10 Ves 107; *Bradley v Millar* (1812) 1 Rose 273.

[2] See *Lindley* (16th edn) para 27–153, where the learned editor doubts whether the rule against 'double proof' still exists.

[3] Ibid.

[4] *Ex p Bate* (1838) 3 Deac 358.

[5] *Ex p Ladbroke* (1826) 2 Gl & J 81; *Ex p Hill* (1837) 2 Deac 249.

[6] See the Insolvency Act 1986, Pts I and III.

[7] See the Insolvent Partnerships Order 1994, art 4 and Sch 1.

The Insolvent Partnerships Order 1994 applies, with appropriate modifications, Pt I of the Insolvency Act 1986, which concerns company voluntary arrangements, to insolvent partnerships. An insolvent partnership as an entity may, therefore, conclude a legally effective arrangement with its creditors, whereby it may discharge its debts and return itself to financial health, without resort by either the partners or the partnership creditors to the drastic insolvency procedures that have been noted above.

The members of an insolvent partnership may propose a voluntary arrangement, but not if the partnership is subject to an administration order,[8] or is being wound up as an unregistered company, or where an order for the winding up of the partnership has been made on the joint bankruptcy petition of the partners. Where the partnership is subject to any of the above procedures, the administrator, the liquidator or the trustee of the partnership may themselves propose such an arrangement. The proposal may take the form of a composition with the partnership's creditors in satisfaction of the debts of the partnership, or a scheme of arrangement of its affairs.[9] The proposal must provide a nominee, who must be a qualified insolvency practitioner, to act as trustee of the voluntary arrangement and supervise its operation.[10]

Where the nominee is not a liquidator, administrator or trustee of the insolvent partnership, he must submit within prescribed time limits a report to the court, stating whether the arrangement is worthwhile, and accordingly whether the arrangement should proceed to the next stage.[11] The next stage is a summoning of a partnership creditor's meeting.[12] The meeting shall decide whether to approve the arrangement with or without modifications. A meeting cannot, in approving the arrangement, affect the rights of a secured creditor, nor that of a preferential creditor, unless the latter concurs with the arrangement. The result of the meeting should be reported to the court.[13] If the meeting approves the arrangement, it binds all creditors, and the court may stay any insolvency proceedings against the insolvent partnership, or discharge any administration order. The court may give directions for facilitating the implementation of the arrangement.[14]

---

[8] See p 339, below for an outline consideration of an administration order.
[9] Insolvency Act 1986, s 1, as modified by Sch 1 to the 1994 Order.
[10] Ibid.
[11] Section 2, as modified by Sch 1 to the 1994 Order.
[12] Section 3, as modified by Sch 1 to the 1994 Order.
[13] Section 4, as modified by Sch 1 to the 1994 Order.
[14] Section 5, as modified by Sch 1 to the 1994 Order.

Certain specified persons[15] may apply to court to have the arrangement revoked, suspended or revised on the grounds, inter alia, of material irregularity of the meeting, or that the arrangement as approved unfairly prejudices a creditor, member or contributory of the partnership.[16]

Subject to the above, the arrangement may be implemented by the nominee, who is now known as the supervisor. A party may apply to the court if he considers the supervisor is carrying out his duties in an unsatisfactory fashion.[17]

The above provisions, appropriately modified, may also be applicable to corporate partners and individual partners who are in their respective capacities subject to an insolvency order, and where an insolvency order is also made against their insolvent partnership. In those cases, Pt I of the 1986 Act applies to a corporate partner's voluntary arrangement and Pt VIII applies to the voluntary arrangement of an individual partner.[18] These procedures may be applied to a corporate or individual partner of an insolvent partnership, whether or not a winding up order has been made against the partnership and whether or not an insolvency order has been made against any respective partner or partners under either the 1994 Order or the 1986 Act.[19]

Administration orders

Another reform of the law of insolvency as it applies to partnerships has been wrought by the Insolvent Partnerships Order 1994. By that order from 1 December 1994, Pt II of the Insolvency Act 1986, concerning administration orders, is applied with modifications, and for the first time, to insolvent partnerships.[20]

Where the court is satisfied that a partnership is unable to pay its debts[1] the court may make an administration order in relation to the partnership. An administrator should be appointed by the court who must be a qualified insolvency practitioner. The purposes of the order which should be specified are:

(1)   to secure the survival of the partnership in whole or in part as a going concern;

---

[15] Section 2, as modified by Sch 1 to the 1994 Order.
[16] Ibid.
[17] Section 7, as modified by Sch 1 to the 1994 Order.
[18] Art 5 of the 1994 Order.
[19] Ibid.
[20] Art 6 of and Sch 2 to the 1994 Order.
[1] For this concept see p 305, above.

(2) to secure the approval of a voluntary arrangement, as has been noted above;

(3) to secure a more advantageous realisation of the partnership property than would be effected by a winding up.[2]

An administration order shall not be made in relation to a partnership after an order has been made for its winding up as an unregistered company, or where the partnership has been wound up on the joint bankruptcy petitions of the members, without the partnership being wound up as an unregistered company.[3]

This procedure is therefore aimed at the rehabilitation of the partnership as a going concern, or at least securing a more advantageous realisation of the partnership assets if it is subsequently wound up.

An application for an administration order may be made by the members and/or the creditors of the partnership. The grounds upon which the order may be made by the court are specified.[4] The court has a discretion as to whether to make such an order or an interim administration order.[5]

The effect of making an application for an administration order is to impose a moratorium on the partnership's affairs from the date of application, ie the presentation of the petition, to the date the court either makes the order or dismisses the petition. The principal effect of the application is that the partnership cannot be wound up in any circumstances. Furthermore, no security over partnership property can be enforced, nor can proceedings be instituted nor execution be levied on partnership assets.[6] These effects are further applied and confirmed if the administration order is subsequently made.[7] In addition, any other insolvency proceedings against the partnership are rendered inapplicable and any receivers appointed in respect of the partnership must vacate their office.[8]

All persons dealing with the partnership during the subsistence of the administration order must be notified of this fact. Every partnership business document, ie letters, invoices, etc must therefore give notice that the partnership is subject to an administration order.[9]

---

[2] Insolvency Act 1986, as modified by Sch 2 to the 1994 Order.
[3] Ibid.
[4] Section 9, as modified by Sch 2 to the 1994 Order.
[5] Ibid.
[6] Section 10, as modified by Sch 2 to the 1994 Order.
[7] Section 11, as modified by Sch 2 to the 1994 Order.
[8] Ibid.
[9] Section 12, as modified by Sch 2 to the 1994 Order.

The administrator shall be appointed either by the administration order itself or, if a vacancy occurs through the death or resignation of the administrator, by the court.[10] An application to the court to fill the office of administrator may be made by the continuing administrator or, where there is no administrator, by the creditors of the partnership, through a creditor's committee[11] or, failing either of the above, by parties making the application the members or a creditor or creditors of the partnership.[12]

The extent of the powers and duties of the administrator during the subsistence of the order are specified.[13] In essence, the powers and duties of the administrator of an insolvent partnership are the same as those of the partners whom the administrator supplants. The administrator may therefore do all things as are necessary for the management of the affairs and business of the partnership and of the partnership property.[14]

Finally, the administrator during the subsistence of the order has power to dispose of, or exercise any powers in relation to, partnership property, notwithstanding that the property is subject to a security, as if the property were not subject to any security.[15] Any party holding any security on partnership property has the right, however, if the property is disposed of by the administrator, to the net proceeds of the disposal in discharging the sums secured by the security. Furthermore, where those proceeds are less than the court considers to be the amount which could have been obtained in the open market by a willing vendor, the party who held the security on the property has a right, in addition to the net proceeds, to such sums as may be required to make good that deficiency.[16] The rights of a secured creditor of the partnership are thus protected, yet the secured property is rendered alienable, and the powers of the administrator remain in this respect unfettered.

[10] Section 13, as modified by Sch 2 to the 1994 Order.
[11] Insolvency Act 1986, s 26.
[12] Section 13, as modified by Sch 2 to the 1994 Order.
[13] Section 14 and Sch 1, as modified by Sch 2 to the 1994 Order.
[14] Section 13, as modified by Sch 2 to the 1994 Order. See also Sch 1 of the 1986 Act as modified by Sch 2 to the 1994 Order, which sets out in detail the powers of the administrator of an insolvent partnership.
[15] Section 15, as modified by Sch 2 to the 1994 Order.
[16] Ibid.

CHAPTER 14

LIMITED PARTNERSHIPS

INTRODUCTION

Despite the enactment of the Partnership Act in 1890, English law continued without a form of business organisation well known in continental Europe and elsewhere – the limited partnership – known in civil law jurisprudence as the commandite system of partnership. The principal characteristics of such forms of partnership are, first, that the liability of some of the partners with regard to the debts and obligations of the firm is limited, and second, that the firm is registered in some way so as to publicise that limited liability applies in relation to the particular firm.

It was hardly surprising that English law still failed to embrace this form of business organisation. The 1890 Act was merely a codification of English common law, and English common law had never developed this particular form of partnership. Nevertheless, when comparison was made with the legal systems of continental Europe, the omission of this particular form from the repertoire of business organisation available to the English businessman was felt to be anomalous. This feeling had, in fact, been expressed even prior to the enactment of the 1890 Act when the common law creation was discussed and evaluated. Writing in 1882, Pollock wrote:

'. . . there is a great want in the English law of partnership. It needs to be amended, not by changes of a detail here and a detail there in the rules which have been laid down by the courts, but by supplying the whole missing chapter. The institution of partnership en commandite, or limited partnership, as we may call it in English, is unknown in the United Kingdom, and in these Kingdoms alone, or almost alone, among all the civilised countries of the world.'[1]

---

[1] *Essays on Jurisprudence and Ethics* (1882) p 100.

The anomalous nature of the position under English law had, in fact, been recognised earlier by two government reports earlier in the century. The reports were inconclusive but, nevertheless, it was felt that the absence of this form of business organisation might have the consequence that British trade and enterprise may not be developed to their very fullest potential, which would not be in the best interests of either capital or labour.[2]

The new form of business organisation was finally introduced in 1907 with the enactment of the Limited Partnerships Act. It is one of the ironies of legal history that a form of business organisation which, if introduced at the beginning of the nineteenth century, might have proved to be an immensely useful creation throughout the golden age of partnership as a commercial vehicle, was not in fact introduced until 1907 when the Companies Act of that year introduced the new private company. It is the latter, together with its big brother the public company, which has dominated business organisations in the twentieth century. However, the limited partnership, while not widely used, has been pressed into service in respect of some businesses[3] and therefore some account of it must necessarily be given in any book on partnership.[4]

The characteristics of the limited partnership are derived from the manner in which it is distinguished from a general partnership. The passing of the 1907 Act enabled a form of partnership to be created which did not display three of the basic principles which characterise a general partnership, namely (1) the unlimited liability of every partner, (2) the right, subject to any agreement to the contrary, for each and every partner to participate in the management of the business, and (3) the implied authority of each partner to bind the firm with regard to all matters falling within the scope of the usual partnership business.

[2] Departmental Report on the Law of Partnership to the President of the Board of Trade, made 1 March 1837, and the Report of the Select Committee of the House of Commons 1851 No 509. The Report of the Select Committee recommended the appointment of a commission of adequate legal and commercial knowledge to consider the matter and make recommendations for change.

[3] While there has been a modest increase in the number of such partnerships registered in recent years they remain few in number compared with general partnerships.

[4] In any event the Partnership Act 1890 also applies to them.

APPLICATION OF THE GENERAL LAW OF PARTNERSHIP

The Limited Partnership Act 1907 presupposes the existence of partnership as a legal vehicle, and merely modifies the application of the rules of partnership law so as to create a new specialist business form. Consequently, limited partnerships remained governed by both the Partnership Act 1890 and the general rules of law and equity except in so far as the 1907 Act necessarily provides otherwise.[5] It is usual, therefore, for a limited partnership to be constituted by a formal partnership agreement in a manner similar to an ordinary partnership.

DEFINITION AND CONSTITUTION

By s 4(1) of the Limited Partnerships Act 1907, limited partnerships may be formed in the manner, and subject to the conditions, provided by that statute. It follows, therefore, from the very words of the Act that partnerships formed in a manner for which the Act does not provide, or which do not meet the conditions set out in the Act, will not be limited liability partnerships within its terms, with the inevitable consequence that the liability of all partners will be unlimited and all the general principles of partnership law applicable.

A limited partnership must consist of (1) one or more general persons or 'general partners',[6] who are liable for all debts and obligations of the firm; and (2) one or more persons called 'limited partners', who must at the time of entering such a partnership contribute *either* a sum or sums as capital *or* property valued at a stated amount, and who are not liable for the debts or obligations of the firm so contributed.[7]

The idea which clearly lies behind this is that the partners with

---

[5] Limited Partnerships Act 1907, s 7.

[6] Section 4(2). A general partner is any partner who is not a limited partner as defined by the Act (s 3).

[7] Limited partners are defined by the Limited Partnerships Act 1907, s 4(2). Whilst the limited partner's liability to creditors is thus limited to the capital which he has introduced, he may still incur greater trading losses for which he can claim tax relief, despite the restriction on his actual liability: *Reed (Inspector of Taxes) v Young* [1985] STC 25. Since the sleeping partner tenders advice only and takes no part in the management of the firm no goods or services are supplied *by him* in the course of the firm's business, and he has no personal responsibility for VAT in respect of them: *H Saunders v Customs and Excise Comrs* [1980] VATTR 53.

limited liability achieve that status by providing capital for the firm.[8] The capital may take the form of cash or other property, but if it is property which is provided then it must be at a fair and accurate valuation. Above all, the capital must be actually provided to the firm. A mere guarantee given by a person in respect of money lent to the firm is not a provision of capital by him, and consequently he does not become a limited partner. Since he has exhibited the intention of becoming a partner it necessarily follows that he will be a general partner with unlimited liability. The position was well stated by Wright J in *Rayner & Co v Rhodes*:[9]

'What the Act contemplates is that either actual money or the equivalent of money in the form of property should be transferred to the company for their use; and while that money or property was actually enjoyed and possessed by the firm . . . the partner was to be under no subsequent liability.'

The facts of that case are instructive. A firm with which Rhodes was connected had breached a contract, and an arbitrator's award had been made against him. Rhodes claimed that he had no personal liability in respect of it since his liability was limited to the capital which he had contributed to the firm. If he was a limited partner, his contention was accurate. In the deed of partnership he was described as a limited partner. However, when his contribution to the firm was examined, it was found that the £5,000, which he claimed as his provision of capital, consisted merely of a running guarantee in the sum of £5,000 given to Barclays Bank Ltd in respect of loans or overdrafts granted to the firm. The guarantee was terminable on three months' notice. In fact, therefore, as the court recognised, Rhodes had contributed nothing to the firm, his guarantee amounting merely to a future contingent liability. Since Rhodes was not a limited partner he could only be a general partner with unlimited liability.

It also follows logically that since limited liability is the quid pro quo for the provision of capital, the limited liability of the partner should not be reduced by subsequent withdrawal of the amount of capital that he has provided. The 1907 Act deals with this issue by providing specifically that once a limited partner has made his

---

[8] By contrast, a shareholder in a private company might indeed finance the business with the provision of a very small amount of paid up capital to purchase a share or shares, and a guarantee of loans which provide the basis of the real capital of the business. Many underfinanced British businesses are financed in exactly this manner.

[9] (1926) 24 Ll L Rep 25.

capital contribution, he must not during the continuance of the partnership, either directly or indirectly, draw out or receive back any part of his contribution, and if he does draw out or receive back any part, he is liable for the debts and obligations of the firm up to the amount so drawn out or received back.[10]

Logically, there is nothing to prevent a limited partner from obtaining his limited partnership status by the provision of a sum of capital, and subsequently increasing his capital contribution. In such a case his capitalisation of the firm is increased by the further amount paid and, if he subsequently withdraws any of his capital, he will remain potentially liable for the debts of the firm up to the level to which his contribution was increased by the subsequent payment. There is no unfairness to the limited partner in this consequence when it is reflected that partnership is a commercial arrangement, and the partner will be advancing further capital against either an agreed share in the partnership profit or his own estimation that the contribution will cause the firm to generate increased profits in the future.

CAPACITY

Any person who has the capacity to enter into a general partnership may become a limited partner, as the 1907 Act imposes no specific restrictions.[11] Indeed, in one respect it is clearer than the 1890 Act in providing specifically that a body corporate can become a limited partner.[12] However, it should always be borne in mind that the capacity of a company is limited by the ultra vires rules, and the provision of the 1907 Act does not confer powers which are absent from the memorandum of association or articles of the company.

NUMBER OF PARTNERS

The 1907 Act has a provision relating to the size of partnership. Like ordinary partnerships a limited partnership must not in general consist of more than 20 persons.[13] However, this general rule has now been modified by two provisions. First, by s 717(1) of the

[10] Section 4(3).
[11] As to which see Chapter 2, p 34, above.
[12] Section 4(4). The capacity of corporate bodies to become partners under general law is discussed in Chapter 2, p 39, above.
[13] Section 4(2), as amended by the Banking Act 1979, ss 46(b), 51(2), Sch 7.

Companies Act 1985 the restriction on numbers does not apply to partnerships carrying on practice as solicitors, accountants or members of a recognised stock exchange, subject to all the partners holding the appropriate professional qualifications. Secondly, the Secretary of State has power by regulation to confer a similar exemption on limited partnerships carrying on other designated businesses. So far he has exercised his power on three occasions. The first extended the exemption to partnerships carrying on the activities of surveying, auctioneering, valuing, estate agency, land agency and estate management.[14] However this requires that three quarters of the partners are members of either the Royal Institution of Chartered Surveyors or the Incorporated Society of Valuers and Auctioneers, and no more than one quarter of them may be limited partners within the meaning of the 1907 Act. The second exempted limited partnerships carrying on business as insurance brokers,[15] and the third limited partnerships, carrying on business as a member firm of the International Stock Exchange of the United Kingdom and the Republic of Ireland Limited.[16]

If the restrictions on numbers are not complied with, the partnership will be illegal, as is also the case with regard to non-limited partnerships.[17] In addition since the conditions for the establishment of a limited partnership will not have been complied with, it follows that the limited partners would, in any event, incur general liability.

DURATION

In general terms, the rules governing the duration of ordinary partnerships also apply to limited partnerships. However, the limited partners have no power to determine the partnership by notice,[18] with the result that, if the partnership is not for a fixed term, it may

---

[14] By the Limited Partnerships (Unrestricted Size) No 1 Regulations 1971, SI 1971/782.

[15] The Limited Partnership (Unrestricted Size) No 2 Regulations 1990, SI 1990/1580. To qualify, the partnership must *both* carry on business as insurance brokers *and* consist of persons each of whom is a registered insurance broker or an enrolled body corporate within the meanings given in the Insurance Brokers (Registration) Act 1977, s 29(1).

[16] The Limited Partnerships (Unrestricted Size) No 3 Regulations 1992, SI 1992/1027.

[17] See Chapter 2, p 49, above.

[18] Limited Partnerships Act 1907, s 6(5)(e).

be determined at any time by notice given by one or other of the general partners,[19] but not by notice from the limited partners. In addition, if the limited partnership is for a fixed period, details must be given as part of the registration particulars, and particulars of any subsequent changes in the length of the term must also be given.[20]

A potential trap for unwary limited partners needs to be noted. If a fixed term partnership expires but the business is continued by the active partners, the partnership continues as a partnership at will. There is no express provision under the 1907 Act to prevent this situation arising in the case of limited partnerships.[1] If it does arise, the change in the term and nature of the partnership would require registration, and failure to register would deprive the non-active partners of their limitation on liability.

REGISTRATION

Publicity that a partnership is in fact a limited partnership is not achieved by any requirement that this should be indicated in the firm name.[2] Instead, reliance is placed on registration. Every limited partnership must be registered as such in accordance with the requirements of the Act, and in default of this is deemed to be a general partnership and every limited partner is deemed to be a general partner.[3] The Registrar of Companies is required to keep an index of the names of registered partnerships.[4] There is no requirement that registration should be effected within any particular period of the partnership, but since no partner has limited liability until such time as the registration has been effected, little would seem to turn upon this.

---

[19] Partnership Act 1890, ss 26(1), 32(c).
[20] Limited Partnerships Act 1907, ss 8(e), 9(e).
[1] Limited Partnerships Act 1907, s 7.
[2] Although, of course, a limited partnership must have a firm name, and that name must be registered under the 1907 Act (ss 3, 8, 9). The members of a limited partnership have the same right as those of an ordinary partnership to trade under a name of their choice (1907 Act, s 7). The choice of a firm name is discussed in Chapter 5, p 91, above. The name chosen may not include the word 'limited' or any contraction or imitation as the last word (Companies Act 1985, s 34).
[3] Section 5.
[4] Companies Act 1985, s 714(1)(d).

Manner and particulars of registration

Registration is carried out by posting or delivering a statement containing the particulars prescribed by the Act to the Registrar of Companies at the Companies Registration Office for the particular part of the United Kingdom in which the firm's principal place of business has been established, or in which it is proposed that it should be placed.[5]

The statement to be registered must be signed by all the partners and must contain the following particulars: (1) the firm name; (2) the general nature of the business; (3) the principal place of business; (4) the full name of each of the partners; (5) the term, if any, for which the partnership is entered into, and the date of its commencement; (6) a statement that the partnership is limited and a description of every limited partner as such, and (7) the sum contributed by each limited partner, and whether paid in cash or how otherwise.[6]

On receipt of the registration statement from the partners the Registrar must file it, and post a registration certificate to the firm.[7] Whilst the certificate is not conclusive that the partnership is registered in accordance with the provisions of the Act, it is admissible in evidence in all legal proceedings, both civil and criminal.[8]

1. EFFECT OF NON-REGISTRATION

Failure to register a limited partnership in accordance with the provisions of the Act does not make it illegal. However, an unregistered partnership is deemed to be a general partnership and every limited partner is deemed to be a general partner.[9] Consequently, the substantial benefits arising from limited partnership do not accrue.

2. FALSE STATEMENTS

It is an offence under the Perjury Act 1911, s 17 for a person knowingly and wilfully to make (otherwise than on oath) a statement false

---

[5] Limited Partnerships Act 1907, s 8. The firm's principal place of business would appear to be its administrative headquarters from which the central control and management is executed: *De Beers Consolidated Mines Ltd v Howe* [1906] AC 455; *Palmer v Caledonian Rly Co* [1892] 1 QB 823.

[6] Section 8. The form prescribed for use for effecting registration is set out in the Appendix to the Limited Partnerships Rules 1907, SR & O 1907/1020, form LP 1.

[7] Section 13.

[8] Section 16(2).

[9] Section 5.

in a material particular which he is authorised or required to make under an Act of Parliament.

There are thus clear criminal sanctions for the filing of false registration particulars. In addition, it is submitted that the sending of false particular results in a failure to comply with the terms of s 8, so that in reality no registration is effected and limited liability does not accrue to the limited partners.[10]

3. REGISTRATION OF CHANGE IN PARTNERSHIP

A requirement that material particulars should be registered on creation of a partnership would mean nothing if there were no further requirement that changes with regard to material particulars should also be registered. Consequently, changes of specified types occurring during continuance of a limited partnership must be given to the registrar by posting or delivering it to that official within seven days, at the appropriate office, giving particulars of the nature of the change. The changes which require registration are those relating to: (1) the firm name; (2) the general nature of the business; (3) the principal place of business; (4) the partners or the name of any partner; (5) the term or character of the partnership; (6) the sum contributed by any limited partner; (7) the liability of any partner by reason of his becoming a limited partner instead of a general partner, or a general instead of a limited partner.[11]

The statement must be signed by the firm. Consequently, the signature of any general partner on behalf of the firm will suffice.

Failure to register changes in accordance with these provisions results in criminal sanctions. In particular a daily fine accrues.[12]

A difficult issue arises as to whether the failure to register details of changes, or the registering of erroneous details, has any consequence beyond the criminal sanctions. It is not immediately obvious that any greater consequences arise, but it is submitted that in fact the result of a failure to register changes results in limited liability being lost. The Limited Partnerships Act 1907, s 5 provides that every limited partnership must be registered as such *in accordance with the provisions* of the Act or, in default thereof, shall be deemed to be a general partnership, and every limited partner shall be deemed to be

---

[10] This is the view of Lindley: see (16th edn) (1990) p 743. But see to the contrary *Re Blair Open Hearth Furnace Co* [1914] 1 Ch 390; and *National Provincial and Union Bank of England v Charnley* [1924] 1 KB 431 on various comparable provisions of the Companies Act.

[11] Section 9(1). The prescribed form under the Limited Partnerships Rules is Form LP6.

[12] Section 9(2).

a general partner. If material changes to the partnership are not registered in accordance with the statutory requirements the limited partnership ceased to be registered *in accordance with the provisions of the Act,* and the rest of the consequences prescribed by s 5 necessarily follow.[13]

4. INSPECTION OF STATEMENT

Registration would be of little use in protecting the public if members of the public had no right to inspect the statements filed with the Registrar. Such a right is conferred generally on all persons by s 16. A small fee is payable.[14] Further, any person may require a certificate of the registration of any limited partnership, or a copy of or extract from any registered statement, to be certified by the Registrar on payment of the appropriate fee.[15] A certificate of registration, or a copy of or extract from, any statement registered under the Act, if duly certified to be a true copy under the hand of the Registrar or one of the assistant registrars (whom it shall not be necessary to prove to be the Registrar or assistant registrar), must be received in evidence in all legal proceedings, civil or criminal, and in all cases whatsoever.[16]

The effect of registration

The effect of correct registration of a limited partnership is, in general, to obtain limited liability for the dormant partners; the effect of correct registration of a change of particulars is to maintain that situation; and the effect of registration of a change to a general partnership is to lose the limited status. However, an issue arises as to whether mere registration and advertisement in the London Gazette is all that is needed in all circumstances for limited liability to be obtained against all classes of creditors. In particular, Lindley[17] suggests that where a general partnership is turned into a limited partnership with some of the erstwhile general partners converting to limited status, specific notice would need to be given

---

[13] This is the view of Lindley (16th edn) p 744, who argues that '[T]here would seem no logical reason to distinguish between an unregistered firm and a firm which is registered with inaccurate particulars, at least so long as the default continues'.

[14] Section 16(1).

[15] Section 16(1). The fee currently is 5p for each inspection, 10p for copy registration form, and 2½p per folio for each document copied.

[16] Section 16(2).

[17] (16th edn) p 745.

to all existing customers of the business. It is the view of the present authors that the 1907 Act is intended to be a self-contained statement of all steps necessary to obtain limited status for a partner and that no action should be necessary beyond carrying out its requirements, the creditors being protected – at least to some degree – by the fact that the firm always contains general partners with unlimited liability. However, an argument can be maintained for the contrary view, and in the circumstances the safe practical course is to give specific notice to existing creditors.

LIMITED PARTNERS AND THIRD PERSONS

The general purpose of the Limited Partnership Act 1907 is to modify the general law applicable to ordinary partnerships. In consequence, the Partnership Act 1890 and the rules of equity and common law apply, in general, to limited partnerships in the same way as they apply to ordinary partnerships, except in so far as they are inconsistent with the express provisions of the 1907 legislation.[18] The general law is modified with regard to the position of the limited partner in the firm, but not with regard to the general partner or partners to whom the ordinary rules of partnership are applicable. The position of the limited partner in principle is that he is a partner by reason of his provision of capital, and this is his sole function. Consequently, a limited partner must not take part in the management of the partnership business and has no power to bind the firm, although by himself or his agents he may inspect at any time the books of the firm and examine the state and prospects of the partnership business, and may advise the partners thereon. If, in breach of this restriction, a limited partner takes part in the management of a partnership business, he is liable for all debts and obligations of the firm incurred while he is taking part in the management as though he were a general partner.[19] Participation in the management of the partnership business is not defined, but would appear to mean undertaking those functions which, either expressly or by implication, are reserved to the general partners.

It will be seen that the loss of limited liability by the limited partner who participates in the management of the firm is temporary. It subsists only so long as he continues to act in the management of the firm, and extends to all debts and obligations of the firm

[18]   Section 7.
[19]   Section 6(1).

incurred during this period. However, by acting as a general partner throughout the period has he created a position in which a change has occurred with regard to the firm which requires registration under the provisions pertaining to registration? By failing to register such a change if necessary, it could be argued that all limited partners, including those who are not participating in the management of the particular firm, lose their limited liability due to lack of registration. This is not, however, the consequence expressly provided by statute, and the better view is that participation by a limited partner in the management of the business without the agreement of all partners does not bring about a change within the partnership business which requires registration. To interpret the statutory provisions otherwise makes nonsense of s 6. In short, it is submitted that acting in the management of a business without the approval of all partners merely removes the limited liability of the partner concerned for the time being, but does not constitute him a general partner. The transformation from limited partner to general partner would require the approval of all partners to a complete change of status; activities not agreed by all partners, or which fall short of being a complete change of status, do not create a general partner out of a limited partner.[20]

The principles (1) that a limited partner has no authority to bind the firm, (2) that he may not participate in the management of the business, and (3) that if he does participate in the management of the business his limited liability is lost, must be set against the application of the general principles of agency which still apply except where excluded. In general, a limited partner who purports to act on behalf of the firm in the management of the business of the firm will not be bound, but the partner may find himself liable in damages for breach of warranty of authority under general agency principles. However, it may be that his co-partners have expressly given him authority to undertake the particular act. In such a case there is express authority and the firm is bound, but by participating in the management of the business the agent partner will have forfeited his limited liability.

Loss of limited liability

It is, perhaps, helpful at this point to draw together and list the three circumstances in which a limited partner will lose his limited

---

[20] There are strict requirements to be carried out when such a change is effected in ss 9 and 10 of the Act (discussed at p 350, above).

liability, in whole or part. They are: (1) if the firm is not properly registered; (2) if the limited partner participates in the management of the business; and (3) to the extent that he receives back the whole or any part of his capital contribution.

THE RELATIONS OF THE PARTNERS AMONGST THEMSELVES

Participation in the business

As the position of the limited partners in relation to third parties is modified by the 1907 Act, so also modifications are made to the relations of partners inter se. As has been noted, a limited partner is excluded from participating in the management of the partnership business, and has no power to bind the firm.[1] Consequently, the Act is structured so that the management of a business is confined to the ordinary partners. In particular, s 5 of the 1907 Act provides that any difference arising as to ordinary matters connected with the partnership business may be decided by a majority of the general partners, subject to any agreement, express or implied, between the partners. If there is no such agreement, the general partners may decide the differences in question without seeking or taking into account the views of the limited partners. However, whilst this seems to postulate the general concept that matters should be resolved without reference to the limited partners, it does allow for agreements to be made which would allow their views to be taken into account.

What is far from clear here is what is intended to be achieved by this provision. Is it intended that the limited partners can participate in decisions affecting ordinary matters connected with the partnership business, or merely that there can be a machinery by which their views can be expressed? If it is read as a mechanism by which limited partners can participate in decisions relating to ordinary matters connected with the partnership business, then what, if anything, is the distinction between this and participating in the management of the business? The difficulty is compounded by the realisation that those decisions which would require the agreement of all partners under general partnership law (such as the admission of new partners, or changes in the nature of the partnership business) equally require the concurrence of all partners in the case of

---

[1] Section 6(1).

unlimited partnership, and therefore do not form part of the management of the business. If provision is to be inserted into the partnership agreement varying the general provisions of s 5, the only safe way of confronting the issue is merely to create some formal channel through which the views of the limited partners are made available to the general partners for the latter to consider in making the actual decision.

Liability for losses

The general provisions of partnership law with regard to participation in the capital and profits of the business apply. Inevitably, however, the position with regard to losses is modified in respect of limited partners so that in general their responsibilities do not extend beyond the capital provided.

However, this is not invariably the case. The limitation of the limited partner's liability to the amount of his capital contribution is the position vis-à-vis the firm's creditors, and prima facie also as between the partners. It is therefore possible that, as between the partners, agreement may be reached under which the partners agree that, as between themselves, any trading losses of the firm will be divided without limitation, and if they do so agree, the courts will give effect to their agreement as it did in the case of *Reed v Young*.[2] This was a case on the tax treatment of losses sustained by a limited partner. In the House of Lords Lord Oliver said:[3]

'The profits and losses with which we are concerned are the profits and losses of the partnership from the carrying on of the trade as shown by its annual profit and loss account . . . The assessment of tax on the individual partners is by reference to their respective shares as set out in the partnership deed and has no necessary relation to what may ultimately turn out to be the proportions in which the partner is called upon to contribute to payment of the firm's debts – for instance if one of his partners is insolvent. Thus, the partnerships trading losses are conceptually quite distinct from the debts and liabilities of the firm and from the assets which are available to meet them.'

---

[2] [1986] 1 WLR 649.
[3] At 653.

Introduction of new partners

The position with regard to the introduction of new partners to a limited partnership also differs in some respects from that applicable to general partners. With regard to ordinary partnerships it will be remembered that no new partner can be introduced without the consent of all existing partners.[4] In the case of limited partnerships there are two modifications to this basic rule. First, subject to any agreement express or implied between the partners, a limited partner may, with the consent of the *general* partners, assign his share in the partnership, and upon such an assignment the assignee becomes a limited partner with all the rights of the assignor.[5] Such an assignment must be advertised in accordance with provisions mentioned below.[6] It should, of course, be remembered that a partner in an ordinary partnership may assign his share but, as a result, the assignee is only entitled to receive a share of the profits and acquires no other rights beyond that simple right.[7] The rights conferred in favour of a limited partner pursuant to this exception are therefore more extensive. However, for the exception to be useable, the consent of the general partners must be available. An assignment without their consent would take effect under general partnership law and would, therefore, be a simple assignment of profits only. The second modification to general partnership law applicable to limited partnerships is that a person may be introduced as a partner without the consent of the existing limited partners, unless there is an express agreement to the contrary.[8]

DISSOLUTION AND WINDING UP

Dissolution

The general provisions with regard to the dissolution of partnership are applicable to limited partnerships, except where the 1907 Act makes contrary provision. The exceptions arising expressly or by implication from the 1907 Act are as follows.

---

[4] Partnership Act 1890, s 24(7).
[5] Limited Partnerships Act 1907, s 6(5)(b).
[6] See p 359, below.
[7] Partnership Act 1890, s 31.
[8] Limited Partnerships Act 1907, s 6(5)(d).

1. DEATH OR BANKRUPTCY OF SOLE GENERAL PARTNER

Since a limited partnership must have at least one general partner it follows that the death or bankruptcy of a sole general partner must dissolve the partnership, regardless of any provision in the partnership articles to the contrary, unless a new general partner is immediately admitted to the firm to allow it to continue.

2. DEATH OR BANKRUPTCY OF A LIMITED PARTNER

The death or bankruptcy of a limited partner does not automatically dissolve a limited partnership.[9] These are considerable modifications of the rules applicable to ordinary partnerships[10] and, indeed, provide a solution in the case of death or bankruptcy of a limited partner which is the converse of that generally applicable. It should, of course, be borne in mind that these differing provisions applicable to limited partnerships are applicable to the limited partners only; the position of the general partners is governed by general partnership law.

3. CHARGE ON LIMITED PARTNER'S SHARE

A further provision creating a direct contrast to that applicable under general partnership law deals with charges on the limited partner's share. Subject to any agreement between the partners, whether express or implied, the other partners shall not be entitled to dissolve the partnership by reason of any limited partner suffering his share to be charged for his separate debts.[11] Again, the provision relates only to charges on a limited partner's share; charges on the shares of general partners remain governed by general partnership law.[12]

4. NOTICE

The power of a limited partner to dissolve the partnership is modified by the 1907 Act. Subject to any agreement, express or implied, between the partners, a limited partner is not entitled to dissolve the partnership by notice.[13]

---

[9] Ibid, s 6(2).
[10] See Chapter 12, p 263, above.
[11] Limited Partnership Act 1907, s 6(5)(c).
[12] See Chapter 9.
[13] Section 6(5)(e).

WINDING UP AND DISSOLUTION BY THE COURT

In general, the courts' jurisdiction to dissolve or wind up a limited partnership is the same as that to wind up a general partnership.[14]

1. MENTAL DISORDER OF A PARTNER

Where a *general* partner suffers from a mental disorder a judge of the Court of Protection will have the usual powers to dissolve the partnership.[15] However, the 1907 Act makes special provision for the mental disorder of a *limited partner* by enacting that the mental disorder is not a ground for the dissolution of the partnership by the court unless 'the patient's share cannot otherwise be ascertained and realised.'[16] Clearly, this envisages some situations in which the partnership can continue in these circumstances. However, unless the afflicted limited partner can dispose of his share, either to the continuing partners or a third person, it will be necessary for the partnership to be dissolved for his share in the assets to be ascertained and realised given the very nature of partnership property.[17] Consequently, it would appear that this provision is effective only in these situations.[18]

2. WINDING UP AS COMPANY

As has been noted, in certain circumstances ordinary partnerships may be wound up by the court as unregistered companies under the companies legislation as an alternative to winding up under the Partnership Act 1890.[19] In the case of limited partnerships it appears that the principle built into the 1907 Act was that limited partnerships should always be wound up as companies,[20] but the relevant subsection was quickly repealed.[1] This, for a short period, left the limited partnership in the position where it could be wound up under either of the two possible regimes available to ordinary partnerships. However, the possibility of winding up as an unregistered company was then removed with effect from 1 January 1914.[2] The result was undoubtedly something of an anomalous tangle and

---

[14] As to the winding up of partnerships generally, see Chapter 12.
[15] See Chapter 13.
[16] Limited Partnerships Act 1907, s 6(2).
[17] See Chapter 9.
[18] A view with which Lindley agrees: see (16th edn) p 766.
[19] See Chapter 12.
[20] Limited Partnerships Act 1907, s 6(4).
[1] Companies (Consolidation) Act 1908, s 289.
[2] Bankruptcy Act 1914, s 24, continued by the Companies Act 1948, s 398.

very rightly the legislature gave it attention in the wholesale reform of insolvency law effected by the Insolvency Act 1986. The option of winding up an insolvent partnership as an unregistered company was reinstated, and a petition seeking this result may be presented with or without concurrent petitions against one or more partners.[3] There are, however, restrictions on the freedom of the partners to serve such a petition.

Winding up

On the dissolution of a limited partnership the task of winding up its affairs is that of the general partners unless the court otherwise orders.[4] However, whilst a limited partner is thus in general excluded from winding up the affairs of the limited partnership, no restriction is placed by the legislation on his right to apply to the court to order that the business and affairs of the firm be wound up. Given the general exclusion of a limited partner from participation in the management of the business it may well be that the court will only entertain an application from a limited partner in exceptional circumstances, such as the misconduct of the general partners.

Advertisements

Notice of any arrangement or transaction under which any person will cease to be a general partner in any firm and will become a limited partner in that firm, or under which the share of a limited partner will be assigned to any person, must be forthwith advertised in the London Gazette. Until notice of the arrangement or transaction is so advertised it is deemed, for the purposes of the Act, to be of no effect.[5]

INSOLVENCY

Application of the Insolvency Act to limited partnerships

The Insolvency Act 1986 is applied to partnerships by the Insolvent Partnerships Order 1994.[6] The order does not in general draw a

---

[3] Insolvency Act 1986, s 420 and the Insolvent Partnerships Order 1994, SI 1994/2421.
[4] Limited Partnerships Act 1907, s 6(3).
[5] Ibid, s 10.
[6] SI 1994/2421: see Chapter 13.

distinction between ordinary and limited partnerships. This gives rise to difficulties. In particular, the approach of the insolvency legislation is to treat the partners of a company as its officers and directors, so that the partnership is equated with the company as a business organisation. However, the particular status of the limited partner, who may not participate in the management of the business if he is to retain his limited liability, is ignored by this approach. Thus, under the Insolvent Partnerships Order 1994,[7] where an insolvent partnership is being wound up as an unregistered company under Pt V of the Insolvency Act 1986, certain of the provisions of the Company Directors (Disqualification) Act 1986 are applicable to partners, who may be subject to a disqualification order under the Insolvency Act 1986 if they are deemed to be unfit officers of the partnership. Since a limited partner could also be regarded as an unfit officer of the partnership it follows that he is also subject to the above provisions, although his right to participate in the firm is severely curtailed by the 1907 Act.[8] In any event, a limited partner is a contributory in the insolvency,[9] but only to the extent of his capital contribution to the firm.[10]

Petitions by limited partners

The limited partners in a limited partnership are prohibited from presenting a joint debtors petition except where the firm is itself wound up as an unregistered company. There is no such limitation on the general partners.[11]

Petitions against limited partners

In certain circumstances, where concurrent petitions are presented both against the firm and against one or more of the partners, a limited partner may obtain the dismissal of the petition against himself, even though an order is made against the firm. He may do this either by lodging in court 'sufficient money or security . . . to meet his limited liability for the debts and obligations of the partnership, or by satisfying the court that he is no longer under any liability in respect of such debts and obligations.'[12] Since a limited partner

---

[7] Art 16 and Sch 8.
[8] See Chapter 8, p 168, above.
[9] Insolvency Act 1986, s 226(1).
[10] Limited Partnerships Act 1907, s 4(2) as modified by s 264 of the 1986 Act.
[11] Insolvent Partnerships Order 1994, art 11 and Sch 7.
[12] See the Insolvency Act 1986, s 125A(7), as substituted by the Insolvent Partnerships Order 1994, SI 1994/2421, art 10 and Sch 6.

need contribute no more than his capital contribution, it would seem that he may rely on this provision either by showing that he has made that contribution of capital and has not withdrawn it or, if it is not possible for him to establish that his capital contribution is retained, by lodging in court a sum equal to the amount of his contribution.

Partnership property and the partner's estate

The new insolvency regime is similar to the old bankruptcy law in one important respect. The joint debts of the partnership are principally payable out of the partnership property, and the separate debts of the individual partners are principally payable out of their respective separate estates.[13] This principle was expounded by Farwell J in *Re Barnard, Martin's Bank v Trustee*[14] and the case still remains good law. In that case, Barnard was the sole general partner in two limited partnerships, W H Barnard and the Scrap Metal Co. Both firms had limited partners. In the case of the first firm there was one limited partner and, in the case of the second, three. Five bills of exchange had been drawn by the Scrap Metal Co and accepted by Barnard as the general partner. In June, a receiving order was made against Barnard, and Barnard himself was adjudicated bankrupt. The following month a receiving order was made against Scrap Metal Co and again Barnard was adjudicated bankrupt. The holder of the bills of exchange lodged a proof of debt against Scrap Metal Co, but subsequently sought to prove in the bankruptcy of W H Barnard. The court allowed the proof to be admitted. In dealing with the complicated interrelation of the two firms and Barnard, and the availability of the resultant assets, Farwell J explained the position with incisive clarity:

'The Barnard firm assets must first be applied in discharging the firm's debt, ie the debts incurred by or on behalf of that firm. The surplus must be applied in paying the limited partners their actual contributions. The balance will form part of Barnard's separate estate, and out of that will be paid Barnard's own private debts and any other debts incurred by him on behalf of other limited partnerships.

The same thing applies mutatis mutandis in the case of the Scrap Metal Co. The debts proved in the bankruptcy which have

---

13 See Chapter 13.
14 [1932] 1 Ch 269.

been incurred on behalf of the firm will be payable out of that firm's assets. The balance will be applied in the first instance in repaying the limited partners, and the surplus will be part of Barnard's separate estate available for payment of his private debts, and debts incurred by him on behalf of some other limited partnership, which for that purpose must be treated as separate debts.'[15]

The effect of this is that if there is a surplus of assets of one firm to meet the liabilities of the particular firm, the surplus is applied by repaying to the limited partners their actual contributions. Thus, the contributions of the limited partners do not become liable for the individual responsibilities of the insolvent general partner, whether his own normal debts or his personal liabilities arising from his connections with other insolvent firms.

---

[15] [1932] 1 Ch 269 at 274.

CHAPTER 15

THE TAXATION
OF PARTNERSHIPS

A partnership, irrespective of the nature of its business or its size, is not generally subject to any special rules of taxation. Accordingly, the normal principles governing the collection of income tax, capital gains tax, and inheritance tax are usually applied to each partner as an individual. The application of these taxes, as well as value added tax and stamp duty to partners and partnerships, are the subject of this chapter.

INCOME TAX AND PARTNERSHIPS

Partnerships in existence prior to 6 April 1994

Notwithstanding the above, a partnership which commenced business prior to 6 April 1994 is, for the purposes of the assessment and collection of income tax, treated, at least in part, as an entity distinct from its members. A trading partnership of this kind is taxed under the rules of Schedule D, Case 1 and a professional partnership under Schedule D, Case II.

For the purposes of the assessment of income tax of a partnership which commenced business prior to 6 April 1994, the senior partner[1] should make a return of partnership income.[2] This does not preclude the need for each individual partner[3] to make his own tax return in which he will make his claim for his own personal allowances.[4] On the basis of these returns the Inland Revenue will make a joint

---

[1] Or the partner whose name appears first in the partnership deed.
[2] See the Taxes Management Act 1970, s 9, as amended by the Finance Act 1994, s 179.
[3] Ibid.
[4] Income and Corporation Taxes Act 1988, s 227 hereafter referred to as the Taxes Act 1988.

assessment to income tax in the partnership name.[5] In these cases the tax payable by the partnership is the combined tax liability of all the partners as regards their share of partnership profits, less their personal reliefs and permitted deductions.[6] The Revenue will provide the partner who made the return on the partnership's behalf with information which sets out how the Revenue has calculated the partnership tax bill. Accordingly, the individual tax liability of the partners can be established. The tax should be paid, as in all cases of Schedule D, Case I and II tax, in two equal instalments on 1 January and 1 July in the year following the relevant tax year.

Whatever arrangements are made by the partners inter se for the payment of any partnership tax bill, the liability of the partners for the bill is joint, but not several. Accordingly, where the tax bill of the partnership remains unpaid, the Revenue may institute proceedings to recover the full tax bill from a single partner. The latter may, of course, join his fellow partners as co-defendants in respect of any such action.[7] The effect of the above rule imposing joint liability is that the bankruptcy of a partner will not prejudice the position of the Revenue, who may recover the tax which the bankrupt partner is liable to pay from the remaining solvent partners. Where a partner dies, his estate is released from any liability in respect of any unpaid partnership tax. This is, however, subject to one exception, namely where the deceased partner was the last surviving partner. In that case the deceased's estate is liable for all unpaid partnership income tax, although his estate has the benefit of a right of contribution from the estates of his former partners.[8]

Calculation of partnership profits for the purposes of income tax

The calculation of the profits of a partnership for the purposes of assessment to income tax, be it a professional or trading partnership under Schedule D, Case I or II, follows the same procedure for the calculation of the profits of a sole trader or practitioner.[9]

---

5   Taxes Act 1988, s 111.
6   Such matters are outside the scope of this book. For the best review of this area of the law see Whitehouse Stuart Buttle *Revenue Law Principles and Practice* (12th edn); Tiley *Butterworths UK Tax Guide 1994–95* (13th edn).
7   See RSC Ord 15, r 6.
8   *Harrison v Willis Bros* [1965] 3 All ER 753; *Stevens v Britten* [1954] 3 All ER 385.
9   See *Whitehouse Stuart Buttle*, Chapter 6 for a consideration of the procedure for the calculation of such profits: *Connelly & Co v Wilbey* [1992] STC 783; *MacKinlay v Arthur Young McClelland Moores & Co* [1989] STC 898.

Accordingly, business expenditure incurred by a partnership will not be deductible unless it is wholly and exclusively laid out or expended for the purposes of the business or profession.[10] It follows that, as a general rule, no sums paid out by the partnership to a partner can amount to a deductible business expense.

Basis of assessment to income tax of partnerships carrying on business prior to 6 April 1994

For partnerships carrying on business prior to 6 April 1994, income tax for a given year of assessment is levied on the profits or gains of the business or profession, on the preceding year basis, and by reference to the profits earned in the partnership's accounting year which ends in that preceding year. The special rules for the assessment of income tax of such a partnership where it commences its business may be summarised as follows. Where the partnership is commenced within a tax year, tax is charged for this first year on the profits earned up to the next 5 April. The tax for the second year of business is calculated by reference to the profits of the first 12 months of trading and the third year on the preceding year basis, but only where there is a complete 12-month accounting period ending in the second tax year. The partnership can, however, elect that for *both* the second and third years of assessment tax be levied on a current year basis.[11]

If the partnership ceases to trade or carry on its business, income tax for the year of assessment in which the business or enterprise discontinues is levied on the profits of that year, and not on a preceding year basis.[12] A discontinuance for these purposes will also arise where there is a change of partners within a partnership. For a partnership existing prior to 6 April 1994, a change of partnership membership has the same consequences for income tax purposes as a partnership which merely ceases to carry on its business.[13] However, there are two exceptions to this rule; thus where there is merely a change in trustees or personal representatives of a deceased partner there is no discontinuance of a partnership, nor does the entry or withdrawal of a corporate partner constitute a discontinuance for the above purposes.[14] It should also be noted that

---

10 Taxes Act 1988, s 62.
11 Taxes Act 1988, s 60.
12 Taxes Act 1988, s 63(1)(a).
13 Taxes Act 1988, s 113.
14 Taxes Act 1988, ss 113(7), 114(3)(b).

where there is a discontinuance of the partnership business following a change in membership, any losses may be rolled forward by the remaining partners, if they carry on the business, against their share of the profits earned after the change in the membership of the partnership.[15]

It is possible for the continuing partners, in cases where there has been a change of partners, to elect that the business should for the purposes of the assessment of income tax be regarded as continuing without any discontinuance. Such an election must be made within two years of the change. However, an election, once made, can be subsequently withdrawn. Where an election for continuance is made by a partnership, the income earned by the partnership in which the change of partners occurred is allocated between the partners as if there had been no such change, and is apportioned as may be fair and just.[16]

Income tax and partnerships

1. THE NEW RULES

In a case of a partnership formed and carrying on a business or trade on or after 6 April 1994, and from 1996–97 for *all* partnerships, the rules for the assessment of income tax have been fundamentally altered by the Finance Act 1994. In these cases the effect of this new legislation is that the partnership is no longer to be treated for the purposes of the levying of income tax, or for the application of the Tax Acts in general, as an entity which is separate and distinct from its members. The profits of the partnership are to be calculated as if the partnership were itself an individual.[17] A partner's share in the partnership profits for any given period is, for the purposes of income tax assessment, determined by reference to the partner's interests in the partnership during that period. The new legislation also regards each partner as carrying on his or her own trade, profession or business. Such a trade, profession or business is deemed to have commenced when the individual concerned became a partner.[18] If the partnership business has been carried on prior to a given individual entering into the partnership, that

---

[15] Taxes Act 1988, s 385(5).

[16] Taxes Act 1988, s 113(3)(a).

[17] The effect of this provision is that the partners must each forward a tax return disclosing profits earned by their involvement in the partnership together with a statement of the partnership income for the relevant year of assessment.

[18] Taxes Act 1988, s 111(3)(a), as substituted by the Finance Act 1994, s 215(1).

individual's deemed business is nevertheless regarded as having commenced when the actual partnership business commenced.[19] The new legislation also provides that the 'deemed' trade, profession or business of an individual partner is to be regarded as coming to an end when he ceases to be a partner. Where the actual partnership business, trade or profession is subsequently carried on by him alone the deemed business of such an individual ends when the actual business is permanently discontinued.[20] The effect of these new legislative provisions is that partners are individually responsible for the tax on their own share of the profits of the partnership business, and that their taxable share is computed by reference to the actual share of the profits enjoyed by the relevant partner. Each partner is therefore subject to the new tax regime as if he were a sole trader or practitioner. The principles of income tax assessment applied to partnerships are accordingly applicable to each partner's affairs, and govern his tax liability for income earned as a partner.

It will also be noted that a further consequence of the new legislative provisions is that once the relevant business, trade or profession has commenced, there will be no *deemed* discontinuance of the partnership business merely because there is a change in partners. One of the most fundamental changes wrought by the new legislative provisions in respect of the taxation of income earned by partnerships is the phasing out of the preceding year basis of assessment. This aspect of the new legislation is discussed below.

For all partnerships commencing their business on or after 6 April 1994, and for all partnerships from 1996–97, the assessment of profits for the purposes of income tax is by reference to the current year of trade or business. This new basis of assessment should ensure that, over the lifetime of a partnership, the profits which are subject to income tax will, in general, be the profits which have been actually earned by the partnership.

2. OPENING YEARS

For a partnership which is commenced on or after 6 April 1994, special provision is still made for assessing income tax during the opening years of the business. For a partnership which is commenced within a given tax year the basis of assessment for the first year of business is the profits of the business arising in that tax year. This means that the profits earned up to and including 5 April of the relevant tax year will usually be calculated by reference to the

---

[19] Taxes Act 1988, s 111(3)(b), as substituted by the Finance Act 1994, s 215(1).
[20] Taxes Act 1988, s 111(3)(c), as substituted by the Finance Act 1994, s 215(1).

appropriate proportion of the accounts for the opening period of the business.[1] For the second year of the partnership the profits of the first 12 months of the business will be the basis of assessment. Where the first 12 months of the business accounts also fall within the first year of the business the relevant overlapping accounts will thus be taken into account twice.[2]

For subsequent years the profits on which income tax will be levied may be calculated by reference to the profits of a given basis period[3] rather than the actual profits of a year of assessment. However, in those cases the basis period will be required to end in the actual year of assessment and not, as previously, in the year preceding the year of assessment.[4]

At the actual cessation of the partnership[5] the profits for income tax purposes will be calculated from the end of the basis period in the last complete year of assessment, prior to the year in which the partnership ceased to carry on its business, and up to the date of discontinuance of the partnership.[6] This period can run for more than 12 months, and this ensures that there will be no earned profits of the business which will not be subject to income tax. It should be noted that any profits which have been taken into account twice during the continuance of the partnership[7] may be deducted in calculating the profits of the business for this final period.

3. TRANSITION PROVISIONS

In respect of a partnership which commenced its business prior to 6 April 1994 the new basis for the assessment of income tax will begin to bite from the tax year 1996–97 and be fully implemented from 1997–98. If the partnership has not effected any change in its accounting date, the profits for the tax year 1996–97 will be calculated by reference to an averaging of the profits for that and the previous tax year. From 1997–98 the partnership will be taxed on the current year basis of assessment as considered above. Thus, for the tax year 1997–98 the partnership will be taxed on the basis of the profits for the 12-month accounting period, ie the basis period

---

[1] Taxes Act 1988, s 61 as substituted by the Finance Act 1994, s 201.

[2] See the Taxes Act 1988, s 63A(5) as added by the Finance Act 1994, s 205.

[3] For the concept of the basis period which in essence is the accounting period of the partnership see p 369, below.

[4] The Taxes Act 1988, s 60(2) as substituted by the Finance Act 1994, s 200.

[5] See p 367, above for a consideration of the position where there is a change of partnership members and the effective abolition of the deemed discontinuance concept.

[6] Taxes Act 1988, s 63 as substituted by the Finance Act 1994, s 204.

[7] As at the commencement of the business: see p 368, above.

which ended in the tax year 1997–98.[8] Where a partnership ceases to carry on its business before 6 April 1997 the old rules relating to discontinuance noted above will apply.[9]

4. THE BASIS PERIOD

The new provisions considered above seek to levy income tax on the profits of the relevant year of assessment. The calculation of income for these purposes is by reference to a basis period, in which income is earned, and which will *usually* be a period of 12 months.[10] The basis period for a year of assessment may be determined by reference to the Taxes Act 1988, s 60(3). This section utilises for the purpose of defining the basis period the concept of the accounting date, which is defined in relation to the relevant year of assessment, and thus means a date within the year of assessment to which the relevant partnership account is made up.[11]

The above section goes on to provide that if a given year is the first year of assessment in which there is an accounting date which falls *not less* than 12 months after the commencement date of the partnership,[12] then the basis period for the business is the period of 12 months ending with that accounting date. The section provides an alternative method of determining a basis period for a partnership. The section states that if there is a basis period for the year immediately preceding the current year of assessment and that basis period has not been determined during the year of the commencement of the business or in the following year,[13] the period of 12 months beginning immediately after the end of that basis period may be selected by the partnership as its basis period. This latter method of determining the basis period is not dependent on the concept of an accounting date.

For the year in which the partnership is set up the basis of assessment is prescribed by s 61 of the Taxes Act 1988.[14] This section provides that:

---

[8] See the Finance Act 1994, Sch 20, paras 1–2.

[9] See the Finance Act 1994, Sch 20, para 3.

[10] Taxes Act 1988, s 60(2), as substituted by the Finance Act 1994, s 200.

[11] Note where there are two or more dates the accounting date is the latest of those dates: see the Taxes Act 1988, s 60(5), as substituted by the Finance Act 1994, s 200.

[12] The commencement date means the date on which the partnership business was set up: Taxes Act 1988, s 60(5), as substituted by the Finance Act 1994, s 200.

[13] Section 61 of the Taxes Act 1988 determines the basis of the assessment during the year of commencement of the partnership business.

[14] As substituted by the Finance Act 1994, s 201.

'. . . where the year of assessment is the commencement year the computation of the profits chargeable to income tax are the profits arising in that year.'[15]

Where the year of assessment is the year next following the year of commencement of the partnership business and there is an accounting date falling in that year which is less than 12 months from the commencement date of the partnership the basis period for that year is the period of 12 months beginning with the commencement date of the business.

5. CHANGE OF BASIS PERIOD

The new legislation, like the previous legislation, governing the income tax liability of partnerships, has regard to the fact that the accounting dates of a partnership may change during the continuance of that partnership.[16]

The new legislation permits, subject to conditions, a partnership to change its accounting date.[17] The conditions are:

(1)   that the first new accounting date must not exceed a period of 18 months;
(2)   that notice of a change of accounting dates must be given to the Revenue no later than 31 January following the year of assessment.

Furthermore, there must either have been no accounting change in the partnership business in the previous five years of assessment, or the notice of change to the Revenue must set out the reasons for the change. In the latter case, the Revenue must be satisfied that any change of accounting dates is made in good faith for commercial reasons. This would not include the partnership gaining a tax advantage by instigating such a change. If the Revenue is not satisfied with the reasons for the change, notice must be given to the partnership within 60 days. An appeal may be made by the partnership against any Revenue notice to the commissioners.

Where the above conditions are satisfied, the accounting date of a partnership may be changed. The new accounting date is determined by reference to the concept of the 'relevant period'. This

---

[15]   See pp 367 and 369 above.
[16]   Special provision is made where there is a change in accounting dates in the second or third year of assessment under the Taxes Act 1988, s 62(1)(b).
[17]   And therefore the basis period for the assessment of income tax. See the Taxes Act 1988, ss 62 and 62A, substituted and added by the Finance Act 1994, ss 202 and 203.

period is defined as beginning immediately after the end of the basis period for the previous year of assessment and ending with the new accounting date. This new accounting date will determine the new basis period for the assessment of income tax.[18] The accounting period which covers the extent of the relevant period may exceed 12 months but, as has been noted above, this accounting period may not exceed 18 months. Where the relevant period is less than 12 months, the basis period is 12 months for this accounting period ending on the new accounting date.[19] Where the above conditions are not satisfied, the basis period for this accounting period will be a period of 12 months, which will end on the previous accounting date. Apportionments may be made between actual accounts as necessary in order to determine the tax liability between the transitional relevant period and the new year of assessment determined by the new accounting date.[20]

6. DISCONTINUANCE

The rules governing the calculation of income tax liability on the discontinuance of a partnership have been considered above. It should be noted that where a partnership business is permanently discontinued, the basis period for the year of discontinuance will, in general, be the period beginning immediately after the end of the basis period for the preceding year of assessment and ending on the actual date of discontinuance. Such a period may exceed 12 months.

---

[18] Taxes Act 1988, s 62(2), as substituted by the Finance Act 1994, s 202.

[19] Such circumstances may give rise to overlap relief for profits which may, under the change in accounting dates, be taxed twice. Such relief is calculated by reference to a formula set out in s 63A of the Taxes Act 1988 and inserted by the Finance Act 1994. The formula is as follows:

$$A \times \frac{B - C}{D}$$

where –

A = the aggregate of any overlap profits less the aggregate of any amounts previously deducted under s 63A(1) of the Taxes Act 1988;

B = the number of days in the basis period;

C = the number of days in the year of assessment;

D = the aggregate of the overlap periods of any overlap profits less the aggregate number of days given by the variable 'B – C' in any previous applications of s 63A(2).

[20] Taxes Act 1988, s 60(3)(b), as substituted by the Finance Act 1994, s 200.

7. SUPPLEMENTARY PROVISIONS

The new provisions governing the assessment and levying of income tax on partnerships considered above are supplemented by provisions governing, inter alia, the nature of and contents of tax returns both by partners and by the partnership.

Any tax return by a partner may, as in the case of any individual, include a self-assessment of the income which on the basis of the information contained in the return is chargeable to income tax. Such a self-assessment will not be required, however, if the return is forwarded to the Revenue within a prescribed period.[1]

8. PARTNERSHIP RETURNS

By s 12AA of the Taxes Management Act 1970[2] the Revenue may, for the purposes of facilitating the assessment of each partner to income tax for a year of assessment, require a partner to make and deliver a return, containing any information which the Revenue may reasonably require. Any individual partner may also be required to deliver with the return any accounts or statements which it is reasonable for him to supply. Every return should include the following:

(1)   a declaration of the name, residence, and tax reference of each of the persons who have been partners for all, or any part, of the period for which the return relates; and

(2)   a declaration by the partner making the return that it is to the best of his knowledge correct and complete.

Such a return should also include a partnership statement which sets out, inter alia, the income, losses or charges in income relating to the partnership for the relevant period of assessment. The statement should also include the amount of any income, losses or charges which are to be enjoyed or borne by the individual partner. There is power to amend obvious errors in the partnership statement.[3]

By s 12AC of the Taxes Management Act 1970[4] the Revenue is

---

[1]   As part of the new self-assessment procedures: Taxes Management Act 1970, s 9, as substituted by the Finance Act 1994, s 179. See also s 9A of the 1970 Act as inserted by the Finance Act 1994, s 180, which empowers the Revenue to inquire into a return.

[2]   See Finance Act 1994, s 184.

[3]   Taxes Management Act 1970, s 12AB, as inserted by the Finance Act 1994, s 185. Such amendments, if made by the Revenue, will result in the Revenue issuing a notice to the partners amending their self assessments under s 9 of the 1970 Act: see above.

[4]   As inserted by the Finance Act, s 186.

empowered to enquire into any return made by a partner under s 12AB of the Taxes Management Act or any amendment of that return upon giving notice to the party who made that return. The notice must be given within the prescribed time.[5] The giving of such a notice is also deemed to include the giving of notice under s 9A (1) of the Taxes Management Act 1970, which empowers the Revenue to enquire into any return made by a party under s 9 of the Taxes Management Act 1970.[6]

9. CONSULTANCIES AND INCOME TAX

In the case of a professional partnership, a senior partner may upon retirement be appointed a consultant. Such an individual will usually receive a substantial fee from the partnership in return for services to the partnership. The position of a consultant may be regarded as being similar to the position of many salaried partners, ie he is to be regarded as an employee of the partnership and not a partner. In that case any remuneration he receives will be taxable under Schedule E, being income derived from an office or employment. The effect of such a payment on the partnership is that it will constitute a deductible expense of the business under Schedule D, Case II, but only if the partnership can establish that the expenditure was wholly and exclusively laid out or expended for the purposes of the partnership business.[7]

Where a consultant acts in that capacity for a number of enterprises, he may be able to establish that he is carrying on a profession or vocation. In that a case any income he receives in that capacity may be taxable under Schedule D, Case II.

In the case of a partnership which retains the services of a partner on a consultancy basis, consideration should be given not only to the tax situation, but the overall cost of utilising the partner's services. Where the sum negotiated for those services is high, and the partner is no longer a partner, but is occupying the post as a Schedule E office under the PAYE scheme, then the cost of meeting the accompanying national insurance contributions may offset any advantage to the partnership in deducting the expense of employment of the former partner against the partnership income. In a case where the cost of employment of a former partner is high it may be preferable to seek to retain the services of the partner, not in the guise of a consultant but as a partner, yet nevertheless to have

---

[5] See s 12AC(2).
[6] See above.
[7] *Copeman v Flood* [1941] 1 KB 202; *Earlspring Properties Ltd v Guest* [1993] STC 473.

his remuneration measured by reference to a reduced share of the profits of the partnership.

10. RETIRING PARTNERS AND INCOME TAX

The final issue to consider as regards income tax and partnerships is the consequences that follow the retirement or death of a partner. The partnership agreement will frequently provide that, in the event of the death of a partner, or his retirement, the partnership will pay him or his estate an annuity. In the case of the retirement of the partner the annuity is usually paid in consideration of the retiring partner waiving his right to share in the continuing goodwill of the partnership business or its assets. The calculation of this annuity, ie whether it is determined by reference to a percentage of partnership profits or a fixed sum, is a matter for the partnership deed or the agreement of the parties. The cost of an annuity in the circumstances noted above is generally borne by the continuing partners, in the same proportion as they share in the profits of the business. Any payments made to a former partner, or his dependant or dependants, are to be regarded as effective annual payments.[8] This means that in paying the annuity, *basic rate* income tax is not directly assessed on the recipient,[9] but is deducted by the partners in making the payment to the recipient.[10] Such annuities are thus outside the scope of s 347A of the Income and Corporation Taxes Act 1988.[11] This section provides that an annual payment, ie including an annuity which would otherwise be within Schedule D, Case III,[12] and which is not expressly excluded by the section, is to be neither a deductible expense, nor an allowable charge on the income of the payer, nor taxable income of the recipient. However, the 1988 Act excludes annual payments including annuities paid to former partners or their dependants by the partnership from the ambit of this provision if the following conditions are met:

---

[8] If certain conditions are fulfilled: see below.
[9] See below for a further consideration of this matter.
[10] See the Taxes Act 1988, ss 348 and 349.
[11] Inserted into the Taxes Act 1988 by the Finance Act 1994. In respect of payments prior to the enactment of s 347A and which, if still in existence, are governed by the law in existence prior to enactment, all such annuities and annual payments are to all intents and purposes deductible in calculating the total income of the payer, although generally the effect of such transfers or settlements were and are restricted to basic rate income tax.
[12] Although usually with a credit for basic rate tax deducted at source.

(1)   that the payment is made for bona fide commercial reasons and in connection with the partnership business.[13] This clearly includes such partnership annuities as have been considered above;

(2)   that the annuity while payable under the terms of the partnership agreement to either:
  (a) a former partner or
  (b) his widow or dependent(s)
  is payable by virtue of a liability incurred for full consideration;

(3)   that where the former partner is dead, the annuity is not payable for more than ten years.[14]

It should also be noted that annuities as considered above are also outside the ambit of s 674A of the Income and Corporation Taxes Act 1988.[15] This provision determines that income arising under a settlement (which would include an annuity) is to be treated as that of the settlor for all purposes, unless a settlement is excluded from the ambit of the provision. The settlements thus excluded consist, inter alia, of annual payments made under the terms of a partnership agreement to a retired partner or the widow or dependant of such a partner.[16]

The party receiving an annuity will be taxed on the annuity, under Schedule D, Case III, although with a credit for basic rate tax which has been deducted at source.[17] Such an annuity will be taxed as earned income, only to the extent that the annuity paid does not exceed one half of the average of the retired partner's best three years' profits, received during the last seven years of his involvement in the partnership. For the above purposes, involvement requires a partner to devote a substantial part of his time to the partnership. Furthermore, the retired or deceased partner's share of the partnership profits for the first six of the seven years, are to be increased to reflect increases in the retail price index up to December in the seventh year.[18] Any income received in excess of the prescribed amount is regarded as unearned or investment income.[19]

As an alternative to an annuity, partners may make provision for

---

[13]   See the Taxes Act 1988, s 660(3).

[14]   An annuity will also be an annual payment within the terms noted above, if it is paid in connection with the acquiring of a share in the partnership business of the outgoing partner.

[15]   Inserted into the Taxes Act 1988 by the Finance Act 1988.

[16]   Taxes Act 1988, s 683.

[17]   See p 374, above and the Taxes Act 1988, ss 348, 394.

[18]   Taxes Act 1988, s 628(3).

[19]   Taxes Act 1988, s 628.

insurance against death or early retirement by way of personal pension scheme arrangements. These forms of provision are, however, outside the scope of this chapter and have been mentioned solely for completeness.[20]

Companies as partners and income tax

It only remains to consider in outline the position of a partnership which includes a company as a partner. In cases where a company is a member of a partnership the profits of the partnerships are computed for the purposes of the levying of tax as if the partnership were a company, with the company's shares ascertained and subjected to corporation tax. Income tax remains chargeable, however, on the share of the profits attributed to the non-corporate partners.[1]

This outline consideration of the principal incidents which attach to the taxation of partnership income cannot cover the complexities of the law governing the levying of income tax on businesses. It is not intended to be comprehensive in its coverage. Reference should therefore be made to leading standard works on Revenue law.[2] This chapter will now consider the liability of partnerships to capital gains tax.

CAPITAL GAINS TAX AND PARTNERSHIPS

The application of capital gains tax to a partnership and its transactions is fraught with difficulties. In part this is due to the failure of the legislation to distinguish clearly between partnership property and a partner's share in a partnership. Neither does the legislation seek to identify and assimilate such forms of property one with another. The Revenue has sought to avoid the difficulties that a purely technical and mechanical application of the legislation governing capital gains tax would produce in respect of partnerships. It has, accordingly, produced a practice statement which sets out the principles by which it seeks to apply capital gains tax to partnerships.[3] The guidance determines that partnership dealings are treated as being made by the partners and not by the partnership.[4]

---

[20] See the Taxes Act 1988, ss 619 and 630-655.
[1] Taxes Act 1988, s 114(3).
[2] See fn 6, p 364, above.
[3] See Statement of Practice D12, *Simon's Taxes* Division H34.
[4] See Taxation of Chargeable Gains Act 1992, s 59.

Thus, capital gains tax is brought into operation by a disposal by the partnership of a partnership asset which is nevertheless treated as a disposal by the partners individually. Although the assessment to capital gains tax is by reference to the partners as individuals, the returns are made by the partnership.[5] The individual assessment to capital gains tax upon a partner is determined by reference to the proportional share he enjoyed in the disposed asset and thus the proportional share he enjoys in the surplus created by the disposal of that asset.

The proportional share enjoyed by a partner in any partnership asset will be determined generally by the partnership deed. Where the partnership deed is silent with respect to any particular asset, any liability to capital gains tax arising on its disposal will be assessed by reference to the profit-sharing arrangements enjoyed by the partners. This particular means of determining liability to capital gains tax does not take into account a partner's contribution to the capital of the partnership. It is therefore advisable for the partnership deed to provide a means of determining both the proportional right to share in the surplus created by the disposal of a partnership asset and the consequential liability to capital gains tax, by reference to the proportion in which the partner has contributed to the capital of the business. Nevertheless, it should be emphasised that the difficulties of determining in a particular instance whether an asset is a partnership asset, or is the exclusive property of an individual partner which the latter permits the partnership to use, remain an inscrutable problem.[6]

OUTLINE OF CAPITAL GAINS TAX

Although a full consideration of capital gains tax falls outside the ambit of this book, it would be helpful to outline some general principles applicable to the tax.[7] Capital gains tax is charged on chargeable gains realised by an individual, during a year of assessment. A chargeable gain occurs where there is a chargeable disposal of a chargeable asset.[8]

Capital gains tax is independent of income tax, and capital gains and losses cannot be set off against gains and losses incurred in respect of income tax and vice versa. Tax is levied on the difference

---

[5] Taxes Management Act 1970, s 12(4).
[6] See *Faulks v Faulks* [1992] 1 EGLR 9.
[7] For a full discussion of this tax see *Whitehouse* and *Tiley*.
[8] For a definition of disposals see the Taxation of Chargeable Gains Act 1992, s 7.

between the base cost of the asset, ie its value at the time of acquisition, and its value at disposal, less any incidental costs of disposal, and any indexation allowance to take account of inflation.[9]

Losses are calculated in the same way as gains; losses must be set off against capital gains within the same year of assessment,[10] although unrelieved losses may be carried forward to later years. Usually, capital gains tax is due on the 1 December which follows the end of the year of assessment or, if later, 30 days after the assessment notice is issued.[11] In cases of hardship, the tax may be paid by instalments. There is an annual exemption for gains accruing in any year of assessment; the exemption is index linked, although this may be disapplied and was done so for the year 1994–95.[12] Spouses are each entitled to an exemption. Chargeable gains are charged at income tax rates, the chargeable gain being regarded as the top slice of income of an individual. Nevertheless, the tax which is charged remains capital gains tax. If spouses are living together, any disposal of an asset inter se is regarded as giving rise to neither a gain nor a loss.[13]

Assets for the purposes of capital gains tax includes all forms of property such as options, debts, incorporeal property and copyright, as well as tangible property including all currencies except sterling.[14] Every asset which is disposed of is treated as a distinct and separate item, with the expenditure incurred in disposing of that asset set off against the gain. Certain assets are non-chargeable assets, and their disposal does not give rise to capital gains tax.[15] Certain disposals are exempt from the tax, for example where the asset is the only or main residence of the party disposing of the asset.[16]

Transactions between partners

The general principles governing the liability to capital gains tax are modified under the Revenue practice statement when the disposal

---

[9] Indexation cannot increase a loss or convert a gain to a loss for any disposal after 30 November 1993: see Taxation of Chargeable Gains Act 1992, as amended by the Finance Act 1994, s 93.
[10] Taxation of Chargeable Gains Act 1992, s 2(2)(a).
[11] Taxation of Chargeable Gains Act 1992, s 7.
[12] Taxation of Chargeable Gains Act 1992, s 3(3); Finance Act 1994, s 90.
[13] Taxation of Chargeable Gains Act 1992, s 58.
[14] See *O'Brien v Benson's Hosiery (Holdings) Ltd* [1979] STC 735.
[15] See the Taxation of Chargeable Gains Act 1992, ss 5(1), 124, 204, 210, 252(2), 263, 268, 269.
[16] Taxation of Chargeable Gains Act 1992, s 222.

of a chargeable asset takes place between partners. Thus, a change in the profit-sharing ratio enjoyed by the partners including where such a change is effected by the admission of a new partner will give rise to the possibility of capital gains tax liability. Similar considerations also arise on the expulsion or retirement of a partner, or on the change or amendment of the terms of the partnership deed. This is because such a change involves a disposal by some partners of a fraction of their share in the ownership of the capital assets of the partnership, and a consequential change in their entitlement to any surplus realised on such assets, together with a corresponding acquisition of such rights by other partners. The Revenue is prepared to accept any disposal of a partnership asset or assets in such cases as taking place at a deemed consideration, which, nevertheless, it regards as giving rise to neither a gain nor a loss.[17] The consequence of this practice is that the base cost of a share in a partnership asset vested in a partner will be reduced if his share in the asset is reduced, with a corresponding increase in base cost for any partner whose share in the asset is increased. In effect, the payment of any capital gains tax by a partner is postponed until there is a disposal of any relevant partnership asset. A simple fractional basis is used in determining, post-transaction, the value of each share in a partnership asset vested in each of the partners, and therefore any notional gain made by a partner, and not the formula used when an individual or partnership makes a partial disposal of an asset. In the latter case it is necessary to determine the actual gain made on the partial disposal of the asset. The formula for determining the original value of part of an asset which has been disposed of and the resultant gain made is as follows:

$$C \times \frac{A}{A + B}$$

Where: C is all the deductible expenditure on the whole asset including acquisition cost.

A is the sale proceeds of the part of the asset sold.

B is the market value of part of the asset remaining in the disposer's hands, at the time when the part disposal was made.[18]

---

[17] Statement of Practice D12, para 4.
[18] Taxation of Chargeable Gains Act 1992, s 42.

Indexation is applied for part disposals as for whole disposals, but only the apportioned expenditure is index linked.[19]

Although the practice statement is ambiguous, it would seem that indexation should be permitted in the case of transactions between partners in determining the value of the deemed consideration. This is important for any future disposals of the relevant partnership asset(s).

Notwithstanding the above, the Revenue may, in certain circumstances, substitute the market value as the disposal consideration in any transaction between partners, rather than a deemed consideration, which does not give rise to a gain or a loss. The potential for capital gains tax may thus arise in such cases. The circumstances where the Revenue *may* adopt this position are as follows:

(1)   where the partners are connected persons, other than their connection as partners, including any transaction between partners who are related by blood or marriage. However, market value will not be substituted in such partnership transactions if the consideration passing between the partners is not less than the consideration which would have passed between the parties if it had been a transaction at arm's length;[20]

(2)   where the consideration in respect of a partnership transaction cannot be valued, irrespective of whether the partners conducted the transaction at arm's length;[1]

(3)   where, prior to the relevant transaction, there has been an adjustment through the partnership accounts of the partnership assets, ie a revaluation of those assets. In that case any subsequent change in the profit-sharing ratios of the partners will be treated by the Revenue as a disposal of fractional shares in those assets between the partners for a consideration equal to each partner's share of the revalued amount, which will be greater or less than the original base cost for each partner's share in the relevant partnership asset;[2]

(4)   where there has been a payment outside the partnership accounts. This usually involves payments by an incoming partner in respect of a share of the goodwill of the business, although such payments are not included in the partnership balance sheet. Such payments will give rise to capital gains tax.[3]

---

[19]   Ibid.
[20]   Statement of Practice D12, para 7.
[1]   Taxation of Chargeable Gains Act 1992, s 17(1)(b).
[2]   Statement of Practice D12, para 5.
[3]   Statement of Practice D12, para 6.

Goodwill

It will be noted from above that goodwill is for the purposes of capital gains tax a chargeable asset. Any disposal of a partnership's goodwill may therefore give rise to capital gains tax. It is a practice for many partnerships, especially professional partnerships, not to charge incoming partners for any share in the partnership goodwill. This may give rise to problems for existing partners. In essence, these partners will in such cases write off the goodwill in the partnership balance sheet. If any of these existing partners originally made payment to the partnership in respect of goodwill when they became partners, they may seek to claim immediate capital gains tax loss relief. It would appear that an allowable loss for capital gains purposes will be permitted in the above circumstances on an actual disposal of the goodwill, either on retirement of the partner claiming relief or where actual disposal is made to an incoming partner. Furthermore, where the goodwill of a partnership has been written off in the balance sheet, the partners may seek to claim immediate loss relief on the basis that the Revenue is satisfied that the value of an asset, ie the goodwill, has become negligible.[4] It seems that most Revenue inspectors do not accept that the writing off of goodwill in the circumstances noted above renders the goodwill an asset of negligible value. This is logical, since any sale of a partnership business will take into account as part of the consideration the goodwill of the business. Nevertheless, it appears that a few inspectors are prepared to admit such a claim.

Annuities and capital gains tax

It has already been noted that the payment of an annuity to a retiring partner or his dependants may give rise to a liability for income tax. Where the capitalised value of the annuity is treated as consideration received by the retiring partner for his share in the partnership, the annuity may give rise to a chargeable gain as it may be treated as consideration for the disposal of a share in partnership assets.[5] The Revenue has formulated the following practice, and will only seek to levy capital gains tax on any resultant gain enjoyed by a partner in the following circumstances:[6]

---

4 Taxation of Chargeable Gains Act 1992, s 24(2).
5 Taxation of Chargeable Gains Act 1992, s 37(3).
6 Practice Statement D12, para 8.

'The capitalised value of the annuity will only be treated as consideration for the disposal of his share in the partnership assets, if it is more than can be regarded as a reasonable recognition of the past contribution of work and effort by the partner to the partnership. Provided that the former partner had been in the partnership for at least ten years an annuity will be regarded as reasonable for this purpose if it is no more than two-thirds of his average share of the profits in the best three of the last seven years in which he was required to devote substantially the whole of his time to acting as a partner. For lesser periods the following fractions will be used instead of the two-thirds:

Complete years in partnership	*Fraction*
1–5	1/60 for each year
6	8/60
7	16/60
8	24/60
9	32/60'

Where a retiring partner receives both an annuity and a lump sum, the Revenue will not seek to charge capital gains tax on the capitalised value of the annuity, provided that the annuity and one ninth of the lump sum when added together do not exceed the relevant fraction of the retired partner's average share of the profits as set out above.[7] Although a lump sum will always be chargeable to capital gains tax, a lump sum paid with an annuity may also cause the capitalised value of the annuity to be taxed.

Reliefs and partnerships

A gain made on the disposal of an asset may not be chargeable, because the gain is exempt or because the asset is not defined within the governing legislation as a chargeable asset. Furthermore, even where a gain is chargeable, there may be various reliefs applicable whereby the capital gains tax otherwise payable can be lessened or even deferred indefinitely. There are various reliefs which apply to partners as they apply to sole traders or any other individuals. The purpose of such reliefs is to enable a business to be carried on or its assets transferred without the threat of capital gains tax crippling the enterprise. These reliefs take the form of an indefinite deferral of capital gains tax. They may be listed as follows.

---

[7] Practice Statement SP1/79.

1. HOLD OVER RELIEF

Hold over relief may apply to any gain on a gift or a sale below market value of a chargeable asset. A chargeable asset for the purposes of hold over relief may include a partnership share, or assets which are either partnership assets or assets owned by an individual partner, but they must within the context of a partnership or its members be business assets of the partnership.[8] If both parties to any such transaction agree the chargeable gain otherwise accruing to the transferor is reduced by the amount of the 'held over' gain,[9] with a corresponding reduction in the transferee's acquisition cost. Where the transaction is a sale at below market value, but nevertheless the consideration paid exceeds the base cost of the asset, the held over gain is reduced by that amount. The relief here takes the form of a deferral of any capital gains tax liability. Such liability to capital gains tax will arise when the asset is disposed of by the transferee. The liability for payment of the tax lies principally and initially with the transferor.

It has been noted that this relief applies to business assets. The relief therefore applies only to disposals of an asset or interest in an asset used in the transferor's trade, profession or vocation, or to such assets or interests used in his personal company's trade or shares or securities in such a company. This relief can be claimed in addition to any retirement or reinvestment relief.[10]

It should be noted that where the gain arising could be significantly reduced by the annual exemption, or by an allowable loss, the use of hold over relief may be disadvantageous, because the legislation does not permit a partial hold over. In such cases either the whole chargeable gain must be held over, or be subject to capital gains tax, but with the benefit of the annual exemption or any allowable loss. Accordingly, reliance on the annual exemption to reduce the gain, with the payment of a small payment of capital gains tax, may be more economical than relying on hold over relief.

2. RETIREMENT RELIEF

This relief will be available to a partner if he makes a material disposal of his partnership share[11] but only if he has either:[12]

---

[8] Finance Act 1980, s 79; Taxation of Chargeable Gains Act 1992, s 165.
[9] This is calculated by reference to the market value of the asset at the time of its acquisition by the transferee minus the chargeable gains which would otherwise accrue to the transferor on the disposal.
[10] See below.
[11] But see p 384, below.
[12] Taxation of Chargeable Gains Act 1992, s 163.

(1)   attained the age of 55; or
(2)   retired before the age of 55 on the grounds of ill health. In this case the retiring partner must submit appropriate medical evidence to the Revenue.[13]

The relief may be extended to cover the disposal of an asset owned by a partner if it has been used by the partnership and has been disposed of by the partner in conjunction with his disposal of his partnership share.[14] The relief is not restricted to a partner who is retiring, unless the partner is under the age of 55. In cases of a partner over the age of 55, the relief may be claimed if he is simply disposing of his partnership share.

3. ROLLOVER RELIEF

Any chargeable gains realised by partners on qualifying business asset, ie assets used for the purposes of the business, may be rolled over against their shares of expenditure on the purchase of new qualifying business assets, either within the partnership, or even in relation to other trades or professions carried on by the partners.[15]

This relief will also apply to an asset which though owned by a partner is used by the firm. However, the entire proceeds of disposal must be re-invested in another business asset which is then used by the partnership, or is used in a new business which is carried on by the partner.

It should also be noted that if any qualifying asset, and in particular land, is partitioned it will be treated for the purposes of this relief as a new asset, but only if the partnership is subsequently dissolved.

4. INCORPORATION RELIEF

Where all the assets of a partnership are transferred to a company, ie in essence the partnership is incorporated, rollover relief may be available although there has been a disposal of chargeable assets. The relief will only be available where shares are received in exchange for the business.[16] Furthermore, the relief would seemingly be available only where the partnership *business* in whole or in

---

[13]   Taxation of Chargeable Gains Act 1992, Sch 6, para 3.
[14]   Taxation of Chargeable Gains Act 1992, s 164(6).
[15]   Taxation of Chargeable Gains Act 1992, s 152. Rollover relief may also be partial, if the acquisition cost of the new asset is less than the disposal proceeds of the old asset: s 153.
[16]   Taxation of Chargeable Gains Act 1992, s 162.

part is transferred to a company, and not where a partner merely transfers his share of the business to a company.

Assessment of capital gains

Capital gains tax, as has been noted above, is a tax charged on chargeable gains accruing to an individual during a year of assessment. Although it is a tax distinct from income tax, it shares a number of common features. The principle feature it shares with income tax is the machinery relating to assessment. Thus, tax returns of partners should where appropriate include, inter alia, self-assessments as to the chargeable gains made by the partner in the relevant year of assessment. The Revenue may also inquire into the accuracy of such self-assessments, in so far as they relate to capital gains tax.[17] The relevant machinery of assessment has been considered above in relation to income tax. Reference should therefore be made to the section concerning assessment of income tax for a fuller consideration of the procedures to be followed, and the legislative provisions which govern the assessment of capital gains tax.[18]

European Economic Interest Grouping

Groupings of business organisations formed in pursuance of Council Regulation (EEC) 2137/85 and known as European Economic Interest Groupings[19] are treated for the purposes of capital gains tax in a broadly similar fashion to partnerships. Accordingly, the members of such a business organisation are taxed separately on any chargeable gains.[20] Furthermore, disposals of chargeable assets by a member of such an economic grouping are deemed to take place if a party joins or leaves such a grouping, or his share in such a grouping changes.[1]

---

[17] See the Taxes Management Act 1970, ss 9, 9a, as substituted by the Finance Act 1994, ss 179 and 180.

[18] Also note that a partnership may claim a capital allowance; this permits the partnership to set off the cost of a business asset against the profits of the partnership. Conversely, if an asset for which a capital allowance has been claimed is sold at more than the written down value, there will be a corresponding balancing charge which negates any earlier set off: see the Taxation of Capital Gains Act 1992, s 37(2).

[19] The full nature of which falls outside the ambit of this book.

[20] Taxes Act 1988, s 510A(b); Taxation of Chargeable Gains Act 1992, s 59.

[1] Taxes Act 1988, s 510A(3b).

Conclusion

This section has sought to give only an outline of some of the principal features of capital gains tax as it applies to partnerships. It is not intended to be comprehensive in its coverage. For a detailed discussion of capital gains tax and its application to partnerships reference should be made to appropriate books of authority.[2]

An outline consideration will now be given to the application of inheritance tax to partnerships and partners.

INHERITANCE TAX AND PARTNERSHIPS

Inheritance tax is a tax on the transfers of capital, usually by way of gift, and is designed to operate principally on transfers which occur on the death of the transferor. The tax also operates retrospectively on transfers made by a person within seven years of his death. Furthermore, transfers made outside this seven-year period may be regarded as 'gifts with reservation' and are potentially subject to inheritance tax; such transfers are transfers where the donee, inter alia, does not have full enjoyment and possession of the property. The tax is cumulative, and levied on transfers made within any given seven-year period during the transferor's lifetime until his death.

Inheritance tax is primarily charged on all 'chargeable transfers of value', which is defined as a disposition which causes loss to an individual's estate and which is not an exempt transfer.[3]

A transfer of value is a disposition whereby the value of a person's estate is reduced. At the time of writing the first £150,000 of any chargeable transfers of value within any seven-year period attracts a zero rate of tax. Above this limit there is a single rate of 40%, levied on any chargeable transfers, and 20% for lifetime chargeable transfers. There are various transfer of value which are exempt from the tax.

There are also various reliefs.[4]

---

[2] See *Whitehouse* and *Tiley*.
[3] Inheritance Tax Act 1984, s 3(4). For exempt transfers see p 387, below. Note also the potentially exempt transfer of value which may become chargeable if the person dies within seven years of the transfer: Inheritance Tax Act, s 3A. Note that reference to the Inheritance Tax Act 1984 is permitted by the Finance Act 1986, s 106. Prior to this legislative provision the Inheritance Tax Act was entitled the Capital Transfer Tax Act 1984.
[4] See p 387, below.

Exempt transfers

The three principle forms of exempt transfer are:

(1) transfers between spouses;
(2) transfers up to £300 each tax year;
(3) outright gifts of up to £250 per year to any number of different persons.

The tax is levied on transfers which are transfers of value. Accordingly, in a transaction at arm's length between persons not connected with each other *or*, if the persons are so connected, the transfer was such as might be expected to be made in a transaction at arm's length *and* the transfer was not intended, and was not made in a transaction intended, to confer a gratuitous benefit on any person, any such transaction will be regarded as a commercial transaction and will not constitute a transfer of value.[5] In these cases no inheritance tax liability is incurred. Therefore, although a gratuitous transfer of partnership assets between the partners or to their dependants would attract inheritance tax, any such disposition where there is full consideration between the parties would not constitute a transfer of value. Even where a retiring partner transfers his share to the continuing partners for less than full consideration, the transaction may still be regarded as a commercial transaction, as has been noted above, and may thus escape inheritance tax.

Reliefs

Any liability to inheritance tax may be reduced or entirely remitted by the operation of certain reliefs. The reliefs which are appropriate to transfers of value by a partnership or a partner operate by reducing the value transferred. The relevant reliefs are as set out below.

1. BUSINESS PROPERTY RELIEF

Relief by the reduction in the value transferred of either 100% or 50% for transfers of value after 10 March 1992 is applied in the case of transfers of certain types of business property. Such relief is not available, however, if the relevant property is the subject of a contract of sale at the time of transfer. The conditions for the application of business property relief are:

---

5 Inheritance Tax Act 1984, s 10.

(1)   that the asset is relevant business property;
(2)   that the business is a qualifying business;
(3)   that the asset has been held for the minimum period of ownership;
(4)   that the asset is not an excepted asset.

Each of these conditions will now be considered in turn.

Asset relevant business property[6]

For a partnership this means either:

(a)   property consisting of a business or interest in a business. (The relief in this case is 100%); or
(b)   any land or building, machinery or plant which, immediately prior to the transfer, was used wholly or mainly for the purposes of a business carried on by a partnership of which the transferor was then a partner. (The relief in this case is 50%.)

Relief is also available if the business asset is held on trust, but is used by a life tenant who is also a partner in the partnership business.

A qualifying business

The business from which the business assets are transferred must be a qualifying business. This will include a partnership whose partners carry on a trade or exercise a profession.[7] A qualifying business does not include a business carried on otherwise than for gain[8] – a definition which, by the nature of a partnership, ensures that all partnerships are prima facie qualifying businesses. However, even a partnership may be excluded from the definition of a qualifying business if its essential or primary business is speculation in securities or land.

Period of ownership

The relevant business property must have been owned by the transferor throughout the two years immediately prior to the transfer.[9]

Excepted assets

This condition excludes the private assets of an individual from being disguised as partnership or business assets. Accordingly,

---

[6]   Inheritance Tax Act 1984, s 105(1) and (6).
[7]   Inheritance Tax Act 1984, s 105(3).
[8]   Section 106.
[9]   Section 106.

assets which have not been used wholly or mainly for the purposes of the partnership business throughout the whole of the last two years prior to transfer will be an excepted asset.[10] The consequence of this is that a transfer of value of such an asset by the transferor is liable to inheritance tax.

Business property relief is applied to the value which is transferred, and not to the chargeable transfer, or to the property transferred. This means that the relief is applied before any other relief that might also be applicable to the transfer.

A problem in the application of inheritance tax to a partnership or partners is that a transfer may be potentially exempt at the time it is made, but may subsequently be liable to inheritance tax if the transferor dies within seven years of the transfer. Business relief in such cases is only available on the death of the transferor if two conditions are satisfied at the date of death[11] as follows:

(1)   the original property the subject of the transfer must have been *owned* by the transferee from the time of the transfer down to the date of death of the transferor or, if earlier, the date of death of the transferee[12]; and
(2)   the property the subject of the original transfer must still qualify and be determined as relevant business property, if it was the subject of a hypothetical transfer by the transferee at the date of death of the transferor, or if earlier the date of death of the transferee.[13] In making this determination at the time of the notional transfer, the condition as to two years' ownership noted above is disregarded.[14]

The rationale behind business property relief is to prevent a business such as a partnership from becoming financially crippled by the imposition of inheritance tax. The above conditions, if applied without any exception, would severely restrict the application of business property relief, since the asset transferred could not be exchanged for new assets without the party who is liable for inheritance tax losing the benefit of business property relief. The legislation therefore permits the transferee, for legitimate business reasons, to replace the asset the subject of the transfer without

---

[10] Section 112.
[11] Inheritance Tax Act 1984, s 113A as added by the Finance Act 1986, Sch 18, para 14.
[12] Inheritance Tax Act 1984, s 113A(3)(a), (4), added by the Finance Act 1986, Sch 19, para 21.
[13] Inheritance Tax Act 1984, s 113A(3)(b), (4), added by the Finance Act 1986, Sch 19, para 21.
[14] Inheritance Tax Act 1984, s 113A(3)(b).

losing any business property relief which might be applicable.[15] However, the property which was the subject of the original transfer and the property acquired to replace it must be the subject of an arm's length transaction. Furthermore, the whole of the proceeds received by the sale of the original asset must be used in the acquisition of the new property. Finally, the replacement must occur within a prescribed or allowed period, after the disposal by the transferee of the original property.[16] Where transfers of value of the original property have been made on or after 30 November 1993, the above-mentioned period is three years or a longer period if the Revenue will allow. The conditions which must be satisfied in order for business property relief to apply to any transfer of value must be separately applied to each asset which is the subject of a transfer of value. Where the transferor of the original property dies before the transferee, but the latter has disposed of the property, he can replace the property within 12 months of the disposal and still claim business property relief.[17] Similar provision is made for the case where the transferee predeceases the transferor.[18] The above provisions also apply where only part of the original property is replaced.

Agricultural relief and partnerships

Partnerships which are engaged in the agricultural industry may claim a special relief against liability to inheritance tax in respect of the transfer of agricultural property. Such agricultural relief applies to lifetime transfers, transfers on death, and even applies to settled property.

This relief applies to forms of property, which may be termed 'agricultural property'.

Agricultural land or pasture

This term includes woodlands, but not any timber on such land. Also comprised within this term, for the purposes of agricultural relief, are buildings on agricultural land which are occupied for the purposes of intensive fish farming, livestock rearing or stud farming. Any buildings on agricultural land which constitute a farm building,

---

[15] Inheritance Tax Act 1984, s 113B added by the Finance Act 1986, Sch 19, para 21.
[16] Inheritance Tax Act 1984, s 113B(2)(a), as amended by the Finance Act 1994, s 247(1) and (3).
[17] Inheritance Tax Act 1984, s 113B(5).
[18] Section 113B(4).

a farm house or cottage and which are of a character appropriate to agricultural property are also eligible for agricultural relief.[19]

Any claim to relief will be lost if the property which is the subject of the transfer of value is the subject of a contract of sale, unless the sale is to a company which the transferor controls.[20]

The nature of the relief is broadly similar to the business property relief noted above. It takes the form of a reduction in the transfer of value. It is thus the agricultural value of the property which attracts relief. This may be defined as the value which the property would have if the property was perpetually restricted to agricultural use. Any value derived from development potential is therefore not subject to agricultural relief; this excess may, however, be subject to business property relief. The rates of and conditions upon which agricultural relief may be claimed are as follows:

(1)   for transfers after 10 March 1992 the rate of relief on the transfer of value is 100%. This is conditional, however, on the transferor having vacant possession of the property *or* the right to obtain the same within 12 months.[1] Where the relevant property is jointly owned, whether under a joint tenancy or a tenancy in common, the joint owners must collectively enjoy the right to vacant possession;[2]

(2)   where a transferor of the relevant agricultural property has been entitled to the property since before 10 March 1981, and would have been entitled to agricultural relief under the rules subsisting prior to the above date, but he has no right to vacant possession. This situation may arise, for example, because the relevant agricultural property is currently leased out to an agricultural tenant holding the land under an agricultural tenancy, and the tenant was an employee or relative of the transferor, and the latter has retired, or transferred his interest to a partnership of which he is a member. The relief in such cases is nevertheless 100%.

In virtually all other cases where the transferor is the landlord of agricultural property the rate of relief is only a 50% reduction in the transfer of value.[3] Any reduction is excluded by business relief reduction if the latter applies. The reduction in agricultural relief

[19] Section 115.
[20] Section 24.
[1] Inheritance Tax Act 1984, s 116(2)(a), as amended by the Finance (No 2) Act 1992, Sch 14, paras 4 and 8.
[2] Inheritance Tax Act 1984, s 116(6).
[3] Inheritance Tax Act 1984, s 116(2)(b), (4), as amended by the Finance (No 2) Act 1992, Sch 14, paras 4 and 8.

applies to the value of the relevant property, before any exemptions, but also before any grossing up.[4]

One of two prescribed conditions must be satisfied before agricultural relief may be claimed in the above circumstances, these are that the transferor must:

(a) have occupied the property for agricultural purposes for the last two years; *or*

(b) have owned the land for the last seven years and throughout this period the land has been used for agricultural purposes, and been occupied by the transferor or an agricultural tenant of the transferor.[5]

In calculating any period of occupation or ownership as required by the above conditions the legislation provides guidelines.[6]

Where a party becomes beneficially entitled to agricultural property following a death, his occupation or ownership runs from the date of death. However, if the deceased was a spouse of the party beneficially entitled to the property, the former's period of occupation or ownership of the property may be taken over by the latter.[7] Provision is also made for the occupation or ownership periods noted above to be maintained, and satisfied even when agricultural property is sold and replaced by the transferor. Thus, the prescribed period of occupation under (b) above is satisfied by including any agricultural property which has been occupied by the transferor within the last five years.

Furthermore, in respect of the prescribed period of ownership under (b) above, any agricultural land which has been owned by the transferor within seven of the last ten years may be taken into account[8] in order to satisfy any ownership or occupation requirement. If the agricultural properties concerned in any situation of replacement differ in value, the property with the lowest agricultural value will qualify for agricultural relief.[9] There are, however, special rules in this regard relating to partnerships. The rules may be summarised as follows:

---

[4] Inheritance Tax Act 1984, s 116(7): for grossing up see *Whitehouse*. As a simple definition of grossing up it may be said that the concept involves a transfer of value which is transferred to a transferee net of tax. In such a case the tax on the transfer is to be paid by the transferor, and the actual reduction in the transferor's estate requires the transfer to be grossed up in order to take into account the tax to be paid.

[5] Inheritance Tax Act 1984, s 117.

[6] Section 120(1).

[7] Section 120(2).

[8] Section 118(1).

[9] Section 118(3).

'In the case of partnerships, changes resulting from the formation, alteration or dissolution of a partnership shall be disregarded.'[10]

Provision is also made to deal with the situation where the agricultural property has not been owned or occupied by the transferor for either of the prescribed periods noted above and cannot qualify for relief on any transfer, although the property was acquired by the transferor on a transfer which did so qualify. In such a case relief may nevertheless be available for any subsequent transfer, but only if the following conditions are met. First, it must only be the conditions as to occupation or ownership that prevent relief in the case of the subsequent transfer and, second, either this transfer or the previous one should be on death.[11] Agricultural relief will also be available in the cases noted above even where there has been a replacement of agricultural property between the two transfers. The rules of replacement are the same as those which govern the replacement of agricultural property considered above.[12] Where the first transfer only attracted partial relief, only the same relief will be permitted on the subsequent transfer.[13]

An individual may have made a transfer of agricultural property which is exempt from inheritance tax but which becomes chargeable on his death. Furthermore, a transfer which was chargeable to inheritance tax may be subject to additional tax on the death of the transferor. Agricultural relief may be available in these circumstances, but only if two conditions are satisfied:

(1) that the original agricultural property transferred must be owned by the transferee from the time of the transfer down to his death, or the death of the original transferor, whichever occurs first;[14] and

(2) that the relevant property which is the subject of the original transfer should be agricultural property immediately prior to the death of either the transferor or transferee, whichever occurs first, and the property should have been occupied by the transferee, or another for the purposes of agriculture throughout the relevant period.[15]

Notwithstanding the above, the agricultural property may be

[10] Section 118(4).
[11] Section 121.
[12] Section 121(1).
[13] Section 121(3).
[14] Section 124A(3)(a), (4).
[15] Section 124A(3)(b).

replaced and agricultural relief may still be claimed within the circumstances noted above. However, the disposal of the original property and the acquisition of any replacement property must be a consequence of an arm's length transaction, or on terms which would be arrived at within such a transaction.[16]

As in the case of business relief, the replacement property must be acquired within three years of the disposal of the original property, or such longer period as the Revenue may allow.[17] Similarly, as in business property relief, the conditions for the application of agricultural relief are applied to the original and replacement property.

The instalment option

It should be noted that after the deduction of business property relief the reduced value of the business assets transferred may still attract, or be chargeable to, inheritance tax. The normal inheritance tax exemptions and reliefs[18] may be deducted after the application of business relief. Furthermore, should any inheritance tax be payable, it may be spread over ten years and be paid by annual interest-free instalments. The election to pay by instalments is only available in respect of lifetime transfers if the inheritance tax is paid by the transferee. If the transfer is on death, the election should be made by the personal representatives.[19]

Inheritance tax and the accrual or acquisition of partnership shares

It has been noted above that neither business property relief nor agricultural property relief is available if the relevant property is subject to a contract of sale at the time of the transfer. It follows from this that a partnership share subject to a contract of sale could not attract either form of relief. Accordingly, if the partners wish for any deceased or retired partner's partnership share to pass to the continuing or surviving partners, with the benefit of either business

---

[16] Section 124B(2).
[17] Inheritance Tax Act 1984, s 124B(2)(a), (5)(b), as amended by the Finance Act 1994, s 247(2) and (3) for transfers made on or after 30 November 1993.
[18] See *Whitehouse* for a consideration of these exemptions and reliefs. For an outline of the principal exemptions see p 387 above.
[19] Inheritance Tax Act 1984, ss 105(1)(a) and 227.

property or agricultural relief, the partnership deed should not
impose an obligation upon the remaining partners to acquire such
a share, nor should it provide for automatic accrual of the share.
The deed should, instead, give the continuing or surviving partners
an option to purchase the partnership share.

This outline consideration of inheritance tax as it applies to partnership is not intended to be comprehensive. For a full
consideration of this tax as it applies to partnerships reference
should be made to the standard works on Revenue law.[20]

VAT AND PARTNERSHIP

Value added tax is chargeable on any taxable supply of goods or services in the United Kingdom made by a taxable person in the
course or furtherance of any business.[1] A taxable supply is a supply
of goods or services made in the United Kingdom, other than an
exempt supply.[2] A taxable person is any person who is either:

(1)   required to be registered for the purposes of VAT, whether or
      not he is registered; or
(2)   eligible to be, and is actually, registered.[3]

This definition includes a partnership. A party who exceeds the
threshold limits[4] is a taxable person, whether he has taken steps to
register or not. Once discovered, such a party must be registered,
and the registration is backdated to the date he was liable to be registered. He must account for any VAT from that date.[5]

Although it is persons, not businesses who are subject to registration, special provision is made for partnerships. The Value Added
Tax Act[6] provides that:

'The registration under this Act of persons –
   (a) carrying on a business in partnership, or
   (b) carrying on in partnership any other activities in the course
       or furtherance of which they acquire goods from other mem-
       ber States,

[20] *Whitehouse* and *Tiley.*
[1] Value Added Tax Act 1994, s 4.
[2] Value Added Tax Act 1994, ss 4 and 96(1).
[3] Value Added Tax Act 1994, s 3(1).
[4] A person including a partnership becomes liable to register for VAT purposes if
their business turnover exceeds the threshold limit, this is considered at p 398
below.
[5] *Whitehead v Customs and Excise Comrs* [1975] VATTR 152.
[6] Section 45.

may be in the name of the firm; and no account shall be taken, in determining for any purpose of this Act whether goods or services are supplied to or by such persons or are acquired by such persons from another member State, of any change in the partnership.'

The above section does not preclude the commissioners from insisting that each partner registers for VAT purposes as an individual, although it seems that such a power is rarely exercised. In general, the partnership will be registered for VAT in the firm's name.

There is a further special provision relating to a partnership with regard to VAT. Viz:

'A form known as VAT 2 must be annexed to the notification of liability to register for VAT which is forwarded to the commissioners by the partnership. This form shows the name and address of each partner, and it must bear each of their signatures.'[7]

Furthermore, for registration purposes a partnership is treated as a continuing business. Therefore, any change in the membership of the partnership is disregarded, although any change must be notified to the commissioners within 30 days.[8] Any partner who leaves a partnership is nevertheless regarded as a continuing partner for the purposes of value added tax until his retirement from the partnership is notified to the commissioners.[9] Partners have a joint *and* several liability to give any notice which is required under the Value Added Tax Act 1994 or any regulations made thereunder. Nevertheless, a notification given by one partner to the commissioners will constitute sufficient compliance.[10] Notwithstanding s 45 of the Value Added Tax Act 1994, it seems that separate partnerships with *identical* partners are not entitled to separate registrations.[11] By way of contrast, it has been held that separate registrations of partnership with identical partners are permitted in the case of limited partnerships in which the role of limited partner is fulfilled by different individuals in each of the relevant partnerships.[12]

[7] VAT (General) Regulations, SI 1985/886, reg 4(1) and Sch Form 2.
[8] Value Added Tax Act, s 45(2); VAT (General) Regulations, SI 1985/886, reg 4(2); *Customs & Excise Comrs v Evans* [1982] STC 342.
[9] Value Added Tax Act, s 45(2) and (4).
[10] VAT (General) Regulations, SI 1985/886, reg (1).
[11] *Customs & Excise Comrs v Glassborow* [1974] STC 142, [1974] 1 All ER 1041.
[12] *Saunders v Customs & Excise Comrs* [1980] VATTR 53.

A new registration for VAT, or a transfer of an existing registration, is necessary where a sole trader takes on a partner, or a partnership is dissolved but the partnership business is carried on by a former partner as a sole trader.

A business enterprise such as a partnership may seek to reorganise its business into more than one activity, and to ensure that the various activities are performed by different members of the business. Such 'business splitting', where each activity has a turnover below the registration threshold,[13] may avoid the need for any part of the business to be registered. The commissioners are empowered, however, to counteract such a practice under a direction originally issued under the Value Added Tax Act 1983.[14] Thus, partners who seek to split the various activities of the partnership into separate business activities will continue to be recognised as a partnership, carrying on a single business. Individuals engaged in a partnership will still be regarded as carrying on their separate activities within the context of their partnership for VAT purposes in the following circumstances:

(1) if the taxable supplies made by the various individuals in the course of their activities are properly to be regarded when taken together as the activities of the partnership;
(2) if the combined value of those supplies exceeds the registration limits;
(3) if the activities have been carried on separately, solely or principally so as to avoid the liability to registration.[15]

Even where individuals are associated with one another in a business context but they are not formal partners, they will be deemed to be so for the purposes of VAT under the terms of the above direction and under the same circumstances, as have been noted above. The persons concerned will be known as 'constituent members'.

It follows that a partnership, either actual or deemed, becomes a 'taxable person' liable to registration. A 'taxable person', be it a partnership or deemed partnership, should be registered in such a name as the members or constituent members nominate. If they fail to make a nomination, a name may be specified by the commissioners. Goods and services supplied to or by the members of the partnership, be it actual or deemed, are treated as if made by the so-defined

---

[13] For the current threshold, see p 398, below.
[14] Sch 1, para 1A (2) (b)-(7)(e). See now the 1994 VAT Act, Sch 1.
[15] *Osman v Customs & Excise Comrs* [1989] STC 596; *Hundsdoerfer v Customs & Excise Comrs* [1990] VATTR 158.

taxable person, as are any acquisitions made by the actual or constituent members of the business.

A constituent member who is registered for VAT ceases to be liable to be registered from the date when the 'taxable person' of which he is deemed to be a member itself becomes liable to be registered. Nevertheless, any constituent members are jointly and severally liable for any VAT due from the 'taxable person'. Any failure, therefore, by the 'taxable person' to comply with the relevant legislative provisions governing VAT is treated as a failure by each of the constituent members. In such cases their liability is several.

A constituent member will cease to be a member of a deemed partnership if the commissioners are satisfied that he is no longer to be so regarded, and the commissioners give notice to that effect. Such a person from that date ceases to be liable for any VAT due from the relevant 'taxable person' and any failures of the constituent members of the latter to comply with any VAT legislation.

The VAT threshold

A trader or a partnership is a taxable person, and is required to register for the purposes of VAT, inter alia, if he or it makes taxable supplies in the United Kingdom in the course or furtherance of the business above a prescribed threshold.[16] An unregistered person or partnership is therefore liable to registration at the end of any month (the relevant month) if the taxable supplies of the business in the period of one year then ending exceeds £45,000.[17]

Such a business does not become liable to registration in the circumstances noted above if the commissioners are satisfied that the taxable supplies in the coming year would not exceed £43,000.[18] If a business has previously been deregistered on the basis of a full disclosure of all relevant facts, the value of any taxable supplies made prior to deregistration must be disregarded.[19]

A partnership which becomes liable to registration because its annual turnover at the end of any month, ie the relevant month, exceeds £45,000, must notify the commissioners within 30 days of the end of the relevant month. The partnership must still make notification, even if the partners are of the opinion that the turnover of the business in the coming year will not exceed £43,000. The

---

[16] Value Added Tax Act 1994, s 4 and Sch 1.
[17] Schedule 1. The prescribed rate at the time of writing.
[18] Schedule 1. The prescribed rate at the time of writing.
[19] Schedule 1.

commissioners cannot, unless the partnership makes such a notification, satisfy themselves that the partnership turnover for the coming year will not exceed the prescribed threshold. If a partnership is registered for VAT it is registered from the end of the month which follows the relevant month. For other grounds for registration see fn 2, below.[20]

Cancellation of registration

A partnership ceases to be liable to be registered for VAT with the consequence that the commissioners may cancel the registration if they are satisfied that:

(1) the partnership has ceased to make taxable supplies;[1]
(2) the partnership is neither liable, nor entitled to registration under any other provision;[2]
(3) the taxable supplies in the forthcoming year will not exceed £43,000;[3]
(4) (a) the value of the partnership's relevant acquisitions in the previous calendar year did not exceed £37,600;[4] and
     (b) the commissioners are satisfied that the relevant acquisitions in the current calendar year will not exceed £45,000; and

---

[20] In particular fn 2, below. Note that where a party is unregistered but acquires a business from a taxable person as a going concern he is liable to registration if the taxable supplies of his acquired business within the previous year of acquisition exceeded £45,000 and will in the first year of operation by him be likely to exceed £43,000 or there are reasonable grounds for believing that the value of taxable supplies in the first 30 days after the transfer of the business will exceed £45,000. Value Added Tax Act 1994, Sch 1.

[1] See fn 2, p 395, above.

[2] Such other provision would include the following. A partnership which either: (a) makes a relevant supply of goods subject to excise duty; (b) supplies goods not subject to excise duty which have a cumulative value exceeding £70,000 in the current calendar year; (c) supplies goods not subject to excise duty affected by a place of supply option made under the law of the EC member state where the supplier is registered; (d) if at the end of any month he makes relevant acquisitions of goods for the current calendar year exceeding £45,000 or if there are reasonable grounds for believing that the value of his relevant acquisitions in the next 30 days will exceed £45,000 see also p 398, above. If any of the above cases apply the partnership would need to be registered for VAT purposes: see the Value Added Tax Act 1994, Sch 1.

[3] Value Added Tax Act 1994, Sch 1.

[4] Value Added Tax Act 1994, Sch 1.

(c) there are no reasonable grounds for believing that the value of relevant acquisitions in the next 30 days will exceed £45,000.[5]

It should be noted that a partnership may be *exempt* from registration. This will occur if the supplies of the business would, if the partnership were registered for VAT, be in any event zero rated. The partnership must apply for such exemption and the commissioners must think the application fit and proper.[6] A partnership registered for VAT could seek to be deregistered on the same grounds. Exemption from registration may also be sought on the grounds that the acquisitions of a partnership would, if the partnership were registered, be zero rated acquisitions. A partnership already registered could apply for deregistration on the same grounds.

Transfer of registration

When a business is transferred as a going concern, the parties to the transaction may elect that the purchaser is registered under the seller's VAT registration number. However, the following conditions must be satisfied before such a procedure can take place:

(1)   the business must be a going concern;
(2)   the seller must cease to be liable to registration, although his registration is not cancelled;
(3)   the purchaser must either:
       (a) become liable to be registered; or
       (b) be entitled to registration and the commissioners agree to register the purchaser;
(4)   the prescribed form VAT 68 must be submitted by both parties to the transaction. VAT 68 is the form which constitutes notification that the seller of the business has ceased to make taxable supplies.[7]

Office held by partners

The Value Added Tax Act 1983 provides:[8]

---

[5] Value Added Tax Act 1994, Sch 3.
[6] Value Added Tax Act 1994, Sch 1.
[7] VAT (General) Regulations, SI 1985/886, reg 4(4), (5), Sch 1, para 7, Sch Form 3.
[8] Value Added Tax Act 1994, s 94(4).

'Where a person, in the course or furtherance of a trade, profession, or vocation, accepts any office, services supplied by him as the holder of that office are treated as supplied in the course or furtherance of the trade, profession or vocation.'

The terms of the above subsection should be noted. A partner who as a consequence of his membership of, or in connection with, his partnership, provides services as the holder of an office, such services will in general be regarded as those of the firm for the purposes of VAT. The above provision does not apply, however, to services supplied by a partner under a contract of employment.[9]

There will be no taxable supply of services by a partnership as a result of services supplied by a partner as an office holder, even though the latter may account for such fees as he receives to the partnership, but only if the following conditions are satisfied:

(1) the relevant office is a private arrangement between the partner and the third party. Furthermore there is no written agreement between the latter and the partnership relating to that office;
(2) the relevant office holding has arisen by virtue of the financial or personal or other interests of the partner, and not through the professional interests of the partnership;
(3) the duties of the office do not involve the partner using, to a significant degree, the skills which the partner uses in the partnership, trade or business, unless such services are separately charged for by the partnership.

It is now settled that where a partnership permits a partner to use partnership assets for the latter's personal benefit, the partnership is to be regarded as having made a taxable supply of services.[10]

Sale of partnership assets

Whenever goods forming part of the partnership assets are sold or transferred, any such disposition will generally be regarded as a taxable supply, except in relation to an asset which is for the purposes of VAT exempt.[11] It would seem that the goodwill of the partnership is for the above purposes to be considered as a partnership asset.[12]

---

[9] *Lean & Rose v Customs & Excise Comrs* [1974] 1 VATTR 7.
[10] *Border Flying Co v Customs & Excise Comrs* [1976] VATTR 137; Value Added Tax Act 1983, Sch 2, para 5(3).
[11] Value Added Tax Act 1994, s 94(6).
[12] Value Added Tax Act 1994, Sch 4.

Where the partnership is sold as a going concern the Value Added Taxes Act 1994 provides that:[13]

'The disposition of a business as a going concern or of its assets or liabilities (whether or not in connection with its reorganisation or winding up) is a supply made in the course or furtherance of the business.'

It should be noted that partnership assets which are exempt from VAT will not form part of any taxable supply on any disposition of the partnership business or its assets, within the terms of the above provision. The registration for VAT purposes of the party acquiring the partnership business has been considered above. If the person to whom the partnership business has been transferred is a taxable person, or will become a taxable person by virtue of the need to register as a result of the transaction, the sale will not in general be regarded as a supply of goods or services.[14]

If a partnership ceases to be a taxable person, the commissioners may, on the application of the partnership, cancel its registration. The grounds upon which a partnership may seek cancellation of its registration have been considered above. However, in such a case, any goods forming part of its partnership assets will generally be regarded as having been supplied in the course or furtherance of its business immediately before the partnership lost its status as a business entity liable or entitled to registration.[15] Such a supply will be deemed to be at an open market value.[16]

The general dissolution of a partnership will, within the terms of the Value Added Tax Act 1994,[17] generally involve the partnership making taxable supplies, since this will involve the sale or transfer of partnership assets. All such dispositions of partnership assets made during the termination or intended termination of the partnership will thus be supplies made in the course or furtherance of a business. Any partnership assets still owned by the partnership will, immediately prior to the partnership ceasing to be a taxable person, be the subject of a deemed supply.[18] Once a final deemed supply of the partnership assets has been made, any further dealings with those assets will not be subject to VAT, that is, unless the dealings

---

[13] Value Added Tax Act 1994, s 94(6).
[14] See the Value Added Tax (Special Provisions) Order 1981, SI 1981/1741, art 12; *Customs & Excise Comrs v Dearwood Ltd* [1986] STC 327.
[15] Value Added Tax Act 1994, Sch 4.
[16] Section 19(3).
[17] Section 94(5). For dissolution of a partnership see Chapter 12.
[18] Value Added Tax Act 1994, Sch 4. As is the case where registration is cancelled.

are made in the course or furtherance of a new business carried on by the partners and for which they would be required to be registered for the purposes of VAT.[19]

It may be cogently argued that a transfer of a partnership share by one partner to the other partner(s) cannot constitute a supply of goods or services, and is therefore a transaction which cannot be subject to VAT. Certainly, s 45(1) of the Value Added Tax Act 1994 can be so interpreted, since it determines that 'no account shall be taken . . . in determining whether goods or services are supplied . . . of any change in the partnership'. However, it would seem that a transfer of a partnership share by a partner to a third party who does become a partner is potentially chargeable to VAT. Such a transaction must constitute a taxable supply of goods or services made in the course or furtherance of a business carried on by the transferor partner. There is authority for the proposition that a partnership share, for the purposes of VAT, constitutes a right of each partner to a direct beneficial interest in a particular partnership asset.[20] This view gives rise to an inference that a partnership share is, for the purposes of VAT, merely a conglomeration of such interests in the partnership assets and a transfer of a share of such assets via a partnership share could therefore constitute a taxable supply. Furthermore, it may be argued that a partnership share can constitute a business carried on by that partner. In such a case, a disposition of a partnership share as a going concern would under s 94(6) of the Value Added Tax Act 1994[1] be treated as a supply in the course or furtherance of a business and therefore potentially chargeable to VAT. It must, however, be emphasised that the question whether a transfer of a partnership share to a third party who does not become a partner is a transaction which is potentially chargeable to VAT has not, at the time of writing, been unambiguously resolved.

In conclusion it must be emphasised that the above is an outline consideration of VAT as it applies to partnerships, and is not intended to be comprehensive. For a full consideration of VAT and partnerships reference should be made to the standard texts on Revenue law noted above.[2]

---

[19] *Marshall v Customs & Excise Comrs* [1975] VATTR 98.
[20] *Border Flying Co v Customs & Excise Comrs* [1976] VATTR 137 at 138.
[1] See fn 11, p 401, above for a consideration of this subsection.
[2] See fn 6, p 364, above.

STAMP DUTY

General principles

Stamp duty is a tax on documents, and not on transactions, or persons. The imposition of the tax is governed by numerous statutory provisions, the principal legislative provisions being the Stamp Act 1891 and the Stamp Duties Management Act 1891.[3] For a document to be chargeable to the tax it must fall within one of the heads of charge. If the document falls within more than one head, the Revenue are only entitled to one of the duties. Nevertheless, the Revenue may, in such a case, select the head of charge which will produce the higher or highest duty.[4] Where there is more than one document relating to a transaction, it is the principal document which is charged ad valorem duty. All other documents are subject to a charge of 50p.[5] The heads of charge applicable to partnerships and partners are as follows.

1.   CONVEYANCE OR TRANSFER ON SALE[6]

This head of charge will cover any conveyance or transfer on sale of any property. In respect of partnership property the rate is 1% of the value of the transaction, although the rate is nil if the consideration does not exceed £60,000,[7] and the document contains a certificate of value. The certificate must state that the transaction which has been effected by the document does not form part of a larger transaction or series of transactions which in aggregate exceed in value the sum of £60,000.

2.   CONVEYANCE OR TRANSFER NOT ON SALE[8]

This head of charge concerns documents which effect transfers of property, inter alia, between beneficial owners and nominees. These documents attract a charge of 50p.

---

[3] As amended by various Finance Acts and revenue statues. The Finance Act 1990, ss 107–108 provides for the future abolition of all stamp duty charges.
[4] *Speyer Bros v IRC* [1908] AC 92.
[5] Stamp Act 1891, s 58(3).
[6] Stamp Act 1891, Sch 1.
[7] At the time of writing.
[8] Stamp Act 1891, s 62.

3. LEASES AND AGREEMENTS FOR LEASES[9]

This head of charge does not include documents which concern leases of movable assets but is limited to leases of land, tenements and other heritable rights. A lease or agreement for a lease for seven years or more must be produced to the Revenue and stamped with a produced stamp. Fixed duties are charged on short term leases at low rents, and ad valorem duty on leases for more than a year and on periodic tenancies.[10]

4. THE SALE OF A BUSINESS/BUSINESS ASSETS

The Stamp Act 1891[11] provides that:

'Any contract or agreement for the sale of any equitable estate or interest in any property whatsoever, or for the sale of any estate or interest in any property except lands, tenements, hereditaments, or heritages, or property locally situate out of the United Kingdom, or goods, wares or merchandise, or stock, or marketable securities, or any ship or vessel, or part interest, share or property of or in any ship or vessel, shall be charged with the same ad valorem duty, to be paid by the purchaser, as if it were an actual conveyance on sale of the estate, interest, or property contracted or agreed to be sold.'

Ad valorem duty is therefore payable on sale contracts of equitable interests in assets situated in the United Kingdom other than contracts for the sale of interests in land. However, if a subsequent document or transfer is then executed, vesting the legal interest (as opposed to the mere equitable interest) in the purchaser under the contract of sale, this latter document is not subject to further ad valorem duty. Such a transfer should, however, be stamped with a denoting stamp.

5. EXCHANGE OR PARTITION[12]

This head of charge covers documents effecting exchanges or partitions of real or personal property. Generally, duty is a fixed duty of 50p.

---

[9] Stamp Act 1981, Sch 1.
[10] For the current rates see *Whitehouse*.
[11] Section 59.
[12] Stamp Act 1891, s 73, Sch 1.

6.   OTHER DOCUMENTS SUBJECT TO STAMP DUTY

Fixed duty is chargeable on the following documents:

(1)   conveyance or transfer of any other kind –50p;
(2)   duplicate or counterpart of any instrument chargeable with duty – maximum 50p;
(3)   a document effecting an exchange or partition relating to realty where the amount of the equalisation payment does not exceed £100 – 50p;[13]
(4)   lease of a furnished letting for a definite term of less than one year where the rent for the whole term exceeds £500 – £1;
(5)   leases not stampable under any other head – £2;
(6)   a document effecting a release or renunciation of any property or interest in property and which is not subject to sale duty – 50p;
(7)   surrender of any kind which is not chargeable to sale duty – 50p.

Exemptions and reliefs from stamp duty

Certain documents are exempted from duty; these include:

(1)   wills;
(2)   contracts of employment;
(3)   mortgages.

Consideration is now given to the aspects of stamp duty which are particularly pertinent to partners and partnerships.

Formation of a partnership

Stamp duty is only chargeable on documents; accordingly, changes wrought within a partnership which can be effected without a document being brought into existence are not subject to this tax. Where a partnership is formed by a partnership deed or agreement, stamp duty will only be chargeable if the document conveys or transfers assets. Furthermore, even if the document is a deed under seal, it will not require a deed stamp. This remains the case even if the partners agreed to contribute assets or cash to the partnership, since there is still no conveyance or transfer on sale[14] within the terms of

---

[13]   The rate at the time of writing.
[14]   See p 404, above and the Stamp Act 1891, s 1, Sch 1; *McLeod v IRC* 1885 22 SLR 674.

the Stamp Act. Where a partnership agreement or deed provides for any capital provided by a partner to be credited to another partner's capital account, as the consideration for a share in the partnership, such a document may well be regarded as a conveyance or transfer on sale. In such a case the document may well be chargeable to stamp duty, as it could be regarded as a de facto sale or transfer of partnership assets, which has been disguised as a partnership deed.[15] Any document which transfers, for a consideration, a partnership share or a part of such a share from one partner to another partner will constitute a conveyance or transfer on sale, and will be subject to ad valorem duty. Where the document affects a rearrangement of partnership shares or entitlements between the partners, and constitutes an exchange, a fixed duty of 50p will be payable.[16]

Change in partnership membership

Where a partner retires from a partnership, and effects by a document an assignment of his share in the partnership to the remaining parties for consideration, the document will be subject to ad valorem duty.[17] If an assignment of the partnership share is effected, however, without the execution of a document but, subsequent to the assignment, a document is brought into existence merely evidencing the assignment, no duty will be payable.[18]

In all of the above cases, any contract or agreement for the sale, assignment or transfer of a partnership share or part of a share may be chargeable to ad valorem duty.[19] If a retiring partner merely withdraws any capital profits due to him for which he gives a receipt, it would appear that no ad valorem duty is chargeable on such a document.[20]

Where an individual, on joining a partnership, purchases a share in the partnership, any document which effects the purchase constitutes a conveyance on sale and will be chargeable to ad valorem duty. Such a document will remain a conveyance on sale chargeable to ad valorem duty even if the consideration provided by the incoming partner is not a tangible asset, eg the partner agrees to devote his full time or special skills to the partnership.

15 *Ingram v IRC* [1986] Ch 585.
16 But see fn 12 and p 405, above, where such forms of document may be subject to ad valorem duty.
17 *Christie v IRC* (1866) LR 2 Ex Ch 46.
18 *Garnett v IRC* (1899) 81 LT 633.
19 See fn 11 and p 405, above and the Stamp Act 1891, s 59.
20 *Fleetwood-Hesketh v IRC* [1936] 1 KB 351.

Dissolution of a partnership

Where, on the dissolution of a partnership, a document effecting the dissolution provides for the partnership shares of certain partners to be bought by the other partners, then any such document is as a conveyance or transfer on sale subject to ad valorem duty. By way of contrast, there can be no charge to stamp duty if the dissolution document merely provides for each partner to take out of the dissolved partnership his share of the partnership assets and profits, as a sum of cash.[1] Where, however, the dissolution document provides for a partner to take out his share of the partnership assets in the form in which they existed within the partnership, a fixed duty of 50p will be payable on the document.

If the dissolution is effected without a document, but subsequently a document comes into existence which evidences the terms of the dissolution,[2] then the document is not chargeable to stamp duty. Before such a document is brought into existence, however, the former partners should ensure that they can establish that the dissolution of the partnership has taken place. Furthermore, the document should, in so far as it refers to the distribution of partnership assets, unambiguously declare that the document has not effected such a distribution, but is merely reciting a fact which took place before the document came into existence.

As in the consideration of all the other taxes in this chapter as they apply to partnership, the above discussion concerning stamp duty is not intended to be comprehensive. For a full consideration of this tax and its application to partnerships, reference should be made to the standard works on Revenue law noted above.[3]

---

[1] *Garnett v IRC* (1899) 81 LT 633; *Fleetwood–Hesketh v IRC* [1936] 1 KB 351.

[2] This may be desirable if, eg the partners have agreed to restraint covenants. For such covenants see Chapter 5.

[3] See fn 6, p 364, above.

INDEX

Account stated
  action on, 53
Accountants
  size of partnership, 41, 347
Accounts
  access to, 248
  accounting basis, 255
  accumulation of profits, 259–260
  adjustment of, 288–292
  balance sheet, 72
  basis on which prepared, 73
  books. *See* BOOKS
  capital, 257–258
  common law and, 247
  compensation payments, 256
  consolidated accounts exemption, 252
  current accounts, 257–258
  date of preparation, 73
  dissolution, settling after, 288–292
  division of profits, 257
    final, 259
  1890 Act and, 78, 247
  failure to keep, 247–248
  finality of, 260
  generally, 70, 246
  gifts, 256
  inspection of, 248
  interest, 258–259
  limited companies. *See* LIMITED
    COMPANIES' ACCOUNTS
  manner of keeping, 254–260
  obligation to keep, 247–248
  partnership agreement and, 72
  partnership books. *See* BOOKS
  payments, 256
  profit and loss, 253–254
  purpose of, 72–73
  receipts, 255–256
  right of access to, 248

Accounts – *contd*
  salaries, 259
  signature of partners, 260
  signing of, 73
  special revaluation reserves, 258
  special tax reserve account, 258
  stock valuations, 256–257
  winding up and, 288–292
  work in progress, valuations of,
    256–257
Acquiescence
  actions for account, 227
  actions between partners, 243–245
Actions
  account, for. *See* ACTIONS FOR
    ACCOUNT
  account stated, for, 53
  aliens, against, 38
  dissolution, for, injunctions, 237
  firms, against. *See* ACTIONS AGAINST
    FIRMS
  firms, by, 158–159
  illegal partnerships and, 52–53
  partners, between. *See* ACTIONS
    BETWEEN PARTNERS
  recovery of premium, for, 43
  specific performance, for, 239–240
Actions for account
  acquiescence, 227
  Anton Piller order, 225
  arbitration award, 230
  costs of, 231–232
  defences
    arbitration award, 230
    denial of partnership, 227–228,
      239
    generally, 230–231
    payment in lieu of all demands,
      230
    release, 231

Goods
pledging of, in trading partnerships, 120
purchase for firm, 118
sale of, 117
Goodwill
capital gains tax and, 381
consideration for, 43–44
contractual provisions, 202–203
creation of, 204
employees and, 203
firm name and, 64
generally, 201–202
increase in value of, 70
misrepresentation and, 204–205
name, registration of, 203–204
non-contractual protection, 203–204
ownership of, 202
partnership agreement, 75–76
partnership property, 201–206
passing off, 203, 204–205
payment for, 202
place of business and, 63–64
protection of
non-contractual, 203–204
restraint of trade and, 203
sale of partnership, on, 202–203
registered trade marks, 203–204, 205–206
See also TRADE MARKS
retiring partner, restrictive covenant preventing competition, 75–76
sale of, 29–30, 43–44, 201
capital gains tax and, 381
for provision of annuity, 29–30
Gross misconduct
partner, of, 236
Gross returns, sharing
generally, 18–19
sharing of profits distinguished, 19
Group partnerships
advantages of, 88
assets of, 89
block vote system, 89
decision-making process, 89
dissolution, 89
1890 Act and, 88
expulsion, 89
generally, 88–89
insolvency, 90
management of, 88–89
meaning, 81, 88
name of, 88

Group partnerships – *contd*
partnership agreement, 89–90
retirement, 89–90
Guarantees
authority to bind firm by, 122
continuing, 150
partner, given by, 122
retiring partners and, 150
trade custom, 122

High Court
dissolution proceedings
jurisdiction, 272
transfer of, 273
Hold over relief
capital gains tax, 383
Holding out
dormant partners and, 157
minors, 36
retiring partners and, 153–154
third parties, liability to, 16
Husband and wife. *See* SPOUSE

Illegal partnerships
account, actions for, 53
account stated, action on, 53
actions between partners and, 52–53
consequences of illegality, 52–53
contribution, action for a, 53
corporate partnerships, 50
criminal activity, 49, 51
dissolution of, 52
enemy aliens, 49
EU and, 49–50
exceeding number of permitted partners, 42
formation of, 49–55
generally, 49
illegal act within legal partnership, 53–54
immediate dissolution, 52
morality, purposes contrary to, 49
professions and, 50–51
public policy, purposes contrary to, 49
purpose forbidden by statute, 51
religion, purposes contrary to, 49
statute and, 50–55
purpose forbidden by, 51
third parties and, 54–55
unqualified member, 42, 51
Illegality
consequences of, 52–53
dissolution due to, 264–265, 268

Partners – *contd*
fiduciary duties – *contd*
of, 170–171
conflict of duty and interest,
177–178
generally, 170–172
lease
renewal for own benefit, 174
reversion of, 174–175
partnership property, 174–175
secret profit and, 173, 175–176
fiduciary relationship, 100, 170–171
former, restrictions on, 101–105
fraud on firm by, 156
fraudulent conduct, 268
goods
purchasing, 118
sale of, 117
gross misconduct of, 236
illegal acts of, 53–54
illness of, 68
implied powers of. *See* IMPLIED
POWERS OF PARTNERS
incoming. *See* INCOMING PARTNERS
individual activities of, 24–25
introduction of new. *See* INCOMING
PARTNERS
liability of. *See* LIABILITY
lien of, 319, 333
management of partnership, right to
participate in, 71–72, 168
mental disorder of, 36–37
minors as, 34–36
misconduct of, 236, 238, 268,
269–270
mutual confidence between,
269–270
names
disclosure of, 91–92
actions, in, 159–160
enforcement, 93
displaying of, 92–93
large numbers of partners,
where, 92
stated in correspondence, 91–92
negligence of, on partnership
business, 128
new. *See* INCOMING PARTNERS
non-equity, 63
non-resident, debts and, 166
notice to, as notice to firm, 139–143
numbers of. *See* SIZE OF
PARTNERSHIP
outside activities, 101

Partners – *contd*
outsiders, relations to, 106 *et seq*
partnership assets, use of, for
personal benefit, 173–174
partnership decisions, 169–170
partnership property and, 174–175
personal benefit, use of partnership
assets for, 173–174
personal representatives as, 40
premises, ownership of, 63–64
private profits, accountability for,
172–173
professional qualifications, 42, 51,
265, 347
profits, private, accountability for,
172–173
ratification by, 142–143
receipts, giving of, 117–118
releases, giving of, 117
representations of, 138–139
responsibilities owed to each other, 3
retirement of. *See* RETIREMENT
rights of, 168 *et seq*
salaried, 26–27, 63, 259
secret profit, 173
unauthorised, by use of
information gained as a
partner, 175–176
sleeping. *See* DORMANT PARTNERS
spouses as, 3–4, 38–39
supervening mental illness, 37
torts of, 2
committed in course of
partnership business,
128–129
transactions between, capital gains
tax and, 378–380
trivial disputes between, 242–243
trustees as, 40
undue influence, 100
use of partnership assets for personal
benefit, 173–174
winding up
position in
contributory, as, 316–319
generally, 315–316
Partnership
See also FIRM; PARTNERS
accountants, 41, 347
accounts. *See* ACCOUNTS
activities outside, 101
actuaries, 41
agreement. *See* PARTNERSHIP
AGREEMENT